BUDDHISM
AFTER
PATRIARCHY

BUDDHISM
AFTER
PATRIARCHY

A Feminist History, Analysis,
and Reconstruction
of Buddhism

RITA M. GROSS

State University of New York Press

Published by
State University of New York Press, Albany

Printed in the United States of America

For information, address the State University of New York Press,
State University Plaza, Albany, NY 12246

Production by Christine M. Lynch
Marketing by Lynne Lekakis

Library of Congress Cataloging-in-Publication Data

Gross, Rita M.
    Buddhism after patriarchy : a feminist history, analysis, and
reconstruction of Buddhism / Rita M. Gross.
        p.   cm.
    Includes bibliographical references and index.
    ISBN 0-7914-1403-5 (ch: : acid-free). — ISBN 0-7914-1404-3 (pb :
acid-free)
    1. Women in Buddhism. 2. Woman (Buddhism) 3. Feminism—Religious
aspects—Buddhism. 4. Buddhism—Doctrines. I. Title.
BQ4570.W6G76   1993   92-9133
294.3'082—dc20   CIP

10 9 8 7 6

To the memory of
HOWARD T. LUTZ

In gratitude
for loving and appreciative companionship

CONTENTS

ACKNOWLEDGMENTS

This book is the result of many years of hard work and contemplation. Without the inspiration of my teachers and the encouragement of my friends, this task would never have been begun or completed.

First I would like to thank my academic teachers. Florence Walzl of the University of Wisconsin–Milwaukee encouraged me to be serious about an academic career at a time when undergraduate women were generally steered in other directions. I am deeply grateful to the late Mircea Eliade, who first suggested that I devote a major portion of my academic research to the study of women and religion. Charles H. Long and Joseph M. Kitagawa, also of the University of Chicago, have continued to encourage this scholarship.

From my *dharma* teachers, whom I encountered much later, I learned different lessons, but they are equally critical. The late Chogyam Trungpa and the late Osel Tendzin were brilliant, outrageous, incredibly kind, and very controversial teachers. They inspired their students to uncommon dedication and courage. They also challenged us to carry forward their own vast vision into all areas of life, to regard living and practicing the dharma as inseparable.

Friends in the many worlds that I inhabit have all encouraged me to continue, have read and commented upon earlier drafts of portions of this book, and have provided sorely needed companionship at critical stages in the process of learning enough to be able to complete this book. In the world of academic scholarship, my dear friend Nancy A. Falk has been a constant source of encouragement and helpful feedback. In the early years of my academic career, the community of young feminist scholars of religion was a sustaining force. Carol Christ, Naomi Goldenberg, Judith Plaskow, and many others, helped give me the courage it took to be a young feminist scholar in the early days of feminist scholarship. Among Buddhist friends, I especially want to acknowledge Jean and Brus Westby, Cassell Gross, and Jaird de Raismes, true companions of the Way. The world of Buddhist-Christian dialogue and encounter has increasingly become a significant community of support and encouragement. I want to thank David Chappell for frequent doses of enthusiasm for my project, Frederick Streng for helpful discussions of methodology, and John Cobb for first challenging me to acknowledge Western roots of my Buddhist feminism. My friend Judith Simmer-Brown is involved in so many common areas of discussion that I am at a loss to place her in a single category. Many other voices the years have aided in giving me strength; I apologize for not mentioning all of them by name.

I must acknowledge the University of Wisconsin–Eau Claire, which generously provided me with a sabbatical during the fall semester of 1990, during which I wrote most of the first draft of this book. The university has also provided me with minor grants over the years to help with various projects necessary to preparing myself to write this book. I especially appreciate the understanding of my former department chair, Bruce Jannusch, who facilitated my need to attend various meditation intensives during the years when they constituted a major part of my training. Many, many students who have taken my classes in Buddhism and in Women and Religion, have forced me to clarify and simplify my presentations. Their appreciation of those classes has also been inspiring to me. Wishing not to omit any of them, I will not attempt a complete list of such students.

Lastly, I wish to thank my editor at SUNY Press, Bill Eastman, who gave extremely helpful suggestions in a kind and warm manner. It is hard to imagine a more co-operative or enthusiastic editor.

I

ORIENTATIONS

1

Strategies for a Feminist Revalorization
of Buddhism

This essay grows out of a complex, unique, and personal blending of three perspectives—the cross-cultural, comparative study of religion, feminism, and Buddhism. Though each perspective is well-known and widely used individually, they are not usually brought into conversation with each other. Even more rarely are they blended into one spiritual and scholarly outlook, as I have sought to do in my personal and academic life. Throughout these pages, I will illustrate the dense, mutually illuminating interplay of these three perspectives as they weave a coherent and uplifting vision. I could tell the story of how these three orientations became allies in my system of understanding and orientation. However, unlike Carol Christ and Christine Downing,[1] I choose not to focus directly on my story, on my personal intersection with these three perspectives, but on the sometimes tension-laden synthesis which I have conjured up out of my studies, my suffering, and my experience.

My primary task in this book is a feminist revalorization of Buddhism. In feminist theology in general, the task of "revalorization" involves working with the categories and concepts of a traditional religion in the light of feminist values. This task is double-edged, for, one the one hand, feminist analysis of any major world religion reveals massive undercurrents of sexism and prejudice against women, especially in realms of religious praxis. On the other hand, the very term "revalorization" contains an implicit judgment. To revalorize is to have determined that, however sexist a religious tradition may be, it is not irreparably so. Revalorizing is, in fact, doing that work of repairing the tradition, often bringing it much more into line with its own fundamental values and vision than was its patriarchal form.

My strategies for this revalorization involve first studying Buddhist history and then analyzing key concepts of the Buddhist worldview from a feminist point of view. Utilizing the results of those studies, I finally pursue a feminist reconstruction of Buddhism.

In the chapters on Buddhist history, I will survey the roles and images of women found in each of the three major periods of Buddhist intellectual

3

development—early Indian Buddhism, Mahayana Buddhism, and Indo-Tibetan Vajrayana Buddhism. In addition to surveying roles and images of women, I will look for some of the most relevant and interesting stories about women found in each period. This survey has a dual purpose. First, someone who wishes to comment on Buddhism and feminism cannot meaningfully do so without some knowledge of the Buddhist record regarding images and roles of women commonly found in the Buddhist past. Second, out of this record of roles, images, and stories, we can search for a usable past, as defined by feminist historians.[2]

These chapters will be followed by chapters detailing a feminist analysis of key Buddhist concepts. Thus, I follow the distinction, often made by Christian feminist theologians, between historical context, which may well reflect very limited cultural conditions, and essential core teachings of the religious symbol system. Like most Christian feminist theologians, I am far more concerned about the gender implications of key Buddhist teachings than I am about inadequate models in the past. In the chapters of analysis, I will argue that the key concepts of Buddhism, in every period of Buddhist intellectual development, are incompatible with gender hierarchy and with discrimination against women (or against men).

In a certain sense, the chapters on history discuss the Buddhist past, how Buddhists have in fact dealt with women throughout time. The chapters of analysis, in a sense, deal with the Buddhist present, for though these key concepts were articulated in the past, they have *present* relevance for Buddhists in a way that historical materials do not. History is not revelatory or normative for Buddhists in the way that it is for some other traditions. Key Buddhist concepts, however, constitute what Buddhists currently believe and, therefore, must be taken very seriously. The chapters on reconstruction look toward the post-patriarchal future of Buddhism, using both the tools of traditional Buddhism and of feminist vision. These chapters explore the contradiction between the egalitarian concepts of Buddhism and its patriarchal history, seeking both to explain that contradiction historically and to rectify that situation in a future manifestation and form of Buddhism. As we shall see, such reconstructions take us beyond, not only the current institutional forms of Buddhism, but also beyond its present conceptual structure.

These sections of history, analysis, and reconstruction are set in the matrix of very specific, and somewhat idiosyncratic ways of thinking about religion and the study of religion, about feminism, and about Buddhism itself. Detailed discussion of these methodological issues and stances is found in the two appendices to the book. My method of dealing with complex issues regarding the interface between theology and the history of religions is dealt with in the appendix titled "Religious Experience and the Study of Religion: The History of Religions." Definitions of feminism, critical for understanding my vision of *Buddhist* feminism, are found in the appendix titled "Here I Stand: Feminism as Academic Method and as Social Vision." This appendix is recommended especially for the reader who is unfamiliar with differing feminist methods and claims. My methods for studying Buddhism are discussed in the chapter immediately following. This chapter, on "Orientations to Buddhism," also serves as an introductory overview of Buddhism for the reader not familiar with Buddhism.

Regarding my methodology, in every case, I combine methods and approaches that most scholars separate. Thus, when thinking about religion and the study of religion, I combine the approaches of history of religions and of theology. When thinking about feminism, I see feminism as both academic method and as social vision. Finally, when studying Buddhism, I seek both the historically and sociologically accurate knowledge of Buddhology and the "insider's" understanding of a Buddhist. Thus, my method might be called a "method of inseparability," bringing to mind connotations of the inseparability of Wisdom and Compassion in some forms of Buddhism.

My method involves a further inseparability, in that all three perspectives—the cross-cultural, comparative study of religion, feminism, and Buddhism—are thoroughly intertwined in all my work, no matter which focus I might be concentrating upon in any given discussion. I am deeply committed to the cross-cultural, comparative study of religion, which for me includes the results of the social sciences, especially anthropology, as well as theology, broadly understood. This perspective, adequately and sensitively pursued, can be the most basic arbiter, judge, and peacemaker between divergent points of view about religion. It is the matrix and container within which any sane, reasonable, and humane religious or spiritual statement must be grounded today.[3] I am equally deeply committed to the feminist perspective, which, in my experience radically changes one's ways of looking at almost every topic for research, as well as one's personal and political affirmations.[4] Finally, for me Buddhism is not merely grist for the comparative mill but also personal perspective. I have invested as much training in Buddhism, utilizing traditional techniques of contemplative study and meditative practice, as I have in more conventional academic studies. Thus, I work simultaneously as a comparativist, as a feminist, and as a Buddhist "theologian"; I also work simultaneously both as an insider and an outsider. I see no conflict is this method; rather, it is a complete and well-rounded approach.

2

Orientation to Buddhism:
Approaches, Basics, and Contours

A feminist history, analysis, and reconstruction of Buddhism draws upon two major bodies of theory—feminism and Buddhism. In addition to the lengthy definition of feminism as academic method and as social vision found in the first appendix, discussions of feminist method and theory regarding specific issues are found throughout this book. However, if one is reasonably unfamiliar with Buddhism, it is difficult to appreciate *feminist* analysis of Buddhist materials. It is very difficult to be introduced to a body of knowledge and to feminist commentary on that body of knowledge at the same time—an ongoing problem for teachers and scholars presenting the women studies perspective in all fields. One aspect of my solution to that problem is to give relatively complete discussions of those aspects of Buddhism upon which I will comment from a feminist point of view during my feminist discussion of them. But I am selecting from the Buddhist record, rather than discussing the entirety of Buddhism, which would be impossible for one author to do within one book. Therefore, the other aspect of my solution to the problem of simultaneous introduction to Buddhism and to feminist perspectives on Buddhism is to begin with an overview of Buddhism.

BUDDHISM: BASIC TEACHINGS

To beginners, Buddhism can seem like an incredibly complex and dense religion, but everything in Buddhism really does go back to a few basic teachings that really do encapsulate the entire tradition. Though simple, they often seem difficult to comprehend because they go against the grain of ordinary hopes and fears.

Buddhism is a non-theistic religion. Its central teachings point out to its adherents the cause of and the cure for human suffering, locating both within human attitudes towards life. Buddhism is non-theistic, or not concerned about the existence of a supreme being, because a supreme being would be unable to relieve human suffering, as it is defined by Buddhists. A supreme being cannot cause human beings to give up the attitudes that produce suffering. Only human beings are capable of that feat.

The foundational spiritual and religious attitudes of Buddhism are summarized and communicated by the Four Noble Truths and their extensions and unfoldings into the teachings of the Mahayana and the Vajrayana.

According to Buddhism, the cause of misery is located in negative habitual patterns common to all unenlightened beings. Succinctly put, human beings suffer because while still unenlightened, all beings strive with all their energy for unattainable goals. Disliking boredom and discontent, they strive for perfect complete bliss. Disliking uncertainty, they strive for perfect complete security. And disliking death and finitude, they strive for complete perfect permanence in personal immortality. According to Buddhism, these desires are completely impossible to attain under any conditions; therefore, striving to attain them is counterproductive, and serves only to deepen the pain of inevitable failure. That is the bad news, traditionally communicated by Buddhism's first and second noble truths—the truth that conventional existence is pervaded with suffering, and the truth that the cause of suffering is desire rooted in ignorance.

The good news, according to Buddhism, is that human beings do not have to remain in such useless and counterproductive, desire-ridden states of being; they can lay down the burden and experience the calm and tranquillity of enlightenment. That is the third truth, the truth of the cessation of suffering. Many attempts have been made to define the essentially ineffable quality of the liberation sought by Buddhism. All such attempts ultimately fail because liberation is a matter of experience, not theory. Perhaps liberation, in Buddhist terms, is best defined as knowing how to untie the knot of existence. To be liberated is to know "things as they are," a classic Buddhist phrase, and to know how to live with those conditions freely and compassionately. The best news of all is that there is a simple and workable path that can be used to good effect by anyone who wants to diminish the burden of excessive desire and compulsion. Buddhism prescribes a clear path, a total lifestyle, that facilitates the achievement of such liberation. The lifestyle is defined in the fourth Noble Truth, the truth of the path. Though the path contains eight elements, it is conveniently condensed into three major disciplines—*shila*, *samadhi*, and *prajna*, or moral discipline, spiritual cultivation, and the pursuit of wisdom.

These basics, found in all variants of Buddhism, are extended and amplified in the other forms of Buddhism which developed out of this foundational worldview. Mahayana Buddhism, which had emerged by about 500 years after the origins of Buddhism, developed specific ways of discussing wisdom and compassion—as emptiness and as complete altruism. Still later, Vajrayana Buddhism developed many ritual and meditative techniques, known as skillful means, that are said to make progress on the path toward enlightenment much more rapid.[1]

BUDDHISM: GEOGRAPHICAL AND HISTORICAL CONTOURS

In addition to its doctrinal complexity, Buddhism involves significant historical and cultural complexities which can seem overwhelming to someone not already familiar with Buddhism. Nevertheless, a few basics can orient someone new to Buddhism sufficiently. This sketch of the historical and geographical contours of Buddhism will emphasize the role of women in each movement within Buddhism, so briefly surveyed.[2]

Buddhism began roughly 2,500 years ago in North India. It was founded by Siddartha Gautama, an upper-caste male of royal status who abandoned his family, his social position, and his wealth to pursue spiritual liberation. Such actions were not unusual in India of that day; liberation was thought to be difficult or impossible to attain while one was involved in domestic and social activities. Therefore, many young (and older) men did as Siddartha Gautama had done. Almost immediately after his enlightenment experience and his first sermon, several other male world-renouncers became his followers. The monastic community grew rapidly.

After some years, his aunt, Mahaprajapati, who had raised him from his birth, approached the Buddha and asked that she and her women companions also be allowed to shave their heads, to put on monastic robes, and to join the renunciate community. At first the request was refused but eventually the institution of the nuns' order was permitted. However, the nuns were required to accept eight special rules as a precondition for their admission to the order; these rules subordinated the nuns' order to the monks' order. Additionally, the comment was made that, since women had been permitted to join the order, the *dharma* (Buddhist teachings) would last only 500 years instead of 1,000 years.

Such restrictions and predictions did little to deter women from entering the renunciate *sangha* (Buddhist community) and had even less effect on their ability to gain the insights required for liberation from *samsara* (cyclic existence). Many women attained *nirvana*, the extinction of craving, which brought cessation of rebirths, the goal and ideal of early Buddhism. These women's moving stories, often in the form of eloquent poems in which the women express their realization and their penetrating insight, were collected as the *Therigatha*, the Songs of the Women Elders. The literature was preserved as part of the canon of Theravada Buddhism, the form of Buddhism found today in Southeast Asia.

However, historians of Buddhism generally conclude that some centuries after the death of the Buddha, attitudes hardened. The monastic *sangha* reserved more and more power and respect for itself. Lay people were thought of *merely* as patrons; despite the *Therigatha*, the belief that women could not attain enlightenment grew popular. At the same time, however, new tendencies were developing. Within 500 years of the Buddha's death, full-blown Mahayana (larger vehicle) Buddhism emerged. In addition to significant philosophical differences with earlier Buddhism, nascent Mahayana Buddhism understood the *sangha*, or Buddhist community, differently. As the monastic *sangha* grew more self-aggrandizing, Mahayanists deliberately emphasized the larger *sangha*, including lay people and women. Therefore, many scholars include greater (or renewed) openness to women among the general characteristics of the Mahayana.

Indeed, many of the most famous and influential Mahayana texts explicitly take up the question of how much a woman can attain, concluding, in some significant cases, that women's abilities are unlimited and equal to men's. Often the Mahayana *sutra*-s (texts attributed to the Buddha) are staged as a debate between a highly developed female and a male representative of the older viewpoint. He is always astounded and disgruntled by the woman's intelligence. She always confounds him in debate. He always asks her why, if she is so realized, she is not a man. At this point two motifs end the story. In one variant, the female then magically transforms her body into a male body. In the other, she retains her female body, demonstrating by logic or magic the utter relativity and unimportance of sexual differentiation.

These narratives do not answer another important question: can a woman attain complete perfect enlightenment, or Buddhahood? One of the critical developments in Mahayana thinking was the Bodhisattva path toward complete enlightenment, recommended now for all serious practitioners. Instead of striving for individual *nirvana* bringing release from cyclic existence, Mahayana Buddhists were encouraged to take the Bodhisattva vow to attain enlightenment for the sake of all sentient beings. Few doubted that women could achieve the inspiration to take the Bodhisattva vow, but some contended that at some point in the progression toward complete perfect enlightenment and Buddhahood, the future Buddha would stop being reborn as a female. Thus the Bodhisattva would repeat the pattern of the historical Buddha, Siddartha Gautama. Commonly, in the sequence of stories about his previous lives, he stopped being reborn as a female quite early, before he stopped being reborn as an animal. Many Mahayana texts simply saw womanhood and Buddhahood as antithetical to each other. But other texts state that Buddhahood is neither male nor female, beyond gender altogether, while a few texts may possibly portray a Buddha in female form.

Still later, Vajrayana or Tantric Buddhism, which is based one the Mahayana but also goes beyond it, developed in India and then spread to Tibet.

Vajrayana Buddhism is often regarded as the form of Buddhism that most radically includes women and the feminine. This form of Buddhism has been much maligned in Western scholarship and is also suspect in many Buddhist circles, precisely because of its appreciation of women and the feminine principle. In addition, its widespread use of sexual symbolism has frequently been misinterpreted as permission for wholesale and indiscriminate sexuality. Basic Vajrayana imagery portrays all the Buddhas and Bodhisattvas as partners—male and female—in sexual union. The fundamental pair consists of discriminating awareness (*prajna*), which brings insightful liberation, and her partner, compassion (*karuna*). Though she represents the epitome of realization, she is not isolated, but is joined in male-female union with compassion, understood as activity to save all sentient beings. No wonder this version of Buddhism reveres many important female leaders and founders, especially in Tibet. No wonder the most popular figures in Tibetan devotional Buddhism include female figures. Nevertheless, women as a class, did not experience anything close to equality with men as a class, over time, even in Tibetan Vajrayana Buddhism.

Southeast Asia received the older, Theravada form of Buddhism, often considered to be the most conservative towards women. Though the nuns' order was transmitted to Sri Lanka, and was once strong there, it has died out in all current forms of Theravada Buddhism. Contemporary attempts to revive nuns' ordination lineages are extremely controversial and are often met with extreme skepticism, or even hostility. Furthermore, in Theravada countries, the monastic-lay hierarchy is quite strong and lay Buddhists are not usually expected to be seriously involved in meditation or in philosophical studies of Buddhism. Thus, women's options are quite limited. Women can take on a renunciate's lifestyle, but usually they are not officially recognized as monastics and their status is much lower than that of the monks. The most common role for women is that of a pious, but largely invisible, lay donor. Furthermore, low evaluations of women's potential for Buddhist practice and realization are common. Nevertheless, strong movements for lay practice are springing up in some Theravada contexts and a few women have become well respected lay meditation teachers.

East Asian Buddhism, both in China and in Japan, presents a different and more complex picture. Though East Asian forms of Buddhism are institutionally male dominated, Buddhism did bring new options to women in these societies. Furthermore, in East Asian Buddhism, some aspects of Buddhism favorable to women are highlighted more than in other forms of Buddhism. The full ordination of nuns has been preserved in China and Korea. These lineages of ordination, unique in the Buddhist world, are critically important in contemporary Buddhism, for they will be the source for renewing nuns' ordination lineages in other parts of the Buddhist world. Today, the nuns' *sangha* is healthy and prosperous in both Korea and Taiwan, with many young, well-educated women joining the order.

Japanese forms of Buddhism do not generally practice the same kind of strict monasticism as is found in the rest of the Buddhist world. Though monks were once ordained according to Indian norms, the traditional nuns' ordination never occurred in Japan. Eventually the bodhisattva precepts replaced the monastic precepts and a married priesthood gradually became the norm for Japan. Contemporary Japanese nuns receive these precepts, but they practice a lifestyle that is actually very similar to that of ancient Indian nuns, since, unlike their male counterparts, they usually do not marry or drink alcohol. Sometimes, these nuns may also fill the role of "temple priest," carrying out leadership and liturgical functions in their communities. As in Tibet, popular devotional forms of Buddhism, both in China and in Japan, do give significant reverence to female mythical and iconographical representations of Buddhas and Bodhisattvas.

The most recent development in the long history of Buddhism is its transmission to the West, which began early in this century. Since the mid-sixties, many more Asian teachers have taught in the West and Buddhism has grown exponentially. Currently, all forms of Buddhism can be found in Western countries, not only among Asian immigrants, who maintain Buddhism as part of their ethnic tradition, but also as the religion of choice of an articulate, well-educated, and dedicated minority of Europeans and Americans of European descent. This event provides the greatest opportunity in Buddhist history for Buddhist institutions to manifest, rather than to contradict, Buddhism's worldview and vision regarding gender relations. In the West, currently, women are active and influential in all forms of Buddhism.[3] It is too soon to tell whether women will continue their strong presence and influence in future generations of Western Buddhism. With neglect, with too much complacency about possible patriarchal backlash, this exemplary situation could be destroyed in subsequent generations, as has happened previously, not only in Buddhism, but also in other major religions.

BUDDHISM: AUTHOR'S APPROACHES

My feminist history, analysis, and reconstruction of Buddhism is a task not heretofore undertaken by Buddhists or by scholars of Buddhism. It is also a task that can be undertaken only by combining, without confusing, the "insider's" and the "outsider's" understandings of Buddhism. This task requires the outsider's Buddhological and feminist knowledge. Those lacking the outsider's academic accuracy often misrepresent and whitewash aspects of their tradition that they find unpalatable. They also often lack historical accuracy and willing-ness to critically evaluate their tradition. As a practicing academician and comparative scholar of religion, I find such omissions unacceptable. As a feminist, I cannot simply accept what any tradition may say about the proper roles for women or the supposed inherent limits of being female. Therefore, all my skills and training as a historian of religions and as a feminist will be employed fully throughout this history, analysis, and reconstruction.

On the other hand, someone who is only an outsider would not take the risks involved in analyzing and reconstructing Buddhism from a feminist point of view, nor would such a scholar be interested in the kind of feminist history of Buddhism with which I am concerned. I care, not only about scholarly accuracy, but about Buddhism after patriarchy. My interests in Buddhism are not merely or purely academic. I have invested as much in Buddhism as I have in feminism and in the academic study of religions and I have utilized tradi-tional Buddhist methods of training equally with more conventionally academic approaches. Therefore, I am not satisfied by accounts of Buddhism that are limited to technical expertise but lack depth of insight into the tradition. To me, such accounts of Buddhism misrepresent the tradition as much as do historically inaccurate or uncritical insider's accounts of the tradition.

In this task, I will use the tools of the history of religions and the values of feminism to look at Buddhism, working as a Buddhist "theologian," if that word can carry an extended connotation in this non-theistic case. In this work, I do not intend to function mainly as a reporter or commentator on the opinions and works of others, nor will I function only a replica of my Buddhist teachers, mimicking what they have said. I will work as a Buddhist engaged in world-construction, using all of the tools at my disposal. This stance is unusual for Western writers on Buddhist topics, some of whom claim that scholarship and world-construction are incompatible with each other. As I argue extensively in the appendix on the history of religions, such an attitude is riddled with contradictions and is outdated. To engage in such world-constructive work is a privilege long given to scholars writing about Christianity, Judaism, or even feminism, but long denied to Buddhist scholars. It is time to break this taboo.

Buddhism is too vast for one author or one book to be able to discuss all its variants. Though I attempt to be as broad and non-sectarian as possible, my feminist history, analysis, and reconstruction of Buddhism necessarily reflect my own orientations within Buddhism, as well as the limits of my academic training.

When I function as an outsider, I am much more a historian of religions or a comparativist than a Buddhologist or a philologist and translator. Furthermore, my academic and linguistic training is in South Asia, though I have also taught myself enough about East Asia to teach undergraduate courses.

As an insider, I am trained in Tibetan Vajrayana Buddhism, and within that framework, in the Karma Kagyu school. As a result, I see Buddhism in the "three-yana" perspective. This perspective stresses stages of spiritual development from the foundation of the basic "hinayana," which *does not* refer to contemporary Theravada Buddhism, to the more encompassing "mahayana," and into the indestructible "vajrayana." I will use this framework for organizing both my comments on the history of the roles and images of women in Buddhism and my feminist analysis of key Buddhist teachings.

The historical chapters, on the roles and images of women in Buddhism, will be largely limited to Indian and Tibetan Buddhism, given my academic and my *dharmic* specializations. However, the analysis and reconstruction are not similarly limited, since almost all major Buddhist teachings of all forms of Buddhism developed in India. A feminist analysis of the basic concepts of Buddhism, found in early Indian Buddhism as well as in all other forms of Buddhism, is, by definition relevant for all forms of Buddhism. Likewise, a feminist analysis of Indian Mahayana Buddhist concepts is relevant for East Asian forms of Buddhism, since they are grouped within the Mahayana camp. A feminist analysis of Vajrayana concepts and imagery is, of course, most relevant for Vajrayanists, though in the modern Buddhist world, characterized by efficient communication and a lessening of sectarianism, other Buddhists may find relevance in Vajrayana materials. Clearly, the feminist reconstruction I propose, though it owes something to Vajrayana inspiration, is quite non-sectarian and relevant to Buddhists of all schools and persuasions.

Finally, in this book, Buddhism is discussed as a religious and spiritual system aiming toward liberation. Buddhism could also be studied as a philosophical system. While these materials are important, I will avoid more technical aspects of Buddhist philosophy because, in my view, philosophy is secondary in Buddhism, a teaching tool for spirituality and an *upaya* (skillfully used method) for fostering insight beyond words and concepts. It is not an end in itself and does not communicate the heart of the tradition. Alternatively, Buddhism could be discussed in terms of its social, economic, and political developments. While sometimes critical for understanding some developments within Buddhism, I do not regard social, economic, or political factors as sufficient to provide an understanding of Buddhism.

II

TOWARD AN ACCURATE
AND
USABLE PAST:

A Feminist Sketch
of Buddhist History

3

Why Bother? What Is an Accurate and Usable Past Good for?

Siddartha Guatama, the Buddha, abandoned his wife and new-born infant because he was convinced that they were an obstacle to his own spiritual development. Nevertheless, he resisted women's attempts to abandon their domestic responsibilities and to seek their own spiritual development and liberation. Can a religion founded by such a man possibly serve women's interests and needs?

These two stories are well-known and often repeated. But how do they "read" from the point of view of feminist history? The first story, which is exceedingly familiar, is rarely heard or told from the point of view of the woman left behind. That the act of the future Buddha could have been radically misogynist, or simply irresponsible and cruel, that his actions probably left her emotionally and economically vulnerable, are not generally perceived in the Buddhist world. Rather, this story is lovingly retold and re-enacted as an indication of the future Buddha's concern for universal rather than private well-being.

The second story narrates that after he became the Buddha, the young man who had abandoned his wife and child was very reluctant to allow women, led by his aunt, who was also his foster-mother, to practice the same methods he had found so effective and which he taught without reservations to men. That many contemporary scholars and Buddhists question the authenticity of this story does not undo the fact that it has had great impact, usually negative for women, in Buddhist history.

On the other hand, the same set of texts that preserve these stories also recount that women were eventually allowed to found their own monastic order, which was successful both in recruiting women to its ranks and in producing women elders who achieved the highest goals of the spiritual life as formulated by early Buddhists. For many of the women who joined the nuns' order, it provided an important and liberating option and alternative to the lifestyle usually prescribed for women in north India of the sixth century B.C.E. Their songs of triumph, the *Therigatha*, were preserved as scriptural record by these early

17

Buddhists. That they may be less well-known does not obviate their existence and preservation for well over two thousand years.

Considering these stories, familiar and unfamiliar, gives us a preview of the kind of re-orientation to the familiar that is essential to a feminist reading of Buddhist history. The familiar stories and their familiar androcentric interpretations may give way and become less obvious, less clear-cut. Unfamiliar stories, largely ignored by androcentric commentators, may become central resources. A past for Buddhist women that is both accurate and usable will be a combination of re-orientation to the familiar and discovery of the unfamiliar. Avoiding both androcentric complacency and feminist rage regarding both these stories and these omissions, a new picture of the roles and images of women throughout Buddhist history emerges.

WORKING THROUGH QUADRUPLE ANDROCENTRISM

The Buddhist feminist scholar taking on the task of finding an accurate and usable past for women in Buddhism takes on a formidable task. She must work through a quadruple androcentrism to find that accurate and usable past. On the first level, when Buddhists chose which documents to keep and whose experience to preserve in their historical records, they usually operated with an androcentric consciousness and set of values. Stories about men and men's statements were far more likely to be recorded than were stories about women or what women said. As recent feminist hermeneutics have demonstrated, this choice limits, but does not cripple the contemporary scholar, if s/he wishes to do androgynous scholarship. At the second level, even when Buddhists did preserve significant records by or about women, later Buddhist traditions tend to ignore those stories in favor of stories about male heroes. The *Therigatha* were recorded and preserved, but many Buddhists throughout most Buddhist history believed that women needed to be reborn as men before they could attain enlightenment. Third, most Western scholarship on Buddhism is quite androcentric and often agrees with the biases of Buddhist records, to the point of further ignoring the few records about women or even ridiculing the women in them.* Finally, not only are the Buddhist past and Western scholarship on Buddhism thoroughly androcentric; contemporary Buddhism itself, both Asian and Western, is unrelenting in its ongoing androcentrism.

Western scholarly literature on Buddhism is androcentric, not only because it is working with androcentric documents, but because of the values of conven-

---

*For example, H. Kern, *Manual of Indian Buddhism* (Dehli: Motilal Barnasidass, 1974, reprint of 1893), p. 31, tells the story of the founding of the nuns' order, presenting the Buddha as "fully aware of the dangerous consequences attending on the admission of women." He delights in following this allegation with assertions that the nuns immediately engaged in scandalous behavior. He does not discuss their achievements.

tional Western scholarship. Western scholarly literature on Buddhism ignores women as much as does the scholarly literature about any religion, Western or Asian. Therefore, when one reads general works in Buddhist history, whether philosophical or social, one finds that few scholars have bothered to say much about the participation of women in Buddhist history or their exclusion from Buddhist institutions. For the most part, the role of women, aside from a few comments and stories, is simply *terra incognita* in the standard scholarly literature on Buddhism.

For some Western religions, the women studies perspective has begun to provide a wide range of books focusing specifically on women, even if the "mainstream" scholarly literature is quite androcentric. For Buddhism, even this has not yet been accomplished. Aside from the chapters on women in Buddhism found in the surveys of women in world religions that have appeared in recent years,[1] one cannot find a comprehensive source on women in the Buddhist tradition as a whole. Instead, we have a few books on women in specific periods of Buddhist history and a growing number of articles on various aspects of women and Buddhism. Additionally, the contemporary Buddhist world itself, both Asian and Western, is quite androcentric and patriarchal. Contemporary Buddhists are often quite uninformed about the roles of women in Buddhism historically and are indifferent or hostile to input from a Buddhist feminist movement. In Asia, feminist or women studies movements in Buddhism are small and often led by Western or by Western-educated Asian women. Often the (male) hierarchies, both scholarly and religious, of the Asian Buddhist world are indifferent or hostile to these movements. Certainly they are not quick to integrate the criticisms and knowledge generated by feminism into their curricula and institutions.

AN ACCURATE AND USABLE PAST

Working through this quadruple androcentrism, a feminist historian seeks a past that is at once accurate and usable. "Accuracy" has more to do with the women studies agenda, with feminism as an academic method, while "usability" has more to do with the feminist agenda, with feminism as social vision.

The quest for an accurate history stems from the conviction that androcentric history, by definition, cannot be accurate. It will be riddled with omissions about women, but will also, in most cases, whitewash many negativities about the patriarchal past. The women studies perspective claims, quite reasonably, that a recounted past which ignores data about the female half of the population cannot be accurate. Accurate history is always preferable to inaccurate history, simply because of its accuracy. Therefore, part of the reason to investigate the history of the roles and images of women in Buddhism is simply to recount and recover what is usually not included in histories of Buddhism.

Recognizing that our record of the past is always a *selection* from the past, that the past is always constructed when it is recounted, feminist historians ask the embarrassing question of *how* scholars choose "relevant" data. Recognizing that history is never neutral and objective, but always reinforces certain values and perspectives, the feminist historian seeks a past that is not only accurate, but usable. S/he seeks historical models, often ignored in androcentric record keeping and interpretations, of historical events that empower, rather than disempower, women. Eleanor McLaughlin, writing of the same issue in connection with Christian history, states that the androgynous scholar seeks a past that is:

> at once *responsible*—that is, grounded in the historicist rubric of dealing with the past on its own terms—and *usable*. I mean by the search for a usable past . . . an examination of . . . history with a new set of questions that arise out of commitments to wholeness for women and for all humanity. Following from new questions, this is a history that redresses omissions and recasts interpretations." [2]

Since history is always a selection from the past, it can only be more or less accurate and complete. *What* is selected and *what* is omitted, the reasons for including or excluding certain data, always coincide with certain uses of the past. Feminist history is concerned both with the uses to which an androcentric past has been put and what would constitute a usable past for women. The uses to which one would want to put the past reflect one's current values. An androcentrist is content with a record that focuses on men; the androgynous scholar, on the contrary, will seek "a history that redresses omissions and recasts interpretations."[3]

A "usable past," is important precisely because a religious community constitutes itself by means of its collective memory, the past that it recalls and emulates. Whether or not this record is completely accurate by the standards of modern empirical history is somewhat irrelevant from the religious point of view; its remembered past is being used by the religious community to perpetuate itself. This is the case even for Buddhism, in which history is not normative or revelatory, as it is for the Western monotheisms. When the record discounts or ignores women, the community is telling itself and its women something about women's potential and place in the community. Likewise, when women studies discovers a past for women, even a heroic past, in some cases, the whole community is reshaped. Therefore, the stories that people tell, the history they remember, are crucial to empowering or disempowering whole segments of the community.

One of the most important elements for a feminist usable past is good stories, whether legendary or historical. They serve as myth-models and myth-mirrors that the aspirant can take seriously and inspirationally. The centrality of story, of biography and autobiography, for understanding who people are and why they have the ideologies they hold is a well-established feminist method, which accounts for frequent self-disclosure on the part of feminist authors, myself included. Traditional Buddhism, likewise, has always recognized the value of such stories. Traditionally such stories, usually about male myth-models, are lovingly and frequently retold. Fortunately, there are many such stories about Buddhist women, many more than I would have expected from reading standard histories of Buddhism, though they are less well-known, both to Buddhists and to Western scholars of Buddhism.

When the roles and images of women throughout Buddhist history are studied as part of a feminist revalorization of Buddhism, the quest for an accurate past intertwines with the quest for a usable past, and each enhances the other. An accurate record, corrected for the omissions of androcentrism, demonstrates two things very clearly. It demonstrates that women have participated in the Buddhist past in varied and significant ways, and that their roles and images are discussed relatively frequently in Buddhist texts. On the other hand, looking specifically at women's roles and images throughout Buddhist history also demonstrates quite clearly the patriarchal inadequacies of that past. These two accurate conclusions are both usable, in different ways.

The guidelines quoted above call for studying the past in a way that is responsible, that deals "with the past on its own terms"[4] Responsibility involves not projecting the values and questions of the present onto the past, which for feminist history means avoiding the temptation to see the historical record as either black or white in terms of that tradition's attitudes toward women. Frequently, feminists who explore history report only a depressing record of prejudice, misogyny, and exclusion, accompanied by a condemnation of the people whose history is being recounted. Sometimes, less frequently, a feminist will find that her favorite past is extremely favorable to women, at least as compared with other pasts. It is much more difficult to stay with the subtlety of a mixed record and to refrain from praising or blaming the past, both of which result from a projection of feminist agendas onto the past.

However, at the same time, it is equally important, on the basis of an accurate, rather than a whitewashed, record, to call that past "patriarchal" when the assessment fits. Having enough information to be able to make this judgment is critically important for a feminist revalorization of Buddhism. Without this information, many conservative Buddhists claim that the Buddhist treatment of women is without problem and does not need to be reconsidered and reconstructed. In countering their complacency, it is useful to be able, accurately, to point out ways in which the Buddhist treatment of women has been inappropriate, neither in accord with the ideals and norms of Buddhism nor with other, more egalitarian, examples from the Buddhist record. At this juncture in history, given the promise inherent in the auspicious coincidence of Buddhism and feminism, such information and such awareness are especially critical.

SOME GENERALIZATIONS REGARDING AN ACCURATE AND USABLE BUDDHIST PAST

In accurate history, it is important to differentiate clearly among "androcentrism," "patriarchy," and "misogyny" and to apply these terms precisely. "Androcentrism" and "patriarchy" usually go together. "Androcentrism" is a mode of consciousness, a thought-form, a method of gathering information and classifying women's place in the (male-defined) "scheme of things." Patriarchy is the social and institutional form that usually goes with androcentrism. As is clear, patriarchy involves a gender hierarchy of men over women. Men control women, or at least like to think that they do.

"Misogyny" is a term that should be saved for phenomena that demonstrate its literal meaning—"hatred (or fear) of women and femininity." An individual in any kind of society could be a misogynist and not all patriarchs are misogynists. Patriarchs often praise women "in their place," but they could become misogynists vis-à-vis women who leave their assigned place for a self-determined one. A true misogynists hates or fears all women and anything connected with them. He regards them as intrinsically, categorically, and essentially evil or inferior. He would prefer life without women. It should be clear that I am defining "misogyny" very closely and will use that label as sparingly as possible, since, in my view, misogyny is much more damaging and destructive than patriarchy or androcentrism. I do not find widespread misogyny in the Buddhist tradition, using this definition.

However, feminist analyses of classical Buddhist thought and institutions will still conclude that, for the most part, traditional Buddhism is relatively androcentric and that those who formulated the tradition and wrote the texts operated with an androcentric worldview. In fact, most of the things that will make feminists most uncomfortable with traditional Buddhism stem from its androcentrism, which is assumed, unquestioned, and deeply held in all periods of Buddhist history and in all traditional Buddhist settings. Socially, androcentric consciousness manifests in male-controlled institutions, i.e. in patriarchy. Thus one should not be surprised that Buddhist institutions often excluded women from valued pursuits and leadership roles. Therefore, though "the woman question" comes up over and over again in Buddhist history, it almost always comes up in an androcentric fashion. The question, the issue, is always what to do about women, what special rules they would have to observe, whether or not they can become enlightened, whether they could progress as far as men on the Buddhist path. . . . In characteristic androcentric fashion, women are experienced and discussed as the other, as objects, as "they" rather than "we," as exceptions to the norm that need to be regulated, explained, and placed in the world.

The assessment that historical Buddhism is androcentric in its thought-forms and patriarchal in its institutions is an *analysis*, an *accurate description*, but not an *accusation*. One cannot reasonably accuse or condemn the past of anything, though one may express relief at not having lived under such conditions. It is not an inappropriate projection of feminist values onto the past to describe and analyze its thought-forms and institutions accurately, using categories available to scholars who have made the transition from androcentric and androgynous methods. We would be guilty of an inappropriate projection of feminist values onto the past only if we did not stop with an analysis of its thought-forms and institutions, but also railed against the humans who participated in those modes of thinking and living. We shall save those emotions for those in the *present* who try to cling to an outmoded, and now cruel, androcentric and patriarchal way of being.

Surprisingly, once one becomes attuned to looking at the Buddhist past with the goal of finding accurate information about women, one discovers that the role of women is explicitly discussed in texts from all major periods of Buddhist history. For someone seeking a usable past, this is important information. Given this information, it can not be contended that concern about women's proper position in Buddhism is only a modern issue. Since the issue of women's proper involvement in Buddhism was frequently discussed over long periods of history, and since there are significantly differing opinions on the topic, a feminist analysis of these statements could not be dismissed as a mere projection of modern values and concerns onto a past that was indifferent to such questions.

An accurate survey of this androcentric and patriarchal, but not highly misogynist record, will reveal that throughout the centuries, two basic assessments of women are repeated in numerous variations. One conclusion asserts that there is some basic problem with the female gender. Women are thought to be much less likely than are men to make significant progress on the path and Buddhist men declaim on the preferability of maleness over femaleness. The variants of this conclusion range from hostility toward and fear of women to pity for the misfortune of female rebirth. This "solution" to the question of sexual differentiation is probably more frequent and more popular than the second conclusion.

However, the second conclusion, that being female presents no barrier to the achievement of liberation, is much more normative—a conclusion that becomes obvious when one analyzes major Buddhist doctrines with respect to their implications for gender issues. Whether or not one were to conclude that this second position is more normative for Buddhism, one cannot dispute the existence of this position throughout Buddhist history, which again demonstrates that a "quasi-feminist" position promoting women's equality and dignity is not merely a modern position dependent on modern values. Just as the existence of this position in familiar traditional texts disputes the position of those who would contend that feminist issues in Buddhist thought are a modern innovation, so these texts also confound a common allegation of other feminist critics of religion. One of the important positions in feminist theology and spirituality claims that *all* major current religions are essentially patriarchal and serve men's interests but not women's. Usually formulated against Judaism and Christianity, this position nevertheless includes Buddhism in its sweep. Those who advance this generalization about Buddhism usually quote a few of the most negative texts and stories found in Buddhist thought, but, as will become clearer and clearer, such easy generalizations are superficial and inaccurate for Buddhism. Traditional and revered important Buddhist texts do claim that femaleness is no barrier, just as they also proclaim, in other contexts, that it is.

In fact, the position that femaleness is no barrier to the achievement of the Buddhist human ideals takes two forms in Buddhist texts. The much more common variation on this theme essentially proclaims that "the *dharma* is neither male nor female," that gender is irrelevant or even non-existent when one truly understands the Buddhist teachings. One also finds infrequent claims that in fact, for those with good motivation, femaleness is actually an advantage. Though that assessment is not by any means common or well-known, its very existence is important for gathering the fullness of an accurate record of Buddhist attitudes toward gender.

WESTERN BUDDHISTS AND BUDDHIST ANDROCENTRISM

Accurate history is important and interesting for scholars. Usable and accurate history is even more critical for world-construction within a tradition. The utility of a usable past is clearest to those who have some stake in the future of the tradition. Therefore, I am more concerned about the attitude of Western Buddhists toward Buddhist androcentrism than about either the oversights of Western scholarship or about androcentric Asian Buddhist attitudes. This is because I am writing as a Western Buddhist and am convinced that many of the most significant and necessary developments in Buddhism regarding gender issues will first be articulated by Western Buddhists. Therefore, I find the complacent or unaware attitudes of most of my fellow Western Buddhists to be a problem. Though not traditional or patriarchal in their *practice* of Buddhism, many Western Buddhists are nevertheless ignorant about the androcentric values prevalent throughout most Buddhist history and hostile to an articulate and self-conscious feminist Buddhist position. This stance is quite dangerous to the long-term health of Western, possibly of world, Buddhism.

Most Western Buddhists, as members of the first-generation of a new religious movement, are far better informed about their tradition than is typical of the rank and file membership of most religious movements. They are especially knowledgeable concerning the philosophical and doctrinal components of their religion and tend to be relatively well informed about the history of their particular sect of Buddhism, though they are less well informed about Buddhism in general, whether past or present. Unfortunately, they are far less well informed about women's roles throughout Buddhist history and often assume that women have always participated in Buddhism to the extent that is normal in present-day Western Buddhist communities. They tend to be totally ignorant of Buddhism's patriarchal record and to lack specific information about women's roles in Asian Buddhism. Sometimes they do have some acquaintance with a few of the outstanding female figures in Asian Buddhist history and take them to be far more normal and far less token figures than they are. Therefore, they tend to regard feminism as unnecessary in a Buddhist context and Buddhist feminists as traitors, if not as heretics, who just don't understand that detachment is the heart of Buddhist teaching.

Unfortunately, Western Buddhists are usually so unaware of *women's* situation in Asian Buddhism they do not realize how different their own situation is. Instead, they take those differences for granted, assuming them to be normal, which is a rather shortsighted approach. For it has been noted, though not frequently or forcefully enough, that the single biggest difference between the practice of Buddhism in Asia and the practice of Buddhism in the West is the full and complete participation of women in Western Buddhism.

This difference is forcefully demonstrated visually if one compares photographs of the *Sadhana* (assigned spiritual practice) of Vajrayogini being performed at Rumtek monastery in Sikkim and in Boulder Colorado by Western Buddhists. Since this *sadhana* is widely practiced in the Buddhist sect in which I participate, and since this practice has been very important to me personally, these pictures always stab my heart. In the photographs from Rumtek, only men perform the *sadhana*; in the photograph from Boulder, women are also very much in evidence.[5]

Unfortunately, ignoring and indifference can be so rampant that Western Buddhists, including women who value their own involvement in Buddhist practice, simply *don't notice*. The reactions of some of my friends is typical. A large number of Western Buddhist students had just viewed a spectacular video filmed at Rumtek monastery. It presented such a sympathetic portrait of the beauty and simplicity of life at Rumtek that one could hardly avoid longing to participate. The only woman in the film was a laywoman, shown climbing the steps, twirling her prayer wheel, to leave offerings outside and then depart. But my women friends noticed, not that they would not be admitted either, but the appeal of the place. Many of them enthusiastically proclaimed that they were ready to go. Not one of them remarked that she *wished* she could go, and would go, *were it not for the physical entrance requirement she could never meet*. They were too blind to the most significant deviation of Western Buddhism from Asian models even to notice how important it was for them. And they became hostile to me when I pointed out their potential problem.

Study of the past is often recommended as the alternative to repeating the past. My reasons for wanting to look at the history of women in Buddhism are partially motivated by such considerations, as well as by the desire simply to *know* that past, for scholarly reasons. It is important for Western Buddhists to know what the past involves, so that they can make informed decisions about retaining worthwhile traditions or reshaping inadequate heritages from the past. An analysis of the past record that emphasizes the subtlety, complexity, and ambiguity of traditional Buddhist resources on questions of gender will indicate both how appropriate and how inappropriate those resources can be. Seen from the point of view of the values of contemporary feminism, Buddhist resources are neither black nor white, neither wholly patriarchal nor wholly non-patriarchal, but quite mixed. With these resources available, the contemporary Buddhist seeking to construct an equitable position on gender issues can readily see *both* how "good" and how "bad" the Asian models are. One can readily see that there is a traditional basis from which to argue for more equitable gender relations as the norm for Buddhism, as well as a need to toss out certain conventions because they are so hopelessly sexist. Using this strategy allows one to maintain continuity with the tradition and with the past when it is possible to do so without violating standards of gender equity—always a useful feminist strategy in my opinion.

Additionally, Western Buddhists stand at the confluence, the "auspicious co-incidence," of two of the world's most powerful movements toward liberation—Buddhism and feminism. Therefore, Western Buddhists have a unique opportunity, as well as heavy responsibilities. Western Buddhists have the opportunity and the responsibility to manifest Buddhism after patriarchy. Given such stakes, it is hard to imagine someone saying "Why bother?" when confronted with the task of studying and analyzing patterns of women's involvement in Buddhism throughout history. Rather, the response should be to study the past so that we can "get it right" this time.

4

Sakyadhita, Daughters of the Buddha: Roles and Images of Women in Early Indian Buddhism

"You are the Buddha, you are the teacher,
I am your daughter, . . . your true child,
born from your mouth, my task done. . . ."*

Therigatha, 336

The first five hundred years of Buddhism represent the first major unit in Buddhist history. By the end of this period, Buddhism was undergoing its first major renovation, or corruption, depending on one's point of view. Though everyone agrees that this new development can be called Mahayana Buddhism, a name for the Buddhism of this first period is a more difficult issue. Though many features of this early Indian Buddhism are kept alive in current Theravada Buddhism, contemporary Theravadin Buddhism is not identical with early Buddhism, especially in practices regarding women. In any case, it is an anachronism to use the term "Theravada," which names one of a number of schools that existed during this early period, for the entire period.

Likewise, the term "hinayana" is no longer used to refer to this early Indian Buddhism. The term "hinayana" has several accurate uses in Buddhism, but none of them names this period in Buddhist history. One use of the term "hinayana," as a pejorative used by Mahayanists of their rivals, is especially offensive to contemporary Theravadins and should, therefore, be avoided. The other use of the term is not well understood, but carries no negative connotations when properly understood. Tibetan Vajrayana Buddhists, speaking out of their familiar "three-yana perspective," call their first *yana* the "hinayana," but do not equate their "hinayana" with contemporary Theravada forms of Buddhism, despite a superficial similarity. Nor do they mean the earliest forms of

---

* *Therigatha*, verse 336, translated by K.R. Norman. The term "Sakyadhita—Daughters of the Buddha" has been taken by a contemporary group of Buddhist women in the lineage of the ancient Theris—female elders—who are so important in this chapter. This phrase from their hymns of liberation evokes the aims of many contemporary Buddhist women.

historical Buddhism. Thus, no name of a contemporary Buddhist denomination can properly be used of the Buddhism of this first period, despite the fact that all forms of Buddhism see themselves as directly in the line of that early Buddhism. When speaking of this historical period, I shall always use the term "early Indian Buddhism" for this distinctive form of Buddhism, which was not completely carried forward into any contemporary Buddhism.

Discovering an accurate and usable past concerning women during this period of Buddhist history involves focus upon two conflicting bodies of literature, both concerning the nuns of early Buddhism. The well-known story of the Buddha's reluctant permission to found the nuns' order contrasts significantly and starkly with the less well-known record of early nuns' success, as recorded in the *Therigatha*.[1] This literature demonstrates that, from its beginnings, Buddhists advocated both that there is some problem with women and that women are just as capable as men of achieving Buddhism's goals. From the beginning, the Buddhist position is unclear and ambiguous. By quoting only part of the record, one could easily paint a portrait of Buddhism as hopelessly negative to women or as very egalitarian in its treatment of men and women. Included in this literature are many stories of many women for whom Buddhism was deeply liberating and satisfying, women who manifest that women are highly capable of achieving Buddhism's goals, women who can still inspire their spiritual daughters. We also find many stories, including many elements of the Buddha's own story, that do not indicate an auspicious or positive relationship between women and early Indian Buddhism.

Perhaps because Western scholarship on Buddhism is androcentric, the story of the Buddha's reluctance to ordain women receives much more attention than the achievements of the nuns. Perhaps this imbalance also stems from the long-term failure of the nuns' order; because it did not fare well historically, it is easier to explain its poor record if the Buddha's reluctance, rather than the strengths of the early order, is emphasized. However, if one reads the literature of this period using androgynous methods, one cannot fail to be impressed by the dignity, strength, and size of the women's order, as portrayed in the *Therigatha*. One wonders why these stories are not more strongly emphasized, more frequently recounted. Certainly if they were, our stereotypical impressions of women in early Indian Buddhism would be significantly changed. My own reaction, on first reading them, was to wonder how, with such a strong record of women's achievements in early Buddhism, so much male-dominance came to characterize the tradition and to seem, to most observers, to be the norm for Buddhism. When I made this comment to someone else, she replied, "No. What's difficult to explain, given the predominance of patriarchy in that era, is how such extraordinary literature came into the record at all or was preserved."

Either way, real consciousness of the *Therigatha* and their contents must change one's perceptions of early Indian Buddhism from what one receives in standard readings of that period.

WORLD RENUNCIATION AND EARLY INDIAN BUDDHISM

All opinions and stories about women in this period of Buddhist history are imbedded in the social and spiritual phenomenon of world renunciation. Without understanding the worldview and the values that led both men and women to renounce their birth-given social ties and wealth and to regroup in the alternative society of world renouncers, one cannot hope to understand early Indian Buddhism. Because we are familiar with parallel Western forms of asceticism motivated by a different worldview and different values, Indian world renunciation is frequently misinterpreted by assumed similarities with Western asceticism. As is now well-known, Indian religious thought affirms both the ascetic world-renouncer and the householder, but it is important for each person to recognize her appropriate path. Worldly life is not condemned as worthless, for it provides opportunity to accrue merit and good karma and is the matrix of recruitment and support for world renouncers. But, according to early Indian Buddhism, the householder's lifestyle is not conducive to the final goal of *nirvana*, and is, therefore, an *inappropriate* lifestyle for someone set on that final goal. The literature of early Indian Buddhism, unlike much Hindu literature, primarily reflects the values of world renouncers set on the final goal. The frequent less-than-flattering comments on the householder's lifestyle should be seen, not as universal condemnation of all householders, for many people are not suited for the lifestyle of the monks and nuns, but as reflecting the struggle of renunciates to break free, often against the wishes of their nearest kin.

But why is the world renouncer's lifestyle considered to be so superior? Answers to this question often make false analogies with Western asceticism. For the Buddhist world-renouncer, the body, wealth, family ties, or sense pleasures are not to be avoided because of their intrinsically evil nature, for these things are not viewed as evil. Rather, the attachment and confusion that they tend to breed must be overcome to achieve spiritual liberation. Early Indian Buddhism, like much Indian spirituality of that time, sees little hope that anyone could attain detachment and insight while pursuing sense pleasure, bodily enhancement, or family stability and wealth; these things are too distracting. They are inappropriate concerns for someone set on liberation because they produce emotions that are the polar opposites of detachment, insight, and freedom. These values motivated the women who renounced the world as much as they motivated the men. But many questioned whether it was as appropriate or as possible for women to renounce the world or properly to cultivate detachment. Herein lies much of the ambiguity and tension found in early Indian Buddhist literature regarding women.

RELUCTANT APPROVAL: THE BUDDHA AND THE NUNS' ORDER

Five years after his enlightenment experience and the founding of both the renunciate order for men and the lay sangha, the Buddha received a visit from his aunt, also his foster-mother, Prajapati, accompanied by a large group of women. Three times they asked to be admitted into the monastic order, but each time were told, "Enough, O Gotami, let it not please thee that women should be allowed to do so." The women left weeping, but they persisted. They cut off their hair, put on saffron renunciates' robes, and travelling on foot, went on to the Buddha's next stopping place. Their pitiful condition when they arrived is stressed in many retellings of the story.

At this point, Ananda, the Buddha's as-yet-unenlightened attendant, took up the women's case with the Buddha. Again the request was put forth three times and refused three times. Then Ananda, according the text (*Cullavagga*, x1.3), approached the Buddha with another argument, asking, "Lord, are women, having gone forth from home into homelessness in the *dhamma* and discipline proclaimed by the Truth-finder, able to realize the fruit of stream-attainment or the fruit of once-returning or the fruit of non-returning or perfection?" The Buddha replied they would be able to realize all these goals. Then Ananda argued that since women would be able to benefit from the practice of renunciation and since Prajapati had been so kind to Siddartha, " . . . it were well Lord, that women should obtain the going forth from home into homelessness in the *dhamma* and the discipline proclaimed by the Truth-finder." The Buddha replied "If, Ananda, the Gotamid Pajapati the Great accepts eight important rules, that may be ordination for her." The Buddha recited the rules to Ananda, who conveyed them to Prajapati. She accepted them without reservation.

The Buddha is reported then to have uttered the oft-quoted statement:

> If Ananda, women had not obtained the going forth from home into homelessness in the *dhamma* and discipline proclaimed by the Truth-finder, the Brahma-faring, Ananda, would have endured for a thousand years. But since, Ananda, women have gone forth . . . in the *dhamma* and the discipline proclaimed by the Truth-finder, now Ananda, the Brahma-faring will endure only five hundred years.

This prediction is followed by comparisons between a household subject to robbery because it contains many women and few men or crops that do not prosper because of disease, and a *dhamma* that will be short-lived because women have obtained permission to renounce the world and live the homeless life. The section ends with the Buddha's justification for the eight special rules. "Even, Ananda, as a man, looking forward, may build a dyke to a great reservoir so that the water may not overflow, even so, Ananda, were the eight important rules for nuns laid down by me."[2]

Because the impressions one gains from this story and from the *Therigatha* are so irreconcilable, textual and historical studies suggest an easy solution. Many would prefer to regard the Buddha's negative attitudes towards the nuns' order as an interpolation into the tradition, reflecting the values of later, more conservative disciples. Indeed, that solution makes historical sense. It would be difficult to explain how the *Therigatha* could arise in the atmosphere of the canonical accounts of the Buddha's predictions about the long-term effects of the nuns' order on Buddhism's survival. It is not so difficult, given the patriarchy generally prevalent in Indian culture, to imagine less dedicated and less visionary later disciples reverting to conventional practices and attitudes regarding women.

Scholars who have studied this period extensively conclude that, at the time of the Buddha, the situation of women was relatively good, compared with other possibilities in patriarchal societies.[3] Scholars also conclude that attitudes toward women changed slowly during the period of ancient Indian Buddhism, so that by the end of this period, misogyny is far more prevalent in the texts and women are much more frequently presented as less capable than men and as snares to men.[4] For example, the *Jataka* stories (stories of the Buddha's previous lives), which are generally said to be later, present an almost uniformly negative picture of women,[5] which contrasts sharply with more ambiguous portrayals in earlier literature. In an excellent article, Kajiyama Yuichi presents convincing evidence that the prediction regarding the shortened lifespan of Buddhism due to the admission of women to the monastic orders actually dates from the time when early Indian Buddhism was challenged and threatened by the rise of the Mahayana, which had occurred by 500 years after the founding of Buddhism. In the same article, it is also argued that the familiar conclusion that a woman cannot be a Buddha or attain any of the "five stations" cannot be earlier than the first century B.C.[6]

However, none of these explanations was available to the tradition, which simply preserved both sets of texts. Because the historicist's reworking of the accounts has had no impact on the religious tradition itself, I prefer not to rest simply with modern scholarly methods of easing the problems presented by these two contradictory sets of texts.

One wants to try to understand, explain, or explain away the Buddha's reluctance to ordain women into the homeless life because his attitudes, as represented in canonical literature, seem so antithetical to the basic message of

Buddhism. Yet we can only hypothesize. Previous attempts to explain the story just told, such as I.B. Horner's lengthy discussion in her important book,[7] often seem unconvincing to later generations. Each scholar who comments on this text tells us mainly about his or her outlook, not the Buddha's. Yet the outlook demands attention from any Buddhist feminist and teases the scholar's curiosity. As I.B. Horner points out,[8] this is also the only instance on record of the Buddha changing his position due to persuasion and arguments from his disciples. What can one make of the whole story as it stands in traditional texts?

First, I would suggest that it is important to differentiate clearly what is at issue in the full story. *Never* at stake is women's ability to pursue and achieve the early Buddhist goal of *nibbana* or peace. The Buddha is never represented, in earlier texts, as saying that women could not achieve that goal and a number of verses in the Pali canon represent him as saying that women could or did achieve the goal. He does not refuse women on grounds of their inability and is induced to change his mind by Ananda's challenges to him about their ability. Thus, the one thing that seems certain is that the Buddha's reasons for first refusing the women's request are not due to belief on his part that women are inferior or unworthy. The Buddha is not represented as a misogynist in this text (except in the coda that predicts Buddhism's premature decline, the part of the story most likely to be a later addition).

But, especially if misogyny, the superficially most convincing answer, cannot be blamed, we want to know what reasons do make sense within the text and context as a whole. Two important issues are at stake in the text. Should women be allowed to pursue Buddhism's goal of *nibbana* as world renouncers, as homeless mendicants? If women are ordained into world renunciation, what will be their status and relations with the male renunciates? In dealing with these two questions, we will see that though the Buddha is not represented as a misogynist, he does come through as androcentric and patriarchal. And, I would suggest that, while the misogynist comments may well be later editorial comments, the androcentrism and patriarchy are not.

Why would the Buddha not have immediately acceded to Prajapati's request? Why, in fact, did he wait for her to come forward rather than encouraging women to become world renouncers, as he had already encouraged men? This is a sensible question for anyone with feminist values, but it makes no sense in a social world steeped in androcentrism and strong gender roles. The equality and common humanity of women and men was not the Buddha's major perception about gender, even after his enlightenment. Differences between women and men and the tensions that arise from their close proximity seem to have been much more evident to him. In short, seeing the negativities of androcentrism through women's eyes simply was not his issue. It took persistent women, fueled by their own experiences of suffering caused by patriarchy, to challenge him to do something unconventional and out of the ordinary regarding gender arrangements.

This perhaps could be cited as a shortcoming of the Buddha, a limit to his omniscience, but it is also the unfortunate truth that women, not men, are usually the ones who push for non-patriarchal gender arrangements. This is not necessarily due to ill will on men's part, but simply to lack of experience and consciousness. It is relevant, I believe, to cite contemporary parallels in the Buddhist world. The move to upgrade the nuns' order in contemporary times is being led by women. Some men are quite hostile and unsympathetic. Others, such as the Dalai Lama, are supportive, but they are not leaders of the movement. It's not their issue and not enough is at stake for them. I am also instructed by a personal example. My own teacher, when introducing a feature of Tibetan Buddhism that is stereotypically male to Westerners, simply assumed that only men would take on this role. When women objected he acceded quite readily, but it had not occurred to him to include women from the beginning, even though he was usually very careful not to perpetuate Tibetan cultural stereotypes. Thus, it is not too surprising, though it is unfortunate and causes sadness, that the Buddha, in a sex-role ridden and patriarchal society, did not fully welcome women with their request to undertake an unconventional task.

Given the values placed upon the homeless life vis-à-vis the householder's life in early Buddhism, one could argue that it would be pointless to concede that women are not intrinsically inferior to men spiritually if they are not also encouraged, or at least allowed, to take up the homeless life. Why would there be reluctance to ordain women as world renouncers? First of all, though Buddhists approved of world renunciation by young men, many others did not. Critics of the movement saw such world renunciation as highly irresponsible and destructive. Probably many a parent, wife, or child cursed the Buddhist order that took their men away. Dependent on lay donors, Buddhists may have been reluctant to incur further wrath by also taking mothers, wives, and daughters-in-law. Such a double standard is easily arguable in an androcentric value system, just as today many still argue that women should not come home from war in body-bags, though they will accept that fate for men.

A second set of reasons probably was more immediate. Life in and for the monastic order would simply be more complicated if women joined it. Rules would have to be created to regulate the interactions of male and female renunciates, whose relations would be more complicated and direct than those of monks and laywomen. The gossip of laypeople and non-Buddhists concerning how those male and female renunciates actually interacted would have to be counteracted. Records of lay accusations that monks and nuns engaged in sexual relations occur in some texts.[9] Fears that women renunciates would be vulnerable to male violence were realistic. Stories about male violence against nuns do occur, as do regulations designed to prevent it. These regulations usually restrict women from more solitary travel and practices,[10] just as today we often counter male violence against women by encouraging women not to be in dangerous places at unseemly hours.

But probably the overarching and dominant reason for the reluctance to ordain women to homelessness is simple. It was too unconventional. Buddhism was not a socially revolutionary movement seeking to create a reformed society, but a path of individual self-removal from conventional society. Though contemporary Jains probably included female ascetics, the idea of women without social ties was simply too difficult for most of the Buddha's contemporaries to contemplate. For men to take up this lifestyle was already a somewhat common, if not always appreciated, option by the Buddha's time; for women to do it was radically unconventional, and the Buddha was not a social reformer seeking to correct social injustices and inequities. Overcoming androcentric consciousness and patriarchal gender arrangements was not his issue.

THE EIGHT SPECIAL RULES

Presented with good arguments why his order should take on all these difficulties, the Buddha relented and the nuns' order was begun. Regarding the major issue of how the women's order would rank vis-à-vis the men's order, there was far less flexibility. The eight special rules (*garudharma*) were given as condition for Prajapati's ordination as well as the form of her ordination ceremony. The Buddha compared these rules to a dike built to hold in the water of a reservoir so that it wouldn't overflow. But what is being held in? The conventional gender hierarchy of men over women, male control over women, which is central to each of the eight special rules. Any nun, even of great seniority, must always honor, rise for, and bow to each and every monk, even if newly ordained. The nuns must spend the rainy season retreat in a location where they can be supervised by monks. Monks were to determine the dates for the twice-monthly confessional meetings of the order. Monks would participate in the interrogation of nuns who were accused of breaking rules, but the reverse did not apply. Monks would also help determine a nun's penalty for infractions, but the reverse did not apply. Monks must participate in the nuns' ordination, but the reverse did not apply. Nuns could not, under any circumstances, reprimand or criticize a monk. Finally, nuns were not allowed to officially admonish monks, though monks could admonish women.[11]

In ancient India, it was even more unthinkable that patriarchal gender hierarchy could be ignored than that women could live the homeless life without conventional social ties. Maintaining that formal hierarchy was the bottom line in early Indian Buddhism, which not even world renunciation would change. Virtually every other aspect of worldly life was left behind by the renunciates, but this one sign was maintained adamantly. Though Prajapati had at first accepted the eight special rules without hesitation, after a time, she made a request for one boon to the Buddha through Ananda. "It were well, Lord, if the Lord would allow greeting, standing up for, salutation and the proper duties between monks and nuns according to seniority." (*Cullavagga*, x: 2.3) This request, if granted, would have undone the first special rule. The Buddha flatly refused with the argument that even in other sects, which were subject to poor leadership, men did not rise for or salute women under any circumstances. Therefore, it certainly could not be allowed by "the Truth-farer." Additionally, he declared it an offence if any monk should so behave toward a woman. (*Cullavagga* x: 2.3) Thus it seems clear that while many felt that women had genuine spiritual capabilities and were sympathetic to their wish to lead the homeless life, they felt even more strongly that male gender hierarchy and male control over women must be observed, even between world renouncers.

The eight special rules presented no inherent barrier to women's spiritual development. They mandated institutional subordination, not spiritual subordination. This point is still made by defenders of contemporary Theravada forms of male dominance. Women were not given inferior spiritual instructions or practices. Indeed, in these aspects the monastic code dealt with women and men in remarkably similar ways. They lived the same lifestyle, did the same practices, and even looked alike, both having shaved heads and identical robes. Furthermore, the monastic code protected nuns from demanding monks who might ask nuns to do housework for the monks or to give them food and clothing—feminine tasks in the renounced world.[12] Such rulings are remarkably considerate and recognize that women renounce the world for their own religious pursuits, which should not be undermined by the demands of men used to female service.

Superficially, it would seem that formal subordination, when combined with such similarity of treatment and protection from male demands and interference, could hardly have any major negative repercussions. However, as Nancy Falk has pointed out, in subtle ways, this formal subordination worked to undermine the nuns. Because nuns could not admonish monks, and because the orders lived largely separate lives to protect celibacy, women never became important teachers of the community at large, though they made significant progress themselves and often taught other women. Since they did not become major teachers, well known and important to lay donors, they did not attract the same level of economic support as did the monks. In her analysis, this economic disability, wrought by indirect effects of the eight special rules, when combined with the undercurrent of misogyny that surfaced in the story of the Buddha's reluctance to found the order at all, eventually weakened the order until it disappeared in most parts of the Buddhist world.[13] In this complex web of cause and effect, it is difficult to know which is the most important factor. I would suggest that the rules, norms, and conventions that prevented women from becoming major teachers of the community at large were most central. In a tradition that thrives and survives on the transmission of knowledge and insight from generation to generation of teacher and student, any group that is structurally prohibited from becoming important teachers will be seriously demeaned and diminished. Furthermore, the tradition will be seriously impoverished by the lack of their voices and insights. To silence women is a dominant control tactic of androcentric consciousness and patriarchal gender arrangements. Thus this consequence of the eight special rules has the most serious immediate and long-term impact.

THE PAST: USABLE AND NOT USABLE

Acknowledging the existence of this story and trying to find some cogent reasons for the attitudes toward women reported in it are part of the task of the feminist historian of Buddhism. It is important to have an accurate record, even when that accurate record includes important stories that are unpleasant to contemplate. But that is not the sole task of the feminist historian, who is also seeking a "usable past." I suggest that this story, for the most part, though not entirely, simply does not qualify as part of the usable Buddhist past. The values reflected in the story, especially the intense commitment to the idea that women must, in all conditions—even world renunciation—be controlled by men, are incompatible with more basic and fundamental Buddhist values. They are an unfortunate hangover from conventionality that was not or could not be excised from Buddhism in its original period. As such, they are not worth fostering any more. This judgment extends not only to the misogynist coda or to the Buddha's initial reluctance to ordain women, but also to the eight special rules themselves.

Some will, of course, recoil from the suggestion that the Buddha of canonical texts could be represented as subscribing to an outmoded value. The alternative to that conclusion is, however, even more unpalatable. One must become a literalist and fundamentalist vis-à-vis the given text, which is an attitude not traditionally Buddhist and not appropriate even for religions that have a myth of revelation as part of their core symbol-system. Some Buddhists, in shying away from this conclusion, become unwitting fundamentalists for another reason—the Buddha is said to be fully enlightened and omniscient.

How then can we followers of the Buddha pick and choose which of his words we will still take seriously? Indeed, sometimes for shock value, I suggest that if the Buddha made the statements recorded in this story, he could not have been fully enlightened. Certainly he wasn't omniscient. The texts say that the religion will only last 500 years, not a thousand years, because of the ordination of women. But the religion has lasted well more than either figure! Literalist fundamentalists are always selective about which verses they take literally. Those who would argue that we must retain the eight special rules because they are from the Buddha, (thereby concealing their true agenda of maintaining male control over women), would never then conclude that Buddhism should have self-destructed 1500 or 2000 years ago so that the Buddha's prediction could be proved to be literally true!

I suggest a much more sensible resolution of all these difficulties. The omniscience of a Buddha, whatever it may mean, does not include eternally accurate scientific or historical statements, nor eternally valid institutional forms and rules. In dropping outmoded scientific pronouncements or social norms, we are not suggesting that the insights encoded in the Four Noble Truths will be next. It is a matter of distinguishing essential insights from non-essential cultural trappings. Those familiar with Christian feminist theology will notice that this distinction is also critical to Christian feminism, as it must be to any feminist consideration of a current major religion. The only other ethical evaluation, given the evils of patriarchy, is completely to discard the religions.

This story does, however, contain one supremely usable element. The Buddha, persuaded by the logic of the argument that women, who have the same spiritual capabilities and needs as men, would benefit equally with men from the pursuit of the most helpful and appropriate religious disciplines, *changed his mind.* He changed his mind despite misgivings, practical difficulties, and negative anti-women public opinion. This is, in fact, the most usable model we could have, more usable than an omniscient Buddha solving everyone's problems before people realize there is a problem to be solved. It is not reasonable to expect men to determine what women need and be the leaders of a "women's movement." All that is really required is that when women object to unreasonable and inhumane discriminations and present a program that corrects the problem, men not stand in opposition, trying to maintain their gender-based privileges and power. Thus, the Buddha becomes an extremely relevant model for today. Though at first he resisted women's plans to promote their own spiritual and human well-being, he withdrew that opposition in the face of an overwhelmingly logical and humane counterargument. Would that the male hierarchs who hold almost every position of importance in the Buddhist world today would focus on this theme of the story and take it to heart!

Other stories about the Buddha's interactions with women in the canonical literature are significantly different from the story of the founding of the nuns' order, and much more usable. Though in many cases the nuns speak to the Buddha through a monk intermediary, there are numerous stories of the Buddha directly giving women high-quality *dharma* instruction. Especially in the *Therigatha*, the Buddha is not represented as reluctant to minister to his female disciples, whether lay or monastic. Some nuns are sometimes taught by the Buddha in a dream or a vision at an especially critical time in their meditation practice. He declares certain nuns to be experts in various aspects of monastic life, meditation practice or teaching. He takes special care to instruct some women who are brought to him so distraught that they appear to be deranged. That he advises and teaches the nuns wisely and appropriately is especially important as a counter to the impressions left the by narrative about the founding of the order.

One wonders why, in these two conflicting portraits of the Buddha and the nuns, the one has been so widely repeated and reported while the other is virtually ignored. The answer is not difficult to ascertain; it lies with the double androcentrism already discussed—the androcentrism of the Buddhist record itself and the androcentrism of most of its Western students and interpreters.

WAS EARLY INDIAN BUDDHISM MISOGYNIST?

Interpreting the materials already discussed and certain other passages and themes prevalent in the Pali canon, a number of scholars, especially Diana Paul,[14] have evaluated the entire period of early Indian Buddhism as essentially misogynist. To make such an evaluation is, in my view, a rather serious judgment, which should be considered further. This period of Buddhist history is the most difficult to study and reconstruct in feminist perspective because its texts are more ambiguous and self-contradictory regarding women than those from any other period. The issues become even more complex because the form of contemporary Buddhism that most closely resembles ancient Indian Buddhism—Theravada Buddhism of Southeast Asia—is also the form of Buddhism that is least sympathetic to contemporary women's drive for full and dignified participation in their religion. If we concede that ancient Indian Buddhism really was misogynist or anti-women, we strengthen the claim made by some Theravadins that they are simply being faithful to their pristine form of the religion when they oppose a Buddhist women's movement.

I have never been convinced by this claim or argument. Perhaps this is due to my definition of "misogyny" as the fear and hatred of women and femininity, a different phenomenon from male dominance over women. Or perhaps Diana Paul wishes to contrast early Indian Buddhism with her main interest—Mahayana Buddhism. Perhaps this assessment is simply a judgment call—certainly there are plenty of misogynist passages in the literature of early Indian Buddhism, *especially in the latter parts of that period.*

The substantive issue is that some of the literature, themes, and texts that are often presented as evidences of misogyny are, in my view, misinterpreted. A strange consonance in methods of interpreting texts often crops up between patriarchal and feminist interpreters of the same texts. Both argue strongly that the text demands male dominance or demonstrates low regard for women. The patriarchal interpreters, of course, use this interpretation to argue that male dominance is necessary if we are to be faithful to the tradition, while feminists use the same interpretations to argue that the tradition is quite hostile and unfair to women and should be discarded. In my view, conceding that a text really displays misogyny should be the interpretation of last resort. It is not useful, when reconstructing a tradition, to be forced to conclude that a major period of its history is unrelievedly misogynist.

Misogynistic texts, texts which preserve men's spiteful and resentful comments about women, are found among early Buddhist records. This is not surprising, since the literature is large and misogynists exist in all cultures. What we lack, *because of androcentric record-keeping practices*, are the corresponding opinions of women. I have often commented that because only men kept records of their own opinions, religious texts are one-sided regarding statements reflecting cross-sexual tension and hostility. Androcentric texts sometimes present women as concurring with male opinions about female nature, but that does not indicate that women indeed concurred, when among each other, with these assessments. Anyone who has participated in a female subculture, that is to say any woman scholar, knows that a whole oral tradition regarding men's inadequacies and shortcomings is quite prevalent. She also knows that women, in their own culture, simply don't concur with male published opinions about women. However, in a society whose record-keeping is guided by androcentric modes of thought, these women's opinions will not be recorded, which is not to say they are not widespread. Because the record is so incomplete and so androcentric, I believe feminists misplace their ire when they react so strongly to the presence of misogynist passages in a canon. Their wrath should be directed, not at the *presence* of misogyny, but at the *absence* of corresponding records of women's frustrations with men. Here again, the *Therigatha* serves as an invaluable counterbalance to convention. This woman's record does include women's songs of delight to be free of their husbands:

> O woman well set free! How free am I
> How thoroughly free of kitchen drudgery!
> Me stained and squalid 'mong my cooking pots

My brutal husband ranked as even less
Than the sunshades he sits weaving alway.
Purged now of all my former lust and hate,
I dwell, musing at ease beneath the shade
Of spreading boughs—Oh but tis well with me![15]

Some misogynist passages in the Pali canon are simply the emotional outburst of an individual frustrated monk. Such outbursts should not be interpreted as evidence that a whole period or school is misogynist. Much more serious as evidence of misogyny are more detached and abstract doctrinal statements about women's nature or abilities, such as one characteristic (and often quoted statement) put into the Buddha's mouth. "Womenfolk are uncontrollable ... envious ... greedy ... weak in wisdom. ... A woman's heart is haunted by stinginess ... jealousy ... sensuality."[16] An equally misogynist text records that poor Ananda, the champion of the women, was forced, just after the Buddha's death and during the first council, to confess to a number of faults, including two regarding women: he obtained the admission of women into the homeless life, and he allowed women to view the body of the Buddha and defile it with their tears.[17]

Some misogynist doctrines became part of the Pali canon and early Indian Buddhism at some point during this period, though Kajiyama Yuichi and others argue convincingly that these ideas could only have come into the literature late in this period.[18] The doctrine that a Buddha would not be a woman and a woman could not be a Buddha became widespread by the end of this period. The conclusion was often backed up by the reasoning that a woman cannot become a Buddha because she could not fill any of the "five stations" but must bear the "three kinds of subordination."* This reasoning became extremely widespread as justification for and explanation of women's low status in Buddhism. It is used up to the present time, and became especially popular in East Asian Buddhism. According to Church, even *arahant* status is denied to women in some texts, despite the clear record of the *Therigatha*. Words are put into the Buddha's mouth: "It is impossible, monks, it cannot come pass that a woman should be an *arahant* who is a fully enlightened one."[19]

Finally, the necessary and inevitable maleness of a Buddha was projected backwards into his previous lives as well. *Jataka* literature, which is often evaluated as quite misogynistic,[20] became increasingly popular. Though this literature includes many stories of previous lives of the Buddha in which he was still an animal—a male animal—stories in which he was female are either

---

* The "five stations" are to become, during the rebirth process, Brahma, Indra, the four guardian gods, a universal monarch, and an irreversible Bodhisattva, according to one list. The "three subordinations" are to father when young, to husband while married, to son when old. Yuichi, "Women in Buddhism," pp. 54–56.

non-existent or extremely rare.* Some *jataka*-s tell of the future Buddha as a bandit chief or a thief—a *male* bandit-chief or thief![21] Some accounts state when he stopped experiencing female incarnations and place it very early in his career.[22] To see more affinity between male humans and male animals than between female and male human beings must be an extreme of androcentric consciousness in which, more than is usually the case even for androcentrism, women are seen as outside the norm, as a foreign object but not a human subject.

It would be difficult not to evaluate such doctrines and statements as misogynistic and it cannot be denied that a misogynist strain is found in early Indian Buddhism. But the presence of some clearly misogynist doctrines does not mean that the whole of ancient Indian Buddhism was misogynist. Many other stories and statements that are sometimes used to back up the claim that early Indian Buddhism was misogynistic are, in my view, evidence of something other than misogyny and can be interpreted as misogynist only if parallel stories regarding men are discounted or when not all the relevant information is taken into account.

One of the most popular and long-standing Buddhist attitudes regarding gender is the evaluation that female incarnation is an unfortunate existence and a result of inferior karma. Already in early literature, lists of woes specific to women were collected and circulated. I.B. Horner cites a list of five woes[23]— having to leave her family at a young age, menstruation, pregnancy, childbirth, and having to be subservient to a man. Yuichi cites texts that list ten woes specific to women. The lists include both aspects of the female life cycle that are due to patriarchal social arrangements and dimensions of female biology that men, but not women, may evaluate negatively.[24] Though such lists are sometimes cited as evidence of misogyny, I see them more as a recognition that the conditions under which women lived *were* indeed difficult. Women often concurred in this judgment that female rebirth is difficult and unfortunate. One of the *Therigatha* poems puts it very well:

> Woeful is woman's lot . . .
> . . . .
> Woeful when sharing home with hostile wives,
> Woeful when giving birth in bitter pain,

---

* Yuichi, "Women in Buddhism," pp. 66–67, cites the 38th chapter of the Chinese translation of the *Ekottaragama*, a complex *jataka* in which the Buddha was a princess named Muni. She helped a monk honor Buddha Ratnakara, who predicted that the monk would become Buddha Dipankara. The princess also asked for a prediction, but was told it could not be given to a woman and that she (whoever she might be by then) should remake the request to Buddha Dipankara. When the monk became Buddha Dipankara, she became a Brahmin, who approached Dipankara Buddha, who prophesied that the brahmin (the former princess Muni) would become Buddha Sakyamuni.

> Some seeking death, or e'er they suffer twice,
> Piercing the throat; the delicate poison take,
> Woeful too when mother-murdering embryo
> Comes not to birth, and both alike find death.[25]

It is also clear that widespread cultural stereotypes about women sometimes are reflected in Buddhist scriptures. These stereotypes were important in India throughout Buddhism's history. Generally, it was felt that women were weak and could not fend for themselves but always needed to be under a male's protection and care. Women were thought to be foolish, jealous, and greedy. The Indian stereotype is usually that women are sexual initiators and aggressors and that they cannot easily control their passions. The *Anguttaranikaya* quotes the stereotype that women can never get enough of two things, of intercourse and childbirth.[26]

Often those who claim that early Indian Buddhism should be evaluated as misogynist claim that the tradition sees women as temptresses of men.[27] Frequently lumped together with this theme is the claim that the Pali texts also encourage meditators to view the female body, when seen for what it is beneath its painted exterior, as foul and repugnant. This analysis is quite one-sided and incomplete in my view.[28] Certainly both these themes are found. But they are by no means expressed exclusively vis-à-vis women but not men, which indicates that misogyny is not the fundamental issue. Such stories and attitudes, whether involving women or men, express a more basic viewpoint. Sense pleasures, especially sexuality, were considered extremely dangerous and tempting, for both women and men, by early Buddhism. They are primary attractions of conventional householders' existence, which was thought to trap one into continued rebirth in *samsara*. Avoiding them and fighting off attraction to sensuality and sexuality are constant themes in the literature of early Buddhism.

Some passages surface frequently in the case that early Indian Buddhism is misogynist:

> "How are we to conduct ourselves, lord, with regard to womankind?"
> "As not seeing them, Ananda."
> "But if we should see them, what are we to do?"
> "No talking, Ananda."
> "But if they should speak to us, lord, what are we to do?
> "Keep wide awake, Ananda."[29]

To me, this dialogue is not evidence of misogyny or of the claim that women are evaluated as temptresses. Women may be *tempting* to monks, but that alone does not mean that she is a *temptress*. This distinction is critical to an accurate, non-androcentric analysis of this period. In another frequently cited passage, a monk does what men frequently do when they encounter difficulty in maintaining celibacy. He projects his problems onto women and blames them for being attractive. "Monks, a woman even when going along, will stop to ensnare the heart of a man: whether standing, sitting, or lying down, laughing, talking, or singing, weeping, stricken or dying, a woman will stop to ensnare the heart of a man."*

There are many stories of women trying to seduce monks in the literature. One possible conclusion from these stories is that women were viewed as being "on Mara's side"[30] in the battle against entrapment in *samsara*. There are also stories about men trying to seduce or raping nuns.[31] How do we view stories of men trying to seduce nuns? Equally, the men must be viewed as stand-ins for Mara, which indeed seems to be the view of some texts, especially the *Therigatha*. In the fifty-second story in the *Therigatha*, Mara, "in youthful shape" tempted Khema:

> Thou are fair, and life is young, beauteous Khema!
> I am young, even I too—Come, O fairest lady!
> While in our ear fivefold harmonies murmur melodies,
> Seek we our pleasure.

She replies, in true world-renouncer style:

> Through this body vile, foul, seat of disease and corruption
> Loathing I feel, and oppression. Cravings of lust are uprooted.
> Lusts of the body and sense-mind cut like daggers and javelins.
> Speak not to me of delighting in aught of sensuous pleasure!
> Verily all such vanities no more may delight me.
> Slain on all sides is the love of the world, the flesh, and the devil.
> Rent asunder the gloom of ignorance that once beset me.
> Know this, O Evil One! Destroyer, know thyself worsted.[32]

Interestingly, though many modern commentators feel that one of the major concerns of the monastic rules was to separate the monks and the nuns to protect celibacy, neither monks or nuns are tempted by each other, with very few exceptions.† The real struggle is between monastics and laypeople. In that struggle, it is recognized that attraction goes both ways; it is not merely that women tempt men. Though for men nothing is "so enticing, so desirable, so intoxicating, so binding, so distracting . . . such a hindrance to winning the

---

* Falk, "Daughters of Mara", p. 106 quoting *Anguttaranikaya*, IV.8.80. See also Church, "Temptress, Housewife, Nun," p. 55 quoting *Anguttaranikaya*, V.6.5., in which the Buddha states that nothing is so alluring and so tempting, so disruptive and such a hindrance to winning peace as the form of a woman, that "verily, one may say of womanhood that it is wholly a snare of Mara."

† *Cullavagga,* x9.1–2 (363–64). In this narrative, first monks, then nuns show each other their private parts.

unsurpassed peace . . . as a woman's form,"[33] the reverse can also be true for women. "Monks, I know of no other single form, sound, scent, savor and touch by which a woman's heart is so enslaved as it is by the form, sound, scent, savor and touch of a man."[34]

When the various stories of attempted seduction and temptation are analyzed, many variants and motifs, rather than a single theme of misogyny, emerge. One cannot generalize that women are viewed as temptresses or that they are sexually insatiable, any more than one could make the reverse claim, that men should be evaluated as raping aggressors insensitive to women's autonomy. Many stories, narrating a complete description of various human wants and dilemmas, make such easy stereotypes and generalizations inaccurate.

Wives who try to win back their husbands are not usually castigated as evil temptresses. In fact they sometimes give up the struggle to become nuns or lay devotees themselves.[35] Women who seem to be trying to seduce a monk to test their skills are often severely denigrated and called names, but surely that causes no one to feel that the monk is a misogynist. Most often, the story reports that the monk experiences temptation and retreats, horrified, to practice meditation more seriously,[36] though sometimes, as seen above, he does project his temptation onto the women. When men, rather than women are the sexual aggressors who initiate unwelcome advances, women sometimes convert them in the process of resisting them.[37] Generally, nuns experience much less temptation sexually than do monks. From this, one could deduce, as contemporary Chinese nuns sometimes do,[38] that women, if they decide to become nuns, are more suited to the task than are men who decide to become monks.

One should similarly evaluate the claim that women, more than men, oppose world renunciation, making things more difficult for men who want to leave behind the trivial householder's life. True, some women, most often wives, are not thrilled by the idea, but other women, often mothers, encourage their sons to renounce the world. Men, often fathers, also make it difficult for men to become monks. Likewise men are also the culprits who try to restrain women from renouncing the world. Especially husbands are often no keener on losing their wives than wives on losing their husbands. The difference we see in these texts is not a difference in the portrayal of male versus female human nature. The difference is that in a patriarchal society, men simply left their wives, without a mutual agreement; wives then tried to seduce them back. By contrast, wives who wished to become nuns usually had to wait until their husbands died or granted them permission to leave. But not *all* husbands are so obtuse and self-centered. Some quickly realized that their wives or fiancees needed to become nuns and helped them.

The well-known episode from the Buddha's life story, in which he is tempted by the "daughters of Mara" during his enlightenment experience is often cited as evidence that early Indian Buddhism was misogynistic. Again, this is a partial and selective analysis, which does not take the whole story into account. Clearly, *one* of the temptations placed before Siddartha during the night under the Bodhi tree was the temptation of sensuality, represented by Mara's three daughters. But *males* also tempted the Buddha, both with offers of power and with terrifying threats. And Siddartha's greatest ally and defender was the Earth Goddess, who testified to his generosity when he had no other witnesses. It seems much more cogent to interpret the various temptations of Mara as personifications of various root defilements (*klesha-s*), than to single out the Daughters of Mara from the rest of the narrative, as if they were the sole tempters when they may not even be the primary tempters. They are not even included in some retellings of the story.[39] That the Daughters of Mara represent the temptation to sensuality more than they demonstrate misogyny in early Buddhism is also indicated by the fact that narratives in the *Therigatha* in which nuns are tempted sexually often depict Mara himself as the tempter. Perhaps we could conclude that the texts are definitively heterosexist in their orientation, but we cannot conclude that women, more than men, are sexual tempters or are unable to withstand sexual temptation.

But is not misogyny demonstrated by frequent evaluations of the foulness of the female body beneath its painted and alluring exterior? Because monks had more difficulty with celibacy than nuns, one might expect such literature, especially from monks who blame women for their problems. However, except when resisting temptation to a specific woman, contemplations on the body usually do not distinguish between a male and a female body. The human body is frequently compared to a bag tied at both ends, filled with foul substances, and attractively decorated on the outside. Both monks and nuns recite such litanies to themselves and to others. The exercise breaks attachment to the body—their own or others—and to sense pleasures, including sexual excitement, which are located in and aroused by the body, whether one's own or another's. The lists of foul inner substances that are recited do not mention either specifically male or female liquids or body parts. Usually sex organs are not discussed at all. These contemplations are not especially anti-female, though they certainly are anti-body.

Finally, it is important to evaluate a suggestion made by Nancy Falk in a provocative article titled "An Image of Women in Old Buddhist Literature: The Daughters of Mara." Though not claiming that early Indian Buddhism is essentially misogynist, she does suggest that one could explain the declining status of women in this period by a symbolic equation that was being drawn between women and the realm of becoming—*samsara*—which the world-renouncers are trying to overcome.

> Conservative Buddhism drew a sharp line between two states of "existence" nirvana or liberation ... and samsara, or becoming. ... Samsara was the enemy—a realm of ceaseless generation and destruction that inevitably bred suffering. It had to be broken—overcome—for the desired liberation to occur. Yet, as we have seen, a woman was a veritable image of becoming and of all the forces of blind growth and productivity which Buddhism knew as samsara. As such she too was the enemy—not only on a personal level, as an individual source of temptation, but also on a cosmic level.[40]

Falk herself admits that this equation between women and *samsara* never became full-blown in Buddhism and that Mahayana thought took such symbolic equations in entirely different directions. Falk is suggesting that in ancient Indian Buddhism, we already find a kind of feminine principle—a negative feminine principle, unlike the highly positive feminine principle that later developed in Mahayana and Vajrayana Buddhism. Because the feminine principle does become so important in later forms of Buddhism, it is important to examine this suggestion carefully. The logic is certainly clear, but in my view, the kind of archetypal, mythic, and symbolic thinking that is so much a part of the feminine principle is entirely foreign to the thinking of early Indian Buddhism. Stories from this period include allegorical characters, such as Mara, or Mara's daughters, but these allegorical figures are not archetypal and do not have the depth and numinosity of archetypal symbolism characteristic of a genuine feminine principle. I do not think that Woman is a Cosmic Enemy in this literature.

POSITIVE IMAGES OF WOMEN IN ANCIENT INDIAN BUDDHIST LITERATURE

When we finally turn from material that is negative towards women or has been interpreted as negative to women to materials that are unambiguously positive in their portrayals of women, we should not expect to double the number of citations. It would be foolish to claim that statements which somehow compromise women, and statements with which a contemporary Buddhist feminist could identify, balance each other. It is only being claimed that the record is not completely useless and depressing, and, when viewed accurately, much more usable than first impressions often lead one to believe.

Despite all the negative things about women put into the Buddha's mouth, he is also credited with statements to the contrary. Supposedly, he told a king, disappointed by the birth of a girl, that a girl "may prove a better offspring than a boy."[41] As already pointed out, according to the *Therigatha*, he often taught both nuns and laywomen directly and appropriately, with great compassion and skill. He praised them lavishly for high achievements and for generosity. And he is recorded as having stated, quite decisively, "Monks, among these some women disciples are streamwinners, some once-returners, some non-returners. Not fruitless, monks, are all these women disciples who have met their end."[42] Even more straightforward is the verse cited by Horner:

> And be it woman, be it man for whom
> Such chariot doth wait, by that same car
> Into Nirvana's presence shall they come.[43]

Such statements should always be kept in mind and emphasized, since androcentric record-keeping, combined with androcentric scholarship, tends to give us an overabundance of quotations about keeping awake in the presence of women.

The most positive images of women tend to be found in story form however, in the *Therigatha*, and in other records such as a long poem about the laywoman Vishakha. This literature thus provides portraits of the two lifestyles available to Buddhist women of this period, that of nun or that of a lay woman. At least some of this literature is from the women's point of view, for the *Therigatha* seem to be records women themselves kept, which were somehow included in the Pali canon when men collected and edited the scriptures. Without that text, our picture of early Indian Buddhism would be much more limited, for the nuns' stories do not figure prominently in the far more numerous records kept by men. Without the *Therigatha*, we would know of the nuns' order, of course, but mainly as something about which even the Buddha was quite ambivalent, at best. The records that men kept deal far more with laywomen than with nuns.

Laywomen, as we have already seen, sometimes are negatively portrayed as wives who try to regain their husbands or otherwise present obstacles to men. The stories of these women were of no interest to either the monks or the nuns and their voices are probably irretrievably lost. But another class of laywomen also figures prominently in the men's records. These are pious laywomen donors—the women who come off best in early Buddhist literature as a whole. As Nancy Falk has pointed out: "the grand heroine of Buddhist storytelling is not the nuns' founder, Mahapajapati, as one might expect, but Vishakha, a prominent merchant's daughter and wife who belonged to the early community and who never took the nuns' vows."[44]

This trend continues down into some relatively recent Western considerations of this period. In his generally well-regarded anthology of some 495 pages, *Buddhism in Translation*, Henry Clark Warren devotes 29 pages to

Vishakha and six to the nuns of early Buddhism.[45] Vishakha was never discouraged in her vocation, as Prajapati was, and she is praised extremely highly and frequently. She has easy access to the Buddha, seemingly easier than the nuns, who sometimes rely on Ananda as an intermediary. The Buddha is said to rely on her advice on some occasions and she was able to visit him even at "an unseemly hour" when distressed,[46] apparently without arousing gossip such as is reported to have occurred when monks visited the nuns' quarters for legitimate purposes.[47] Her wealth was immense and her generosity unparalleled. She was quite competent in argument and zealous to promote Buddhism, converting her wealthy and powerful father-in-law. Lacking nothing, she was also incredibly beautiful, bore ten sons and ten daughters, lived to be 120 years old and still looked sixteen, without a single grey hair![48] Clearly, she was a great favorite of the record-keepers and it is hard to avoid the conclusion that they preferred her to Mahaprajapati.

Her story presents two common themes in Buddhist literature—the importance of laywomen donors to the religion and the tendency of androcentric record-keepers to prefer such women to female world-renouncers, to nuns. These two themes need to be evaluated differently. Neither Buddhists nor scholars of Buddhism should neglect the importance of the laity to Buddhism, a religion that easily is subsumed into its monastic elite. Accurate record-keeping is always fostered if the activities of women are recorded and their importance recognized. And usable lay models are as crucial in feminist reconstructions of Buddhism as are nuns' stories.

But something else is also occurring, demonstrated especially by the contrast between the whole-hearted approval of Vishakha and the ambivalence shown to Prajapati. Against the logic of their religion, early Indian Buddhists often seemed to prefer laywomen to nuns. As Nancy Falk has put it so well, "Buddhists, like Hindus, honored fecund housewives, especially if they were also pious laywomen. We can therefore suspect that many Buddhists, like Hindus, also preferred to see women at the hearth rather than on the road or within a monastery's walls."[49] It is not to hard to imagine why. The fecund housewife did not challenge or break stereotypes of women. Presumably happily married, she did not threaten the monk sexually. She was modest and humble. She was honored by the monk's presence and deferred to him. And she always provided what the monk needed, before he even asked and without expecting anything in return. In short, she met men's needs without challenging or threatening them in any way. Unlike the nuns of the *Therigatha*, she is an androcentric creation. These stories present a dilemma. They preserve a measure of accuracy, in that the importance of laywomen is recognized. They present a needed model—that of the Buddhist laywoman. And they manifest something somewhat rare in Buddhist literature—a female figure who is whole-heartedly and completely praised and venerated. Nevertheless, we do not find here a usable model but an enabler—something that is not rare in androcentric records.

In addition to all the texts already quoted from, early Indian Buddhism also preserved, despite mainly androcentric record-keeping practices, a remarkable document which may record more from women, from an earlier period, than any other set of religious literature. This document is, of course, the *Therigatha*, the "psalms of the sisters," referred to and quoted so many times already. I could not restrain myself from imagining, if there were a parallel document for early Christianity, how much helped Christian feminists would be. Here is a clear, unambiguous, and straightforward account, from women with high spiritual achievements, of what Buddhism meant to them, of the freedom and joy they eventually found in its practices. Here we find no doubts about women's abilities, no successful attempts to seduce them or demean them, no misogyny. These are not male fantasies or projections about women. These are not hypotheses that such women must have existed but were excised from the patriarchal record. These are not isolated instances of a few women lost in an overwhelmingly male record.

There are many *theri*-s, women elders, who left the world, meditated, taught, and brought others into the path. Nor are these many women monolithic in their social origins or their reasons for leaving the world to become nuns. Young and old women, widows, wives, fiancees, mothers, and daughters, wealthy and poor women, privileged women and prostitutes, all followed the Buddhist path, won Buddhism's goal, and sang of their experiences. And we somehow have their poems! No summary of its contents could replace reading the entire *Therigatha*.

It is reassuring to know that, even though Buddhism made no attempt deliberately and directly to be a social reform movement intending to improve women's situation, so many women found liberty in early Indian Buddhism. The feminist historian's quest for a usable past and for good stories could hardly be more successful, at least when she operates within an androcentric and patriarchal past. I can think of no Buddhist resource that is so underutilized, both by Buddhists and by scholars of Buddhism.[50]

The theme of freedom, both spiritual and social, dominates these poems. These poems contrast significantly to culturally dominant stereotypes about women as subservient to men and dependent upon them.

> I'm free, totally free in freedom
> from those three hideous shapes:
> my grindstone, my pestle,

and my hunch-backed husband.
I'm free from birth and death—
my ties to life are broken.[51]

Another noteworthy poem takes up directly the question about women's intellectual and spiritual abilities. Despite all the doubts recorded about them in other texts, the nuns themselves do not agonize over, or even consider, the issue of whether they are up to the task of world renunciation or can attain Buddhism's goals. Some of them have a hard time and despair, to the point of suicide, before they break through to enlightenment, but there are parallel stories of desperate slow learners among the men. One woman's verse takes up the question explicitly. Fortunately, her verse is often quoted, but it cannot be repeated too often. The nun Soma was tempted by Mara, not sexually, but with the taunt that women possessed only "two finger intelligence," enough to measure rice, but not enough to attain release. She replied:

> How should the woman's nature hinder us?
> Whose hearts are firmly set, who ever move
> With growing knowledge onward in the Path?
> What can that signify to one in whom
> Insight doth truly comprehend the Norm?
> To one for whom the question doth arise:
> Am I a woman in these matters, or
> Am I a man, or what not am I then?
> To such a one are you, Sir, fit to talk![52]

Notice that her argument turns on the insight that "male" and "female" are irrelevant designations—an argument that is widely used by Buddhists who try to prove that men are not more adept at spiritual practices than are women and that it is un-Buddhist to discriminate religiously between women and men.

Another woman, whose name is unknown, heard Prajapati, the founder of the nun's order, preaching and wished to leave the householder's life. Her husband would not allow it, so she practiced meditation while doing her housework. One day, when her cooking fire ran out of control and burned the food she was cooking, she experienced deeply the truth of impermanence. After that she would no longer wear jewels and ornaments. When her husband asked why, she replied that she felt incapable of living a domestic life any longer. Her husband then brought her to Prajapati so that she could be ordained. Eventually she became an *arhant*.[53] Note the effect of Prajapati's powerful preaching, women-teacher to woman-student. Note also the patriarchal control under which this woman labored. In the monks' verses, the *Theragatha*, men with that level of insight simply walked away from their wives, who sometimes then tried to seduce them back.

A great favorite of many commentators is Kisa-Gotami, who was so grief-crazed by the death of her son that she refused to let his body be burned, but instead, carrying his body on her hip, frantically asked everyone for medicine for her son. People finally directed her to the Buddha, who promised to cure her son if she could bring him a mustard seed from a house in which no death had occurred. She was immensely relieved, but soon realized that she would never find the required mustard seed. "Thrilled at the thought, she left the town and laid her child in the charnel-field." Cherishing her deep insight into impermanence, she returned to the Buddha, saying, "wrought is the work, lord, of the little mustard. Give thou me confirmation."[54] Usually the emphasis in interpreting this story is on the Buddha's immense skill-in-means in teaching a rather crazy woman. One could as well emphasize that the Buddha did not discriminate in the quality of teaching given to the woman or hesitate to teach her. And Kisa-Gotami is no slow learner! She had attained Stream Entry by the time she returned to the Buddha and quickly attained arhantship. Eventually the Buddha "proclaimed her first among the wearers of rough raiment."[55]

The story of Bhaddha Kapilani, told partly in connection with her husband's verses in the *Theragatha* and less fully in connection with her own verses in the *Therigatha*, contains different motifs from any other *Therigatha* story, showing how varied this resource is. Kassapa the Great, her husband, had promised to take care of his parents while they lived, but refused to marry, saying he would renounce the world after their deaths. By a stratagem his mother succeeded in securing an engagement, but Bhaddha, his fiancee, similarly did not wish to marry but to become a nun. By another stratagem, their wedding was performed nevertheless, but they spend their wedding night "separated by a rope of flowers." Eventually his parents died and the two consulted. They cut off each other's hair, put on robes and took begging bowls. Leaving home together, they walked down the road to find the wanderers, but quickly decided that their actions could easily be misinterpreted if they stayed together. Therefore, they parted at the crossroads. Both became arhants and important leaders in the Buddha's community. She was ranked first among those who remember past lives by the Buddha. In her verses in the *Therigatha*, she celebrates both her own achievements and his, as well as their shared vision:

> We both have seen, both he and I, the woe
> And pity of the world, and have gone forth.
> We both are Arahants with selves well tamed.
> Cool are we both, ours is Nibbana now.[56]

With a resource such as the *Therigatha* available, there is no reason to ignore it while repeatedly quoting conversations about how important it is to keep wide awake in the presence of women! Clearly, women and men can co-operate with each other's world renunciation and achievement of liberation and peace. Clearly women are fully capable of achieving that goal. And clearly, the historical record includes many non-misogynist resources, if one chooses to ferret out this fully accurate record. The quests for an accurate and a usable past are more in harmony with each other than androcentric impressions of early Indian Buddhism would lead us to believe.

Therefore, consideration of this period concludes as it began, with an emphasis that an accurate portrait of this period is ambiguous, presenting both "positive" and "negative" images of women that are more or less usable. It must also be emphasized that many of the texts and stories found in this period are easily misinterpreted, presenting a portrait of almost unrelieved misogyny. Nevertheless the existence of the *Therigatha*, with its sympathetic portraits of women who took Buddhism's message fully to heart and achieved its goal of peace and release, stands as a challenge to all Buddhists of all times who would prefer women to do less.

5

Do Innate Female Traits and Characteristics Exist? Roles and Images of Women in Indian Mahayana Buddhism

Sariputra: "Why don't you change your female sex?"

Goddess: "I have been here twelve years and have looked for the innate characteristics of the female sex and haven't been able to find them."[1]

Goddess chapter, *Vimalakirtinirdesa* Sutra

The origins of Mahayana Buddhism are difficult to ascertain. Much debated are the times and the places in which Mahayana tendencies and schools emerged from the context of early Indian Buddhism. Also at issue is the question of which Mahayana concepts emerged first. However, little disagreement is found surrounding several important issues. Mahayana Buddhism did not emerge suddenly, as a fully formed, self-conscious sectarian reform.[2] Rather, it developed very gradually, only later becoming a self-conscious ideology complete with extensive and colorful anti-"hinayana"* rhetoric. Furthermore, few disagree that the emergence of Mahayana ideology made little practical difference. Because the rules of monastic discipline (*vinaya*) were not at issue, it was quite possible for "hinayana" and "mahayana" monks to live together in the same monastery. Such cases were apparently not uncommon.[3] As Snellgrove has demonstrated well, despite their differing intellectual frameworks, the lifestyle and behavior of the Mahayana monk was little different from that of his non-Mahayana counterpart.[4] Additionally, though theoretically Mahayana Buddhism promoted lay practice, monks continued to be revered and central in everyday practical religious life.

---

* Used correctly, as a Mahayana polemical term, such usage does not indicate a judgment on the part of the author.

Eventually, the development of Mahayana Buddhism did produce a major split, intellectually and geographically, in the Buddhist world. With the demise of Buddhism in India, where the two forms could sometimes encounter each other, they lost contact with and direct knowledge of each other until the nineteenth century. Mahayana Buddhism travelled north and east, while the earlier forms of Buddhism travelled south and east. The two forms of Buddhism assess this split quite differently. Stated most polemically, from the viewpoint of the older forms of Buddhism, Mahayana forms of Buddhism are simply unwarranted innovations, deviations created out of whole cloth by lax and backsliding students. Stated equally polemically, the Mahayanists claim true descent from Buddha Shakyamuni, who warned that in the future, uninsightful monks bent selfishly on individual liberation would fail to appreciate the full *dharma*.

Today, members of both sects generally manage to avoid these polemical extremes, but both forms of Buddhism equally claim to represent the full message of the Buddha, despite their marked theoretical differences. The Theravadins can claim the oldest scriptures and a close resemblance to the forms observed by the early Buddhists. Mahayanists claim that their teachings represent the unfolding of the Buddha's original message, making manifest what had been less clearly and fully understood earlier. Mythically, this belief is expressed in the story of the *Naga*-s, who guarded the Buddha-word of the Mahayana *sutra*-s until the world of humans was ready to receive them. The historian, of course, sees change in religious doctrines and forms as inevitable, without, *qua* historian, evaluating whether the changes fulfill or deviate from earlier doctrines and forms.

An important issue dividing these schools of Buddhism concerns the proper images and roles of women, though that sectarian divergence is less noted in androcentric scholarship. How and why did attitudes toward women become so important in the split between Mahayana and Theravadin Buddhism? While I do not believe that one can dispose of anti-women statements placed in the mouth of the Buddha by declaring them to be later interpolations from conservative disciples, it does seem reasonable to me to conclude that during the Buddha's life and shortly thereafter, women's position in Buddhism was not a burning or a controversial issue. The idea of a woman's monastic community does not seem to have originated with the Buddha and he may not have been enthusiastic about it. But, for a while, the very existence of the nuns' *sangha* and its members' spiritual achievements meant that there could be little controversy about women and their options within the Buddhist community, though individuals may have voiced misogynist opinions.

Later, with growing divergence in the Buddhist world, anti-women opinions and rhetoric became more prevalent. The nuns' order could not be abolished, but attainments for women could be curtailed. It could be claimed that Buddhas always embody as males, that all important slots in hierarchy and mythology must be filled by males, and even that women could not win enlightenment. Such hardened, anti-women doctrines, which are quite different from the misogynist outbursts of a frustrated monk, were probably not characteristic of early Buddhism. But they became quite common by the time Buddhism was starting to split apart. Some even blamed the split itself on the presence of the women's order, as we have already seen.

At the same time that more extreme anti-women doctrines began to be widespread, others argued the opposite point of view equally strongly. Some texts are quite anti-women, more so than is the norm for texts from early Indian Buddhism. But other texts, especially in full-fledged Mahayana writings, go much further in proclaiming women's capabilities than almost any text from early Indian Buddhism. For various reasons, by the time the split between older forms of Buddhism and Mahayana Buddhism became clear-cut, those who argued that women could have great religious insights and spiritual attainments were usually in the Mahayana camp. The Mahayana camp also included some who expressed quite negative attitudes toward women. But no one who strongly advocated women's positive qualities seems to have been in the camp of the more conservative, older forms of Buddhism. This long-standing divide on women's issues is important today, for it is difficult to avoid the impression that the Mahayana forms of Buddhism provide more suitable ground for serious women practitioners and a feminist transvaluation of Buddhism than do the Theravada forms.

WOMEN'S ROLES IN MAHAYANA BUDDHISM:
THE HISTORICAL EVIDENCE

The vast majority of sources from this period are textual and "mythic," rather than documents from which one could reconstruct social history. Though women figure prominently in many stories from this period, it is difficult, if not impossible, to link them with any figures recorded in historical annals, or even to regard them as historically realistic characters. Instead, these women are characters used allegorically and fictively to prove doctrinal and ideological points, rather than flesh-and-blood women. This situation contrasts significantly with the historically believable women of the *Therigatha* and the clearly historical heroines whom we will meet in the Vajrayana period. But the mythical quality of the women we meet in Mahayana texts does not decrease the usability of their stories. They simply represent a different genre of religious text and a different type of religious character, which must be interpreted using methods appropriate to that genre.

Historical records concerning both nuns and laywomen are rather sparse for this period. A rather large gap between the conditions often portrayed in texts and the everyday situation in Buddhist institutions seems evident. Making doctrinal points about the universal availability of enlightenment, the typical heroes and protagonists of Mahayana texts are often laypeople, not monks; often famous monks of early Indian Buddhism are named as their rigid, uninsightful opponents. Needless to say, these monks usually look silly by the end of the debate. In many cases, the Mahayana protagonist is not only lay rather than monastic, but also female rather than male, and young rather than mature and educated.

However, sociologically and historically, there is no evidence to suggest that this literary motif reflects lay or female dominance in Mahayana Buddhism, though it does reflect a different evaluation of the spiritual capabilities of laypeople and women. In fact, monks continued to be the leading spokespersons and innovators in Buddhism. Historical records give no indication that nuns played much part in these developments. In fact the opposite was probably true. The economic and social factors set in motion by the eight special rules had already seriously weakened the nuns' order. Lay supporters had picked up the cue, implicit in these rules, that nuns were less worthy and important recipients of their generosity than monks. By the seventh century C.E., the Chinese pilgrim I Ching wrote of the Indian nuns: "Nuns in India are very different from those of China. They support themselves by begging food, and live a poor and simple life. . . . The benefit and supply to the female members of the Order are very small, and monasteries of many a place have no special supply of food for them."[5] Not only were the nuns generally poor and undersupported. They are largely unrecorded and few are even named.[6] Nuns are not recorded as having participated in the great intellectual developments of the day; they do not seem to have been a significant part of the student body at the great Buddhist universities which were "the central gem in the crown of the monk's order, an order which was extensive, prosperous and productive of extraordinary thought and art."[7]

Additionally, no historical records of educated and influential Buddhist laywomen give flesh to literary portraits of such women. Female donors, however, continued to be recorded and, according to Janice Willis, became even more crucial as supporters of Buddhism during the Mahayana period and in newly missionized countries than they had been in the period of early Indian Buddhism.[8] Thus, despite a strong literary movement to defend women's spiritual capabilities, the conditions under which women lived seem to have changed very little. Pious, supportive laywomen are still acceptable, but the nuns, at least in India, seem not to have benefited at all from Mahayana Buddhism's use of the wise female student of the *dharma* as a stock character. In fact, in one case, not typical to be sure, but nevertheless preserved, monks are advised to avoid all women, *even if they are nuns.*[10]

This bleak historical portrait of women, especially nuns, during the Indian Mahayana period contrasts sharply with evidence from other parts of the Buddhist world during this period. I Ching compares the nuns of India with those of China, who are "very different." Seemingly, the nuns of China, at least at this period and somewhat before, were much more numerous, prosperous, respected, and influential than were their Indian counterparts. Nancy Schuster attributes some of the well-being of the Chinese nuns' order to the popularity of these Mahayana scriptures with their strong and highly advanced female literary characters.[11] The nuns of Sri Lanka were also doing relatively well at this period; they sent delegations of nuns to China to help establish ordination lineages for Chinese nuns.[12]

LITERARY IMAGES OF INDIAN BUDDHIST NUNS

When Indian literature about nuns, rather than historical evidence about nuns, is considered, a rather different picture comes through. Though literature about nuns is not nearly so popular or influential as literature in which laywomen star, several Indian texts describe nuns far more elaborately and extensively than in any text from early Indian Buddhism. In the major sourcebook on women in Mahayana Buddhism, *Women in Buddhism*, Diana Paul, with the help of Frances Wilson, translated, for the first time, a section from the conclusion of the *Avatamsaka Sutra*, which portrays the nun Lion-Yawn. She is sought out by a young man who wants instruction on how to train as a Bodhisattva. He finds her seated on a teaching-throne, surrounded by great retinues, proclaiming the *dharma* to various classes of beings, each of whom hears a message appropriate to his or her station, so that every one of them becomes destined for Supreme, Perfect Enlightenment.* She then instructs the young man individually, telling him of her high level of understanding and giving him directions to his next teacher, also a woman.[13] While highly exaggerated and "mythical," this portrait is also remarkable, for the nun is pictured not only as highly accomplished but as an impressive, highly competent teacher with multitudes of students. She teaches the *dharma* with a style and an authority usually reserved for a Buddha or a highly advanced Bodhisattva in much Mahayana literature.

---

* This is a technical term in Mahayana Buddhism for the goal toward which the Mahayanist works and which Mahayanists oppose to the inferior private enlightenment of an *arhant*, the goal of early Indian Buddhism.

Another long portrait of a Buddhist nun is quite different. Written in Tamil, it seems, at least according to the English summary, not to have much Mahayana content. According to Paula Richman, this text was written to introduce an audience unfamiliar with Buddhism, and with the idea of female renunciation, to that possibility. Written in epic form, the text focuses on the emotional and intellectual struggle of a young woman of the courtesan class to renounce her suitor and become a Buddhist nun. After that story is completed, the epic concludes with a detailed account of the heroine's Buddhist higher education in logic and philosophy.[14] It is quite interesting that, at this late date (sixth century C.E.),[15] when the nuns' order already seems to have been in decline, an entire epic would be devoted to the theme of an ordinary woman taking up the path of a Buddhist nun. Her philosophical training is also noteworthy, given the lack of other evidence for nuns' participation in the great Buddhist universities. Perhaps they did indeed study and even teach at these universities, but those who kept the records did not feel it was necessary to mention their presence. This story is also much more human in scale than the stories recounted in many Mahayana scriptures, which indicates that at least some accounts like those of *Therigatha* continued to be written.

FEMALENESS AND BUDDHAHOOD: LIKE OIL AND WATER?

More abstract discussions of women's abilities are common in Mahayana literature. As is the case for early Indian Buddhism, these texts are highly contradictory, with very strong statements both that something is wrong with female birth and that women can be highly developed on the Buddhist path. If anything, the Mahayana texts contain more extreme statements of each position than was the case with early Indian Buddhist materials. As with earlier texts, some of the materials are usable, even inspiring, while others are difficult for a Buddhist feminist to appreciate.

The opinion that there is something wrong with female birth is quite easy to find in Mahayana texts. It had become a strong theme late in the previous period of Buddhist thought and Mahayanists were well aware of it, whether they reacted in agreement or disagreement. However, it is important to distinguish and consider separately two variations on the theme that something is lacking in women. On the one hand, we find full-blown misogyny in doctrinal form, not merely as the emotional outburst of a frustrated, uninsightful monk. On the other hand, often seriously confused with misogyny by some commentators, we find many comments on the misfortunes and difficulties of female rebirth and many prescriptions to cure it. Such comments are not based on fear and hatred of women, but on pity and compassion for beings occupying a difficult and often painful slot in the scheme of things.

As with earlier Buddhism, Mahayana Buddhism existed in the context of a patriarchal society strongly informed by androcentric values and modes of thought. Gender stereotypes of the surrounding culture were a constant influence on both women and men. And, as for earlier Buddhism, those gender stereotypes suggested that women are less intelligent than men, less able to control themselves sexually, more interested in worldly concerns, especially reproduction, and less inclined toward spiritual disciplines. In fact, the words put in the mouths of the conservative representatives of older Buddhism in Mahayana texts probably accurately summarize popular attitudes toward women. In most of the texts to be considered in detail, those misogynist attitudes are countermanded, retracted, or demonstrated to be false. But in some documents, they stand. A particularly virulent example, the opinion of an important philosopher, is found in Asanga's *Bodhisattvabhumi*, an important text. He explains why Buddhas are never female:

> Completely perfected Buddha-s are not women. And why? Precisely be-
> cause a bodhisattva, from the time he has passed beyond the first incalcu-
> lable age (of his career) had completely abandoned the woman's estate
> (*stribhavam*). Ascending (thereafter) to the most excellent throne of en-
> lightenment, he is never again reborn as a woman. All women are by nature
> full of defilement and of weak intelligence. And not by one who is full of
> defilement and of weak intelligence is completely perfected Buddhahood
> attained.[16]

This passage refers directly to the most misogynistic doctrine current in Buddhism of that time, and still carried forward in many circles. This doctrine, debated and refuted in other Mahayana texts, but not here, states that female-ness and Buddhahood are mutually exclusive. A Buddha will never appear in female form and a woman cannot be a Buddha. Various additional reasons were utilized in other Mahayana contexts. A woman must observe the "three subserviences"; she must be under the control of her father, her husband, or her son, but a Buddha is obviously not under anyone's control. The issue of male control over women, so important in the eight special rules, again appears. That this idea is essential to the Hindu and the Confucian social codes, but really has nothing to do with Buddhist *dharma*, is not sufficient to deter Buddhist patriarchs from using it.

Much more frequently cited in Mahayana literature, however, are arguments utilizing the "five stations" and the "thirty-two marks." In an extremely important text that we will discuss again, the *Lotus Sutra*, Shariputra, a famous monk of earlier Buddhism, tells a young woman that she cannot possibly complete the vows she has just undertaken because:

Good daughter, even a woman who does not falter in diligence for many
hundreds of eras and performs meritorious acts for many thousands of eras,
completely fulfilling the six perfections still does not realize Buddhahood.
Why? Because a woman still does not realize five types of status. What are the
five types? (1) The status of Brahma, (2) the status of Sakra (Indra), (3) the
status of a great king, (4) the status of an emperor, and (5) the status of an
irreversible Bodhisattva.[17]

The argument recurs in many places, with the third station often being that of
Mara, the mythical Buddhist tempter. Though this list is imbedded in Indian
mythology, that mythological context does not need to be explicated for the
essential point to come through. Before a being can become a Buddha, it must
exhaust and experience a multitude of other conditions, especially those of great
power in the Indian social and religious universe. Those positions of extreme
power, whether positive or negative, were simply not available to women, under
any possible circumstance, in fact or fantasy. In Mahayana texts, including the
Lotus Sutra, that difficulty eventually is overcome when the female magically
transforms her body into that of male Buddha after she demonstrates her
profound understanding of Buddhist teachings. A contemporary feminist commentator might well respond with a simpler solution—well, then let's have
some affirmative action and open up these positions to females! But such a
solution was not available to the Indian imagination of the time.

Protecting the maleness of the Buddha by declaring that a Buddha must
first undergo experiences that only a man could have was not the final argument,
however. A Buddha, as well as a universal monarch (the usual translation for
the fourth station listed above), were also said to display the "thirty-two marks"
of a superior being. These are all unusual physical traits that could be seen on
the body of a Buddha, at least by spiritually advanced seekers. The tenth of them
is "the concealment of the lower organs in a sheath. The Chinese translation . . .
means that the Buddha's private parts are hidden like those of a horse."[18]

Thus it would seem, superficially to be incontrovertible; one needs a penis,
albeit an hidden one, to be a Buddha and women don't have penises! However,
even traditionally there were refutations to this argument and suggestions that
it should not be taken literally. The point of the hidden penis is not to emphasize
the Buddha's maleness, but to emphasize his asexuality—a point that would
seem clear to all but misogynists bent on finding any arguments, no matter how
undignified, to disqualify women from high spiritual attainments. Another
argument, not especially used to promote the idea of female Buddhas traditionally, but which could be used in that fashion, is that "the Tathagata [a title for
the Buddha] cannot be seen by his marks, rather he is to be known from his
characteristic of having no marks."[19] A modern non-traditional refutation of the

interpretation that the tenth mark means that a Buddha must be a male would look more seriously and closely at female anatomy. The usual bearers of a *sheathed* "penis" are not men at all, but women. Perhaps, equally ridiculously, we could turn tables and argue that the tenth mark really means that a Buddha would never be an anatomically normal male and would most likely be female! I am not, of course, making a serious suggestion, but, by role reversal, showing to what ridiculous lengths androcentric interpreters of texts will go.*

AVOIDING THE WOES OF FEMALE REBIRTH

Often Mahayana texts gave advice on how to avoid female rebirth. Usually, these texts consider female rebirth to be undesirable because of its difficulties. However, in some texts, women are advised to seek male rebirth because women are by nature morally defective—just as Asanga had argued in explaining why women can't be Buddhas: "The female's defects—greed, hate, and delusion, and other defilements—are greater than the male's. . . . You [women] should have such an intention. . . . Because I wish to be freed from the impurities of the woman's body, I will acquire the beautiful and fresh body of a man."[20]

Fortunately, however, usually women are encouraged to seek male rebirth by religious leaders who feel, not misogyny, but pity and compassion for women living in a male-dominated society that believes very strongly that female rebirth is a liability and a limit. An extremely widespread Asian (and Western) view holds that female birth is a misfortune. Indeed, in a patriarchal society, that conclusion is difficult to avoid, for women's lives, objectively, are more difficult and less rewarding than are men's. Social and religious woes are heaped on top of biological woes. Married young and without birth control, life becomes an unending series of pregnancies, many of which end with the mother mourning another dead infant or child. Sexual satisfaction is probably not an expected part of a woman's life. Co-wives and mistresses are common, at least among the upper classes. Lower-class women labor very hard at family occupations in addition to their reproductive labors. These conditions are intensified, rather than eased, by the social world in which they were set. Women are often unwelcome at birth and are always supposed to be under male authority. The social system frequently pits women against each other. Women are usually not educated and are taught that they are sensual, stupid, emotional, jealous and quarrelsome, that they have little spiritual depth, and that, though they should

* Gender role reversal fantasies are often used as an effective technique for consciousness raising in feminist interpretation. In such role reversal fantasies, what is normally done to women is done to men instead, which usually make people who have not thought about the prison of gender roles extremely uncomfortable. When exegeting religious texts, interpretations utilizing such gender role reversals readily demonstrate that literalist understandings of a passage, such as the requirement that a Buddha have a sheathed penis, are quite ridiculous.

be pious and obedient, they do not have the capabilities for genuine spiritual vocation. Under such conditions, no wonder people regard female rebirth as a misfortune. This conclusion is shared by both women and men.

The classic Buddhist solution to this problem is to provide hope that such rebirth could be avoided in the future. With belief in karma and rebirth deeply held, present conditions were accepted with complacence by both women and men. According to classic and widely accepted beliefs, everyone's present birth, no matter how fortunate and lofty, no matter how unfortunate and miserable, was the result of karma accrued in past lives. Rather than seek to change one's present conditions, one should serve well in one's allotted role, knowing that such good acts would produce merit leading to a more fortunate rebirth in the future. Thus women are simply reaping the results of past karma and could do better in the future. Many a Buddhist text took pity on women and provided practices they could do to assure them that they could avoid female rebirth in the future, while others speculated on what past misdeeds had led to present rebirth as a woman. For example, in one of the *Maharatnakuta sutra*-s, a woman who has just discoursed in a learned and advanced manner with the Buddha asks him what a women must do to change her female body. He replies that she must be obedient and pious, that she must:

> avoid envy, stinginess, flattery, anger, be truthful, slander no one, abandon desire, and all wrong views; revere Buddha and Dharma, make offerings to monks and to Brahmanas, give up attachment to home and family, accept the precepts, have no evil thoughts, become indifferent to her female body, abide in the thought of enlightenment and the dharmas of the Great Man, regard worldly life as like an illusion, like a dream."[21]

Another text makes avoiding future rebirth as a woman dependent on arousing "the thought of enlightenment," the profound change of heart that sets one on the Mahayana path of bodhisattvahood:

> If women can accomplish one thing, they will be freed of the female body and become sons. What is that one thing? The profound state of mind which seeks enlightenment. Why? If women awaken to the thought of enlightenment, then they will have the great and good person's state of mind, a man's state of mind, a sage's state of mind. . . . If women awaken to the thought of enlightenment, then they will not be bound to the limitation of a woman's state of mind. Because they will not be limited, they will forever separate from the female sex and be sons.[22]

Still another text details not only how a woman can be reborn as a man (by building images of the Buddha), but also why a woman would be reborn again as a woman and why a man would be reborn as a woman. The woman is reborn as a woman again if she indulges in:

(1) Love for the body of a woman; (2) attachment to the passions of a woman; (3) constant delight in the beauties of a woman; (4) insincerity of heart to hide her wicked deeds; (5) weariness and contempt for her husband; (6) constant thoughts of other men; (7) ingratitude for the kindness of others; and (8) wicked adornment of her body for the sake of deception.

The man is reborn as a woman for four offenses:

(1) Disrespectfully laughing and shouting at the Buddhas or bodhisattvas; (2) slandering one who is pure in keeping the precepts, saying he does not keep them; (3)flattering and fawning in order to deceive; and (4) envying the happiness of other men.[23]

These various texts are quite uneven in the quality of their *dharmic* advice. The recommendation to arouse the thought of enlightenment is good advice for any Mahayanist, male or female. The requirements for avoiding female rebirth in the last set of quotations involve petty conventional morality, while the reasons for women to continue to be reborn as women obviously reflect male complaints vis-à-vis women.

The most famous and important solution to the problem of female birth is found in the *Sukhavativyuha Sutra*, in connection with Amitabha's Pure Land. As is the case with all the Buddha-fields created by the great Buddhas, who dedicate their infinite store of merit to conjuring up such a place, in Amitabha's Pure Land, there will be no unfortunate births of any kind. For Amitabha's paradise, this means that there will be no female birth and the name of "woman" will not even be heard. This vision of the Western Pure Land contrasts significantly with the vision of Akshobya's much less well-known and less popular Eastern Paradise. There, in contrast, no sexual desire or jealousy are found. Women are wonderfully beautiful, and are "freed from the curse of menstruation." They become pregnant without sexual intercourse and both mother and child "are safe and unsullied from conception to birth."[24] But Amitabha had a different vision of how to solve similar problems. About his Pure Land, Amitabha vows:

if, after I have obtained Bodhi [enlightenment], women in immeasurable, inconceivable, immense Buddha countries on all sides, after having heard my name, should allow carelessness to arise, should not turn their thoughts toward Bodhi, should, when they are free from birth, not despise their female nature; and if they, being born again should assume a second female nature, then may I not obtain the highest perfect knowledge.

The methods for assuring rebirth in the Pure Land differed among the various schools of Pure Land Buddhism, but the point is the same for them all. Amitabha vows that women who successfully use the method for gaining rebirth in the Pure Land will be reborn there as men. This form of Buddhism became immensely popular in Japan and the belief that the Pure Land would be free of female rebirth led to the practice of giving women male names during their funeral ceremonies. In a typical Pure Land Buddhist funeral in Japan, the deceased is given a new name, but since there are no females in the next life in the Pure Land, all the names should be male names. This practice continued until very recently.

Difficult as all these passages may be to appreciate, it is crucial to realize that the motivation behind them is not misogyny, but pity and compassion. Women are advised to seek rebirth as men, not "because women aren't good enough"—the almost automatic interpretation of many—but because women's lives are so difficult, given the conditions enumerated above. Under those conditions, who would want to be reborn as a woman, if she had any choice? If she had sufficient merit to obtain a less harsh existence with more autonomy? Today, we might quarrel, not with the motivation behind these texts, but with the methods recommended. Why not eliminate the conditions that make female rebirth so unrewarding and difficult, rather than eliminating female rebirth itself? But that possibility was not available in the Indian imaginative universe of that day, perhaps with good reason.

GENDER-INCLUSIVE LANGUAGE IN MAHAYANA BUDDHISM

Mainstream Mahayana thought includes other methods for dealing with liabilities against women. In every case, though modern feminists might have an initially negative reaction, once one is more familiar with the immediate context, it is clear that Mahayana authors were seeking to correct and overcome, not to increase, negative attitudes toward women. As a prelude to considering major motifs and texts, we should notice several significant stylistic devices, common to Mahayana writings but often overlooked.

First of all, one finds a subtle, but rather widespread, use of gender-inclusive and gender-specific language in many Mahayana texts. Sometimes one almost could imagine that some editor, sensitive to issues of gender-inclusive language had sent out a policy statement requiring avoidance of the generic masculine. One frequently reads of "good daughters" as well as "good sons." (These are dharmic, not kinship relationships. A good son or daughter has taken on the Bodhisattva disciplines of the Mahayana path.) Often the seeker's friends and attendants include equal numbers of women and men.

Good sons and daughters who teach others are called "good friend" (*kalyanamitra*), an extremely important and warm term in Mahayana Buddhism.[26] Women, as well as men, very clearly take on the teaching role of a "good friend." Lion-Yawn, the nun whom we have already discussed, is such a "good friend." Laywomen are also depicted in that role in Mahayana texts. One of the most famous Mahayana *sutra*-s, the *Srimaladevi*, depicts just such a character. Queen Shrimala, the dharma teacher of this text, is sometimes described as a female Buddha because her teachings are so advanced and so effective. Certainly she is also a stunning example of a female "good friend."[27] Given the reluctance in earlier Buddhist texts to portray women as major teachers to the entire Buddhist community, rather than limiting them to teaching only women, these Mahayana portraits of female teachers and "good friends" are deliberate reversals of earlier norms. Since the presence or absence of female teachers is an overriding concern in any feminist analysis of Buddhism, these are significant portraits, even if they reflect mythic rather than historical characters.

MAGICAL SEX CHANGE IN MAHAYANA BUDDHIST TEXTS

Mahayana texts contain surprisingly frequent examples of female teachers and a wide range of attitudes toward them. Many stories in which women are important or advanced teachers also contain other motifs that are difficult to appreciate. A frequent scenario in Mahayana texts recounts a debate between a woman or a girl and a highly respected male elder, often a monk-hero of earlier Buddhism, sometimes a Bodhisattva. The female always demonstrates a extremely high level of dharmic understanding, proving that she is already far advanced on the Bodhisattva path and is moving rapidly towards Buddhahood. The male elders often express amazement that a female could be so advanced on the Buddhist path and contradict or challenge her. The woman and the man may debate about whether maleness and femaleness exist or have any relevance for spiritual discipline. Often the man challenges the female to prove her level of attainment by changing her sex. In some stories, she performs an act of truth, stating that if her aspirations will come true, then she will immediately become a male, which occurs instantly. In other stories, she does not change her sex or brings an unexpected twist to the sex change. In a few texts, the woman is not challenged, but discourses on the *dharma*, with great skill, eloquence, and effectiveness.

Recently, these stories have attracted more attention and have been carefully translated and studied by both Diana Paul and Nancy Schuster. Among these stories, those containing the motif of the "changing of the female sex" have received the most attention. As a result, this motif has sometimes been separated from the rest of the text, from the whole class of Mahayana *sutra*-s that feature a strong female *dharma* teacher and from the arguments about gender that accompany the motif, with unfortunate results. When so isolated, this provocative theme could be used by conservative patriarchs or by skeptical feminists to argue that Buddhism really is male dominant. "See," they can both say, "in the long run you *have* to become a man, even if that happens magically. Women are definitely of a lower order according to Buddhism." However, this interpretation seriously misunderstands the point of the motif.

The story of a female turning into a male before one's very eyes occurs relatively frequently. This odd turn of events is embedded in the context of a debate about the Buddhist path as understood in Mahayana Buddhism. Unlike earlier Buddhism, Mahayanists no longer saw individual enlightenment, resulting in arahantship or personal *nibbana*, the cessation of rebirth, as the appropriate goal of Buddhist practice. Rather, they saw the complete perfect enlightenment of a Buddha as the Buddhist's proper goal, which means that for Mahayana Buddhists, the ideal of eventual Buddhahood is not so unimaginable as it was in earlier Buddhism. For the average practitioner, however, that eventual goal was rather far removed and the practical emphasis was on arousing "the thought of enlightenment" (*bodhicitta*). Inspired by this experience, the practitioner takes the Bodhisattva vow, thereby dedicating oneself eventually to attain complete perfect enlightenment for the sake of all sentient beings. During the long period of Bodhisattvahood, during which the future Buddha returns to *samsara* for continuing rebirths, the good son or good daughter practices simultaneously the disciplines of wisdom and compassion.

Equally important for understanding the motif of the "changing of the female sex" is the Mahayana philosophical emphasis on all-pervasive emptiness, which means there are no fixed, immutable essences or traits anywhere, no inherent qualities in any being or thing. Therefore, one cannot label or categorize one's world or the people one meets on the basis of superficial traits. Perhaps this woman, this girl, or this woman of questionable morals, is not as she appears, but is already well practiced in the Bodhisattva's disciplines. Furthermore, gender itself contains nothing fixed or inherent. One only *appears* to be female or male; because nothing has fixed, inherent existence, it could not be said that one *is* male or female. One needs always to be open-ended and flexible in one's categorization of experience, because nothing is defined or limited by an immutable, fixed essence.

But some Buddhists had become quite inflexible about a number of issues, including women's spiritual potential. They argued as if a fixed essence of femaleness made it impossible for any woman to be spiritually advanced. The opinion that "a woman will not become a Buddha, absolutely holy and perfectly enlightened"[28] was already widespread. Some conservative texts also declared, "It is impossible for a woman to be an arahan, all-enlightened; but it is possible for a man to be."[29] Some conservative Buddhists even denied to women the possibility of making the resolution to attain Buddhahood eventually. "Leave aside Buddhahood; . . . even the mere resolution (for the attainment of Buddhahood) cannot be accomplished by a woman."* If a Mahayanist were to accept such a doctrine, then women would be barred from the religion's most significant experience—rousing the "thought of enlightenment" or *bodhicitta*.

Against this background of extremely fixed opinions about women's dharmic potential, Mahayanists told stories of women and girls who obviously had already made the resolution to attain Buddhahood. Thus, the most restrictive claim of the most misogynist Buddhists, the claim that a woman could not even experience *bodhicitta*, was categorically denied in the stories of the female Bodhisattva who sometimes changed her sex. The more important point in these stories is not that she eventually changes her sex, but that *she already had become a Bodhisattva and had already made the resolution to attain Buddhahood*, which she could demonstrate both by her understanding of *dharma* and by her magical power.

Mahayanists themselves, however, though they generally agreed that a woman could make the resolution to attain Buddhahood, disagreed about whether such a person would *eventually* become a male. Though the majority opinion does seem to be that eventually she would become a male, that is not the point of doctrinal interest. The point of doctrinal interest is that the woman standing here *now* could well be an advanced Bodhisattva and certainly is capable of rousing *bodhicitta*, contrary to conservative Buddhist opponents' opinions about her. Furthermore, magical transformations are entirely compatible with the Mahayana emphasis on the utter fluidity of phenomenal reality. Therefore, for this woman to change her sex on the spot drives home even more forcefully the point that *this woman* is indeed already an advanced Bodhisattva. Even more important, this magical sex change emphasizes that fixed mind, relying on conventional signs, tokens, opinions, and prejudices, such as gender stereotypes, cannot be trusted.

This background is essential for understanding some of the more important versions of this story, which occur already in the oldest Mahayana *sutra*, *The Perfection of Wisdom in Eight Thousand Lines*. In this *sutra*, the sex change occurs not instantaneously, but is predicted for the Goddess Ganga's next birth. Here, in this life she appears before the Buddha and vows to bring the *dharma* to all beings. (Such an aspiration would be impossible for a woman, according to most non-Mahayanists.) The Buddha then predicts that this female will

---

* Buddhaghosa, quoted by Sharma, "Can there by a Female Buddha in Theravada Buddhism," *Bucknell Review: Women, Literature, Criticism* 24 (Spring 1978), p. 76. See also the Jataka discussed by Yuichi, "Women in Buddhism," (pp. 42-3 of this book), in which a woman, who eventually became Siddartha Gautama, was told that a Buddha prediction could not be made about her while she was still a woman. She was told to try to obtain such a prediction later, after she had achieved male birth.

become a Tathagata and gives her a Buddha-name. (Such a prediction would be unthinkable to non-Mahayanists.) Next, he predicts that in her next life she will become male. After this, the Buddha also discloses that this female first made the resolution to attain Supreme Perfect Enlightenment while in a female body, during the life of the previous Buddha, Buddha Dipankara.* That she will become a male soon is rather incidental. What is radical, in the context of opinions widely current at the time of the text, is the claim that she had already, long ago, while a female, made her resolve to attain Buddhahood, and the prediction of her future Buddhahood.

The most famous and influential version of the "changing of female sex motif" is found in the *Lotus Sutra*, one of the most important of all Mahayana *sutra-s*, especially in East Asia. This story involves an instantaneous change of sex, rather than a future change of sex. The heroine is the eight-year-old Naga-princess, whom Bodhisattva Manjusri, just returned from the Naga kingdom, declares to be "superior in knowledge and understanding." He reports that she "has made wide-reaching resolves and practices faultlessly." Another Bodhisattva doubts that she could do this, since the Bodhisattva way is very difficult and takes much time to accomplish.

The Naga princess suddenly appears, praises the Buddha and vows, "Because I wish enlightenment, I will extensively teach the Dharma which liberates from suffering." Shariputra objects that a female simply cannot accomplish that goal because she cannot attain the five stations. (This passage has already been quoted and discussed. See page 62.) She gives the Buddha a jewel, which he immediately accepts. She asks Shariputra to confirm that the Buddha took the jewel quickly, not slowly and says, "Now I shall seize the unexcelled perfect way and achieve supreme enlightenment even more quickly than that."

> Then at that instant in time, before the Elder Sariputra and the entire world, King Sagara's daughter's female organ disappeared and the male organ became visible. She appeared as a Bodhisattva. At that instant in time, . . . he appeared as an enlightened one. Radiating a form having the thirty-two marks . . . he began teaching the dharma.[30]

Though this text could be, and has been, used[31] to challenge women who cannot similarly trade in their female sex organs for male ones, the emphasis, in context, is not on the literal sex change. Rather, the point is that one should not depend on conventional signs and tokens in one's attempt to determine someone's true identity. One moment, an eight-year-old girl, the very next instant a Bodhisattva, yet the very next, a Buddha with the thirty-two marks.

---

* The Buddha immediately preceding the Buddha of our world age, under whom our Budda Shakyamuni, also received his prediction and made his resolve. See Paul, *Women in Buddhism*, pp. 182–4, for the story.

Who is this person, really? Will the real Naga-princess please stand up? The real Bodhisattva? The real Buddha with the thirty-two marks? It is not that one *became* the other, for in emptiness, neither the Naga princess nor the bodhisattva, nor the Buddha has fixed existence. Therefore, one cannot predetermine what any women or any men could do or whom they might be.

Many other versions of the motif of changing the female sex are found in Mahayana scriptures, including some in which the woman performs her sex change as an act of truth.[32] There is no need to summarize all of them, but is impossible to avoid the conclusion that this motif solved an important problem for some Buddhists. Furthermore, those who used this motif intended to emphasize women's possibilities, not to glorify the male sex further. In all cases, the person who undergoes the sex change is already highly advanced while she is in a female body. She proves her capabilities *before* the sex change, which does not add at all to her wisdom. The sex change is a mockery to slow-witted conservatives, who believe in some essence of gender that defines and limits women, not an improvement to the main character. She already is clearly superior to all the males present except for the reigning Buddha.

The use of this motif also demonstrates that, in emptiness, sex is not a fixed or rigid trait, but something that is fluid and changes readily. According to Schuster, in the *Surangamasamadhisutra*, a character says that those who are established in the Mahayana do not see any difference between men and women. "I had a female body, and that was according to my resolve, and now that I have a male body I have not destroyed nor abandoned the characteristics of a female body."[33] In another case, the girl changes herself into a man and then back into a girl again.[34]

Embedded in these stories, but often overlooked by both patriarchal and feminist interpreters, is an important insight for a Buddhist and *dharmic* exegesis of this motif. Dwelling in emptiness, the person who undergoes the sex change is utterly non-fixated and non-attached regarding gender. The woman is not attached to her femaleness but will leave it behind when skill-in-means to teach the *dharma* would be well served by a sex change. For conventional people, no aspect of ego-identity is so fixed and unmalleable as gender identity and sexual form. Would that those who interpret this text to mean that in the long run males are more fit to be Buddhas would contemplate that a Buddha cannot be attached to sex or gender. These women did not change their sex because they *had to*, but because they *could*. If they had to change their sex to achieve Buddhahood, they would not have been able to, since in Buddhist thought, magic can happen only when one is utterly detached and non-fixated.

ROLE REVERSAL AND SEX CHANGE

Nevertheless, it is impossible for someone with feminist sensibilities not to be slightly uncomfortable with the end of the story, especially when we know that men sometimes used this story to challenge female contemporaries who were attempting to take up positions of authority in Buddhism.[35] Luckily, this motif is not the only Mahayana Buddhist answer to the question about the relationship between gender and spiritual attainment. Other texts demonstrate, by logic and by magic, the utter irrelevance of gender, a different and more powerful argument against the presumed female inabilities posited by conservative Buddhists.

A favorite episode of many commentators contains both logic and magic— an unbeatable combination, especially when linked with humor. In the *Vimalakirtinirdesa Sutra*, Shariputra is once again debating and discussing the *dharma* with a female. In this case, she is not a girl, but a mature woman, a "goddess," who has been living in Vimalakirti's palace for twelve years, apparently studying and meditating. Their discussion has gone on for some time and Shariputra has been extremely impressed by the goddess' questions and answers. He says to her, "Why don't you change your female sex?" She replies:

> "I have been here twelve years and have looked for the innate characteristics of the female sex and haven't been able to find them. How can I change them? Just as a magician creates an illusion of a woman, if someone asks why don't you change your female sex, what is he asking?"
>
> Sariputra: "But an illusion is without any determinate innate characteristics, so how could it be changed?"
>
> Goddess: "All things are also without any determinate innate characteristics, so how could you ask, 'why don't you change your female sex?' "
>
> Then the Goddess, by supernatural power, changed Sariputra into a likeness of herself and changed herself into a likeness of Sariputra and asked: "Why don't you change your female sex?"
>
> Sariputra, in the form of a goddess answered: "I do not know how I changed nor how I changed into a female form."
>
> Goddess: "Sariputra, if you can change into a female form, then all women can also change. Just as you are not really a woman but appear to be female in form, all women also only appear to be female in form but are not really women. Therefore, the Buddha said all are not really men or women."
>
> Then the goddess, by her supernatural power, changed Sariputra back into his own form. The goddess questioned Sariputra: "Where are the female form and innate characteristics now?"
>
> Sariputra: "The female form and innate characteristics neither exist nor do not exist."[36]

Clearly, this argument depends completely on the Mahayana concept of emptiness, one of the central Buddhist doctrines to be used in any refutation of belief in fixed gender traits and limitations entailed by such traits. The magic simply gives pith and color to what stands on its own in logic.

NO MAGIC, JUST LOGIC

Not relying upon the advanced technology demonstrated by the goddess, my favorite discussion of this question is less well known, but even more direct. Jewel Brocade meditated upon the Buddha and he appeared before her. She gave him her jewel and made a declaration to attain Supreme Perfect Enlightenment. The elder Mahakasyapa tried to explain, "The Supreme Perfect Enlightenment is extremely difficult to attain. One cannot attain Buddhahood within a woman's body." Jewel Brocade's reply is the last word on the topic:

> The practicing Bodhisattva whose mind is determined and originally pure attains Buddhahood without difficulty. Awakening to the thought of enlightenment, he attains Buddhahood as if perceiving the palm of his hand. . . . You have said, "One cannot attain Buddhahood within a woman's body." Then one cannot attain it within a man's body either. What is the reason? Because the thought of enlightenment is neither male nor female. . . . The one who perceives through emptiness is neither male nor female. The ears, nose, mouth, body and mind are also empty.
>
> Just as the stillness of space is neither male nor female, . . . one who perceives through enlightenment has the dharma which is neither male nor female.[37]

This line of reasoning cannot go further than the realization that the *dharma* is neither male nor female. Androcentric expectations that, of course, Buddhas would be male, are overcome by sex-neutral modes of argumentation and understanding, modes of perceiving and understanding which proclaim that, in truth, at a deep level of understanding, male and female do not really exist. Nevertheless, to some extent the context remains androcentric, in that discriminations against women, *not discriminations against men*, are the problem to be overcome by sex-neutral understandings. One should still question whether the choice between androcentrism and sex-neutral models of humanity and reality gives us all the options we need.

A FEMALE BUDDHA?

In later Mahayana Buddhism yet another option is tentatively suggested. Perhaps a highly advanced being, whether a Buddha or an advanced, so-called "celestial Bodhisattva," could be portrayed in unabashed female form. Such a figure would not undergo a sex change from female to male, nor would she necessarily rely solely on the argument that reality and the *dharma* are sex neutral, "neither male nor female." Her competence and her spiritually advanced state would need no such justification or explanation. This possibility, which is taken further in East Asian than in Indian Mahayana, and much further yet in Vajrayana Buddhism, is found in some Mahayana texts and practices. The main character and *dharma*-teacher of another important Mahayana *sutra*, the *Srimaladevisimhananda Sutra* is the laywoman and queen, Shrimaladevi. She is pictured as ruling her Indian kingdom with her husband, but she is clearly the main focus of interest because of her great understanding of Buddhism and her equally great abilities to teach the *dharma*. Because of her ability to teach, she is said to be one "who has the lion's roar." To have "the lion's roar" is to proclaim enlightenment and to be able to preach like a Buddha. Thus this title, given to a female, is quite provocative and suggestive. Interestingly, this *sutra* is renowned for its presentation of *tathagatagarbha* theory, to be discussed in the next section as one of the Buddhist doctrines most helpful and profound to a Buddhist feminist.

In her story, her parents perceive her exceptional abilities and arrange for her to hear of the Tathagata (Buddha). Immediately upon hearing, she confesses her deep faith and resolve to attain complete perfect enlightenment; she then receives a prediction regarding her eventual achievement of Buddhahood. No sex change is predicted or hinted at anywhere in the story. After vowing to practice the Mahayana disciplines, she preaches "eloquently with the 'lion's roar' of a Buddha." No one ever challenges her and the issue of her female gender is not raised or discussed. In the end, all the citizens of her kingdom, first the women, then her husband, and finally the men, are converted to (Mahayana) Buddhism.[38]

As Diana Paul, who has translated and extensively studied this *sutra*, has argued,[39] implicitly, Shrimaladevi is a female Buddha. She receives a prediction of full and complete Buddhahood in the future. In the present, as a laywoman, she teaches with the eloquence and effect of a Buddha. Refreshingly, in this text, the competent female does not have to explain or justify her competence nor to trade in her female sex eventually. Certainly this story is pre-eminently usable to the feminist historian.

However, some of the uses to which this story has been put in traditional commentaries are in stark contrast with the uses to which a feminist might put this story. Complex Mahayana Bodhisattva theory talks of ten stages in the Bodhisattva's long career and people became interested in the question of assigning a Bodhisattva stage to Shrimaladevi, in her current incarnation as laywoman queen. According to two commentators, she is an eighth-stage Bodhisattva, a very advanced stage also attributed to some of the great mythical male Bodhisattvas of the Mahayana pantheon. However, one of these commentators claims that Shrimaladevi is not "really" a female but a male appearing as a female! Yet another places her slightly lower, as a seventh stage Bodhisattva just about to make the major transformation involved in moving from the seventh to the eighth stage. But another commentator says she is only at the first stage, not nearly so impressive an achievement.[40] Even a highly usable story can be derailed by androcentric commentators.

FEMININE PERSONIFICATIONS OF WISDOM AND COMPASSION IN THE MAHAYANA PANTHEON

Though these stories which have just been summarized and analyzed all appear somewhat "mythical" rather than historical to the modern reader, the characters in them are given homes on earth in the present world-age. They are not mythical characters in another sense of the word "mythical." They are not primarily personifications of various traits, projections created by human imagination and placed in another realm not to be found on this earth. The characters in the texts surveyed thus far are "humans," albeit rather unusual humans, rather then non-human superior beings of another order.

"Mythic," non-human personifications and projections were not an important part of early Indian Buddhism but they did become important to Buddhism during the Mahayana period. Explaining just how this happened and how to fit them into the context of Buddhist non-theism is always a challenge. Nevertheless, eventually Mahayana Buddhism includes a "pantheon" of what are usually called "celestial Buddhas and bodhisattvas." As is usually the case with such divine figures, such projections and personifications, they are gendered, rather than abstract, neutered, non-sexed beings. Many of the figures found in the Mahayana pantheon are male, but two significant feminine figures, Kuan-yin and Prajnaparamita, are present and important. Thus, for Mahayana Buddhism, unlike earlier Indian Buddhism, we can talk of a "feminine principle," though this feminine principle is nowhere nearly as well developed or as important as it will become still later, during the Vajrayana period.

The female manifestations of Kuan-yin are not part of Indian Mahayana, which knows only the male Bodhisattva Avalokitesvara. However, his female counterpart or manifestation, as Kwan-Yin, became immensely popular in East Asian Buddhism. This process of "reverse" sex change (from the ones so frequently seen in this chapter) is not yet well understood or much studied, but in East Asian popular Buddhism, these female forms were often the most loved and cherished figures.

Actually, Avalokitesvara, or, to use the Chinese name, Kuan-yin, the Bodhisattva who embodies and personifies compassion, is not "really" male or female, though the androcentric imagination, whether Buddhist or scholarly, more readily sees "him" as a male who sometimes takes on female form. This being manifests, out of compassion, in many forms. Having very great ability at skill-in-means (*upaya*) he/she takes whatever form will be most effective to help the person who is calling out, whom Kuan-yin compassionately aids. In an immensely popular chapter from a Chinese translation of the *Lotus Sutra*, Kuan-yin is said to assume thirty-three forms, of which seven are female. The purpose for each of the thirty-three forms is that if someone can be saved by a "monk, nun, layman, or laywoman," then Kuan-yin appears in that form. The other five female forms are: woman, housewife, officer's wife, Brahmin woman, and young girl.[41]

In this *sutra*, Kuan-yin also promises to help people with a great variety of needs and wants. Included among the needs Kuan-yin will meet are those of a woman who wants to give birth to a son. She gets a "virtuous and wise son." Kuan-yin is equally kind to the woman who wants to give birth to a daughter, for she will have an "exceptionally refined" daughter with good karma whom everyone will cherish.[42] It is quite interesting to notice that women wanted to have daughters and that their desires are granted equally with the desire for sons.

The other major Mahayana feminine personification, Prajnaparamita, is quite different. She is truly a personification of the transcendent wisdom sought by the Bodhisattva; as such, she is not a saviour to whom one can appeal at all, but a vision of the goal. Some claim that she owes her femininity only to the grammatical accident that the Sanskrit word for Wisdom, "Prajna," takes the feminine gender. If so, that is a happy accident, for the pursuit of wisdom, personified as feminine, became a major and felicitous metaphor and spiritual discipline in Vajrayana Buddhism. Clearly, she belongs on the Wisdom side of the Wisdom and Compassion team that are so important to late Mahayana and Vajrayana thought and practice, just as Kuan-yin clearly belongs to the Compassion side. That is why she is not worshipped or often represented iconographically and why her major qualities are "light, emptiness, space, and a *samsara*-confronting gaze that is both clinical and compassionate."[43] Also unlike Kuan-yin, she is found already in the earliest Mahayana literature, the *Perfection of Wisdom in 8,000 Lines*,[44] in which she is called "mother of the Tathagatas" and "genetrix and nurse of the six perfections."[45]

> The Buddhas in the world-systems in the ten directions
> Bring to mind this perfection of wisdom as their mother.
> The saviours of the world who were in the past, and also are now in the
>   ten directions,
> Have issued from her, and so will the future ones be.
> She is the one who shows this world (for what it is), she is the genetrix,
>   the mother of the Buddhas.[46]

Not only is she the mother, but also the desired lover. In a metaphor that is especially interesting, given the fear of women and sex found so frequently in earlier Buddhist texts, the male student is compared to a man who is in love.In his constant contemplation of wisdom, he is like a man in love who constantly thinks of his beloved, especially when separated from her.[47]

In that same text, not only is the ultimate goal personified positively as feminine. Positive feminine symbolism is also used of the Bodhisattva, the presumably male student and disciple. In his readiness to experience enlightenment, he is like a pregnant women about to give birth. In his practice of compassion for all beings, he is like the mother of an only child in his attentive care.[48] Clearly, in such metaphors, we are approaching androgynous modes of thinking and symbolizing.

Thus, this chapter also ends as it began. During the Mahayana period, the roles and images of women were clearly an important issue. Modern feminists are not the first Buddhists to think long and hard about the question of proper gender roles in Buddhism, nor are we the first Buddhists to suggest that androcentric and patriarchal systems of male privilege and honor are not properly Buddhist. Clearly, then as now, others were uncomfortable with more egalitarian gender arrangements and more positive images of women and femininity. They tried hard to find innate female traits, which they were sure would be limiting and demeaning. In compensation and in compassion, they held out the promise of immediate or future sex change, since they did realize that a religion of compassion cannot condemn half its members to perpetual inferiority. However, those who won the debate placed in a woman's mouth the final argument: "The one who perceives through enlightenment has the *dharma*, which is neither male nor female."[49]

6

The Feminine Principle: Roles and Images of Women in Indian and Tibetan Vajrayana Buddhism

The basis for realizing enlightenment is a human body.
Male or female—there is no great difference.
But if she develops the mind bent on enlightenment,
the woman's body is better.*

Mother of Knowledge

Delineating the historical origins of Vajrayana Buddhism, also known as Tantric Buddhism is, if anything, even more difficult than tracing the development of Mahayana Buddhism out of early Indian Buddhism.[1] Nevertheless, just as the difficulties surrounding the history of Mahayana Buddhism do not undermine our ability to speak of Mahayana Buddhism as a definable and distinct, albeit varied and multifaceted, movement within Buddhism, so the historical difficulties attendant on studying Vajrayana Buddhism do not undercut our ability to speak of Vajrayana Buddhism, both Indian and Tibetan, as a distinctive movement within Buddhism.

In this case, the division is not so sharp, since Vajrayanists do not argue against Mahayana Buddhism, but regard it as part of their vision and practice of Buddhism. In fact, most Vajrayanists would consider themselves to be primarily Mahayanists with some special techniques that speed up the process of achieving enlightenment. Some would say that Mahayana teachings already include all aspects of Wisdom, but that the Vajrayana provides the skillful methods, the techniques, quickly to realize that wisdom.† Thus, discussions of Vajrayana Buddhism focus on extensive descriptions of esoteric meditation techniques; philosophical discussions elaborate on topics and controversies already familiar to Mahayana Buddhism.

---

* Padmasambhava to Yeshe Tsogyel, a quote that sets the tone for one major theme of this chapter.
† Notice the complementarity of wisdom and method, a major theme is Vajrayana Buddhism.

79

However, some of the techniques most utilized by Vajrayana Buddhism imply a radically altered intuition about the environment surrounding the practitioner—an intuition that is more proclaimed than argued. The world of Vajrayana practice is built on an intuition of the primordial purity and sacredness of the phenomenal world, which brings with it an intuition of the inherent workability and transmutability of *all* human emotions and experiences. This insight is the conclusion, put to extremely practical use, of the Mahayana view that all phenomena are empty of inherent existence and defining characteristics. The practical conclusions that are drawn from this philosophical position mean that Vajrayana practices utilize, as essential elements on the path, certain experiences and emotions that were shunned by early Indian Buddhism. Therefore, Vajrayana Buddhism evaluates itself as potentially dangerous and needing to be restricted to properly initiated students. Outsiders, both Buddhist and non-Buddhist, are often and easily scandalized by spiritual practices sometimes undertaken by Vajrayanists.

As with earlier chapters on roles and images of women in the major epochs of Buddhist history, I will discuss typical Indian and Tibetan Vajrayana attitudes toward women theme by theme. Since the lines between Mahayana and Vajrayana Buddhism are not absolute, some of the materials discussed in this chapter are not, strictly speaking, Vajrayana materials. They are not esoteric and do not depend on the Vajrayanist's intuitive sense of the sacredness of phenomena. In that sense, some of these themes might technically be considered Mahayana themes, but they are characteristic of the kind of Mahayana that is interspersed with Vajrayana in late Indian and Tibetan Buddhism.

DUAL ATTITUDES TOWARD WOMEN

The ambiguity characteristic of Buddhist attitudes toward women continues in Vajrayana Buddhism, down to the present day. However, both positive and negative attitudes toward women find unique expression in Vajrayana Buddhism. The doctrinal attitude toward women is very favorable—much more favorable than in any earlier form of Buddhism and among the most favorable attitudes found in any major religion in any period of its development. Vajrayana Buddhism includes an abundance of positive feminine images and symbols, as well as a significant number of women practitioners, both monastics and laypeople, who are highly regarded and respected by both women and men.

This exaltation both of femininity and of exceptional women contrasts significantly with everyday reality, for the folk wisdom of Vajrayana Buddhism continues unabated in its assessment that female birth is unfortunate. Virtually all institutionalized positions of religious power, influence, authority, and veneration were held by men; that such an arrangement is proper was the unchallenged consensus. There were many fewer nuns than monks; they were generally less well educated and less well supported; as a result, they fared less well in every regard. Women who sought to take up serious practice of spiritual discipline, whether as nuns or recluses, frequently were ridiculed and reminded of the expected norms and roles for women.

The contradictions between these views could hardly be greater, and both views are very strongly held, even in contemporary times. It might seem that such a contradiction would be intolerable, but, unfortunately, this is not the only case in world religions in which a symbolic and mythic glorification of femininity coexists with a social reality that sharply limits women. In Tibetan Vajrayana Buddhism, as with most other such situations, the contradiction is not perceived by those who live within the system. Usually, in the case of contemporary Tibetan Buddhism, people say, at one and the same time, that the Buddha's teachings are without reference to sex, so there can be no special issue of "women and the *dharma*," while with the next breath claiming that women are different because of their responsibilities vis-à-vis children. Almost always, male teachers make these proclamations to women questioners. Obviously, something is being overlooked.

"BORN LOW": THE EVALUATION OF FEMALE REBIRTH

The negative attitudes toward women generally are not found in religious texts as formal points of doctrine, the way that they sometimes are found in texts of early Indian or Mahayana Buddhism. Rather, they are deeply embedded and ingrained assumptions of folk wisdom. As such, they insidiously crop up in everyday speech and attitudes, as asides in important religious texts, as androcentric record-keeping and remembering practices, and as accepted norms and practices of Tibetan Buddhist society.

In everyday speech, the attitude that femaleness is an inferior or unfortunate birth is so deeply ingrained, so taken for granted, that the very word for "woman" in the Tibetan language "literally translates 'born low.' This rather alarming signification is not buried in the distant past or in the unconscious. Anyone using or hearing it can tell you precisely what it means." This most widely used term for "woman" is neither slang nor a localism.[2]

> this word carries a conscious social status that Tibetans everywhere recognize as low. Yes, they say, a woman is not as capable as a man, she cannot enter into new areas of development; her place is in the house; she lacks a man's intellectual capacity; she is unable to initiate new things; and finally, she cannot become a Bodhisattva until she is reborn as a man.[3]

In this thoroughly Mahayana country, the last limitation means that, in popular folk wisdom, a woman must wait until male rebirth before she can begin serious progress on the path of *dharma*. Such an attitude may explain why nuns are generally less respected and supported, and why many women are ridiculed when they express a desire to take up serious religious practice.

Because of the understanding that her birth is "low," a woman's institution-alized inferiority begins at birth. "no parent is pleased over the birth of a girl as they are by the arrival of a son. This is not a suppressed value; it is openly stated. And a man without a male heir is believed, and said to be, most unfortunate."[4] By contrast, a boy's sexuality is celebrated and protected by rituals that protect him from being changed into a girl.[5]

Even nuns retain this attitude of regarding female birth as "low." Karma Lekshe Tsomo, a Western woman who as lived as a Tibetan nun in India for many years reports:

> I have spoken with Tibetan women who, on the one hand regret having made prayers for a male rebirth when they were children, yet who have not gained confidence enough to pray for a female rebirth. They still cite the disadvan-tages of enforced dependency and vulnerability to pregnancy as making the female state less desirable both from the worldly and religious points of view. Women even today are seen as requiring more protection and entitled to less personal freedom than men.[6]

As I argued in the previous chapter, I believe that providing women with methods to obtain male rebirth indicates, not misogynistic fear and hatred of women, but pity for those subjected to existence as women in a patriarchal society. Nevertheless, one can only imagine what it must do to a girl's self-concept to be taught such methods as a child. We can see the effects of this attitude on an adult woman, the mother of an incarnate teacher, one of the highest honors available to a laywoman. Her son, the incarnate teacher, relates a story of how he asked her about their family name when he was a very young boy—so young that his mother still lived near the monastery (women are not allowed *in* the monasteries), so that she could visit him and care for him on occasion. She told him the family name, but when he asked if that meant he too carried the name, she hesitated and said "You're Rinpoche," the title of respect, meaning precious one, used of all important teachers. He then asked whether he was her son who had come out of her body. She replied, "Yes. . . . Well maybe I'm an inhuman being, a subhuman being. I have a woman's body; I had an inferior birth."[7] Recently, I asked a prominent Tibetan woman teacher, Jetsun Kushala, of her opinion about such attitudes. Refreshingly, and unhesitatingly, she said that in America, one didn't need to say such prayers, but she did not elaborate why not.

"BORN LOW" AND BEING A MOTHER

Women's maternal role and responsibility are used frequently by Buddhist teachers both to explain and to justify women's frequent limited participation in Buddhist spiritual and philosophical disciplines. I myself have received that answer on occasion when questioning teachers about why there are so few great women teachers in the history of Buddhism. The contemporary Tibetan women who are still somewhat negative about their femaleness cited vulnerability to pregnancy as a liability of being female. In the views of both women and men, motherhood is regarded as the inevitable fate of women, a fate that both limits and defines them.

Pregnancy itself is often regarded as a painful state for both mother and fetus, though the supposed indignities suffered by the fetus are stressed much more than are the difficulties of the mother. This is typical of androcentric thinking, in which the author identifies more readily with a fetus than with a female human being. The womb is often called a "foul place." Perhaps the most famous instance of this attitude is the oft-quoted metaphor for Inherent Buddha-nature (*tathagatagarbha*). "Like a king-to-be in a foul female womb . . . even so is the Buddha-sphere to be found in living beings."[8] The judgment that the womb is a place of "unbearable stench" is also frequent. Gampopa, an important eleventh-century Tibetan teacher, in his manual for Bodhisattva practice, *The Jewel Ornament of Liberation*, writes a long description of pregnancy, including a week by week narration of what happens to the fetus. Every week brings new pain, and the whole process is summarized as "having been boiled and fried in the womb's heat as in a hot vessel for a long time."[9]

The tendency to identify with the fetus rather than with women continues in an identification with the new baby. Stereotypically, the baby is pictured as receiving lavish and totally selfless care from the mother. A few pages after discussing the stench of the womb, Gampopa talks of mother as one's greatest benefactor because she does everything for the infant and suffers greatly from all her exertions.[10] While such a description contains a certain accuracy, it also involves unfortunate consequences. Fathers are absolved from similar responsibilities to nurture their infants. Mothers are idealized as completely self-giving. The effect of such idealized descriptions of mother may well be to make actual mothers feel guilty for being anything less than totally self-giving, since mothers inevitably fall short of that mark. At the same time, such one-sided idealizations of the mother-role also discourage and denigrate women who don't want to be physical mothers, especially since no highly valued alternatives are given.

When we turn to legendary literature about women, we find a much more wrenching, but more accurate picture. Nangsa Obum, whose story is set in eleventh-century Tibet, is torn between her desire to practice *dharma* full time and her little son. Crying as she nurses her baby, she sings, "This woman wishes to become accomplished in the dharma! My son, children are like a rope that pulls a woman into Samsara."[11] Clearly she feels affection and concern for her child, but he is not her only reason for existence, nor does he meet her existential need to live her own life and understand reality herself. Though her attitude is not normative for women in patriarchal societies, and is, in fact, discouraged, it probably comes much closer to revealing most women's actual experiences than the androcentric ideal of the woman who lives only to minister to her children.

The whole picture for women presented in such literature is rather bleak. Women are given no option but to become mothers, but their organs of generation are dismissed as foul and stench-ridden, while their sufferings during pregnancy are ignored in favor of imagined sufferings on the part of the fetus. Once born, the child should be the only thing about which the mother thinks, her sole reason for existence. Fathers are allowed to be rather remote and uninvolved in the whole process. The description of pregnancy and early childhood could hardly be more androcentric.

"BORN LOW" AND BEING MARRIED

In popular attitudes, motherhood is not the only inevitability of the female life cycle which is thought both to define women and to oppose their attempts at serious religious practice. Being a wife is also inevitable and constricting. In almost every case, the biographies of exceptional women recount that conventional marriage was unwanted by them because they feared it as a major obstacle and stumbling block. Yet this course was forced upon them by relatives and society. As was the case for the nuns of early Buddhism, these women encountered far greater opposition than did their male counterparts in avoiding or fleeing conventional marriages.[12]

Yeshe Tsogyel's back was beaten to a bloody pulp by her suitor-captor. When he and his companions passed out after drinking to celebrate her capture and submission, she escaped to live in a cave.[13] Lakshminkara, a Indian Mahasiddha, feigned madness in her husband's palace, tearing off her clothes and destroying her appearance. She escaped the palace and continued to appear as one insane, feeding on food put out for dogs and living in cremation grounds.[14] Nangsa Obum also expressed a wish to avoid marriage, but relented when her parents begged her to accept a royal suitor, arguing that they feared his reprisals if she did not submit. After her child was born, her husband, her sister-in-law, and her father-in-law beat her to death for giving supplies to wandering *yogin*-s. After she magically revived and left her household to practice with a guru, her in-laws came with an army to attempt to retrieve her and to kill her guru and his disciples.[15]

This opposition is rooted in widespread attitudes that women are intellectually and spiritually not suited to *dharma* practice. Mothers seem to be particularly hard on daughters in this regard. Not only do Nangsa Obum's relatives by marriage scorn and impede her aspirations. Her own mother ridicules her:

> If you really want to practice the Dharma, it is very difficult.
> . . . .
> Do not try to do what you are not capable of doing,
> Practicing the Dharma.
> Do what you know how to do,
> Be a housewife.[16]

Another biography narrates the mother as telling her daughter, "My dear, girls cannot practice the Dharma. It would be far better for you to marry now that you have many suitors." The girl does not reply out loud, but thinks to herself, "I will prove to her that girls can practice the Dharma."[17] In the case of this woman, luckily her father recognized that she was "not an ordinary girl," but someone with exceptional potential. He does not make her marry, gives her valuable *dharmic* instructions regarding both study and practice, and eventually made her his lineage heir for his most secret teachings, a rare event in Tibetan accounts of *dharma* lineages.

WOMEN'S OPTIONS: NUNS IN INDO-TIBETAN VAJRAYANA BUDDHISM

Recent commentators on the Tibetan social world who are also familiar with feminist standards of assessment and analysis conclude that Tibetan women did have greater self-determination and freedom and had more options available to them than did women in surrounding Asian societies, whether South Asian or East Asian. They also conclude that, nevertheless, social and religious prestige and power rested almost completely in male hands.[18]

Thus, the situation for Tibetan Buddhism is more complex and variegated than was the case with Indian Buddhism. Women were more free to take up an independent religious vocation, and did so more frequently, than seems to have been the case in India, but they were nevertheless constrained in many ways and many avenues were closed to them. Women practicing Tibetan Vajrayana Buddhism seriously could become either nuns or *yogini*-s. The nuns's code is essentially the same as it had been in India. Tibetan women also continued to become *yogini*-s, full-time religious practitioners whose rule of conduct is neither monastic nor lay.

The Tibetan nuns suffered many liabilities, both vis-à-vis monks and *yogini*-s. First of all, they lived, and most still do even today, as perpetual novices. It is uncertain whether the nuns' ordination was ever transmitted from India to Tibet, but certainly it was not transmitted during the second diffusion of Buddhism from India to Tibet, in the tenth and eleventh centuries, and if it ever had existed in Tibet, it had died out by then. Though novice nuns dress and behave very much like monks or fully ordained nuns, their prestige is much lower. Thus, Tibetan nuns are subject not only to the liabilities of the eight special rules but also to the lowered status of noviceship.[19] Today, most Western nuns who practice in the Tibetan manner receive the full ordination from Chinese or Korean ordination lineages; some Tibetan women are also beginning to receive this ordination. Tibetan male hierarchs show some interest in reinstituting the full-scale nun's ordination in Tibetan lineages, but it is not a high priority for them. They are excessively concerned over the "purity" of the ordination lineages, even though the alternative is continued treatment of nuns as second-class monastics.

Because of their low prestige, nuns and nunneries were subject to other limitations. Nunneries were never politically powerful, as were some monasteries.[20] More problematic, considering the purpose of monastic institutions, educational opportunies for nuns were, and still are, discouragingly limited. Though educational opportunities for nuns are improving, most of the leadership for this movement comes from the nuns themselves, especially from Western-born and educated nuns, sometimes without much co-operation from their male supervisors.[21] Tibetan monks, even in exile in India, are relatively well supported, with sufficient time available for study and practice. By contrast, nuns' living accommodations are so limited that many women are turned away. The nuns themselves must engage in heavy labor to construct their dwellings, to carry water from considerable distances and to split their own wood for cooking fires. As Karma Lekshe Tsomo has observed, these liabilities probably result from "a subtle tendency . . . to place greater value on efforts of men in spiritual matters."[22] "Even a girl of strong spiritual inclinations would not routinely be encouraged by her family to take up the monastic life, whereas a boy of similar disposition would surely be placed in a monastery with pride."[23]

It is not surprising, therefore, that in a society that valued and supported its monastics as much as any society ever has, monks vastly outnumbered nuns. Estimates regarding the number of nuns in Tibet prior to the Chinese takeover vary wildly, from 18,000[24] to 120,000,[25] but even the more generous figure would mean there were nine monks for every nun. It is difficult to avoid the impression that since 1959, preserving the monks' lifestyle has been a much higher priority than preserving or improving that of the nuns.

Under these conditions, few nuns stand out in the historical record of Tibetan Buddhism, but this may have more to do with androcentric record-keeping practices than lack of accomplishments. In the recent record, at least one outstanding nun, Ani Lochen, can be mentioned, in part because a male student wanted to honor her memory in the English-speaking world.[26] How many more such women there were who did not have their biographies recorded will never be known.

WOMEN'S OPTIONS: *YOGINI*-S IN INDO-TIBETAN
VAJRAYANA BUDDHISM

If a woman did not want to become a nun, her other major option was to become a *yogini*, otherwise known as a *tantrika*. The religious lifestyle of the *yogi*-s and *yogini*-s was not found in earlier forms of Buddhism, but became popular and valued in Indian Vajrayana Buddhism. *Yogini*-s were not necessarily celibate and were not so closely associated with a religious order that lived communally as were nuns. Often they wandered freely on religious pilgrimage all over Tibet and into Nepal, alone, with other *yogini*-s, or in mixed company with *yogi*-s. Between or after periods of wandering, such *yogini*-s would settle down in an isolated hermitage for long periods of intensive meditation practice. Constantly practicing various *sadhana*-s and other meditation disciplines, they were usually not highly educated philosophically, but they frequently requested and received empowerments and meditation instruction from the great meditation masters. Frequently, they attained high states of meditational realization and were sought out as meditation teachers by both men and women, both monastics and laypeople. Most of the exceptional women, whose stories are remembered and who were greatly loved and honored in the Tibetan Vajrayana tradition as a whole, belonged to this category of religious practitioner. And the Tibetan tradition did and still does greatly honor such exceptions. If a woman can somehow make it through the maze of negative socialization and gender stereotypes, she will be greatly revered as an exceptionally accomplished *yogini*.

Fortunately, the biography of a recent *yogini*, Ayu Khadro, has been preserved because a male student from one of the elite Tibetan universities studied briefly with her, asked her about her life, wrote down her comments (which he says was unusual for a Tibetan),[27] carried them out of Tibet and made them public.[28] Her biography should be read in full since any summary will highlight some aspects of her life to the detriment of others.

To me, her life story is especially revealing in its portrayal of the freedom that could be experienced by such a *yogini* and in its portrayal of the depth and warmth of spiritual friendship between Ayu Khadro and other *yogini*-s. She lived with her aunt, another *yogini*, from the age of seven till she was eighteen, by which time she had decided that she wanted the *yogini* lifestyle for herself. Her parents forced her to marry at nineteen but after three years she was undiagnosably near death. Her aunt and the resident *lama* insisted that her poor health was due to the forcible interruption of her religious practices. Ayu Khadro characterized her husband as kind, both before and after this diagnosis. He accompanied her back to her aunt's cave and paid for her attendant during her recovery. She remained with her aunt until the aunt died.

Then, when she was thirty, she began to travel around Tibet, first with a nun and a male *Chod* * practitioner. Eventually she met another *yogini* with whom she became close friends. The two of them met several male practitioners with whom they had great rapport; they travelled in a foursome for some time. Eventually after about fourteen years of wandering to important pilgrimage spots, practicing, making retreats, and studying with many important teachers, she returned to her home area. Her former husband, with whom she had very good rapport and to whom she gave meditation instructions, build a retreat hut for her. She remained there for most of the rest of her long life. At one point her *yogini*-friend from her days on the road came and stayed with her "and we did retreat together. This was a big boon for me; it really helped the development of my practices."[29] In 1953 at the age of 115, she died. Namkhai Norbu had recorded her life history about two years before she died. Without this almost accidental preservation of her biography, we would probably have no idea that such a woman had lived so recently. She may not have been as rare as the impression given us by the records that were preserved. She told Namkhai Norbu that her *yogini* friend had also established a hermitage and had many students before she died in 1911. But no one recorded or remembered her life.

REINCARNATING LAMAS: THE BASTION OF MALE PRIVILEGE

The tension between an underground tradition of highly accomplished female practitioners and the institutional preference for male practitioners is greatest in the Tibetan practice of finding and installing successive "reincarnations" of great teachers. The institution of "reincarnating *lamas*," unique to Tibetan Buddhism and best known to the general public in the case of the Dalai Lama, is very widespread. The great teacher, considered to be an emanation of a

---

* "*Chod*" is an esoteric practice first introduced by the Tibetan woman Machig Lapdron (see pp. 98-9). Often practiced in solitary, frightening locations, the meditation practice is designed to cut attachment to ego and conventional reality.

celestial Buddha or Bodhisattva, is successively incarnated, generation after generation, in the young child selected as his successor and trained almost from infancy for that role. No leaders in Tibetan Buddhism receive greater respect, devotion, and honor, or have greater power and influence, than these "incarnations," especially those who are heads of major lineages or important monasteries.

Unfortunately, it is taken for granted that each successive incarnation will be found in a male rather that a female baby. Parents try very hard to present their boy babies for inspection when search parties look for the new incarnation, but parents who brought forward a girl would probably be ridiculed and shamed. The boy chosen as the incarnation brings honor and wealth to his parents. Since he then receives an extremely privileged education, it is no wonder that so many of these boys do turn out to be exceptional people. It would be difficult for a girl to make up for that kind of head start, no matter how exceptional she might be in her endowments.

In Tibet, only one successively reincarnating lineage holder was expected to be female, an incarnation of the major female Buddha, Vajrayogini, a central figure in the Tibetan mythic universe. The present incarnation, thought to be the sixth in the lineage, renounced her position as a "living Buddha" and became a ranking political official in the Chinese-run government of Tibet. She married and had three children. [30]

Tibetan Buddhism also sometimes regards an adult with great spiritual attainment as an emanation of an important mythic Buddha or Bodhisattva, even though such a person is not part of a lineage of successive incarnations. These two practices are often confused with each other, resulting in the claim that female incarnations are not quite as rare as to limited to the single instance of the incarnation of Vajrayogini. The best known Tibetan woman currently teaching in the West, Jetsun Kushula, is regarded as such an emanation. In 1988, an adult American woman was declared to be an emanation of a minor figure. Such recognition is quite different from choosing a baby who will grow up to be a major lineage holder.

The practice of searching for a new incarnation after the death of an incarnate teacher is continuing in the present, outside Tibet. A few non-Tibetan children have been declared to be such incarnations, but, to date, none have been girls. Given the reverence accorded to such incarnations, nothing could demonstrate the essential Buddhist teachings about the irrelevance of gender more readily and forcefully than to have some of these important incarnations appear in female form. What this could do for the self-respect of women practitioners, both Tibetan and Western, is incalculable. No significant religious reasons contradict this possibility and some religious rationales favor it. The much beloved female Buddha Tara declared, in a myth known to many, that she will always take rebirth in female form because so many desire liberation in male form "but those who wish to serve the aims of beings in a woman's body are few indeed."[31] If a male incarnation of Avalokitesvara, the Dalai Lama, commonly takes rebirth, why not a female incarnation of Tara? In addition, as we have already seen, for centuries, exceptional women have been recognized, in hindsight, as incarnations of important female Buddhas or great *yogini*-s. If they can be seen as incarnations in hindsight, why could females not be recognized earlier, in the same way that chosen males are recognized? But it certainly would change the political, social, and religious balance of power between the sexes, which, one suspects, is why it has not been done.

Given these conditions, it is especially depressing to read that a reincarnation of the great nun Ani Lochen, briefly described above, had been found in Lhasa in 1955. "He was a fine little boy who remembered his prayers and many of his disciples and he had just been recognized by the Dalai Lama as the true incarnation."[32]

Today there is some hope among the students of the late Chogyam Trungpa, who was so extraordinary in bringing together the best insights of Buddhism and Western thought, that at least one of his expected incarnations will be female. Four years after his death, however, there is no public discussion of any reincarnations.

INDO-TIBETAN LEGENDS OF DHARMIC HEROS AND ANDROCENTRIC RECORD-KEEPING

Legends of the great practitioners of the past are central in Vajrayana Buddhism. Because Vajrayanists believe that enlightenment can be attained in a single lifetime, stories about people who have accomplished that feat are collected and frequently retold, as inspiration for the present generation of students. Given the value of role models of one's own sex, androcentric record-keeping would be even more destructive in this context than in earlier forms of Buddhism.

The doctrines introduced by Mahayana Buddhism had set the stage for a more egalitarian form of Buddhism and we can read between the lines of many Tantric Buddhist records that women responded to this opening quite forcefully. But often we lose sight of them and even more troubling, when we do see them in the biographies of their male counterparts, we often see them as servants and companions of the men. Their level of insight can be astounding but their insight is presented as if it were intended only to help the male attain enlightenment; his enlightenment is the focus of the story. Such treatment of the women in this literature leaves each new generation to wonder my own most troubling question regarding Buddhism. If, as is so often asserted, the Buddha's teachings are without reference to gender, equally relevant for all sentient beings, and if all beings have Buddha-nature (*tathagatagarbha*), then why are there so few great female teachers? To some extent, especially for Vajrayana Buddhism, the answer may be inadequate androcentric record-keeping, rather than lack of accomplished women, though undoubtedly the folk wisdom and social norms we have surveyed also took their toll.

Accomplished women teachers like Ayu Khadro and her friend do exist, but they did not have the institutional support of their male colleagues; whether they were remembered or not often depended on a chance recording of them by a male student. Since men were more frequently able to read and write, due to the more adequate educational facilities at men's monasteries, men had a monopoly in choosing whose records to preserve as inspiration for future generations of practitioners. Indo-Tibetan Vajrayana is not the only form of Buddhism in which great women were remembered only sporadically. Ch'an Buddhism, which once flourished in China, was theoretically as open to women as is Vajrayana Buddhism, but one of the very few women Ch'an teachers whom we know about is known because a male disciple acknowledged her.[33] It is not without reason that so many feminist scholars of religion see their agenda as giving voice to the "unspoken worlds"* of women's religious lives.

A survey of the most important biographical literature reveals some of the ways in which the voices and records of women are lost, thus impoverishing the generations of practitioners who follow. The trend is already quite evident in the Indian Vajrayana tradition of the Mahasiddhas, great adepts and "crazy yogins" who lived between the eighth and twelfth centuries.[34] Many of them are familiar lineage holders in important Tibetan lineages. They are often considered as a group—the eighty-four Mahasiddhas. Eighty of them are male and four are female. Most of the eighty male mahasiddas had significant and transformative encounters and relationships with females.[35] Yet these women are barely named and are lost as lineage heroines, despite their obvious insight and accomplishment.

The story of the early mahasiddha Saraha, one of the most important of the whole group, bears out this generalization very clearly. He lived with his low-caste consort; "while the master practiced his sadhana, the girl fulfilled his needs and went out begging." One day he asked for radish curry, which she made, but when she brought it to him, she found him in a deep meditation state and withdrew, so as not to disturb him. The meditation state lasted twelve years,

---

* This is the title of a book, edited by myself and Nancy Falk, on women's religious lives. When we chose this title, I did not fully realize how appropriate or profound this title was for the task we were attempting. Androcentric scholars had often assumed that women's religious experiences were non-existent. We find that they are not at all non-existent, but have been silenced by generations of androcentric record-keeping and patriarchal social norms.

but as soon as he came out of it, he immediately asked for his radish curry. She was amazed that after twelve years of deep meditation he was still in exactly the same state of mind—desiring radish curry. She told him that radishes were now out of season. He was taken aback by her comment and said he would go into stricter retreat in the mountains to perfect his meditation. She then told him,

> Physical isolation is not real solitude. The best kind of solitude is complete escape from the preconceptions and prejudices of an inflexible and narrow mind, and moreover, from all concepts and labels. If you awaken from a twelve year samadhi and are still clinging to a desire for your twelve year old radish curry, what is the point of going to the mountains.[36]

He realized that she had given him valuable meditation instruction and took her words to heart. He achieved liberation and became a great lineage holder and teacher. In the end, together with his consort, he went to the realm of the Dakinis. Clearly, the nameless consort understands the *dharma* at least as well as the famous Saraha. To focus of him and forget her is a clear example of what happens in androcentric record-keeping.

In a few cases, both members of a Tantric couple became extremely important teachers and lineage holders. Predominant is the record of Padmasambhava and Yeshe Tsogyel, who together are sometimes credited with establishing Buddhism in Tibet. Luckily we have a very extensive biography of her, the eighth-century Tibetan woman who is said to have attained Buddhahood in a single lifetime.[37] If we only had the biography of Padmasambhava, we would not understand so clearly the accomplishments and importance of Yeshe Tsogyel.

In the case of another couple, Naropa and Niguma, of eleventh-century India, we are not so fortunate. We know that both became important teachers of a cycle of practices called the Six Yogas. The six yogas of Naropa are heard of frequently; the six yogas of Niguma are heard of less frequently but they are no less important.[38] The story of how Naropa and Niguma ended their married life to renounce the world is much better known. As is the case for so many adepts, conventional marriage did not agree with Naropa who, as a male, could leave a marriage more easily than could the female Siddhas. He told Niguma that he was leaving and she could either marry someone else or become a full-time *dharma* practitioner herself. Privately she told Naropa that he couldn't just discard her as if she were a non-Buddhist, but that she would not hinder him. Naropa, with Niguma's prior co-operation, told his parents that since women are full of guile and his wife had countless faults, he could no longer live with her. When the parents asked her about the situation, she too said that she had not a single virtue. The parents agreed to a divorce and both Naropa and Niguma renounced the world. After this point, the story focuses on Naropa.[39] Similarly the highly accomplished wife of Marpa, Dagmema, who was never rejected as a wife by her husband, gets lost in his biography.[40] Both Naropa and Marpa have a position on the Refuge Tree* of Kagyu Buddhism, but their equally accomplished partners do not. Yeshe Tsogyel is the only woman on the Nyingma Refuge Tree, and, to my knowledge, the only woman on the Refuge Tree of any major school of Tibetan Buddhism.

YESHE TSOGYEL: GREAT TEACHER, ENLIGHTENED CONSORT, FEMALE ROLE MODEL

Despite androcentric record-keeping, frustration is not the only response to this literature. As with the *Therigatha*, these stories, in their own right, are extremely moving and inspiring. My own study of the biography of Yeshe Tsogyel has greatly comforted me and from it I drew several conclusions important to me about the *dharmic* conduct, content, and significance of male-female relationships. I am also inspired by her perserverence, by her compassion, by her relationships with male and female students, and by her ways of acknowledging and dealing with emotions. Though embedded in an androcentric context, her story comes through.[41] This is probably the most "usable" story in the Buddhist record, though Vajrayana terminology and conventions may make it seem somewhat ethereal and miraculous to some readers. At other times, extended descriptions of initiations and complex meditation practices may make it sound a bit like the book of Leviticus. In my rather long summary of this eminently usable story, I will try to downplay the esoteric elements and to keep the focus on how Yeshe Tsogyel worked with her world to manifest as a fully enlightened Buddha.

Yeshe Tsogyel's biography in divided into eight chapters. (1) "Yeshe Tsogyel sees that the time has come for her to teach and appear in the world"— which narrates, on the esoteric level, the story of her conception. (2) "The arrival and manifestation of Yeshe Tsogyel in the land of Tibet"—which narrates Tsogyel's exoteric human conception and birth. (3) "Yeshe Tsogyel recognizes the impermanence of all things and relies upon a teacher"—which narrates Tsogyel's failed attempts to avoid conventional marriage, her suffering within conventional marriage, and her eventual union with her guru, Padmasambhava. (4) "Yeshe Tsogyel asks her teacher for instruction in the Dharma"—which narrates Tsogyel's early training and her acquisition, by

---

* A Refuge Tree is an important visualization done in connection with the strenuous initiatory preliminary practices of Vajrayana Buddhism. The meditator visualizes herself standing before a large tree which supports all the objects of refuge, including the lineage gurus of the sect of Tibetan Buddhism in which one is meditating.

buying him out of slavery, of a principal consort, Atsara Sale. (5) "The manner in which Tsogyel did her practices"—which narrates Tsogyel's solitary three-year practice in a cave at the snowline of a Himalayan mountain, the incredible austerity and discipline of those years, and the sexual and other fantasies that were part of her experience in those years. (6) "A summary of the auspicious signs which occurred as Yeshe Tsogyel practiced and the siddhis she manifested after achieving realization." (7) "The manner in which Yeshe Tsogyel acted to benefit sentient beings"—which narrates Tsogyel's enlightened compassionate activities throughout her life. Finally, (8) "How Yeshe Tsogyel reached her goal, achieved Buddhahood and entered the expanse of all that is."[42]

The first two chapters can be considered together, as they tell the same story from two points of view, first from the point of view of enlightenment manifesting in the ordinary world and then from the point of view of ordinary creatures striving to overcome obstacles. This juxtaposition is an important, but difficult, concept in Vajrayana Buddhism. Innate primordial purity and Buddha nature have never been sullied, but ignorant creatures still need the path of practice to uncover that primordial purity. From the first point of view, Tsogyel is a multilayered being who must be understood in terms of the three *kaya*-s, the three levels on which a Buddha is encountered. Her *dharmakaya* form is Samantabhadri—primordial Buddhahood (here with the feminine grammatical ending used in Sanskrit); her *sambhogakaya* form is Vajrayogini—an important *yidam* (personal, non-theistic deity), whom we will discuss again; and in the *nirmanakaya*, the apparition body of ordinary human form, she is Yeshe Tsogyel, eighth-century Tibetan woman, great teacher, enlightened consort.[43] Because she *is* also a human woman, her story should not be seen as irrelevant because of the miracles and magic that seem impossible to us and that make her seem very different from us. Rather, in Vajrayana Buddhist practice, she would be regarded as a myth-model; any of us might emulate her story.

To continue, the story of her conception is told on two levels. On the supramundane level, the guru and *dakini** (Padmasambhava and Tsogyel in supramundane form) meet to engender the human conception of Tsogyel.

> The vajra of the *Yab* joined the lotus of the *Yum* and together they entered the state of great equanimity. . . . The Great Bliss of the *Yab-Yum* penetrated everywhere into all realms of the world, and great tremors and earthquakes shook the universe. Light rays burst forth like shooting stars from the union of the *Yab* and *Yum*. The red letter A came into view, and from it spiralled a

---

* The term "*dakini*" (literally "sky-goer") is used with a wide variety of meanings. See Willis, "Dakini: Some Comments on its Nature and Meaning," *Feminine Ground*, pp. 57-75. Here it is used to connote a feminine principle of enlightenment.

garland of white vowels. The white letter VAM appeared and from it spiralled a chain of red consonants. The lights and letters penetrated into the world, striking the ground . . . in Tibet.[44]

Meanwhile, on the ordinary level,

> One day when the Prince, my father was twenty-five years old, while he and his queen, my mother, were enjoying the pleasures of love-making, my mother had a vision.[45]

Extraordinary visions continued throughout the night for both and nine months later the queen gave birth painlessly to a baby girl with unusual abilities. Almost immediately, it was predicted that either she would become a great religious teacher or the consort of an emperor, an obvious parallel to the life of Siddhartha Gautama.

Despite this extraordinary conception and birth, as is typical in many biographies, Tsogyel's parents had no appreciation for her great potential and were concerned only with making a proper marriage for her. That task proved very difficult, since all the local kings had been driven mad by her beauty and threatened war over her. Finally her parents sent her away with the edict that whoever caught her first could have her and no war would be waged to try to dispossess the winner of his prize. Tsogyel's desire not to enter such a marriage was not taken into account by anyone. When captured, she resisted to the extent that her feet sank into a boulder as if it were mud and only after being whipped "until my back was a bloody pulp,"[46] did she submit. However, she kept her resolution to obtain enlightenment in a single life and escaped after her captors passed out from drinking to celebrate her capture. Living in cave, subsisting on fruit, she was found out and the wars over her threatened to continue. To end the turmoil, the emperor took Tsogyel as his consort. Soon thereafter, the emperor, who was eager to learn the Buddhist teachings gave Tsogyel to the guru as part of his *mandala* offering.*

This turn of events suited Tsogyel perfectly, since she cared only to learn the teachings, and the guru to whom she had been given, Padmasambhava, was willing to teach her. However, after some training, her guru sent her away to make further progress on her own. He told her, ". . . without a consort of skillful means, there is no way that you can experience the mysteries of Tantra. . . . So go to the valley of Nepal where there is a sixteen year old youth with a mole on his right breast . . . find him and make him your ally."[47]

---

* A *mandala* is a diagram emphasizing four quadrants around a center. The diagram is a "map" of both cosmic and psychological reality. "*Mandala* offering" is a ritual done during initiatory practices (*ngundro*) in which the student, symbolically or in actuality, offers the cosmos to the guru.

She found her consort after a long, harrowing journey, but she found him in slavery and had to purchase his freedom. She obtained the necessary funds with which to purchase him by raising from the dead the son of an important Nepali family.

The next major stage of her practice was her three-year solitary retreat high in the mountains. Though the narrative of her retreat is filled with interesting episodes, I select one which tells, from a woman's point of view, a story often told against women. Well into her retreat, she had some interesting visitors.

> Charming youths handsome, with fine complexions, smelling sweetly, glowing with desire, strong and capable, young men at whom a girl need only glance to feel excited. They would begin by addressing me respectfully, but soon they would become familiar, relating obscene stories and making lewd suggestions. Sometimes they would play games with me: gradually they would expose their sexual organs, whispering, "Would you like this, sweetheart?" and "Would you like to milk me darling?" . . . all the time . . . trying all kinds of seductive foreplay. Overcome by the splendor of my *samadhi*, some of them vanished immediately; some I reduced to petty frauds by insight into all appearances as illusion.[48]

To complete her retreat, she practiced "the last austerity practiced for my own benefit. . . . The austerity of the 'seed-essence of coincident Pleasure and Emptiness' " with three consorts, including her redeemed slave. Shortly after this, she left the retreat site to return to her guru Padmasambhava, who confirmed her achievements and praised her realization.

She did several more advanced practices, at least one of which required her to find another consort. However, most of the rest of her biography focuses on her extensive work to establish and spread Buddhist teachings. She gains innumerable disciples, both male and female and brings many of them to high levels of realization. She also did much writing, hiding many of her texts so they could be discovered at a later time.* These activities were carried on both while Padmasambhava was with her in Tibet and after his departure. Her work did not depend on his presence. In fact, she stayed behind when he left "because of her superiority to work for the welfare of beings and to fill the earth with the Guru's teachings."[49]

The final, most advanced, set of practices she did to complete her training involved "the exchange of my *karma* for that of others,"† which perfected her compasssion and ability to work on behalf of others. In this practice, she took

---

* Yeshe Tsogyel is the source for many of the *terma* texts written in "*dakini* code" that are "discovered" and deciphered by a teacher skilled in such activity when the time is ripe. Such attributions are important in Tibetan Buddhism.

† As a meditation practice, such an exchange is an important aspect of Mahayana training in the three-*yana* perspective of Tibetan Buddhism.

on the sufferings of others and gave them what would relieve their sufferings. She says, "I gave my body to ravenous carnivores, I fed the hungry, I clothed the destitute and cold, I gave medicine to the sick, I gave wealth to the poverty stricken, I gave refuge to the forlorn, and I gave my sexual parts to the lustful."[50] The greatest needs which she encountered involved a man who needed body parts for a transplant operation and an extremely repulsive, diseased man who longed for human and female companionship. She met the needs of both. This kind of self-sacrifice, however, should not be seen as everyday practice or the inevitable lot of a woman. She is nearing Buddhahood by the time it is appropriate for her to take on such self-sacrifice on behalf of others.

When she can completely give herself for others, she is able to manifest emanations throughout the universe to meet people's needs. Many of the needs she satisfies at this stage are very easy to relate to: "To the childless I appeared as sons or daughters, bringing them happiness; to men desiring women, I appeared as attractive girls, bringing them happiness; to women desiring husbands, I appeared as handsome men, bringing them happiness."[51]

After twelve years of such work, Yeshe Tsogyel "composed [her]self in the *samadhi* that brings all things to extinction."[52] In a long concluding narrative, her students ask for and receive final teachings and predictions.

> With this farewell she ended, and light, shimmering, sparkling irridescently in splendid vivid colors, streamed towards the South-west and vanished from sight. All of us who had witnessed this final departure prostrated countless times after her. . . . Then our minds full of grief, our hearts heavy, our stomachs in our mouths, our tears flooding the path, staggering, unable to control our bodies, panting and heaving, we retreated to the meditation cave . . . where we spent the night.[53]

Before we leave Yeshe Tsogyel's story, I would like to comment briefly on two motifs that are woven into the above narrative at various points. Many of Tsogyel's encounters with men, as I think must be obvious, were not positive or pleasant, beginning with the episode in which she tries to escape conventional marriage only to be treated like so much property to be fought over. She uses that suffering as the initiatory ordeal required to launch her on her path of self-discovery and spiritual development. Twice in her travels throughout Tibet, she was waylaid by bands of robbers and on one occasion, late in her life, she was raped by them as well. She was able on both occasions to speak so effectively to them that they were converted to *dharma* and became her students. She did this by giving these aggressive, depraved men insights into the roots of their aggression and keys to handling that energy more effectively.

The other motif that deserves comment concerns her relationships with women, both her students and her companions on the path. She had numerous female disciples and four of her eleven root disciples were women. Two of them were also recognized as emanations of Vajravarahi, just as she was, on one level of analysis, and they too became consorts of Padmasambhava. Almost at the end of her life, just before she took leave of her followers, Yeshe Tsogyel received a visit from Padmasambhava's other main consort, the Indian Mandarava. "Emerging from the sky with her six disciples, she greeted me. She stayed with me for thirty-nine human days and we exchanged and tightened our precepts, making endless discussions on the dharma."[54] Rather than being competitors, these two women are colleagues on the bodhisattva path. Mandarava wishes to continue that relationship in her praise poem to Tsogyel.

> May I be one with you, Mistress of Powerful Magic.
> Hereafter, purity suffusing the sphere of purity
> In your field of lotus-light,
> You and I will project emanations of the Buddha's *karma*
> As light-forms of Guru Pema Skull-Garland's compassion:
> May we empty the depths of the three realms of *samsara*.[55]

OTHER EXEMPLARS

Androcentic record-keeping and remembering continues to the present day and operates in the transmission of Tibetan Buddhism to Western students, who usually learn a great deal about the male figures listed above and very little about the female figures. Tsultrim Allione, a Western women who had lived as a Tibetan nun before her marriages, therefore sought out biographies of women Siddhas and had them translated. Her book, *Women of Wisdom*, which continues the traditional genre of inspirational biography, gathers together many of the stories recounted above (though not Yeshe Tsogyel's) and includes the most complete English account of Tibet's most innovative woman teacher and practitioner, Machig Lapdron.[56] Her story is similar to Tsogyel's, though perhaps not as mythic. In one aspect of her life, she also functions as a model in a way that Tsogyel does not. Unlike Yeshe Tsogyel, she had children. She did not chose to remain with her children once they were somewhat grown. When the youngest was five, she returned to her life of full-time *dharma* practice and her husband cared for the children. Her accomplishments and fame were similar to Tsogyel's. At one point, Tara (to be discussed later in this chapter) manifested to her directly and taught her rare teachings which Machig was then commanded to carry forward. Tara also predicted that Machig's children would continue her lineage for ten generations. Her younger son was thoroughly trained by her and carried on her lineage; her daughter was recognized as a *dakini*. Thus, it does not seem that she harmed her children by pursuing her destiny as *dharma* teacher and practitioner rather than devoting herself completely to their care. Credited with the origins of Chod practice, she is the only Tibetan teacher whose teachings were said to have been taken to India, thus reversing the usual flow of teachings and practice from India to Tibet.[57] Nevertheless, she is not so well known as are many male teachers, founders, and transmitters of important practice lineages.

Jutsun Kushala, probably the best-known contemporary woman Vajrayana teacher, lives in Vancouver, B.C. Born into an elite family, she was given the same education as her brother, the Sakya Trizen, head of the Sakya order. In her early life in Tibet, she was given teaching roles. But later, in exile in India, her family planned a marriage for her. At first she refused, but later consented because her male child was needed to succeed to an important hierarchical position. At that point she stopped teaching and only began again many years later. Her brother the Sakya Trizen and the Dalai Lama asked her to teach again because they were so frequently besieged by questions about female teachers from Western students. Now she heads a *dharma* center and travels to teach on occasion, but, unlike many men with similar responsibilities, she also still works full time.[58]

A WOMAN'S LIFE: TWO VIEWS

The situation of women in the world of Vajrayana Buddhism can most accurately be summarized by quoting two passages found almost side by side in the biography of Yeshe Tsogyel. She complains of her lot as a woman:

> I am a woman—I have little power to resist danger.
> Because of my inferior birth, everyone attacks me.
> If I go as a beggar, dogs attack me.
> If I have wealth and food, bandits attack me.
> If I do a great deal, the locals attack me.
> If I do nothing, gossips attack me.
> If anything goes wrong, they all attack me.
> Whatever I do, I have no chance for happiness.
> Because I am a woman, it is hard to follow the Dharma.
> It is hard even to stay alive![59]

Yeshe Tsogyel is moved to this description of her situation as a woman even though her guru Padmasambhava has only recently praised her accomplishments very highly and uttered a generalization about women's abilities that is as rare in Buddhist literature as in religious literature altogether.

> Wonderful yogini, practitioner of the secret teachings!
> The basis for realizing enlightenment is a human body.
> Male or female—there is no great difference.
> But if she develops the mind bent on enlightenment,
> The woman's body is better.[60]

How can both statements be made almost side by side? How can both be true, as many of us who try to follow in Yeshe Tsogyel's footsteps discover?

THOU SHALT NOT DISPARAGE WOMEN:
A VAJRAYANA COMMANDMENT

These ambiguities and contradictions in the Vajrayana Buddhist tradition are especially difficult to contemplate because they are so at odds with the mainstream *dharma* teachings of this form of Buddhism. The Indian Buddhist texts most negative to women are not central to Vajrayana Buddhism, but the Mahayana texts most positive towards women and conducive to their full involvement in Buddhist practice are extremely central. Furthermore, female symbolism is of central importance to Vajrayana Buddhism and positive to an extent rare in world religions. As a result, despite all the folk wisdom negative to women that we have surveyed, negative comments about women tend to be asides, rather than central components, in most Vajrayana texts. Instead of the debates about innate female traits that were so prominent in Mahayana literature, one will find a brief passing comment, for example, in a discussion of karma in a meditation manual on the practice of the Four Foundations, the arduous Vajrayana preliminary practices, that one gets a male body as the result of accumulating great merit.[61]

For the most part, one can easily look past these asides, for they are very minor compared with much weightier obligations regarding women that are taken up by every Vajrayana practitioner. In the eleventh century Sakya Pandita summarized the obligations of a Tantric practitioner, which must be upheld if the practitioner is to progress on the path, as the Fourteen Root *Samaya* obligations and their opposites, the Fourteen Root Downfalls. *Samaya* obligations are a matter of utmost and unparalleled importance in Vajrayana Buddhism, not to be taken on lightly, and forgotten only with the risk of greatest peril. *Samaya* obligations are taken on by every Vajrayana practitioner, without exception, further demonstrating their centrality. The fourteenth root downfall is worth quoting in full:

> If one disparages women who are of the nature of wisdom, that is the fourteenth root downfall. That is to say, women are the symbol of wisdom and Sunyata, showing both. It is therefore a root downfall to dispraise women in every possible way, saying that women are without spiritual merit and made of unclean things, not considering their good qualities. If one says a little against a woman, that can be purified. But if the woman disparaged is a Vajra sister, and one considers her as one's enemy, that is the third and heavier root downfall. If the woman is not actually a Vajra sister, to give up being friendly to her is the fourth root downfall.[62]

The existence of this *samaya* obligation demonstrates two things. Clearly, women were being denigrated by some Buddhists, since no one makes rules prohibiting activities in which no one is engaged. Also, the authorities who made this obligation so basic to Vajrayana Buddhism were aware that such disparagment is an impediment to the spiritual realization of both women and men. I know of no religious ruling which more decisively outlaws institutionalized or private prejudice against women in any form whatsoever. One could see this semisecret obligation of the Vajrayana practitioner as the antidote to all the anti-women stories and opinions quoted from Buddhist texts and folklore in preceding pages. Certainly this *samaya* obligation provides the strongest justification one could need or want for speaking out against the many residues of patriarchy, sexism, and androcentrism still current in Buddhism. For disparaging women is not confined merely to making unsavory comments about women. It also includes all opinions, stereotypes, and cultural habits that delimit women or confine them to conventional roles and niches in the world at large and in the Buddhist world.

That women are the nature of wisdom and show both wisdom and *shunyata* is the normative position for Vajrayana Buddhism. Women, by their very nature, symbolize central Buddhist insights about reality. Therefore, it is not surprising that feminine symbolism is extremely important to Vajrayana Buddhism, much more so than was the case for earlier forms of Buddhism. From a feminist perspective, a major question about feminine symbolism and imagery concerns whether the symbols are, indeed, useful to women and are accurate reflections of women's realities. It is certainly not unknown for a religious tradition to include feminine symbols that are highly valued by the tradition, but which are not helpful to women, and may even be destructive, because they are androcentric wishes and projections. It has become quite commonplace to point out that the mere existence of goddesses and other exalted feminine symbols does not mean that women will be well treated or appreciated. The Christian use of the Virgin Mary is an oft-cited case in point, for varieties of Christianity with high devotion to Mary are often rather derogatory in their opinions of empirical women.

In Vajrayana tradition, however, these symbols exist in a religious context that condemned the denigration of women. Furthermore, there is a strong connection between the feminine symbolism and the *samaya* of not disparaging women. The reasons given for not disparaging women are quite specific. One should not denigrate women *because they are of the nature of wisdom and show both wisdom and* shunyata. In other words, women manifest directly in their being the goals and ideals of Buddhism, so to disparage women would be, in fact, to disparage Buddhism. This, I believe is what makes Vajrayana feminine symbols quite different from some other exalted feminine religious symbols. Women are not able to be of the nature of the Virgin Mary in Christianity and do not show her nature to Christians. In fact, it has been said of Mary that "Alone of all her sex, she pleased the Lord."[63] Such a relationship between women and feminine symbols is completely the opposite of that found in Vajrayana Buddhism, which may explain why the Tibetan women who can make it through the obscurations of misogynist folk wisdom and patriarchal social structures to high spiritual achievements are so unambiguously appreciated. What has not happened to date in the Vajrayana Buddhist world is to take to heart the feminist insight that patriarchal social forms, including ones enshrined in long-standing Buddhist practices, are at least as devastating to and disparaging of women as the most misogynist text preserved in any religious canon.

THE FEMININE PRINCIPLE IN INDO-TIBETAN VAJRAYANA BUDDHISM: PRELIMINARY REFLECTIONS

The Vajrayana command not to denigrate women and its highly positive feminine symbols are firmly grounded in central Mahayana teachings. The tradition of a positive personified feminine principle begins early in the Mahayana, with the veneration of Prajnaparamita as the Mother of all Buddhas. In the Vajrayana, understanding of the feminine principle is deepened and extended and the feminine principle is balanced by a masculine principle. Though major doctrinal analysis of these principles will be found in the next section of this book, some preliminary description and discussion of this image is important in this context.

Vajrayana Buddhism advocates that the most adequate language about "things as they are" is non-dualistic,[64] rather than monistic or dualistic. That is to say, disparate phenomena neither collapse into unity in which their specific qualities are subsumed, so that their specificity and individuality are lost, nor do they stand independent and solidly existing in their separateness. Non-duality, sometimes spoken of as "two-in-one" symbolism, or as the coincidence of opposites, is of critical importance for understanding the Vajrayana view of the proper relationship and interactions between both women and men and between the masculine and feminine principles. Masculine and feminine form a dyadic unity, anthropomorphically symbolized by the *yab-yam* icon of a couple in sexual embrace, so familiar to those with even a passing knowledge of Tantric Buddhism. Many other symbolic pairs are also found—bell and *vajra*,* left and right, sun and moon, vowels and consonants, red and white, to name only a few.

---

* Important ritual implements used in Tantric meditation rituals, they are held in left and right hands and symbolize feminine and masculine, wisdom and method, emptiness and compassion.

They are not two separate entities nor are they one entity; they are a dyadic unity, in which each mutually interpenetrates the other, is inseparable from it, and is co-necessary with it.

In this dyadic unity, the feminine principle symbolizes all-encompassing space, in which phenomena arise and in which they play. Space is emptiness, with all the connotations that term has in Mahayana Buddhism, and space is also wisdom. Thus, if there is a primordial element—but one should be very reluctant to assign priority to either element of the pair—it is space, which is "feminine." Therefore, in many Vajrayana *sadhana*-s, one finds an emphasis on the female sexual organs as awesome and sacred. The primordial source of all phenomena is the "source of dharmas,"[65] a downward pointing pyramid which, when Tantric symbols are homologized with the human body, is located at the position of the womb. (Male practitioners also place the source of *dharma*-s at this place in their bodies when they do *sadhana*-s that call for such a visualization.) That which space accommodates is the masculine principle—form, activity, compassion. They are symbolized as the male deity in the *yab-yum* pair and in many other ways. Nevertheless, though distinctive, the masculine and feminine principles, space and form, are inseparable, for "form is emptiness but emptiness is also form."*

Another major intuition in the Vajrayana approach to spiritual realization is equally important in explaining this Vajrayana commandment not to denigrate women. Vajrayana Buddhism proclaims, and practices in accord with the proclamation, that the phenomena which arise in space are primordially pure. They are not to be dualistically rejected but to be non-dualistically appreciated and liberated. One's world and one's experiences are not to be denigrated, for they are the ciphers of enlightenment and the conduits to it. In a male-centered world, women are easily denigrated; therefore, this androcentric temptation is specifically undercut. The command not to denigrate women is consonant with the spiritual impetus to appreciate rather than to reject one's world and cuts out the heart of a tendency to regard world as enemy to be overcome.

As part of this approach to spirituality which emphasizes appreciating, rather the rejecting the world, Vajrayana Buddhism regards the body, sexuality, and emotions as key components of the spiritual quest, a revalorization for which it is justly famous. Positive feminine symbolism, not out of touch with women's realities, is essential in all three cases.

---

* This phrase from the "Heart Sutra" sums up the entirety of Mahayana and Vajrayana Buddhism. See Trungpa, *Cutting through Spiritual Materialism* (Berkeley: Shambhala, 1973), pp. 187–199, for an illuminating commentary. See also Donald S. Lopez, Jr., *The Heart Sutra Explained: Indian and Tibetan Commentaries* (Albany: State University of New York, 1988).

Tantric commentaries on the body are so voluminous as to defy description. But nothing could be more telling than the first reminder contemplated at length by all Vajrayana students: "precious human body, free and well-favored, difficult to obtain, easy to lose . . ."[66] A woman meditator praises her precious human birth in the same way as does a man. Furthermore, the female organs are sometimes praised and venerated, as already demonstrated by the discussion of the uterine source of *dharma*-s. Sexuality is impossible to avoid in the Vajrayana universe; as phenomenal experience it is appreciated and validated, and as symbol, it is routinely visualized in many *sadhana*-s. By definition, sexual symbolism presupposes feminine symbolism. Finally, appreciation of emotions as the raw material of enlightenment is commonplace in Vajrayana Buddhism. The way in which the five neurotic emotions become the five enlightened wisdoms is a favored contemplative theme. In that contemplation, the emotions are not repressed but freed of their negative dimensions.[67]

In more conventional spiritual practices, which are suspicious of the body, sexuality and the emotions, or consider them to be antispiritual, women are often identified with all three and blamed for arousing them. However, if the body, sexuality and the emotions are seen as integral to the spiritual path, insofar as women are associated with them, then women should not to be denigrated, but venerated. By itself, this would still be a highly androcentric view, but the concomitant Vajrayana emphasis on non-duality discourages projection of emotion onto the other and encourages claiming one's emotions as one's own, a point consistently stressed in Vajrayana meditation training.

Some feminists have voiced suspicions that a genuine dyadic unity is impossible. Put more abstractly, they would have to claim that genuine non-dualism is impossible, that the only options are duality or monism. Whenever two elements are central in a symbolic universe, they would contend, there *will be* hierarchical ranking between the two. In their favor, many systems do retain a subtle dualism, even when they proclaim that both elements of a dyad are critical and necessary. The ambiguity attached to the *yin* element in some Chinese cosmological thinking is a good case in point.* Is there a similar possibility that activity and compassion, the male elements in this dyad, are similarly given a subtly higher value? They are not, which becomes clear in the oral instructions given to the student for internalizing and utilizing the symbols for feminine and masculine principles in Tantric meditation rituals. The inter-

* *Yin*, which is feminine, should be equal opposite of *yang*, the masculine element in Chinese cosmological thinking. In many cases, the two are seen as equally necessary in the scheme of things, though opposites of each other. But, in some contexts, *yin* is associated with evil, which is avoided, while *yang* is associated with good, which one attempts to increase and attract.

play of right and left hands, and of the *vajra* and bell, which stand for masculine and feminine, stress equality, co-necessity, and mutual interpenetration.

A more serious question would concern whether the emphasis on masculine and feminine principles reinforces, rather than undermines gender stereotypes. Are women to be accommodating and space-like, rather than active? Are men to be busy saving the world, but not too spacious and quiet? That humans should emulate and strive to develop only the principle that matches their physiological sex is never taught in Vajrayana Buddhism. Rather, the practitioner always strives to develop both wisdom and compassion, both spacious accommodation and effective activity. Women and men equally are given *sadhana*-s in which they visualize themselves as male or as female *yidam*-s, or as both together. Men and women students may begin their journey conforming to gender stereotypes, but that conformity should decrease, not increase, with practice, which, in my experience and observations, usually happens.

RITUAL SEX: HUMAN AND "DIVINE"

More substantive and troubling questions occur in connection with the ritual sexuality for which Vajrayana Buddhism is so famous or infamous. One frequently reads that practitioners had consorts as part of their religious practice. Furthermore, the *yidam*-s are routinely visualized and portrayed in sexual embrace. On both the human and the "divine" plane, the mere existence of sexual partnership does not guarantee that the female partner is regarded as equally significant with the male. It is possible that ritual sexuality involves a one-sided focus on him and *his* consort, rather than genuine partnership. To put the question most bluntly: is the woman a partner, or a ritual implement, needed by the male to complete himself and do his *sadhana* properly? This question must be asked first of the human partners and then of the divine *yidam* partners portrayed on *thangkha*-s and visualized in *sadhana* practice.

In his massive history, *Indo-Tibetan Buddhism*, David Snellgrove devotes considerable attention to the practices of sexual yoga among Indian and Tibetan Tantric Buddhists. In his view, there is no question that the literal practice of sexual yoga was quite common at one time and that "sexual gratification [is regarded as] a means to enlightenment."[68]

But what of the female partner? Most of the texts and *sadhana*-s *are* written from the male point of view and *do* treat the woman more as is she were an instrument than a partner. Snellgrove translates one text in which the student, "having obtained a fair-eyed Symbol, possessed of youth and beauty, . . . adorns her with fine clothes, with garlands and sandalwood scent and makes a presentation of her" to the teacher. He then worships her and his teacher and the initiation proceeds. The "blissful teacher" unites with the Symbol, and conse-crates his pupil "who (in turn) is united with the Symbol."[69] Is she also being initiated, or is she one of the required ritual implements? How does he obtain his Symbol? What happens to her when she no longer is "possessed of youth and beauty?"

In one of the texts translated by Snellgrove, the male is told to instruct the woman as part of preparing for his initiation. First he practices by himself for one month. Then he "takes this girl with her wide-open arms, endowed with youth and beauty" and instructs her in basic *dharma* and meditation techniques. "Within one month she will be fit, of that there is no doubt. So there is this girl freed of all false ideas and received as though she were a boon."[70] Snellgrove's own conclusion about the issue is quite negative.

Thus despite the eulogies of women in these tantras and her high symbolic status, the whole theory and practice is given for the benefit of males. While the relative neglect of women's interests in pursuing a higher religious life is typical of Buddhism of all periods, simply because her ability to do so is doubted so long as she is encumbered with a female body, this form of tantric Buddhism appears to offer her some hope at last, but in the actual event seems to fail to do so.[71]

While it is difficult to argue with so great an authority, particularly because he is surely correct in many cases, I feel that some evidence indicates otherwise. Women were not always treated as mere ritual instruments rather than full-scale partners. The biographical literature gives a somewhat different picture than the ritual texts, particularly the few biographies of the women, like Yeshe Tsogyel, who also practiced sexual yoga. In the stories of the Mahasiddhas, though the telling of the story is quite androcentric, their consorts are not portrayed as mere instruments at all, but as partners. As already discussed in the story of Saraha, as well as in many other stories in the collection about the eighty-four Siddhas, both partners are accomplished practitioners who go to the realm of the *dakini*-s together. Marpa's song of farewell to India, in which he sings of all the things he will miss, speaks with genuine affection of his ritual consorts.[72] From the women's point of view, some accounts certainly give the impression that proficient and knowledgeable female practitioners of tantra met, of their own accord, with the male practitioners in the sacred places to practice the rituals. The *yogi*-s and *yogini*-s apparently used signs to identify each other as belong-ing to the same sect and lineage "so that they may arouse in them a condition of mutual responsiveness."[73] The impression that women were often regarded as ritual implements rather than as partners may have more to do with an-drocentric patterns of record-keeping and of writing than with the actual practice and experience of those who wrote the ritual texts.

For contemporary Vajrayana Buddhism, much of this discussion is moot, since the usual current interpretation of sexual yoga is as an internal and symbolic process, rather than as a ritual which is performed literally and externally. Sexuality is appreciated as an important aspect of life for non-celibate practitioners, but Tantric feasts, which may involve literally drinking liquor and eating meat, do not involve literal sexual intercourse.

A much more problematic question regarding ritual sex arises in connection with the typical portrayal of the male and female *yidam*-s in sexual embrace. The image is familiar to non-Vajrayanists from *thangkha* paintings and three-dimensional icons, produced, not as art work, but as the support for visualizations that are practical aids for the mental transformations sought in Vajrayana practice. As a symbolic representation of both non-duality and the enlightened state of mind, this sexual image becomes deeply familiar to the student of Vajrayana Buddhism. Therefore, the usual form of this image presents real problems, for the male deity often seems to predominate. The couple is shown with her back and his front facing the viewer. Her face is visible because her head is flung back, while his face looks at the viewer straight on. In some cases, if the two are of similar color, one can barely disentangle her form from the mass of arms, legs, heads and ritual implements. It would be easy to draw the conclusion that she is one of ritual implements being held by the male *yidam*—his anima, necessary for his completion, but not very significant in her own right. In my experience, however, such an impression is always contradicted by the oral instructions one is given if one asks whether she should be regarded as an aspect or extension of him.

Some of these visual difficulties, I believe, do result from subtle androcentrism in the tradition. Others are more due to technical problems, especially in the two-dimensional medium. If he is taller, featuring his back and her front would mean she would be entirely blocked out. If they were portrayed from the side, they would be more equal, but neither face would visible unless they turned their heads toward the viewer—hardly a convincing pose for sexual passion. Nevertheless, I believe this is a problem that must be addressed as Vajrayana Buddhism becomes more sensitive to subtle androcentrism and realizes that it is denigrating to women. For example, the artist can more carefully distinguish her form from his by clear color differentiation and boundaries between the two forms. Some more recent *thangkha*-s are much more careful in this regard than were many older ones.

These visual difficulties are also mitigated by the fact that so many other symbolisms do stress the coeval nature of feminine and masculine principles and these other symbols are being used in ritual *sadhana* at the same time that the *yidam* couple is being visualized. The outsider, looking only at the sexual pose on the *thangkha*, does not have full information. Anyone initiated into the practice of the *yidam* couple is also quite familiar with each of them individually. She is not merely the consort of the male *yidam*, but a centrally important *yidam* in her own right. When portrayed by herself, she loosely holds a staff in the crook of her arm. This staff, mounted with three human heads in various stages of decomposition, from freshly severed to dry skull, is replete with symbolism. One meaning is that the staff represents her consort in a hidden way. Already some feminist women practitioners have found fresh and relevant meanings to this symbolism of the female and her secret consort. "She holds it and yet she does not grasp it. She recognizes it as something she must have near her to use, and yet she recognizes it as something which is separate."[74]

DAKA-S AND *DAKINI*-S IN RITUAL AND LITERATURE

The male-female relationship in Vajrayana Buddhism has other dimensions than ritual sexuality, whether human or "divine." The feminine principle as *dakini* is quite important, both in biographical literature and in Vajrayana ritual meditations. The term "*dakini*" is rather complex[75] and has a variety of meanings.

In the biographical literature, *dakini*-s are enlightened or highly insightful females who often act as messengers, reminders, and revealers to the student of Vajrayana. They can be human or non-human. Many women are *dakini*-s and the Mahasiddhas are constantly encountering them. The human consort of a Mahasiddha is frequently called a *dakini*. So are the mysterious, playful, and elusive females who somehow appear to give the Mahasiddha a reminder or a challenge at some critical point. The great Mahasiddha Naropa was propelled onto his Tantric path by the taunts of a mysterious, ugly old woman who was a *dakini*.[76] *Dakini*-s hold the teachings in their non-earthly realm. An unusually persistent and important Mahasiddha, such as Tilopa, is said to have gotten the teachings by "storming the palace of the *dakini*-s." And when a mahasiddha dies, he is frequently said to go to the realm of the *dakini*-s.

A contemporary Vajrayana student would regularly encounter *dakini*-s in meditation practice. The central *yidam* or *yidam* couple is surrounded by *dakini*-s, according to the visualization instructions in many *sadhana*-s. These surrounding *dakini*-s usually carry important symbolic meanings to the meditator. At other points in a *sadhana* liturgy, one invokes other females as well, to make offerings or run other errands. The net result is a rather heavily feminine visualized universe, in which the only male in anthropomorphic form is the central male *yidam*. If the *sadhana* liturgy focuses on a female *yidam*, there may be no males at all.

It is also important to point out that male equivalents, the *daka*-s, are known and sometimes play their roles in a *sadhana* liturgy. But they rarely figure in the biographical literature. They really are quite insignificant in the total Vajrayana universe and are much less prominent than their feminine counterparts.

What is going on? Is the importance of females being acknowledged? Or is this the ultimate male phantasy of being surrounded by a circle of females dedicated to noticing and helping one's self. And how would genuinely woman-identified practitioners relate with this whole situation? If the tradition were less androcentric and if roughly half of the Mahasiddhas had been women, would we find a similar imbalance of *daka*-s and *dakini*-s? Or would the mythology and symbolism of *daka*-s be more developed?

These are all serious questions that must be dealt with in an eventual androgynous reconstruction of Buddhism. First, the central importance of *dakini*-s clearly does stem from an appreciation of women and their imagination, insight, and provocativeness. It is a refreshing reversal from earlier Buddhist fears about contact with females. It also seems clear to me that when women have more creative input into writing Buddhist literature, the *daka* figure will be considerably fleshed out, a possibility already suggested by Tsultrim Allione.[77] Much still needs to be articulated about the feminine principle and the various Vajrayana representations of the female-male relationship from the female point of view.

However, the need for more exploration of *daka*-s from the point of view of the woman-identified practitioner does not mean that *dakini*-s are irrelevant to women practitioners. The image of a strong, creative, intelligent female, as the *dakini*-s are usually portrayed, is healing and helpful to women, especially in a patriarchal or androcentric context. One of Yeshe Tsogyel's contacts with a *dakini* demonstrates this well. Practicing severe asceticism during her solitary three-year retreat at the snowline, Tsogyel is near death. She prayed to her guru, cried from the depths of her heart to the *yidam* and visualized an unbroken stream of offerings to the *dakini*. "Then I had a vision of a red woman, naked, lacking even the covering of bone ornaments, who thrust her *bhaga* against my mouth, and I drank deeply from her copious flow of blood. My entire being was filled with health and well-being. I felt as strong as a snow-lion, and I realized profound absorption to be inexpressible truth."[78]

TARA AND VAJRAYOGINI: TWO FEMALE *YIDAM*-S

The images of women and the feminine principle found in the Vajrayana are best communicated by the female *yidam*-s, the meditation deities with whom one identifies in Vajrayana meditation practice. This discussion of the roles and images of women in Indian and Tibetan Vajrayana Buddhism ends by considering two of the most significant female *yidam*-s—the gentle and attractive

Tara, known to every practitioner of Tibetan Buddhism, and the much more esoteric, fierce, and compelling Vajrayogini or Vajravarahi.

Tara, the Saviouress, is certainly one of the two most popular meditational deities of Tibet. According to Beyer,[79] one seldom finds a Tibetan shrine that lacks her icon, though it may be surrounded by many other more esoteric *yidam*-s. She is widely prayed to and contemplated by practitioners of every level and lifestyle and her *mantra* is one of the best-known and most widely used. Initiation to practice her *sadhana* is widely available and its practice is encouraged for virtually anyone.

Her well-known story is told on two levels. Though she is said now to be both an advanced Bodhisattva and a fully enlightened Buddha, like all such beings, she was once an ordinary human who aroused the "thought of enlightenment" (*bodhicitta*) and practiced the various disciplines for many eons. Her story is quite relevant to many themes that were prominent in the discussion of Mahayana attitudes toward women. Taranatha, an important Tibetan teacher, wrote the text that has become a standard "history" of Tara in 1608. He relates that eons ago, a princess named Moon of Wisdom made extensive offerings to the Buddha of that eon and to his entourage for a very long time. Finally, for the first time, *bodhicitta* arose in her. Then the monks present suggested, "If you pray that your deeds accord with the teachings, then indeed on that account, you will change your form to that of a man, as is befitting." After a long discussion, she told them, "In this life, there is no such distinction as 'male' and 'female'. . . and therefore attachment to ideas of 'male' and 'female' is quite worthless. Weak-minded worldlings are always deluded by this." Then follows her vow: "There are many who wish to gain enlightenment in a man's form, and there are but few who wish to work for the welfare of sentient beings in a female form. Therefore, may I, in a female body, work for the welfare of beings right until Samsara has been emptied."[80] It is also said that she originated from the tears of Avalokitesvara, the male Bodhisattva of compassion who appears as the female Kuan-yin in East Asia. It is said that Avalokitesvara wept when he saw that no matter how many beings he saved, countless more still remained in *samsara*. A blue lotus (also held by Tara) grew in the water of his tears and Tara was born on that lotus.[81]

Her appearance and activities, frequently described in Sanskrit and Tibetan poetry, are well known and widely contemplated.[82] The best-known set of descriptions is the "Praise in Twenty-One Homages," which gave rise to several traditions of *thangkha* paintings in which a central figure of Tara in her most familiar form is surrounded by twenty-one smaller figures of Tara representing all the activities she undertakes. This set of praises is found in *sadhana*-s composed for meditation on Tara as one's *yidam* and has been widely commented upon.[83]

Rather than trying to summarize these praises, or even to summarize a complete description of Tara, I will quote two verses from one of the many devotional poems composed in her honor. This description includes some of her most important features and explains their symbolic meaning, important to the *yidam*'s form or appearance. Though this quotation is not from a *sadhana*, the description is congruent with the form that would be used for self-visualization of one's self as Tara when meditating using her *sadhana*.

> On a lotus seat, for pure understanding of emptiness,
> Emerald-colored, one-faced, two-armed girl,
> In full bloom of youth, right leg out, left drawn in,
> Uniting Method and Wisdom—homage to You!
>
> Prominent, full breasts, treasures of undefiled bliss,
> Face with a brilliant smile like a full moon,
> Mother with calm-mannered, wide, compassionate eyes,
> Beauty of Khadira Forest—to You I bow![84]

Not explained in the text is Tara's green color. Though there are Taras in other colors as well, the Green Tara is the most popular. In Tantric symbolism, green is the color of the Action Family, of those Buddhas and Bodhisattvas who specialize in the Wisdom of All-Accomplishing Action. This color is consonant with Tara's constant activity to help and save beings. Thus, it is often explained at a Green Tara initiation that her *sadhana* is especially recommended for active people who have major projects under way.

Much of the devotional poetry written to Tara praises her for her many activities. A standard repertoire of activities attributed to her includes saving people from the eight great dangers. Though there are some variants in some lists, or sometimes more than eight dangers from which Tara rescues, a standard list of the eight includes: fire, water, prison, bandits, elephants, tigers (or lions), snakes, and evil spirits.[85] One can appreciate these as troublesome mundane dangers that would worry anyone in the environment of ancient India. Tara is very accessible; she helps people with these everyday worries and does not confine her help to so-called spiritual matters. If one wishes, one can interpret any of the eight dangers in a spiritual way, which was sometimes done by devotees singing her praises.[86]

Among the many stories of how Tara rescued her devotees, I find two narrated by Taranatha especially appealing and whimsical. She saved a devotee from bandits in the following fashion. She appeared in a dream to the master Sanghamitra, telling him to study Mahayana teachings. He set out to go to Kashmir, but on the way he was captured by bandits who said that they needed to worship Durga (a popular Hindu goddess) by offering her warm human blood. They took him to a Durga temple "like a charnel ground." He prayed to Tara, and the Durga image spontaneously split into many pieces. The bandits became frightened and ran away from him. How she saved from tigers is even more intriguing. Master Buddhadasa travelled through an empty town with many tiger dens. When he enquired, he was told that the tigers ate humans every day. "Therefore, great compassion arose in him." He walked towards the tigers, prayed to Tara and sprinkled water over which he had recited mantras. "Through this, the tigers became of peaceful mind; thereafter they did no harm to living creatures but stopped eating and passed away." Things ended well for the tigers, who were reborn in a more fortunate existence in which, presumably, they could subsist as vegetarians.[87] The gentleness of Tara, the peaceful *yidam*, could not be more graphically demonstrated.

The red semi-wrathful Vajrayogini or Vajravarahi, sow-headed, dancing on a lotus, corpse, and sun-disc, is much more esoteric. She is undoubtedly the most important female *yidam* of the *anuttarayoga tantra*-s, the highest and most esoteric class of *tantra*-s according to most classification schemes. In these *tantra*-s, she is celebrated both as the central *yidam* of her own extensive *sadhana* and as the consort of major male *yidam*-s, such as Cakrasamvara and Hevajra. Her initiation is much more difficult to receive than is Tara's and her practice much more restricted because, as a semi-wrathful *yidam*, she can arouse emotions that may overwhelm a student not ready to take on her wild, untamed, fierce energy or her "transcendental lust." Therefore, commentaries about her are more restricted to the oral tradition.

Tangkha-s and line drawings of Vajravarahi are relatively standard.[88] In the *sadhana* text itself, as is always the case, the meaning of each aspect of her form is explained, since the meditator visualizing herself as Vajrayogini is not especially trying to become a red sixteen-year-old, but to take on and manifest the qualities implicit in her form. Thus, for example, she wears a garland of fifty-one freshly severed heads, which represents wearing out the habitual patterns of grasping and fixation. She also carries a hooked knife and a skullcup filled with blood or *amrita* ("deathless" ambrosia—a liquid much used in Tantric ritual liturgies). She holds the *khatvanga* staff, already commented on, in the crook of her arm. She is naked and wearing bone ornaments. She dances on a corpse, sun, and lotus.[89] She is surrounded by four *dakini*-s almost identical to her in form, but in appropriate colors (blue, yellow, red, and green) for the sphere of the *mandala* they embody. Thus her practice involves a complete universe in which all five of the basic energies so important to Vajrayana Buddhism are roused and transmuted.

Because practicing with Vajrayogini as one's *yidam* is considered relatively advanced and dangerous, she is not usually regarded as a saviour and one does not do her practice for relative benefits, but for the ultimate *siddhi*—enlightenment. Therefore, her praises talk of her as promoting, often in terrifying fashion, the states of mind that overcome confusion and clinging. A number of these praises have been translated and ably commented upon in a very illuminating article by Chogyam Trungpa. A few of them will suffice to connote Vajrayogini's immensely compelling, highly charged, and provocative iconography. They also communicate well her activities to promote enlightenment. One praise comments on the meaning of her sow's head as well:

> Your sow's face shows nonthought, the unchanging *dharmakaya*,
> You benefit beings with wrathful mercy
> Accomplishing their welfare with horrific accoutrements,
> I prostrate to you who benefit beings in nonthought.

The efficacy of her wrathful actions is evoked in many praises.

> Naked, with loosed hair, of faultless and terrifying form
> Beyond the vice of the *klesas*, you do benefit for sentient beings.
> You lead beings from the six realms with your hook of mercy,
> I prostrate to you who accomplish Buddha activity.

A concluding praise links her with Prajnaparamita, the Mother of all Buddhas. This certainly sums up the meaning and purpose of her fierce form and activity, which summons primordial energies in the practitioner, familiarizes the practitioner with them, tames them, and harnesses their energy—very quickly and effectively, it is hoped.

> Prajnaparamita, inexpressible by speech or thought
> Unborn, unceasing, with a nature like sky
> Which can only be experienced by discriminating awareness wisdom,
> Mother of the victorious ones of the three times,
> I praise you and prostrate.

Both of these anthropomorphic representations of enlightenment are central to Vajrayana Buddhism. As anthropomorphic representations that can be visualized and related to, they demonstrate more readily than does philosophy, the nature of enlightened mind, which, according to Vajrayana Buddhism, is always there waiting to be realized. If gentle Tara's smile does not push one over the brink from confusion to enlightenment, perhaps Vajrayogini's fang-filled grimace will. But clearly, in consonance with the command not to denigrate women, Vajrayana tradition claims that these wonderful female *yidam*-s demonstrate to the seeker the nature of her or his own mind in its unfettered form as readily as their male counterparts might.

The materials surveyed in this chapter take us to the limit of roles and images of women currently found in any form of Buddhism. Between the central *samaya* command not to denigrate women and the centrality of enlightened female *yidam*-s in Vajrayana Buddhism, it is difficult to imagine a religion more potentially favorable for the spiritual development and maturation of women as well as men. (Surely men too will develop into gentle and mature human beings more readily in a non-sexist and non-patriarchal environment.) Therefore, the social realities of the historically existing forms of Vajrayana Buddhism cause one more than a little sadness and depression.

7

Conclusions: Tokens and Heroines

This survey of roles and images of women throughout Buddhist history presents an accurate and usable past, beyond the quadruple androcentrism that characterizes most accounts of Buddhism. Now the time is ripe for concluding summaries, generalizations, and assessments. Some are familiar, having been demonstrated in each period of Buddhist history; others are not apparent until the whole sweep of that history is in view.

An accurate record about women's roles and images throughout Buddhist history can be summarized in three major generalizations. The most significant of these is already familiar; throughout Buddhist history, the proper images of and roles for women have always been an issue and there have always been two major attitudes about women. In any major period or form of Buddhism, we can find opinions and texts demonstrating varying levels of negativity to women, from outright misogyny to compassion for beings with such a difficult slot in the *samsaric* ocean. Strong statements and demonstrations to the effect that women have the same spiritual capacities as men, that gender is totally irrelevant to the spiritual quest, or even that, for the unusually motivated person, femaleness is an advantage, are also found. These two attitudes are diametrically opposed to one another, but, nevertheless, they are found, almost side by side, in texts and other evidence from all periods and all forms of Buddhism.

When the long history of Buddhism is considered as a whole, another generalization regarding women's roles and images is obvious. The view that one should not discriminate against women, and that gender is an irrelevant category in the spiritual life becomes stronger and more normative in later forms of Buddhism. Insofar as this generalization is accurate, it involves an interesting contrast with most major world religions, in which the position of women has either degenerated or remained stable.

As we have seen, women's roles and images were probably least consciously at issue during the beginnings of Buddhist history. The nuns' order does not seem to have a high priority for the historical Buddha, but it clearly began during his life and under his direction. As Buddhism began to split apart, opinions about women began to polarize, with some misogynist doctrines, as

115

opposed to individual outbursts of frustration and lust, being expressed. But, while some became misogynists, others argued more directly and forcefully than had ever been done previously that, "the *dharma* is neither male nor female," and that women could be highly developed spiritually. At the same time, positive feminine symbolism began to develop in Buddhism. Finally, in Vajrayana Buddhism, the normative position was stated quite clearly in that the fourteenth root downfall, or violation of Vajrayana vows, is to denigrate women. This command not to denigrate women is accompanied by a symbol system in which the highest goals and values of the tradition are portrayed in feminine anthropomorphic forms.

The third generalization points ahead to the analysis of key Buddhist concepts as well as back to the history of attitudes toward women. Probably throughout Buddhist history, including Vajrayana Buddhism, the attitude that there is some problem with female birth has been far more popular and widespread than the attitude that gender is irrelevant and women are not to be denigrated. Nevertheless, though it was probably always the minority opinion, the attitude that gender is irrelevant to the practice of *dharma* and the pursuit of enlightenment is far more normative and appropriate. As we shall see, every major teaching of Buddhism from each major period of Buddhist development is compatible only with that conclusion. As I shall argue in the next part, if one understands the central Buddhist teachings, one cannot possibly justify or condone sexism, patriarchy, or androcentrism, let alone misogyny, or even be indifferent to their existence, while being faithful to Buddhist insights.

A feminist reading of history seeks not only an accurate record, but also a usable past. In the vast Buddhist historical record, the single most usable dimension of the past is, in my view, the sheer fact that Buddhists have *always* been concerned about women's proper roles and images and that Buddhist tradition includes a long, old tradition of arguing against male prerogatives. The Buddhist traditionalist simply has no basis to argue that feminist concerns have no place in Buddhism or that the effort to safeguard and upgrade women's opportunities within Buddhism stem from "modern" or "secular" concerns and values exterior to Buddhism. Feminists who denounce certain long-standing Buddhist interpretations and practices are more normatively expressing the values of the tradition than are antifeminist "traditionalists." Were it not anachronistic to apply a contemporary term to historical epochs, one could accurately say that there has always been a "feminist" position in Buddhism, and it has been the more normative, if the less popular view.

Paradoxically, at the same time, some "negative" information is also extremely useful. It is useful to know that some Buddhists have, despite Buddhist teachings, drawn misogynist or patriarchal conclusions, that these opinions are quite popular, and that Buddhist institutions, such as monasteries and universities, have favored men over women in all periods and forms of Buddhism. These facts warn those antifeminists who, though not hostile to feminism's goals, wish to draw the conclusion that Buddhism has a clean bill of health and needs no input from feminism. These historically naive commentators believe that Buddhist teachings against gender discrimination are so clear that there couldn't possibly be a problem in Buddhism. As we have seen, such a conclusion ignores massive historical evidence as well as the practices still current in much of the Buddhist world.

Because overt sexism and misogyny are not the party line in most parts of the Buddhist world today, this more covert form of antifeminism is actually very problematic, especially when combined with unconscious androcentrism. I will never forget some of the reactions to my first talk on Buddhism and feminism, which was also the first time the topic was discussed at a major international Buddhist-Christian dialogue conference. Male delegates from an Asian Buddhist country confided to Western male friends of mine that they were totally mystified as to how there could be any need for a feminist critique in Buddhism, though they are somewhat sympathetic to a feminist critique of Christianity. They argued that Buddhism had already had dealt with any problems. "After all," they were quoted as having said, "since, according to Buddhism, worthy women are reborn as men, there's no discrimination against women." Not even noticing that women *are* being discriminated against is a more destructive and dangerous form of opposition to gender equality than outright opposition to egalitarian reforms. Such opposition encourages complacency and brands those who point out the obvious as "too sensitive."

In the usable past, abundant good stories of heroines and potential role models are found. In each of the three major periods of Buddhist history, we found stories, some more historical, others more mythic, of women who persisted in their efforts to practice Buddhism fully and were highly successful. The *theri*-s of early Buddhism, Yeshe Tsogyel, Machig Labdron and other women Mahasiddas, all are inspiring models. Likewise, we find stories from all three major periods of Buddhist history of women who taught eloquently against gender discrimination and demonstrated by their competence that stereotypes about women's spiritual incompetence are inaccurate. The stories of Jewel Brocade, Shrimala Devi, and the anonymous goddess of the *Vimalakirti Sutra* come especially to mind, but early Buddhist nuns and Vajrayana women Siddhas also exemplify this theme.

These stories, neglected by androcentrists, are inspiring and should be brought into the record. However, though these stories are highly useful, their utility is also limited. These women are heroines, but they are also tokens in an androcentric and patriarchal past. We need to know about and celebrate our heroines and role models, but on the other hand, it is important not to overcompensate by making more of them than is justified. They can also be used against us. In my conversations with more conservative and antifeminist Buddhists, I often encounter the statement that, since some women have been acknowledged by Buddhist tradition as enlightened beings, Buddhism is not sexist or patriarchal, and feminism is irrelevant to Buddhism. Their opinion seems to be that women themselves are to be blamed for the fact that so few women are recognized as Buddhist exemplars. Such reasoning continues: "if a few women made it, then anyone can; if a woman doesn't achieve success, or even aspire to it, that's due to her own inadequacies, not to any institutionalized sexist practices." Thus, the outstanding, exceptional women in a male-dominated system are used to discourage and denigrate, rather than to encourage, the vast numbers of women who are not truly extraordinary, but who are as competent as the many average males who are fostered and encouraged in their intellectual and spiritual quests. The only women who will succeed must be well beyond the norm for even outstanding males. Though such exceptional women are heroines, they are also tokens—and tokens do not even begin to address the issues brought up in a feminist critique of a situation that produces only token heroines from among the voluminous ranks of its female members.

Buddhist women find themselves in a strange and complex situation vis-à-vis their tradition if they are such "unusual" or "atypical" women. Those women who do not conform to the feminine stereotype, but are "more spiritual," may face an initial ignoring of their potential, and even hostility, demonstrated in the many stories of female siddhas being railroaded into conventional marriages. But once they establish themselves as "exceptions," they are encouraged and honored, though they are still regarded as exceptions whose existence has no implications regarding the accuracy of conventional stereotypes about women.

This impression is formed not only from stories of female Siddhas but also by a vivid personal experience that has always stood out in my memory as a good description of the ambiguities of being a token "exceptional female" in a patriarchal system. During my first trip to India, the guru with whose household I was living took me to his personal astrologer to have my horoscope done. The astrologer gave a reading that emphasized intellectual creativity, but his main focus was on supposed significant spiritual capacities, which he saw as reflecting many lifetimes of serious spiritual practice.

A few days later, my horoscope was done by an old, learned Brahmin Sanskritist, almost for the fun of it. He gave an identical reading to the professional, but mentioned nothing about spirituality. After he asked me a number of times whether I had any more questions, I shyly asked him about spiritual potential. He looked at his chart again, became very excited and ran to the guru, saying to him, "Look, look—she has incredible spiritual potential!" Then he turned almost full circle to me and said very sincerely, "I didn't check your horoscope for that. In India, we don't expect girls to be spiritual." He was excited and glad that I was an exception and he did everything he could after that to foster my alleged spiritual inclinations. But to him I was always a fortunate anomaly.

How many women never ask? How many baby girl *tulku*-s or incarnate teachers are overlooked because, in the Tibetan system, girls are never checked? How many women are so brainwashed by gender stereotypes in their socialization that they cannot imagine themselves to have spiritual inclinations? To allow exceptions who somehow make it through a patriarchal system to do their exceptional thing does nothing to address the fundamental misjudgments and faulty preconceptions of the whole system.

For this reason, I am ambivalent about the usability of the token heroines of the Buddhist tradition. All patriarchal traditions have a few of them. Women are so incredibly competent as members of the human species that no system is able successfully to keep all of them in their conventional slots. The part of Buddhist tradition that is much more precious and rare is its consistent, though never completely successful, critique of androcentric assumptions and institutions. This thread, running through the entirety of Buddhist history, should be focused on over and over against all attempts to summarize Buddhism as a tradition that is consistently negative toward women, or as a tradition that would be forced into new, foreign, "un-Buddhist" territory, if it took feminism seriously.

When all is said and done, it is impossible to avoid the overarching generalization and conclusion that Buddhism, as it has manifested itself thus far in history, is thoroughly and completely androcentric, though it is not especially misogynist. In every case, with the possible exception of Vajrayana discussions of masculine and feminine principles, *when the issue of women is discussed, it is always from the male point of view. And men are always perceived as the norm for humanity, while women are debated about, analyzed, classified, and evaluated.* Such a way of perceiving and conceptualizing is very far removed from an androgynous perception and conceptualization of the problem. *The problematic is not women at all. The problematic is human sexual differentiation.* Until maleness and femaleness are equally considered variant modes of the human, Buddhist thought will continue to be riddled through with androcentrism. This is the most serious issue facing the feminist historian of Buddhism, for though this generalization is accurate, there is nothing useful, for a feminist, in androcentrism.

When all these generalizations are kept in mind, the feminist historian of Buddhism seeking an accurate and usable past reaches a complex and ambiguous conclusion. Clearly, Buddhism has a usable past, but, as model for the future, it is neither sufficient nor adequate. At one and the same time, it is important to know and utilize the past, while not being bound by it. Buddhists sometimes call this kind of balancing act the "Middle Way," or "riding the razor's edge."

Before moving on to feminist analysis of key Buddhist concepts and post-patriarchal reconstruction of Buddhism, it may be interesting to comment, from both a feminist and a Buddhist point of view, on these conclusions and challenges.

There is a strong consonance between these conclusions and an important feminist point of view. Feminists frequently discuss the pain and the challenge of living in a world without adequate models, which is the case with the Buddhist past. Therefore, Buddhism cannot be dismissed or criticized too severely for not providing what no other culture or religion has provided in recent history—a setting in which women flourish as human beings.

Some feminists might counter at this point that we do have an adequate model in the past—the supposed pre-patriarchal goddess-worshipping religions of pre-classical, pre-Biblical, and pre-Buddhist times. I would reply that such situations do provide us with examples of religions and cultures in which women were not denigrated, as they have been in patriarchal cultures and in the religions, both Biblical and Indian, that flourish in patriarchal cultures. But they do not provide us with models that we could adopt completely as an adequate blueprint for today. Gender roles in these societies were too rigid to serve as a current model, even though the gender stereotypes were not negative to women. More importantly, the central focus was to link femaleness with maternity and to emphasize women's reproductive roles and capacities, an option that is counterproductive to women's needs today. Thus, though these pre-patriarchal goddess-worshipping societies provide some important clues, they do not serve as an adequate model. As feminists, we are left without adequate models from the past. Our task is more challenging—to conjure them up out of experience, reflection, and knowledge.

The conclusions drawn from our study of Buddhist history are quite challenging to Buddhism. How would Buddhists respond? Some, of course, will ignore and deny the issues. That response is, unfortunately, present in all religions that emerged and developed under patriarchal conditions. But, for less defensive and more reflective Buddhists, the challenge should not be so overwhelming. Buddhism does, after all, teach that all-pervasive impermanence is the nature of things. To regard patriarchy as an impermanent set of social conditions, destined to give way to other conditions eventually, is both a welcome view to feminists and more in accord with fundamental Buddhist teachings than to regard male dominance and male privilege as unalterable and unchanging constants. If everything is subject to impermanence, there seems to be no reason to exempt male dominance and male privilege or to try to preserve them.

Furthermore, for a Buddhist, history does not have the same normative quality that it does for Biblically based religions. The fact that certain social conditions have been relatively constant throughout Buddhist history does not sanction them as unchanging *dharma*. Historical precedent and all historical events are simply part of the ceaseless rise and fall of phenomena, not ultimately meaningful or relevant patterns. Therefore, there is no reason to try to fight change or to cling to traditional ways of doing things. Much more normative for a Buddhist than historical precedent is the *dharma*, the truths pointed to by the central teachings of Buddhism, but not encapsulated by them. If the *dharma* indicates that certain practices should be dropped, then all historical precedents to the contrary become irrelevant. If it is in accord with the *dharma* that patriarchal institutions and practices give way to egalitarian ones, then 2,500 years of Buddhist patriarchy have no countervailing merit. In Buddhist perspective, truth is not found in the realm of historical precedent or the way things have always been done, though some Buddhists reluctant to treat women humanely would argue to the contrary.

The implications of these Buddhist emphases on impermanence and the non-normative quality of historical precedent can best be summed up in a story which has now become apocryphal. One of the Western women who became a Buddhist nun in the Tibetan tradition was once discussing the poor conditions of nuns throughout much of Tibetan history with one of the highest of the male hierarchs. He was encouraging her to go through with receiving the precedent-setting full ordination in a Chinese nuns' ordination lineage, rather than to remain content with the novice ordination available through Tibetan lineages. Of the whole long process that resulted in the loss of the nuns' ordination in many forms of Buddhism and of the often sorry state of nuns throughout the Buddhist past, he said, "That's history. Now it's up to you."

Like the sword of *prajna*, this statement cuts two ways at once. It cuts those who oppose changes in Buddhist practices regarding gender because they go against precedent. Equally, it cuts those who feel burdened by and trapped within the limitations of the Buddhist past, who do not have the vision or the courage to challenge and to change the patterns bequeathed from the past.

III

"THE *DHARMA* IS NEITHER MALE NOR FEMALE":

A Feminist Analysis of Key Buddhist Concepts

8

Resources for a Buddhist Feminism

Building upon the foundation an accurate and usable past, one is in a good position to move forward to feminist analysis of key Buddhist concepts and to feminist reconstruction of Buddhism. When making claims about the feminist implications of certain key Buddhist concepts and when suggesting reconstructions of Buddhist institutions and concepts, historical depth strengthens one's insights and arguments. Without such historical knowledge, which commentators on issues pertaining to women and Buddhism often lack, the discussion is one-dimensional, limited to the Buddhist experience of a fairly small, and perhaps atypical, group of contemporary Buddhists. However, feminist discussions of religious traditions are more concerned with the present and the future than with the past. Information about the past of the tradition is used to foster feminist analysis and reconstruction of the tradition, rather than being an end in itself.

In Buddhist feminist discussion, the transition from history into analysis and reconstruction involves moving into almost completely uncharted territory, which is both extremely painful and quite exhilarating. Though there has been little, if any, previous *feminist* historical scholarship on Buddhism, at least there have been discussions of the history of women in Buddhism. But, except for the discussions contained in Buddhist texts themselves, many of which were surveyed in preceding chapters, little attention has been paid to the implications of Buddhist doctrines for gender issues. Even fewer suggestions for reconstruction of the Buddhist world in accord with feminist values are found in existing literature.

THE RESOURCE OF WESTERN FEMINIST THOUGHT

One of the great resources for this venture into Buddhist feminist analysis and reconstruction is, of course, the immense body of feminist thought that has so radically altered scholarship and understanding in the past twenty years. No academic certitude or conventional truth has been left untouched by this revolution of consciousness, discussed in some detail in the methodological appendix on feminism both as an academic method and as a social vision. Much of a feminist analysis and reconstruction of Buddhism will involve making connections between these two vast and profound modes of understanding experience—Buddhism and feminism.

Therefore, this venture will bear some resemblance to a similar venture—Christian feminist thought, which makes connections between the Christian and the feminist understandings. Christian feminist thought is far more developed and has far more proponents than its Buddhist counterpart. Nevertheless, most of the questions faced by a Buddhist or a Christian feminist are similar, as are most of the strategies employed by each. Therefore, it should not be surprising that those who are familiar with both Christian feminist thought and with Buddhism will notice similarities between much Christian feminist thought and much of what will follow. Such similarities should not be mistaken for imitation.

At the beginning of the Christian feminist movement, two decades ago, the essential first question was posed. Is it possible to work within this tradition, to find a non-sexist core that is compatible with feminist vision? Or is it impossible for anyone who regards women as genuine and valuable human beings who deserve dignity and self-determination to work within this tradition? Religious feminist thought coming out of the Christian context roughly divides into two camps in answering these questions.

One the one hand, we find a large body of Christian and a smaller number of Jewish feminist theologians who fully are committed to "reconstructing traditions."[1] These thinkers argue that the core symbols of the tradition are not inherently sexist, misogynist, or patriarchal, but are fundamentally egalitarian and liberating for all human beings. However, long-standing cultural practices and biases in favor of men and against women have seriously tainted this pristine core. Such theologians go on to argue that, if the tradition contains a pristine, but tainted, core of egalitarian teachings, that situation not only allows but requires reconstruction of the tradition.

On the other hand, we find a smaller number of "post-Christian" or "post-Jewish" feminists, who argue that such reconstruction is impossible and that the only viable alternative is withdrawal from the traditions altogether, a fresh start (sometimes with alleged pre-Christian symbols and rituals), and the "creation of new traditions."[2]

Within this camp, we find two arguments as to why reconstruction is impossible. Some argue that the symbols of the religious system are so hopelessly patriarchal that if the patriarchy is cut away from the symbols of the religious tradition, nothing will be left. Therefore, there is nothing to reconstruct. It is easy to see how one could make such a case for a religious symbol system of male monotheism, though counterarguments can also be made.*

---

* Beginning with *Beyond God the Father*, Mary Daly has become the foremost proponent of the point of view that male monotheism is unreconstructable. Rosemary Ruether's many books focus on reconstructing the symbols of monotheism.

Others argue that, though reconstruction of the symbol system is not necessarily impossible, the hierarchical powers that control the religion are so unsympathetic to women's concerns that they will never allow the necessary reconstructions to be made. With such a situation, heartbreak and burnout are the only possible results of trying to work within the system. In order to survive, one must found or find an alternative community. Some of these communities, such as the "Womanchurch" movement,[3] do not see themselves as totally separated from their community of origin and draw upon its traditions, though in most cases, their practices would be rejected as legitimate expressions of the faith by those in formal authority within that tradition. Other communities, collectively known under the heading of the "women's spirituality movement" or "feminist wicca,"[4] are definitely both "post-Christian" and "pre-Christian" in their orientation and ideology. They argue, not only for the bankruptcy of the institutional systems of authority, but also for the total unworkability of the symbol systems of Judaism and Christianity.

Buddhist feminist analysis and reconstruction will involve parallels with the above categories. Obviously, if we are at the midpoint of a feminist history, analysis, and reconstruction of Buddhism, this feminist discussion of Buddhism argues that Buddhism is reconstructible. Furthermore, Buddhism is reconstructible, it will be argued, because the fundamental teachings and symbols of Buddhism are essentially egalitarian and liberating for all, equally relevant for and applicable to all beings. The main chapters of this section of the book will make that case in a systematic and detailed fashion. After this case has been made, we then face the basic question of what kind of reconstructions must, can, or should be made, which is the question that will occupy the final part of the book. We then will face the fundamental, but presently unanswerable question, of whether those currently holding positions of authority in Buddhism have the courage and the will to incorporate such reconstructions. In that part, we shall find that reconstructions relevant to Buddhism involve certain parallels both to the "Womenchurch" and the "women's spirituality" movements.

A BUDDHIST DEFINITION OF FEMINISM

Buddhism and feminism can be brought into relationship with each other through a third definition of feminism*—a definition of feminism in Buddhist terms, which I often use when trying to present feminism to Buddhists. According to this definition, feminism involves "the radical practice of the co-humanity of women and men." I focus on each word of the definition. "Radical"

---

* The first two definitions of feminism—as academic method and as social vision—are discussed in detail in the appendix entitled "Here I Stand: Feminism as Academic Method and as Social Vision."

simply means "going to the root of things," a very Buddhist approach to major existential questions. In Buddhism, one does not rest on the surface of things, with appearances or conventional understandings. Feminism asks us to question conventional gender arrangements and stereotypes in a similarly radical way. Buddhism, strangely, has never applied its usual radicalism to the gender stereotypes and arrangements that it accepted and utilized.

Moving next to the end of the definition, note that the conventional word order has been reversed to "women and men." Serious attention to linguistic precision has always been a concern of Buddhist philosophy, even though Buddhism does not regard verbal expressions as capable of capturing ultimate truth. Feminism also is serious about words, often to the exasperation of those who cannot see the subtle link between language and consciousness and, therefore, object to the use of "she" as a generic pronoun. Not in every instance, but in this case, the conventional word order is reversed as a deliberate consciousness-raising devise.

Nevertheless, equally important, is the emphasis on the co-humanity of *men* and women. That is to say, men too can become fully integrated human beings. With this statement I am disassociating myself from versions of feminism that see men as unworkable, essentially flawed beings who cannot get over being patriarchs, sexists, and misogynists, despite the fact that those values are wrecking the planet and lead inevitably to war, oppression, and rape.*

To see feminism as a "practice" is not usual in feminist circles because the language is so very Buddhist. Buddhism is at root a "practice," a spiritual discipline; various meditation techniques are the heart of the tradition, and its method for achieving its goals of calm, insight, and liberation. "Theory," or philosophy, in Buddhism grows out of practice and gives the meditator some motivation and faith, but it is the handmaiden, not the queen, of the tradition. Feminists, more used to the Western predominance of theory over practice, are prone to talk of "feminist theory," but feminism really involves a fundamental reorientation of mind and heart that cannot bear fruit if it is merely theoretical. To be effective, feminism needs to become an ongoing practice of changing one's language, one's expectations, one's ideas of normalcy, which happens as soon as things "click," as soon as one "wakes up," using Buddhist language, to feminism's fundamental and outrageous truth of the *co-humanity* of women and men.

---

* Daly, *Gyn/Ecology: The Metaethics of Radical Feminism* (Boston: Beacon Press, 1978), pp. 252–55, contrasts male energy, which she claims is essentially necrophiliac, with female energy, claimed to be essentially biophilic. Charlene Spretnak, *The Politics of Women's Spirituality: Essays on the Rise of Spiritual Feminist Movement* (Garden City, NY: Doubleday, 1982), pp. 565–73, locates these differences in physiology rather than cultural conditioning. While I agree with Daly, Spretnak, and others who claim that masculinist culture and values are inherently unhealthy and are wrecking the planet, I do not believe that men are doomed to remain in a masculinist value system.

Central to feminism is an androgynous, two-sexed model of humanity. To bring this concept into relationship with the central Buddhist concepts of the six realms and the preciousness of birth in the human realm is to make an extremely potent connection between Buddhist and feminist understandings of humanity and to begin the demonstration that the key concepts of Buddhism and the key claims of feminism mutually entail each other.

Often in public forums, outsiders or beginners ask, "What about women and the *dharma*?" Buddhist teachers, especially those coming out of the Tibetan tradition, usually reply that there can be no real questions about women or men in the *dharma*, since the Buddha's teachings are relevant universally, not only for humans, but for all sentient beings. Classical Indian thought, Hindu as well as Buddhist, sees the universe as a vast, interdependent system of beings located in one of six realms.

Interpretable as both psychological experiences and as realms of psycho-physical rebirth, these realms are, in descending order, the realm of pleasure-bound divine beings (*deva*-s), the realm of the ambitious semidivine beings (*asura*-s), the realm of humans, the realm of animals, the realm of homeless, hungry wandering spirits (*preta*-s), and the realm of beings bound in the various torturous hells.[5] Notice that there is no separate realm for women—there is only the *human* realm. If we were to take seriously and apply literally some of the more negative views about women and their biological, intellectual, and spiritual incapacities found in the Buddhist texts we have surveyed, there should be a seventh realm, probably between the animal and the human realms, for women. That seventh realm is on no wheel of life* depicting the realms of existence—an instructive point that highlights the internal contradictions in Buddhist tradition between its popular stereotypes and practices and its fundamental vision.

One can only understand how crucial is the lack of a seventh realm when one understands the importance accorded to *human* birth in Buddhism. Often it is said that, though the dharma applies equally to all sentient beings in all realms of existence, only those born into the human realm have a realistic chance of practicing the dharma and thus winning its fruits. This point is made over and over in Buddhist texts, but the one that is seared into my consciousness occurs in the liturgy of the "four reminders which turn the mind to the dharma," recited in connection with the practice of the Four Foundations to Vajrayana practice (*ngundro*).[6] The first reminder reads "Precious human body, free and well-favored, difficult to obtain, easy to lose—now I must do something useful." The traditional use of this reminder is to encourage one to remember the shortness

---

* The reference is to the popular wheel of life depicted on the entrance to all Tibetan monsteries as a summary of Buddhist teachings. See Robinson, *The Buddhist Religion*, p. 18, for a diagram.

of human life and, therefore, to go beyond frivolity. But it could as well be used to point out that the precious human body, not to be wasted, can be of either gender, since there is no separate realm for women in Buddhist cosmology.

A Buddhist antifeminist might try to argue that, just as the *dharma* applies to beings in all realms, but can only be practiced by those in the human realm, so the *dharma* applies to all human beings but can be practiced more effectively by some humans than by others. Probably most Buddhist teachers would agree with this judgment, but one would have to question what would be the motivation to use gender as a criterion for prejudging who might most effectively practice the *dharma*. It is difficult to imagine that there could be a truly *dharmic* motivation, a motivation in accord with basic Buddhist teachings, for using gender as a criterion. Rather, the use of this criterion would derive from reliance on convention or from prejudice, motivations not in accord with the Buddhist ideals of insight and calm or with Buddhist teachings such as egolessness, emptiness, and Buddha-nature.

BUDDHISM *IS* FEMINISM

Some women involved in both Buddhism and feminism simply say "Buddhism *is* feminism!" by which they express intuitively the conviction that when Buddhism is true to itself, it manifests the same vision as does feminism. Though the statement that Buddhism is feminism strikes deep chords in me, the opposite claim, that feminism is Buddhism, could not be made. First, feminism is a broad movement, and not all feminists end up with any spiritual orientation. Certainly they need not be or become Buddhists to be true to the vision of feminism, as Buddhism must, explicitly or implicitly, be "feminist" in order to be true to its vision. Secondly, some versions of feminism, the more militant or separatist versions of feminism would be difficult to reconcile with Buddhism. One could well sympathize with someone, unaware that such versions of feminism are not the feminist norm or vision, who balked at the claim than Buddhism is feminism.

Nevertheless, the intuition that Buddhism *is* feminism, when systematized, is a major resource for a Buddhist feminism. At least four profound similarities between the fundamental orientations of Buddhism and of feminism strengthen the claim the Buddhism is feminism.

First, contrary to most of the Western philosophical and theological heritage, both Buddhism and feminism begin with experience, stress experiential understanding enormously, and move from experience to theory, which becomes the expression of experience. Both share the approach that conventional views and dogmas are worthless if experience does not actually bear out theory. In other words, in a conflict between ones's experience of one's world and what one has been taught by others about the world, both feminism and Buddhism agree that one cannot deny or repress experience.

Allegiance to experience before theory leads to a second important similarity between Buddhism and feminism, the will and the courage to go against the grain at any cost, and to hold to insights of truth, no matter how bizarre they seem from a conventional point to view. In its core teachings about the lack of external salvation (non-theism), about the non-existence of a permanent abiding self (non-ego), and about the pervasiveness and richness of suffering, Buddhism goes against the grain of what religions generally promise. Yet Buddhists continue to see these unpopular religious insights as the only way to attain liberation "beyond hope and fear."* Feminism's equally unconventional and unpopular truths about gender arrangements lead many to ridicule, scorn, or misrepresent it as nothing but the emotional outbursts of a group of unbalanced women who can't conform gracefully to their "natural place." In a time of backlash, it becomes all the more common to read letters to the editor and columns proclaiming "the failure of feminism," or claiming that feminism is responsible for the woes of economic decline, drug abuse, and domestic violence. Such unreasoned attempts to dismiss feminism's prophetic proclamations against conventional gender privilege and hierarchy make the courage and humor displayed by battle-weary veterans of the first attempts to introduce feminist discourse all the more remarkable.

Thirdly, both perspectives use their willingness to hold to experience over convention and theory and their tenacious courage to explore how mental constructs operate to block or enhance liberation. For Buddhism, this exploration has involved the study of conventional ego, its painful habitual tendencies, and the underlying freedom of the basic egoless state. For feminism, this exploration involves looking into ways in which the social conditioning that produces gender stereotypes and conventional gender roles trap both women and men in half-humanity, encouraging mutual incompetence and threatening to destroy the planet. However, mingled with this fundamental similarity is a basic difference, to be explored more fully in later chapters. Buddhism has never looked deeply into gender conventions as an aspect of *samsaric*, pain-filled ego. Feminism, so caught up in immediate needs, often lacks an ability to convey the deep peace beyond ego. Nevertheless, beneath these important

---

* The Buddhist insight that one needs to transcend not only fear but hope to attain spiritual maturity has long puzzled Christians, who have been taught that hope is a great virtue and saviour. But Buddhism claims that spiritual freedom is found only when we are able to accommodate what is happening, that so long as we hope that things could be different, we are enslaved to our hopes and fearful that they might not be realized. Thus hope and fear are seen as interdependent and interchangeable.

differences is the more profound similarity of outlook. Both Buddhism and feminism explore how habitual ego patterns block basic well-being.

Finally, both perspectives speak of liberation as the point of human existence, the aim toward which all existence strains. The language conceptualizing liberation is superficially different in the two perspectives. For Buddhism, the language wavers between seeing liberation as freedom from the world and freedom within the world—an important internal ambiguity within Buddhism that will be explored more fully later. For feminism the definition of liberation is clearer—freedom from gender roles and gender stereotypes. But to focus on these differences of language and conceptualization is to miss the point. Feminism, like Buddhism and like all other visions of the human spirit, looks beyond the immediate and compelling entrapments of easy solutions and conventional perspectives to the radical freedom of transcending those entrapments.

MUTUAL TRANSFORMATION BETWEEN BUDDHISM AND FEMINISM

Though it is compelling and accurate to speak of Buddhism *as* feminism, that statement is not the complete story. Potential mutual transformation between Buddhism and feminism provides an equally significant resource for Buddhist feminism. When mutual transformation, rather than similarity, is focused upon, the emphasis changes from how compatible the two perspectives are to what they might learn from each other. Made famous by process theologian John Cobb in the title of his book *Beyond Dialogue: Toward a Mutual Transformation of Buddhism and Christianity*, the phrase "mutual transformation," which goes beyond dialogue because it results from genuine dialogue, describes the most appropriate mode of interaction and change between differing spiritual perspectives. Genuine dialogue and the resulting mutual transformation are a middle path between rigid ideological self-justification and syncretistic shopping in the great spiritual supermarket.

The concept of mutual transformation is based on the experience that when one enters into genuine dialogue, one is changed. Genuine dialogue is conversation with the other that abandons, in so far as possible, the agenda of debate, argument, scoring points, or conversion. In genuine dialogue, one seeks only to explain one's self and to understand the other. But such genuine dialogue, in ways that cannot be predicted at the beginnings of the encounter, changes its partners. Therefore, genuine dialogue is inherently risky and threatening to ideologues of any persuasion. The change in the dialogue partners is gradual, almost imperceptible, resulting from a process of inner growth that results from truly understanding the other. The changes are not deliberately sought and intellectualized, but without the protection of ideological self-justification, they will arise organically. Because they arise organically, they are much more authentic than the usual alternatives to rigid self-maintaining ideologies—shopping in the great spiritual supermarket, mindless borrowing, and easy syncretism. Genuine dialogue, resulting inevitably, slowly, organically in mutual transformation, is much more work, much slower, and much more profound.

Mutual transformation is usually thought to result when two partners from different spiritual perspectives interact with each other. In the case of the dialogue and mutual transformation between Buddhism and feminism, the process is usually an internal dialogue within a person seriously committed to both perspectives. That this is an internal dialogue does not make the process less real or less transformative. In my own experience, I was a feminist long before I became involved in Buddhist practice. Quite frankly, I checked very carefully, using feminist criteria, before committing my energies to Buddhist practice. I was not interested in another trip through a religion so sexist in its symbol system or hierarchical structure that I would inevitably be damaged by it. Somewhat warily, I committed, but I fully expected feminism and Buddhism to be two separate and parallel tracks in my life.

It was unnerving and unsettling when, against the rule of geometry, the parallel tracks began to merge and intersect. In my case, feminism was more deeply transformed initially by Buddhist practice than vice versa and this transformation was an ungrounding and profound experience. I continue to believe that Buddhism can make a significant critique of feminism as usually constituted and that Buddhist thought and practice could have a great deal to contribute to feminists. I have written in other contexts on this topic.[7] Here I will only summarize by saying that Buddhist practice has a great deal to offer in helping feminists deal with the anger that can be so enervating, while allowing them to retain the sharp critical brilliance contained in the anger.* Buddhist meditation practices can also do wonders to soften the ideological hardness that often makes feminists ineffective spokespersons in their own behalf. Buddhist teachings on suffering help feminists remember that basic human sufferings and existential anxieties are not patriarchy's fault and will not be eliminated in post-patriarchal social conditions.[8] Finally, Buddhist spirituality, with its long-tested spiritual disciplines, can do much to undercut the tendencies towards trippiness and spiritual materialism that often plague feminist spirituality movements.[9]

At this point, however, my main topic is transformation from the other direction, from feminism into Buddhism. This is a feminist history, analysis,

---

* Gross, "Feminism from the Perspective of Buddhist Practice," *Buddhist Christian Studies*, I. 1980. Known in Vajrayana Buddhism as transmutation, the process of utilizing negative energy, such as that of anger, on the spiritual path is an important spiritual discipline. See Trungpa, *Cutting through Spiritual Materialism*, pp. 223-34.

and reconstruction of Buddhism, not an assessment of "Feminism from the Perspective of Buddhist Practice."[10] What transformation from feminism to Buddhism involves is, in my view, best summed up by saying that I am taking permission, as a Buddhist, to use the prophetic voice. This unusual phrase deserves some explanation, and also some credit. John Cobb first challenged me to acknowledge that some of the things I was saying about women and Buddhism derived, not from classic Buddhist sources, but from aspects of my value system that were part of my spiritual heritage as a Westerner. Feminism, especially the Christian and post-Christian feminist thought with which I am most familiar can, with great cogency, be seen as in direct continuity with Biblical prophecy, in its true meaning of social criticism, protest against misuse of power, vision for a social order more nearly expressing justice and equity, and, most importantly, willingness actively to seek that more just and equitable order through whatever means are appropriate and necessary.

This prophetic voice is the missing element that has allowed Buddhists to tolerate with ease the combination of lofty and extremely refined teachings about compassion, including some theoretical understanding of gender equity, with often extremely repressive social regimes, not only regarding gender, but also regarding politics and economics. Herein lies the major problem for Buddhism. It is not that Buddhism lacks a social ethic, as is sometimes claimed, for Buddhism has an extremely sophisticated set of guidelines for moral inter-actions. But Buddhists have generally not been willing to engage in social action to see the realization of that ethic in realms of politics, economics, or social organization. Probably, most Buddhists have felt that individual transfor-mation and enlightenment are so high a priority, and that society is so intractable and unenlightenable, that social action becomes a diversion and a waste of energy. In any case, there certainly has been more tendency to accept the status quo of politics, economics, and society than to seek to improve it in most forms of Buddhism throughout history.

"Compassion" is a word that comes easily and naturally in Buddhist discussions of social ethics. The word "righteousness" does not. Compassion for those caught in the ocean of *samsara*, suffering all the indignities inherent in such existence, is a prime motivation for and justification of the Buddhist lifestyle. Living the eightfold path of Buddhist individual and social morality involves non-harming and working for the benefit of all sentient beings on all levels. The method, however, has been individual and somewhat passive, especially when compared with ringing calls for and acts on behalf of overall justice and righteousness common to those who use the prophetic voice. In taking permission to use the prophetic voice as a Buddhist feminist, I am seeking to empower compassion, as understood so well in Buddhist social ethics, by direct infusion of concern for righteousness, for the actual manifes-tation in Buddhist societies of Buddhism's compassionate vision.

I most certainly am not content to accept the status quo of gender arrange-ments in most of the Buddhist world. In fact, if I had to be a Buddhist woman under the conditions that exist in most parts of the Buddhist world, Buddhism would not be my religion of choice. Only an auspicious coincidence of Bud-dhism and feminism, central to my vision, permits the internal dialogue. That internal dialogue has resulted in mutual transformation. The prophetic voice, derived from earlier trainings in Western modalities of the spirit, is coming through loudly and clearly in my Buddhist discussions of women. Furthermore, the permission to use that prophetic voice in Buddhist discourse is perhaps the greatest, most necessary, and most useful resource for a Buddhist feminism.

At the same time, mutual transformation comes through from the other side, for Buddhist meditation training and the Buddhist emphasis on gentleness will modulate the prophetic voice, which can sometimes be strident in express-ing its truth and insights. Perhaps we can envision a marriage of compassion and righteousness in social ethics, a gentle and active approach to such issues as gender inequity, privilege, and hierarchy.

9

Setting the Stage: Presuppositions of the Buddhist Worldview

As prelude to a feminist analysis of the major concepts specific to each of the three major doctrinal developments within Buddhism, several presuppositions of the Buddhist worldview should be examined. These concepts represent the background out of which grow the more explicitly and specifically Buddhist teachings. As such, they could be easily overlooked, despite their major significance for a feminist analysis of Buddhism. We first ponder the good fortune that Buddhism lacks two pervasive religious concepts which are very difficult for feminists to reconstruct. Then we will thoroughly investigate the pan-Indian concept of karma, the Buddhist concept most frequently used to defend the practices of gender hierarchy and gender privilege in Buddhism. Finally, we will discuss a question which is very important to feminist analyses and critiques of religious symbol systems: is the Buddhist outlook dualistic and otherworldly?

COUNT YOUR NEGATIVE BLESSINGS: BATTLES WE DON'T HAVE TO FIGHT

Buddhism is a non-theistic religion. That sentence, often presented in elementary textbooks as one of Buddhism's great differences from many other religions, is then followed by discussion of the meaning and rationale of non-theism. Briefly, Buddhist non-theism does not deny the existence of supernatural beings; what it denies is that such beings can confer enlightenment or save sentient beings from samsaric existence. Thus, the briefest possible explanation of Buddhist non-theism states that there can be no vicarious enlightenment (not even in Amitabha's Pure Land), that there is no external saviour. Consequently, Buddhism simply lacks the categories that have so consumed the interest and energies of many other religions—Absolute Supreme Being, Creator, God. . . .

What does this have to do with feminism? Because Buddhism is non-theistic, there is no gendered Absolute or Supreme Being valorizing the male sex among humans as does the deity of male monotheism. In all theistic religions, the Absolute Supreme Being is also personified and given human traits, including gender. In a religion like Hinduism, the deities are, sensibly, symbolized as being of both genders. Such androgynous symbolism is the norm for all theistic religions, with a single significant exception. The three monotheistic religions generally refer to the Supreme Being using masculine pronouns and images. Though they claim that the deity is beyond sexuality altogether, since that is part of His transcendence, most adherents of these religions are quite horrified and offended to hear that deity referred to using female pronouns and images. In Jewish and Christian feminist theology, reams have been written on this problem,[1] which remains, especially at the practical level, one of the most intractable problems for feminists to reconstruct.

In this context, only an outline of the issues can be undertaken. Three important conclusions widely, though not universally agreed upon, most adequately sum up the writings on this most basic problem for Jewish and Christian feminists. The first is that the maleness of the deity and male dominance in society mirror, reinforce, and validate each other. Perhaps the most famous short statement of this conclusion is by Mary Daly:

> The symbol of the Father God, spawned in the human imagination and sustained as plausible by patriarchy, has in turn rendered service to this type of society by making its mechanisms for the oppression of women appear right and fitting. If God in "his" heaven is a father ruling "his" people, then it is in the "nature" of things and according to divine plan and the order of the universe that society be male-dominated.[2]

Secondly, it is concluded that the lack of significant mythic and symbolic feminine figures is a major psychological and spiritual handicap for women. Though the presence of a divine feminine may not secure political and economic freedom and equality for women, at least women's bodies and modes of being are mirrored and validated by powerful and generally venerated goddesses in religions like Hinduism. Even that is lacking in male monotheisms, which are not only socially and economically, but psychologically and symbolically patriarchal.[3]

Third, those feminists who wish to remain within the Jewish or Christian traditions must seek various alternative sets of images about deity that undo the conventional images of the deity as male but not female. Unfortunately, practical changes at the level of liturgy often simply skirt the issue by avoiding any gendered language about deity. Thus pronouns disappear entirely. On other occasions, the language is neutralized by using "Parent" instead of "Father," for example, or by using only very abstract or non-anthropomorphic images for deity. To use feminine pronouns and images is to confront the problem too directly and straightforwardly; nevertheless, as I have argued in my contributions to that debate, nothing short of unambiguously female pronouns and images of deity addresses the issues adequately. Since a theistic religion will always include a gendered Supreme Being, only clearly feminine symbolism and imagery can avoid sexism.[4]

At one point, I participated significantly in such discussions, which I believe address one of the most critical issues for monotheistic feminists. I am grateful that, as a Buddhist, this is one issue that I can leave behind. I can leave it behind for two reasons. First, though some Jewish or Christian feminists might initially expect that the maleness of the Buddha should give me just as big a problem, the Buddha, no matter how interpreted, just isn't as important to Buddhism as God is to the monotheistic faiths. The maleness of the historical Buddha is analogous to the maleness of the historical Jesus—a sociological necessity of his patriarchal times and an accident of his particular personality, not an essential attribute of his being. Second, in forms of Buddhism that have a more abstract and metaphysical concept of Buddhahood, the ultimate level of Buddha (Dharmakaya) is impersonal, while the manifest and relative levels of Buddha (Sambhogakaya and Nirmanakaya) occur in both female and male form according to most schools of Buddhism.Though Buddhism does not have a gendered Absolute Supreme Being who creates and saves, it does have a vast pantheon of mythic, symbolic heros and models with whom one can identify and relate in liturgy and meditation practices. As soon as Buddhism began to develop "deity-like" figures, it developed both male and female celestial bodhisattvas and *yidam*-s.

Their presence has made the greatest difference in my experiences within Judaism and Buddhism. Five previous articles represent a covert autobiography, though that was not the intention with which they were written, of my struggles with the issues of gender, images of deity, and psychological well-being. The first article, the first I wrote after finishing my doctoral dissertation, had nothing to do with the kind of work I was supposed to be doing as a historian of religions. Titled "Female God-Language in a Jewish Context," this essay was reprinted in the widely used anthology *WomanSpirit Rising* and commented up by many. Written out of pain, alienation, and frustration, it contains a theological argument for the acceptability of feminine pronouns for the deity in Jewish and, by extension, all monotheistic contexts. Though I already expressed the conviction that there are links between patriarchal sexism and male monotheism, at that point all I envisioned was the healing involved in being able comfortably to relate to the familiar deity of traditional monotheism as "She" as well as "He." I ended with a confession of inability, at that time, to say anything about the topic of feminine *imagery* for deity; the linguistic revolution involved in allowing "She" into liturgical language was all I could manage.

A few years later, I had begun to utilize the imagery of the Hindu goddesses as a resource for monotheistic thought and published two articles on that topic.[5] My suggestions were much bolder and I felt much more empowered and whole. I developed a slide show around six images of the feminine side of deity, using Hindu icons to illustrate visually theological points relevant to monotheistic god-talk; it was widely and successfully shown. But, while I felt more sane about my own sense of deity, I was also much more alone. Fellow Jews and other monotheists were, at best, curious, but not wholly receptive to direct feminine imagery of "their" deity, and were even less enthusiastic about learning from "polytheistic idolaters."

For reasons having nothing to do with feminism, I had also begun a Buddhist meditation practice at about the same time. My next paper on the topic, "Suffering, Feminist Theory, and Images of Goddess,"[6] already showed a great deal of Buddhist influence; the process of internal mutual transformation discussed in the previous chapter was already much further along than I realized. Again in that paper, I worked with the imagery of the Hindu goddess Kali, showing how her iconography helped me understand and internalize important ideas and begin a critical assessment of limitations in feminist thought. I was more alone in that paper than I realized at the time, for, clearly, I was no longer relating to deity as transcendent other but as myth-model—a transition many other feminists were making at about the same time. But I was not yet genuinely conversant with or initiated into a communal tradition in which deity was commonly related with as "She" or invoked as myth-model rather than as transcendent other.

Five years later, I felt secure enough to present some materials about my experiences with the practice of the *sadhana* of Vajrayogini at a session of the Ritual Studies section of the American Academy of Religion on "Women and Initiation."[7] In that paper, I expressed my "incredible relief" at being initiated into practices "introducing me to myself and to the world as the body and mind of Vajrayogini—this incredibly powerful, magnetizing red woman dancing on a lotus, sun and corpse seat, naked, sixteen. . . ."[8] In that paper, I tried to express some of the empowerment I experience through having access to this *sadhana* involving a *female* myth-model. "She is so strong and beautiful, so fierce and compassionate, so permeates everything; she is my body and mind."[9] I suggested that, though this spiritual practice had not been designed to solve the problems inherent in Western patriarchal religious symbolism, it had done so for me because of the "healing power of non-patriarchal, non-sexist anthropomorphic symbolism."[10]

Thus, Buddhist non-theism turns out to be much more complex than the sheer absence of the Absolute of male monotheism. That absence, that lack, is a powerful presupposition of the Buddhist worldview in all forms of Buddhism. At least no Buddhist feminist has to reconstruct a male Supreme Being that is of ultimate significance in the symbol system of the religion. The unexpected gift available to some Buddhists is the comforting and empowering presence of female myth-models such as Tara, Kwan-yin, or Vajrayogini. Those whose spiritual temperaments long for symbol and liturgy not weighted down by theism or male monotheism can find such a resource intact in some forms of Buddhism. The advantages of not having to "remember" or discover them, as is done in the various feminist spirituality movements, are very great.

Most religions also possess another complex of ideas that is very difficult for feminists to reconstruct. To a greater or a lesser degree, most religions include a complex code of behavior considered to be divinely revealed or cosmically given that regulates daily life, including gender relationships. For Judaism and Islam, the divinely given, minutely detailed code of daily living demonstrates the deity's great concern for His people. Hinduism and Confucianism do not account for their codes of conduct by citing divine authorship of a personal deity. But both perspectives involve as central concepts the idea that a detailed and prescribed code of daily behavior resonates harmoniously with cosmic patterns, and that going against these behavioral norms disrupts the harmony of the cosmos. Both kinds of behavioral code are thought to be immutable and eternal, not something humans constructed or can change easily, if at all.

Both the revealed and the cosmic law codes define gender roles sharply and distinctly. They demarcate certain tasks and privileges as being for males and others as being for females. Usually they also teach that crossing these gender boundaries is extremely disruptive and dangerous, affecting not only the individuals involved, but also upsetting larger cosmic and social harmonies. Needless to say, the law codes of all four religions are also extremely patriarchal. The Hindu and Confucian codes state explicitly that women are never to be independent, but must always be under control of a male, whether father, husband, or son. The Jewish and Muslim codes give public and religious power and authority to men. In fact, in these two religions, it is difficult for women even to practice the more directly religious or spiritual (and highly valued) aspects of the tradition and they are not expected to be interested in them. That a behavioral code with all these traits will be difficult to reconstruct in accord with feminist values is an understatement.

Buddhism has the great good fortune to lack such a rigid and detailed code of behavior for daily living, at least for lay Buddhists. In Buddhism, the legalistic urge is given its due in the *vinaya*, the rules of discipline governing monks and nuns, which is relatively constant throughout the Buddhist world.

By contrast, lay Buddhists have been given only general guidelines for moral conduct, but not detailed codes regarding sexuality, family relations, diet, or even gender roles. Generally, lay Buddhists have followed the norms of their society, rather than a specifically Buddhist code, regarding such matters. Thus, for example, Buddhists have often relied on Hindu or Confucian norms for gender roles, but they do not have the same cosmic significance for Buddhists that they do for Hindus or Confucianists.

For these reasons the greatest legal battles facing Buddhist feminists occur over issues of nuns' ordination and nuns' status within the monastic institutions. These rules are detailed and go back to the origins of Buddhism. But even in this case, the rules are not thought of as a revelation or as something that keeps the cosmos in balance. They are not quite that weighty, venerable as they may be. Nor do they demarcate a women's sphere that is essentially different from a men's sphere; monks and nuns are more alike than different. For non-monastics the situation is much simpler. Lay Buddhists are not breaking with divine command or cosmic models when they break with older gender roles and patterns of gender interaction. They are only changing received social custom. Thus a lay Buddhist male who wants to retain gender privilege cannot call upon God or the cosmos to validate him. It is much clearer that he simply is motivated by his desire to retain his privileged position. This does not mean that change can come easily, for social customs are well entrenched, even among Western Buddhists, but at least feminists do not first have to reconstruct interpretations of divine revelation or cosmic order to make their case.

NEGATIVE KARMA AND FEMALE BIRTH:
SOME FEMINIST COMMENTS

As we have already seen, Buddhists attempt to explain and justify gender hierarchy and male dominance by other means. They appeal to the pan-Indian concept of karma, the law of cause and effect and its corollary, belief in rebirth. Before going on to a discussion of this concept in the context of feminist analysis, it may be useful to discuss the concept more fully. It is important to understand that the so-called "law of karma" is about cause and effect. It is not a theory of reward and punishment, though sometimes it is discussed almost as if it were. It is not a theory of rewards and punishments because there is no rewarder or punisher, and because effects are said to be completely non-arbitrary, which is not always the case with rewards and punishments.

Even more important, karma is not a theory of predestination, though it is often misunderstood in that fashion by Westerners not thoroughly acquainted with the concept. One is not constrained to activate the causes that produce negative effects. Habitual tendencies may make it almost inevitable that certain causes will be activated under certain conditions by the spiritually immature. Nevertheless, through meditation and other appropriate spiritual disciplines, one can slowly undo those habitual tendencies and break the cycle of cause and effect. Once set in motion, however, effect inevitably follows cause; personal choices or decisions, even on the part of a deity, cannot change or alter that inevitability. Thus, much of my present is determined by what has already occurred in the past and cannot be undone or changed. However, my *method of coping* with my present is not predetermined; how I do cope will deeply affect my future.

Traditionally, this law of cause and effect was intertwined with a belief in rebirth and many traditional Indo-Tibetan Buddhists find it almost impossible to imagine being Buddhist without taking belief in rebirth for granted. Nevertheless, most Western Buddhists do not consider belief in rebirth to be central to their understanding of Buddhism or to their reasons for practicing Buddhist spiritual disciplines. For us, the concept of karma explains rather well how specific causes, such as negative habitual tendencies, inevitably produce specific effects, such as psychological anguish, but it does not satisfactorily explain why some people are born addicted to crack, while others are born to loving parents. Even if the law of karma is not used as a universal explanatory framework, it is very useful psychologically and therapeutically in contemplating one's life and one's relationships.

We may now review the traditional application of these concepts to the fact of being female. Traditionally, it would be said that women are in their present difficult situation because of their karma, due to past behaviors. Women have an inferior position in patriarchal societies, and furthermore, are thought by many with sexist values to be deficient and perhaps disgusting, biologically, intellectually, and spiritually. But they are only reaping the effects of past karma. In a certain sense, they "deserve" what they get. Their present sufferings burn out or exhaust the negative karma from the past; coping well with the present situation creates a "bank account" of positive karma to drive future situations. Male rebirth was the promised eventual positive outcome.

We have already looked at textual discussions of how women might overcome female rebirth and what can cause either male or female rebirth. But here, it should be added that such traditional applications of teaching about karma to the fact of female birth can be used very effectively against women who do not have an alternative analysis. Not only are they told they are only reaping what they have sowed and, therefore, have no basis for complaint. They can also be told that if they rebel against the system by trying to change patriarchal norms concerning the treatment of women, they are creating negative karma for themselves.

This traditional line of thinking functions both as an explanation and as a justification of the treatment of women under male dominance. I will analyze its inadequacy on both counts, for there are significant problems with both functions of this line of thinking. As an explanation, it works relatively well within a traditional framework which assumes both the inevitability of rebirth and patriarchal expectations about women. But even within a traditional framework, this reasoning does not work well as a justification for treating women poorly. When used for that purpose, such thinking demonstrates a fundamental confusion between descriptive and normative statements. At most, traditional concepts of karma and rebirth could explain why women have been or are being treated badly. They do not *justify continuing to treat them badly.*

When we examine these arguments closely in a feminist framework, we see that the traditional and the feminist Buddhist agree on one thing only. After that they would disagree on almost all points of analysis. Both the feminist and the traditionalist agree that female existence, *under current patriarchal conditions*, is less than ideal. The traditional Buddhist solves this problem be eliminating female birth, either in the next life, or, taken to an extreme, entirely, as in Amitabha's Pure Land devoid of female rebirth. The feminist would solve this problem by eliminating, not females, but the *conditions*, especially male privilege, that make female existence a liability, recognizing that femaleness itself is only one variant of the human, not a deficient state of being. Had I the merit to create a Pure Land, its pure quality would be its lack of patriarchy, its androgyny, its mutuality between women and men, not its lack of women.

Feminist analysis would also suggest that there are more cogent and more empirical explanations for the liabilities of female existence under patriarchy than the imputed misdeeds, in some past life, of the beings currently embodied in female form. The negativities of women's existence in male-dominated societies are created and maintained by patriarchal social systems, not given in the nature of things, according to feminist analysis. Female biology and reproduction are culturally construed into liabilities in a way that male biology and reproduction are not. Avenues of cultural and spiritual creativity are almost entirely cut off to women, who are then said to less intellectual and spiritual than men. Women are treated as social inferiors, which then is given as one of the reasons why female rebirth is the result of negative karma.

Under premodern condition, women's admittedly difficult existence could, to a certain extent, be explained by lack of safe, effective birth control, a short lifespan spent almost entirely in reproduction, heavy work demands, and other characteristics of premodern agricultural conditions. But the main cause of patriarchal social arrangements and stereotypes has always been habitual patterns and egocentrism, even under premodern conditions. Today, given the dysfunctionality of traditional gender roles and divisions of labor, that is even more the case. In other words, what causes the negativity of women's existence under patriarchy is not women's karma, but the self-centered, fixated, habitual patterns of those in power, of those who maintain the status quo. To fault women's karma rather than habitual patterns of self-interest is to blame the victim—a not uncommon tactic used against women in many patriarchal systems. This explanation, which locates the cause of women's misery under male-dominated systems in *present* ego-patterns and self-interest, rather than in past karma, also has the advantage of being a thoroughly *Buddhist* analysis, in addition to making sense in feminist terms.

Even if we followed the more traditional line of analysis, which locates the cause of women's present patriarchally induced misery in karma-laden past deeds, we have only an *explanation*, not a *justification*, for their current treatment. In other words, someone might look at the situation and analyze that another person's misfortune is due to the karma they have accrued in the past. Even if that analysis is correct, that does not give the analyst *licence* to contribute to the other's misery. In fact, the analyst should be quick to conclude that contributing to the misery of the sufferer would be the cause activating the effect of negative karma to him or herself. Therefore, really integrating teachings about karma into one's life should have the opposite effect from inducing complaisance about the status quo and condoning privilege, even though this has been an unfortunately frequent side effect of this teaching in Indian religions. Rather, one would not be willing to support, passively or actively, fundamentally cruel and oppressive institutions or situations, such as gender privilege, militarism, or economic exploitation. Additionally, contributing ones's efforts to undermining such institutions should, logically, produce positive karma leading to a fortunate future. Seen in this way, the traditional interpretation of the doctrine of karma has serious implications for social policy, which is probably why Buddhists usually advised kings to be kind and just. Unfortunately, such interpretations of the concept of karma, emphasizing its implications for social policy in addition to its implications for individual conduct, have been relatively rare in traditional Buddhism.

This feminist rejoinder to traditional discussions of karma and femaleness depends on one thing that never seems to have part of the traditional Buddhist outlook. That is the willingness and courage to name oppression as *oppression*, not as normal, not as the way things have to be, not as inevitable and unchangeable, but as oppression, deriving from the self-interest and habitual patterns of both oppressors and oppressed. Probably one of the reasons traditional Buddhism promised a way out of female rebirth altogether is that people just didn't think of patriarchy as *oppressive*; they thought of it as inevitable. They did not imagine that there could be other ways to construct gender relationships. In fact, this seems to be a general tendency regarding all social situations in traditional Buddhism. The very word "oppression" isn't part of the vocabulary. Instead people emphasize acceptance of their lot, non-aggression, and forbearance. The term "oppression" fits much more naturally into the vocabulary of social protest and social activism characteristic of the prophetic tradition. Thus, for the feminist to combine discussion of karma with use of the term "oppression" is itself a result of mutual transformation and this use of the term "oppression" grows out of permission to use the prophetic voice within Buddhism, in Buddhist ways. This feminist discussion of karma and female birth could perhaps suggest ways to talk of social activism regarding other issues as well from within a Buddhist framework.

Finally, at another level of discussion altogether, contemplation of teachings about karma can help provide equanimity and deep peace. Ultimately, the things that happen are not the result of the mysterious and arbitrary will of Someone. They are the result of cause and effect and reflect some deep harmony and sanity inherent in the cosmos. First one needs to sort out the things that can be changed and work to change them, rather than passively accepting them as "just my karma." Following that, one can temper potential emotional exhaustion and burnout by contemplating whatever results, whether success or failure, as karma, seeing karma not as a matter of rewards and punishments, but as a matter of inscrutable appropriateness. Such contemplation helps foster a sense of detachment regarding the outcomes of one's attempts to undo oppression—something essential to social activism. This is the razor's edge of the middle way between capitulating to injustice as if it were karmic justice and losing one's self in anger and frustration over what does not change despite one's best efforts. Seen in this way, the teachings of karma can be effective as one of a number of tools provided by Buddhism to provide relief from the burnout and heartbreak that are so often the lot of visionaries.

IS BUDDHISM DUALISTIC AND OTHERWORLDLY?:
AN ESSENTIAL FEMINIST QUESTION

Many textbooks present Buddhism as a world-denying, otherworldly religion. Certainly much within Buddhist tradition fosters that interpretation. Nevertheless, one standing authentically within the Buddhist tradition can accurately see Buddhism as a path to freedom *within* the world process or as a path to freedom *from* the world process. To see Buddhism as providing freedom within the world is much more compatible with post-patriarchal vision than the more familiar interpretation of Buddhism as freedom from the world.

This question regarding proper interpretation of presuppositions of the Buddhist worldview is critical from a feminist perspective. The otherworldly mode of spirituality has been thoroughly delineated and critiqued in the last two decades by many feminist scholars. Usually they evaluate that type of spirituality very negatively because in the West, such spirituality tends to be both misogynist and patriarchal. One of the most widely used tools for both explaining and critiquing patriarchal religion has been Rosemary Ruether's discussion of the dualistic and otherworldly worldview that she sees as dominating the entire Hellenistic world and as critical to the formation of Christianity. According to her analysis, in the late pre-Christian period, people in the Mediterranean world began to lose faith in the cyclic processes and rhythms of the cosmic world of nature. Instead, they sought escape from the finitude and death contained in those cyclic processes and salvation outside and beyond the world of nature. People dichotomized experience into a good-evil duality, with the spirit on the side of the good, while nature and the body, if not intrinsically evil, easily tempted people from the transcendence of spiritual salvation for the soul after death. The dichotomies of this world and the other world, the spirit and the body or nature, the intellect and the emotions, reinforced and intensified the sexual polarity. Women were associated with the body, the emotions, and the realm of nature, all of which had to be rejected and controlled to ensure salvation of the spirit.[11] Ruether and many others see this dualistic and otherworldly outlook as a major contributing factor to classical Christian views of women and misogyny. Furthermore, feminist scholars often find links between otherworldly, dualistic spiritualities and the most serious problems that currently afflict us—widespread glorification of aggression and war as methods of solving conflicts, and the exploitation of global ecology without regard for the earth as a finite matrix of existence. Misogyny and patriarchy are often seen as the critical links between anti-worldly outlooks and aggression or exploitation.

Superficially, at least, Buddhism can appear to be quite similarly, or even more intensely, dualistic and otherworldly in its orientations. I know that this is the impression of many of my colleagues in feminist thought, who wonder why I would take on such a problematic worldview. But I am convinced that this impression is superficial for all forms of Buddhism and incorrect for Mahayana and Vajrayana forms of Buddhism. I also suspect that the ease with which Western interpreters see Buddhism as dualistic and otherworldly owes more to their familiarity with that stream of Western religious thought than to Buddhism itself.

This question can well be discussed by analyzing whether Buddhism seems to be more about freedom *from* the world or freedom *within* the world. The core of the Buddhist quest has something to do with *freedom*. Though it is not a literal translation, what I am calling freedom would roughly correspond to *nirvana* in classical Buddhist and Indian thought. Pinning down precisely what this term means is notoriously difficult; whole books have been written about the question.[12] Nevertheless, one can with some certainty say that *nirvana* means freedom from *samsara*. *Samsara* is easily translated as "cyclic existence," which, by definition is understood to be painful. Therefore, Buddhist freedom involves freedom from painful, cyclic existence—though one can further interpret and debate what precisely such freedom would entail. If one is free *from* painful cyclic existence, what is one free *for*? The answer to that question is less clearly and definitively spelled out in Buddhist tradition, but always involves in some way to help and serve one's fellow sentient beings.

Whether one understands freedom as "freedom from" or as "freedom within" the world, one must begin with the Four Noble Truths, the conceptual heart of Buddhism and the existential discovery of every Buddha in her or his enlightenment experience. Freedom is proclaimed in the third truth, the truth of cessation. Cessation of what? Cessation of the causes of suffering, proclaimed in the first and second truths. The first truth states that (conventional) existence inevitably produces suffering. That suffering, according to the second truth, results from the desire and ignorance that characterize conventional existence. But, according to the third truth, if one can be free from such desire and ignorance, one can be free from the suffering they produce. The fourth truth declaims the lifestyle that is conducive to such freedom. One should pursue wisdom, moral discipline, and spiritual depth—the classic goals of *prajna*, *shila*, and *samadhi*.

One of the most influential Buddhist conceptualizations of the meaning of freedom from suffering has been that such freedom means freedom from rebirth. Birth into the world inevitably brings the pain of "birth, old age, sickness, and death"—an unenviable lot. Rebirth into those patterns is inevitable for all who are not free from desire and ignorance. Easily, this interpretation of Buddhism leads to otherworldly and anti-worldly concerns. (re)Birth is undesirable; far better to remain in the timeless "untime" of the unborn than to take form in the realms of "birth, old age, sickness, and death." Life, as known by those of us who inhabit human bodies in this realm, is inadequate and undesirable compared to some other transcendent state of existence. Furthermore, that other state of existence is attainable by those who can properly renounce the usual human mode of existence and emotionality. Those who no longer experience ignorance and desire will never again be reborn into *samsara*, or cyclic existence, and will live out the remainder of this life in tranquillity, undisturbed by conflicting emotions.

Clearly, this classic interpretation of *samsara* and *nirvana* is otherworldly and anti-worldly, seeing existence as the problem and release as freedom from existence. This dualistic and anti-worldly interpretation of Buddhism can be further intensified by familiar and popular descriptions of the lifestyle that will promote freedom from desire and ignorance. As is well-known, the preferred Buddhist lifestyle in traditional Buddhist countries has always been the monastic lifestyle. One of the primary motivations for this preference is the observation that family and profession, the lot of ordinary people, tend to enmesh one in desires, negative emotions, and large-scale ignoring. Those who have no families and professional concerns will be more likely attain *nirvana* and cessation, both of conventional concerns and of conventional existence.

Alternatively, and, in my view, more appropriately, one can also interpret Buddhism, not as freedom *from* the world, but as freedom *within* the world. To do so, we must return to the discussion of *samsara* and *nirvana*, and to the Four Noble Truths. Freedom remains *the* essential term, but freedom that merely escapes the world of conventional existence may not be real freedom and in fact may well be impossible. Rather, the only freedom is, in the perceptive words of Suzuki Roshi, to find our composure in the truth of impermanence.[13] Dissatisfaction with impermanence, which is to say dissatisfaction with the inevitable finitude of our existence, *rather than* impermanence and finitude themselves, is *the* fundamental unfreedom. As the Four Noble Truths state, we suffer because of our desires; the most basic desire is for things to be different than they are. Conventionally, our deepest desires are for permanence (immortality), ease or bliss, and security, but these desires are unfulfillable, despite the fact that whole religions are based on promising these impossible goals. Thus, the real problem addressed by Buddhism is not an unsatisfactory world that we somehow transcend or escape *from*, but improper and unsatisfactory desires regarding that world. Freedom, the cessation proclaimed by the third noble truth, remains the heart and core of Buddhism. And, as Buddhism always proclaims, that freedom is achieved when the desires and ignorance that cause suffering rather than freedom are given up.

But is cessation of desire really a matter of "renouncing the world" rather than "living in the world?" To transcend desire and ignorance, one needs to change one's attitudes, which is not guaranteed by a change of lifestyle. The world we live in, the existence we experience, are not the problem, are not the source of suffering and the barrier to freedom. Rather, the problem is unrealistic hopes and demands regarding that world—essentially hopes and demands for permanence, ease, and security. We need to go beyond these attitudes to be truly free. When this occurs, we are not, in fact, free *from* the world process, since we are still, inevitably subject to "birth, old age, sickness, and death," as well as impermanence, lack of security, and insufficient ease or pleasure. In short, finitude is, was, and will be our lot. However, to "find our ease in impermanence" is to live and die untroubled by finitude, untroubled by our world and by the conditions of our existence. We are free *within* the world and therefore, are unlikely to be otherworldly or anti-worldly in our basic values and orientations. We live, in the classic words of Buddhist vision, "neither wandering in *samsara* nor dwelling in *nirvana*." *

Both interpretations of Buddhism, as freedom from the world, and as freedom within the world, are authentic and traditional. Though they intertwine throughout Buddhist history, an accurate generalization would see the anti-worldly and dualistic interpretation of Buddhism as dominant in early Indian Buddhism, while the non-dualistic interpretation of Buddhism as freedom within the world becomes more important some centuries after the historical Buddha, but never entirely displaces the earlier emphasis. Thus Buddhism follows the general lines of religious evolution from a more otherworldly to a more this-worldly orientation pointed out by Robert Bellah in his classic essay on that topic.[14] My own sympathies lie completely with the understanding of Buddhism as freedom within the world, which is the dominant emphasis of Western Buddhists, if not of Buddhism throughout the world today. Because to me it makes so much more sense to see Buddhism as providing freedom within the world than freedom from the world, feminist suspicions about Buddhist as a dualistic, otherworldly, and, therefore, inevitably patriarchal religion do not seem well-founded to me.

Furthermore, I do not share the general feminist conclusion that anti-worldly and otherworldly spiritualities will inevitably develop misogyny as well. Dualistic, otherworldly spiritualities should be rejected, not because historically, in the West, they were linked with misogyny, but because they are inadequate spiritually. If we were convinced that freedom from the world really is our proper spiritual goal, then our task would be to engage in the social reconstruction that would permit a non-patriarchal and non-misogynist, but otherworldly spirituality. But very few are today convinced that anti-worldliness really is our true spiritual goal. Whatever once made otherworldliness spiritually attractive, those forces now are exhausted, at least in the non-popular level of religious practice where the leading edge of religious and spiritual thinking is found. Today we seek non-dualistic, world- and life-affirming spiritualities. Some of us also seek post-patriarchal spirituality. These two goals are compatible, but do not logically entail each other. Recognizing this complexity helps us avoid the rather simplistic conclusions that otherworldly spiri-

---

* A phrase from a tradition Tibetan Buddhist liturgy, the *sadhana* of Vajrayogini.

tualities developed because only men were the religious elite in them, or that women could create and favor only this-worldly spirituality. However, Buddhism understood as freedom *within* the world *and* informed by the concerns of feminist and post-patriarchal women (and men) will undoubtedly address concerns and issues unthinkable to patriarchal and male-created Buddhism understood as freedom from the world.

10

Strategies for a Feminist Analysis of
Key Buddhist Concepts

A major strategy of feminist thinking in any major religion is to demonstrate that the central concepts of the tradition not only are *compatible with* feminism but also *require* a feminist, rather than a patriarchal, structuring and interpretation of the religion. In other words, the symbols and doctrines of the tradition do not support the patriarchal institutions and practices of the tradition. They more sensibly would support an egalitarian and non-discriminatory manifestation of the religion.[1]

In traditional Buddhism, except for the teachings about karma, no major teaching has been used to explain or justify male dominance. As is the case for most major religions most of the time, the core texts present the major teachings in a sex-neutral manner. One would easily form the impression that they describe the human condition and prescribe ways of dealing with it that apply equally to women and men. Many Buddhist teachers reinforce that impression implicitly or explicitly in their teaching style. Nevertheless, Buddhist institutions, both lay and monastic, are riddled with male dominance. As is so common, we find gender-neutral teachings appropriate to all human beings linked with male dominance of the religious life and institutions.

Therefore, something more is needed. It is necessary explicitly and directly to tease out the implications about gender issues implicit in the major doctrines of Buddhism and apply those findings both to current Buddhist practices and to contemporary gender questions. The primary theses of this part of this book are that no major Buddhist teaching provides any basis for gender privilege or gender hierarchy and that these doctrines, in fact, mandate gender equality at the same time as they undercut the relevance of gender. Furthermore, it is also my thesis that these major teachings are much more compatible with feminist than with patriarchal manifestations of Buddhism. In other words, to be true to its own vision, Buddhism needs to transcend its androcentrism and patriarchy.

Most knowledgeable Buddhists would, I believe, agree with me in these assessments. However, many would probably be reluctant to criticize Buddhism severely and to advocate changes in long-standing practices prevalent in the Buddhist world. More to the heart of the matter, many would not share the urgency with which I contend that gender privilege is totally at odds with the *dharma* and, therefore, completely inappropriate in the Buddhist world.

To demonstrate these theses regarding Buddhist doctrines, we shall again survey the development of Buddhism. This survey, however, focuses not on external history or on attitudes toward women. This survey discusses the major doctrines of Buddhism as they are taught, practiced, and presented by a major form of contemporary Buddhism, Tibetan Buddhism, especially of the Kagyu and Nyingma schools. Thus, in this survey, all the doctrines are "contemporary" in that they are existentially vital to contemporary Buddhists, whatever their historical origins may be. But they are presented and practiced in developmental sequence and build upon one another conceptually.[2] This developmental sequence is important for ordering and making sense, both psychologically and conceptually, of the vast array of Buddhist teachings that eventually became current in Buddhist thought.

The conceptual schema that I shall use to survey key Buddhist doctrines relevant to gender is that of the "three turnings of the wheel of *dharma*."[3] This metaphor uses the old idea that when the Buddha first taught, he set in motion the wheel of *dharma*, which reverses another wheel, the wheel of samsaric existence. According to this schema, the wheel was rotated twice more, which indicates the perception that later developments in Buddhism represent decisive fresh starts. Possibly the wheel will turn again. The most complete discussion of women in Western Buddhism is titled provocatively *Turning the Wheel: American Women Creating the New Buddhism*.[4] On the other hand, it is equally important to emphasize that Buddhists see these turnings or stages as building upon one another. As a practitioner, one cannot start with the third turning and skip the first two. In the same way, the "new" feminist, androgynous Buddhism would incorporate the previous turnings.

Historically, these teachings developed sequentially over a long period of time. But the emphasis here is psychological or spiritual; these are the stages of development a practitioner goes through on the path to freedom and enlightenment. Practically speaking, we must also recognize that in some sense, to say there have been three turnings is somewhat arbitrary. As Reginald Ray points out, the Theravada Buddhist would see the full teachings contained in what the Tibetan tradition calls the first turning, while many East Asian schools of Buddhism discuss the full development of Buddhist teachings as going through five stages.[5]

The first-turning teachings are those attributed to the historical Buddha. When the schema of the "three *yana*-s" or the three vehicles, also highly favored by Tibetan Buddhists, is combined with the "three turnings" schema, the first turning teachings are called the "Hinayana." This use of the term has nothing to do with the pejorative use of the term that so angers contemporary Theravadins. It does not mean the "lesser vehicle" in this case, but the "foundation vehicle." These teachings, basic to all forms of Buddhism, are the Four Noble Truths, the Eightfold Path, the Three Marks, and Co-dependent Co-arising.

Second-turning teachings are associated especially with the Madyamika school and its teachings concerning emptiness or *shunyata*. Also taught as second-turning teachings are the concepts of the two truths and the Bodhisattva path that one enters upon after the experience of *bodhicitta*, or rousing the "thought of enlightenment." These latter concepts are general Mahayana concepts, not specifically Madyamika doctrines however.

The third-turning teachings are straightforwardly associated with the major teachings of the other major Mahayana school of philosophy, the Yogacara.[6] Ray sees the major point of third turning teachings as a more developed view of emptiness. "Whereas the second turning is concerned to emphasize what *sunyata* is *not*, the third turning is concerned to emphasize the point that *sunyata is not nothing*." [7]Thus major doctrines of the third-turning include Buddha-nature (*tathagatagarbha*) and the closely related concept of Suchness or Things-As-They-Are (*tathata*). When the *yana*-s are superimposed on the turnings, both the second and the third turnings are included in the Mahayana. The Vajrayana, with its emphasis on non-duality and on the masculine and feminine principles grows directly out of the third-turning teachings and will be analyzed within the third turning.

To conduct this feminist analysis of the key concepts of Buddhism, I will focus on the philosophical or psychological concept central to each turning or *yana* and on correlate ethical precepts. In so far as is feasible, I will weave the other major concepts of each turning or *yana*, around the discussion of the concept upon which we are focusing, though I am not attempting an exhaustive survey of Buddhism in this analysis. Interestingly, each of the three turnings provides a major concept that invites an extremely provocative discussion of gender, even though in classic Buddhist sources, the implications of these teachings for gender issues have been noticed only with the second turning. And with each turning, we will discover a progressively richer and fuller basis for reconstructing androgynous Buddhism.

11

Gender and Egolessness:
Feminist Comments on Basic Buddhist Teachings

First turning teachings can be organized and summarized in many ways. In this chapter, I will organize my comments around the three major components of the eightfold path that describe the overarching Buddhist way of life. The eight elements of the path are often condensed into three—*prajna*, or wisdom, *shila*, or morality, and *samadhi*, or spiritual discipline. The feminist implications of each of these three major components of the Buddhist lifestyle is significant, but the majority of my comments consist of a feminist discussion of right view,* or wisdom, as understood by the hinayana.

PRAJNA, GENDER, AND EGO

From its beginnings to its current manifestations, Buddhism has stressed the fundamental first-turning teaching of egolessness and, by implication, the counterpart and opposite of egolessness—ego. What Buddhists mean by these terms has troubled and confused many, both inside and outside Buddhism. As with other key Buddhist doctrines, a full explication of the many nuances of this doctrine in the full range of Buddhist literature would be an immense undertaking in itself. Here, I will try to present some relatively simple and straightforward explications of these concepts in the matrix of other relevant first-turning teachings. Then I will discuss how Buddhist teachings about ego and egolessness, when combined with feminist analysis, could serve as a powerful critique of Buddhist patriarchy and tool for a feminist-androgynous interpretation of Buddhism.

Earlier, when discussing the intuition that Buddhism *is* feminism,[1] I wrote that both "explore how patterns of mental constructs operate to block or enhance liberation." For both Buddhism and feminism, conventional patterns of thinking and perceiving are deeply flawed and cause great suffering. This is a major, uncanny similarity, especially given that, superficially, many do not expect such consonance between these two systems.

---

* This is the first of the eight elements of the eightfold path.

157

Nevertheless, Buddhism has never looked into gender constructs and gender identity as an aspect of ego. Both Anne Klein[2] and myself[3] have noted this oversight in previous articles. With twenty years of feminist reflections behind us, it seems inconceivable that a tradition so dedicated to noticing and reflecting on habitual patterns of conventional ego could have so completely overlooked such a basic dimension of ego. Feminist thought has made us intensely, acutely aware of how extensively our perceptions of and reactions to the world are dependent on gender, as well as on class, race, and ethnicity. Feminist thought has also made us aware of the extent to which gender is socially constructed, not given by biology—a conclusion that I think would have shocked most previous Buddhist commentators on the undesirability of female rebirth. Feminist thought has also explored how thoroughly gender stereotypes, when internalized, as they usually are in non-reflective people, shape and limit the possibilities one can envision or undertake. On the other hand, for all its explorations of the problems of male and female egos as constructed in patriarchal societies, feminism is only beginning to explore what a healthy, post-patriarchal sense of self might involve. Buddhism, with its long tradition of cultivating and exploring egolessness, has delved into this topic considerably, both theoretically and practically. Thus, these two systems of talking about the problems of ego have much to say to each other.

First, we must try to explicate what Buddhists mean by "ego" and "egolessness," especially since many feminists, on first hearing, think that Buddhist concepts of egolessness are completely irrelevant for them. Many terminological difficulties are encountered, since Western psychology usually sees the goal as developing a healthy ego, while Buddhists regard ego as the problem causing mental ill health. It should be obvious that the two traditions are using the same word in radically different ways.

Egolessness is one of the three basic traits of all sentient beings. It, along with suffering and impermanence, can be seen as the most basic Buddhist diagnosis of the human condition. Without exception, when analyzed realistically, all beings share this same fate; they suffer anxiety, they experience unending impermanence, and they lack a permanent soul-entity. Impermanence is the pivot point of these three traits as well as the easiest to grasp and concede, at least superficially. Surely everything changes. At some level, everyone can grasp that basic fact. But people resist change, which inevitably causes suffering and mental anguish. Furthermore, if everything is constantly changing and impermanent, how can we exempt our self, our ego, our identity from this general rule? We are fundamentally egoless, but that state of being is difficult to bear, so we constantly create styles of ego or self, which often cause us great problems. Furthermore, we almost constantly are subject to the illusion that our self must have some permanent core somewhere, so that the veil of ego becomes so thick that we cannot imagine being without it.

Buddhism constantly shifts between metaphysical and psychological meanings of the terms "ego" and "egolessness." Both are equally important in understanding what Buddhists mean by these terms, but the philosophical meanings are easier to grasp. Philosophically, the teachings about egolessness deny that there is any permanent, abiding, unchanging essence that is the "real person," whether the essence denied is the Hindu *atman*, which was the case in the philosophical milieu of early Buddhism, or the more familiar Christian personal and eternal soul. Often egolessness is seen as the companion of non-theism. "Two ideas are psychologically deep-rooted in man: self-protection and self-preservation. For self-protection, man has created God. . . . For self-preservation man has conceived the idea of a immortal soul or *Atman* which will live eternally."[4]

Two methods of demonstrating the truth of egolessness are important in Buddhism. The more familiar method is the analytical method, which looks deeply into the assumed self of conventional thinking. The self is broken down into its component parts, but no real essence is discovered underneath these component parts. "There is no unmoving mover behind the movement. It is only movement."[5] The synthetic method shows that there can be no essence that demarcates an individual as existing in reality, rather than merely at the level of conventional appearance, because all things are interdependent. As important, perhaps more important, than the theory of karma in explaining cause and effect, this concept of interdependent, co-arising (*pratityasamutpada*) emphasizes that nothing exists independent of its matrix, but only in interdependence with it. Thus, there can be no self, as anything more than a convenient and useful label for a particular momentary configuration of events in this vast web of interdependence and relationality.

The psychological experience of egolessness is more important, but also more difficult to catch, even though Buddhists say that flashes of intuitions into egolessness are constantly occurring.

> Fundamentally there is just open space, the *basic ground*, what we really are. Our most fundamental state of mind, before the creation of ego, is such that there is basic openness, basic freedom, a spacious quality; and we have now and have always had that openness. Take, for example, our everyday lives and thought patterns. When we see an object, in the first instant there is a sudden perception which has no logic or conceptualization at all; we just perceive the thing in the open ground.[6]

It is important, however, to undercut some common misconceptions about egolessness by stating what it is *not*. Egolessness is not a nihilistic condition nor the attainment of non-existence, as opposed to existence. It is not a blank vacuous state of non-perception and non-thinking. It is not an indifferent state of not caring what happens to one's self or others and it certainly has nothing to do with being so psychologically beaten and victimized that one acquiesces in whatever happens. It has nothing to do with being spineless and indifferent, with being a pushover for others' aggression. An egoless person is quite the opposite of a zombie. Rather, she is cheerful, calm, humorous, compassionate, empowered, and energized because she has dropped the burden of ego. She has found a sane, healthy, and mature way of being free *within* the world; she has discovered how to "find [her] ease in impermanence," to return again to that utterly clear comment from Suzuki Roshi.

Nevertheless, in the Buddhist diagnosis, that fluid, open, non-fixated way of being is too much for ordinary people to maintain. The discussion of egolessness quoted above moves directly into a discussion of the construction of ego. "Then immediately we panic and begin to rush about trying to add something to it, either trying to find a name for it or trying to find pigeon-holes in which we could locate or categorize it."[7] The panic results in oppositional duality—me and my perceptions, conceptions, states of consciousness dependent on objects experienced as "other." Gradually, we build a habitual, familiar and conventional style of reactions that is "ours," that allows us to cope in one way or another with all the stimuli and otherness that seems to be barraging us from all directions. We develop a sense of being an isolated entity confined in our subjectivity, of being or having an ego which we evaluate as more or less healthy, with which we are often dissatisfied. We also worry a great deal about protecting that ego, which is beginning to cause us a good deal of suffering. We cling to things that seem to be desirable; we fight off other things aggressively; and everything else we ignore.* Along the way, we have also somehow come to feel that this vague "sense of me-ness" deserves to be permanent and eternal. We have moved from experience of a psychological ego to belief in a Soul.

The link between this psychological or metaphysical ego and ethical dilemmas is very close.

> According to the teachings of the Buddha, the idea of self is an imaginary, false belief which has no corresponding reality, and it produces harmful thoughts of "me" and "mine," selfish desires, craving, attachment, hatred, ill-will, conceit, pride, egoism, and other defilements and impurities and problems. It is the source of all the troubles in the world from personal conflicts to wars between nations. In short, to this false view can be traced all the evils in the world.[8]

---

* These are the "three poisons," found at the hub of the "wheel of becoming" that appears so frequently in Tibetan Buddhist art.

In these few brief comments on ego and egolessness as they are understood in Buddhism, all the other major doctrines of the first turning are implicated. Ego protection is the prime motivator of the addictive clinging and fixation that inevitably produces suffering—the root problem to be solved by Buddhist disciplines. And, in many ways, egolessness is synonymous with the freedom proclaimed in the third noble truth. Thus, we clearly have touched a major nerve center of first-turning teachings, closely connected with all the other major strands of basic Buddhist teaching.

It is difficult to summarize feminist thinking on these issues in a similarly succinct way because feminism lacks a similar consensus on these issues. Nevertheless, when we bring these Buddhist ideas into feminist discussions of the same territory, which emphasize that egos are gendered, we should not be surprised if the results are potent for both systems. Except for the fact that Buddhism has not looked at gender as a component of ego, a major oversight that, when corrected, has very significant implications for Buddhism, the two systems are remarkably consonant, despite rather sharp differences of terminology. Regarding issues of gender and ego, Buddhism and feminism are more like each other than either is like Western patriarchal thought, in that both explore how dysfunctional habitual patterns of mind cause great suffering.

First, we should discuss several objections to these Buddhist ideas that one frequently hears from feminists. The classic apocryphal story concerns the puzzled feminists who have just listened to a Buddhist speaker discussing how ego is the source of all human problems and how by dismantling ego, we can achieve some freedom. They comment, "That sounds like a good religion—for men!" Some assume that the Buddhist situation is like the Christian situation, as analyzed by Valerie Saiving[9] and others. She points out that men, who tend toe self-aggrandizing, preach the need for self-effacement to congregations full of women who have already internalized that virtue and need more self-confidence. This frequent comment results from misunderstanding the Buddhist use of the term "ego," and probably from Buddhist speakers who are not alert to their potential to confuse listeners by their use of the term. In popular conventional Western usage, it is assumed that everyone has an ego, that you can't function without one, but that it is somehow measurable or quantifiable, and that some people have "too much ego" while others have a "weak ego." Often, women, who tend to define themselves through relationships more than do men, are thought to have "weak ego boundaries," which some see as a problem and others laud. But it is often claimed by feminists that Buddhist concepts of ego and egolessness would be more relevant for men than for women because many women "need more ego, a stronger self-concept, not less ego."

From the Buddhist point of view, someone who is intensely co-dependent and someone who is intensely macho or self-aggrandizing suffer equally from ego. Ego, as we have seen, is any style of habitual patterns and responses that clouds over the clarity and openness of basic human nature. Self-effacement is just a style of ego different from self-aggrandizement, but both equally cause suffering to self and others. "Ego" names the defence mechanisms, projections, and other tactics habitually used to cope with and ward off direct experience. All ordinary people have some ego-style, some style of grasping and fixation. The amount of ego really isn't quantifiable; someone who is forceful doesn't have "more ego" than someone who is shy and retiring.

Feminists, concerned with the kinds of problems women develop in patriarchal systems, might not immediately see the relevance of this more inclusive and generic discussion of ego. However, it is helpful to see clearly that people with "weak egos," in Western terms, don't really need to build up a "strong ego," in Western terms, before they can get on to the basic task of becoming healthy, no longer needing to cover over the openness and fluidity of basic enlightened human nature. One can go directly from the unhealthy and often overly weak or co-dependent ego styles that characterize women in patriarchy to the health of egolessness.

Though I have already tried to defuse some of the more common misconceptions about egolessness, the tendency to equate a deficient ego-style characterized by weakness or excessive timidity with "not having enough ego" justifies some further comments. Buddhists have never meant by egolessness to deny that we have some identity and sense of self. They have simply meant that identity involves no reified Self. They have also meant that, unless we have worked through considerable psychological material by means of appropriate meditation and contemplation, our sense of self will be unhealthy and cause great problems. But a healthy, functioning sense of self is perfectly okay from a Buddhist point of view. That's not what's being dismantled when ego is dismantled. In fact, that healthy sense of self or identity is necessary for further spiritual development. As Westerners, also familiar with various therapies become more involved in Buddhist spiritual disciplines, it becomes clearer that a severely emotionally damaged person from an extremely dysfunctional situation needs a healthy sense of self to pursue Buddhist spiritual disciplines, which, by themselves, may not be sufficient to heal the emotional deprivations. That healthy sense of self arises with awareness* and gives rise to calmness, equanimity, and energy. This is the same thing as being aware of feelings in a healthy way, not overwhelmed and possessed by them, as is the case with an

---

* See Ann Klein, "Finding a Self," pp. 196–99, for a very helpful discussion of the role of awareness, as defined by Buddhists, in finding a healthy functioning self.

ego-ridden sense of self. An egoless person is not one who has suppressed feelings, as is so often mistakenly stated, but one who can accommodate all feelings well.

The feminist contribution to discussions of ego and egolessness, as defined by Buddhism, is to demonstrate, incontrovertibly and powerfully, the extent to which gender-fixation is part of ego, and therefore, damaging and destructive. As already mentioned several times, this aspect of ego has been totally over-looked by Buddhism, but bringing together these two methods of understanding ego is quite provocative. In feminist analysis, one's ego includes and is conditioned by gender identity. According to classic feminist analysis, in patriarchal societies, the male takes on the ego of being an autonomous self who objectifies the world around him, including women. He then projects repressed ego traits onto women, and other groups whom he identifies as "other." Women then, to a greater or a lesser degree, internalize and manifest those qualities that have been projected onto them—passivity, intuitiveness, emotionality, concern with relatedness, lack of independence, etc. The stronger and more rigid the gender roles in a society, the more likely it is that egostyles will conform to gender stereotypes. Nevertheless, women always find some ways of coping with and fighting against what is projected onto them as well,[10] which means that their egos are not wholly determined by male projections.

Nevertheless, according to feminist analysis, patriarchal societies or societies with strong gender roles, can never be adequately described generically. One needs to pay attention to the specifics of women's experiences. Furthermore, according to feminist analysis, probably no aspect of experience is so central or so conditions one's ego as one's gender identity. This becomes all the more so when one's social and economic options are almost completely constrained by one's gender, as is the case in so many patriarchal societies. So for Buddhist analysis to overlook how massively and centrally gender constitutes and creates ego is rather serious.

Feminist analyses of gender and ego include two rather distinctive tendencies, both of which have Buddhist parallels. In earlier feminist thinking the dominant tendency was to emphasize the negativity and limitations of femininity, as constructed by patriarchy. The emphasis was on what men do to women, how damaged women's sense of self becomes under such conditions, how women are limited and denied fulfillment of their potential by patriarchal gender roles. Important also to these discussions of feminine ego as constructed by patriarchy were demonstrations that women actually don't conform to the stereotypes of femininity, nor men to stereotypes of masculinity, for that matter. These analyses deconstruct masculinity and femininity, showing that behind the ideals or the stereotypes, there is little corresponding reality. This line of argument is quite similar to the Buddhist analytic demonstration that behind the component parts of the personality, there is no reified self. In both cases, we think we are a certain way, but when we examine ourselves, what seems so solid and definite fractures and disappears. We think we are feminine, but discover that doesn't mean anything specific that we can really define. We think we exist as substantial (and feminine or masculine) selves, but there is nothing behind the shifting moving components of personality.

Later feminist analysis of ego does tend to find significant differences between the typical feminine and masculine egos. A significant group of thinkers[11] stresses that women tend to define their identity more in terms of their relationships than do men, who are more likely to seek, pursue, and value autonomous selfhood. Many feminist analysts link these gender differences in ego-style with patriarchal child-rearing practices, which give women almost total responsibility for nurturance and early child care.[12] But something else has changed. The earlier feminist analysis disliked femininity and wanted to free women of feminine egos. It is difficult to read later feminist literature without the impression that what is being deconstructed is not femininity but the autonomous ego more likely to be valued by men. Women's sense of relatedness and interconnectedness, while it can become unhealthy co-dependence, reveals a deep truth about what it is to be human. We are not separate egos. This analysis is strikingly similar to the Buddhist synthetic demonstration that ego really does not exist as a reified entity because all things arise in dependence upon causes and conditions and mutually condition all other things. In both cases, the related self, the interdependent self, is all that there is. Further comparative studies of feminist analyses of the ego as related self and Buddhist theories of interdependence could be quite valuable and illuminating.

Buddhist and feminist discussions of ego involve another important similarity. Buddhist analyses, quoted earlier, speak of the creation of ego as the creation of an oppositional duality that covers over basic openness and fluidity. Once the basic openness and spaciousness of human nature is forgotten, everything becomes a matter of self and other, with the tremendous self-referencing and duality of ego dominating all perceptions and conceptions. This Buddhist discussion of ego as the creation of the duality of self and other is almost identical with the feminist discussion of what men do to women in patriarchy.* In the process of creating language, culture, and society, men arrogate selfhood to themselves and regard women as the other whom they may treat as objects,

---

* This comment refers to Simone de Beauvoir's classic discussion of woman as "other" in male-dominated modes of thought, utilized heavily in the feminist methodological appendix of this book and frequently quoted.

a process almost identical with the Buddhist understanding of how ego is formed by reference to "other." [13]

Buddhists would probably argue, rightly in my view, that women also go through this process in forming egos, even when they are forming a dependent ego based on patriarchal projections. The process is too basic to having a human psyche, to being in the human realm, to be limited to men. In this situation, however, women, by virtue of being "the other," of being outsiders in patriarchal society, are in a better position to become aware of such oppositional duality and to think past it than are men, who, not being the victims of duality, frequently cannot imagine any other mode of being in the world. Therefore, much current feminist thought is an attempt to verbalize ways of knowing and being that do not depend on oppositional dualities. Buddhists have long recommended the same thing with their concept of egolessness. Therefore, discussions of the egoless state of awareness, tranquillity, and energy, and the methods of cultivating it practiced by Buddhist spiritual disciplines, might be quite useful to feminists.

Useful as the Buddhist non-dualistic understanding of egolessness may be to feminists, the feminist understanding of gender is even more useful to Buddhists. Feminist discussions of gender provide a major critique of conventional Buddhism. Ego has often been called a pigeon-holing device by Buddhists. It allows one to objectify phenomena and distance one's self from the immediacy, brilliance, and vividness of experience. Certainly one of the most pervasive and powerful pigeon-holing devices of all is gender. "That's a man. I can expect these behaviors. I should behave in this way." "That's a woman. She can't do these things. She will demonstrate these traits and characteristics. Her function in life is to do the following." Such subconscious gossip is almost continuous. And in terms of Buddhist analysis, there's no place to put it except in the category of "ego," as well as the category of *samsara*. One certainly couldn't place it within the mode of egoless, enlightened being in the world!

Nevertheless, much of the Buddhist institutional world is constituted by patterns of ego that rely on gender to pigeon-hole the world. Stereotypically, males are thought to be more "spiritual" and able to develop calmness and tranquillity, even though male anatomy itself seems to war against these qualities. In every realm, religious or secular, men have precedence and dominance over women, as is evidenced by the eight special rules subjugating nuns to monks. The preference for maleness extends even to the next life. All these practices of gender privilege and gender hierarchy encourage clinging to male ego; they do not encourage egolessness. Strangely, quite un-Buddhist attitudes—pride (in being male), scorn for other beings, clinging to and fixation upon being male—are condoned and encouraged by this situation. Thus,

Buddhist institutions promote one of the more painful and pervasive manifestations of ego, an untenable situation, to say the least. It has always seemed strange to me that a tradition so keenly aware of the perils and pitfalls of ego has not been equally keen in its recognition that gender-privilege is one of the more destructive manifestations of ego.

One can see all these attitudes quite rampantly displayed in a contemporary Buddhist account of the nuns' order. After explaining that women, because of their biology, have more suffering than men and more suffering *does* mean inferior karma, the author begins to explain the rules for nuns. But before launching into the discussion, a warning must be given:

> It is possible that the facts presented so far and the account of the establishment of the Bhikkunni-Sangha below may displease some women. The truth, however, is not always palatable and pleasing. In case displeasure or anger should arise, these manifestations of aversion should be examined: from whence to they arise? Wounded vanity? Damaged pride? Then this is conceit, a mental factor as far from the practice of Dhamma as humility is near to it.[14]

One could as readily ask this author to examine from whence comes his pride in being male, his assurance that things are as they should be regarding gender hierarchies, and his condescending attitudes toward women? The answer would be that they come from a socially constructed male ego that is *samsaric* and unenlightened—not from anything close to an egoless perspective.

If gender, or at least using gender to confer privilege, is one of the deep-seated tricks of ego, how would one correlate gender with egolessness? Would someone who does not use gender to pigeon-hole the world not know whether she was male or female? Would she be unable to determine the sex of someone whom she encounters? I doubt it! But he would not use sex as a basis to organize the world or the *sangha*; she would not use people's sex to limit her expectations of them; most of all, she would not limit or categorize herself based on sex. If we may make the distinction between sex as a biological given and gender as an ego-filled and ego-ridden social construct based on sex, the enlightened or egoless person would be aware of sex but would have transcended the need to rely on gender. Such a person would become androgynous, perhaps even in physical appearance, as is the case with some old adepts who have practiced the egoless life for a long time.

Using the analytic categories of feminism and the insight born of the feminist understanding that gender is an aspect of ego, we can generate a powerful critique of conventional Buddhist habits and stereotypes. Seeing gender fixation and gender privilege as an aspect of ego makes Buddhist patriarchy inadmissible *on Buddhist grounds*. This critique is much more powerful to a Buddhist for we have shown that gender privilege is not compatible with Buddhism on Buddhism's terms, not just on feminism's terms. A Buddhist patriarch could ignore feminism with ease, and probably would. He should pay more attention to Buddhist demonstrations that patriarchy is contrary to Buddhism, that in fact it fosters one of the most basic *samsaric* traps discovered by Buddhist spiritual practice, that it fosters ego rather than egolessness.

GENDER AND THE ETHICS OF NON-HARMING

The second component unit of the eightfold path consists of *shila*, which connotes both discipline and ethical conduct. Right speech, right action, and right livelihood, often taught by "negative language" (one is told what to avoid, rather than what to cultivate), are the classic content of Buddhist ethical conduct. As *shila* is taught in the three-*yana* perspective (though not necessarily in the Theravada perspective), the message is one of restraint, of self-cultivation through non-harming and contemplation. At this stage of development, it is important to pull back for a while, to pull into one's self and to develop the foundations of sane and wholesome habits and modes of interacting. In the beginning of the journey, one does not have the capacity or the ability to worry about saving others. It is enough to take care of one's self and to tame habitual negative patterns to some extent. If one's negative patterns are tempered, that will be quite helpful, not only to one's self, but also to others. The statement that stays with me, almost like a slogan, suggests that if only we could all stop doing all the negative, destructive, harmful things, stemming from passion, aggression, and ignorance, that we do to ourselves and to other people, the world would be immensely improved. But if we are not content with restraint and inaction while we purify negative habitual patterns, if we insist on saving the world while we still act mainly out of passion, aggression, and ignorance, we don't have much to work with and create more harm than help. Thus, the whole ethic of the first-turning adds up, in one word, to non-harming. All the ethical guidelines of first-turning teachings are geared to help a person to restrain negative tendencies, thereby promoting non-harming.

Insofar as Buddhism encourages self-development, restraint, and non-harming as the basis of ethical life, it sometimes accused of being "selfish." Some judge that there isn't enough outgoing compassion and concern for the world. But in the "three-*yana*" perspective, such focus on one's self is the immediate first step. The fruition of the *hinayana* is said to be "individual liberation,"[15] personal freedom from negative habitual tendencies, at least to some extent. Buddhists disagree over what should come next; the major debate between early Indian Buddhism and Mahayana Buddhism was whether individual liberation was sufficient or whether it was the foundation for a further journey onto the Bodhisattva path. But there is no disagreement that self-development, leading to individual liberation, must be the first step. In Buddhist perspective, such attention to self-development is the most compassionate thing one could possibly do; otherwise one will be trying to help others aggressively, on the basis of one's own confusion and negativity.

This interpretation of *shila* intersects well with feminist concerns and has implications for gender issues, some of which will be explored here and others of which will be discussed as part of a feminist reconstruction of Buddhism. To emphasize non-harming and self-development as the basic step in the Buddhist ethical path affords feminists both a rationale to slow down when necessary and a very powerful critique of the status quo.

For women, socialized not to take themselves seriously, to take care of everyone else before attending to their own needs, such a map of the spiritual path is welcome and relevant. The permission granted to stop, to contemplate, to assess one's direction, is not often given to women. Beyond that, the permission to develop one's self along fruitful lines that meet with one's own vision is routinely denied to women. Often they are taught to think of themselves as selfish if they even long to take time, take stock, and develop themselves in response to their inner voice. How refreshing to hear the message that this is the most useful and compassionate thing they could do, both for themselves and others.

Useful as this map of the path of ethical development can be, it can be used in unfortunate ways, as a tool against those, such as feminists, who are involved in social action, who organize, demonstrate, or otherwise make visible their unhappiness with the status quo and their vision for an alternative order. Many American Buddhists became Buddhist after considerable involvement with various protest movements of the sixties. After some years of serious involvement with Buddhist spiritual disciplines, they often look back upon their pre-Buddhist involvements and see a great deal of ego and anger in themselves and their companions in the movement. They then draw the conclusion that meditating in order to dismantle ego is superior to being involved in causes. Because their own pre-Buddhist involvement in social action was ego-filled, they draw the conclusion that social action inevitably feeds the ego and damages the spirituality of those who become involved in causes. Many Buddhist women no longer see feminism as something with which they wish to be involved for such reasons. Often I have been chided by both male and female Buddhists for "not getting over feminism." A Buddhist should not be involved in any position, I am told, but should be detached.

In one form or another, this line of argumentation crops up again and again in Buddhism. On this basis, criticisms of passivity and lack of social ethics are leveled, sometimes fairly, against Buddhism. To Buddhists who make such arguments, and to their critics, one can only reply that certainly the emotional tone of one's involvement in social causes changes radically with long-term spiritual discipline. But being involved in social causes is not antithetical to spiritual development, despite what some jaded Buddhists say. And detached social activism is not acquiescence, despite what some social activists say. Rather, the two enhance each other in ways that are immensely helpful for feminists or anyone else who takes permission to use the prophetic voice within Buddhism.

When one combines spiritual discipline with continued social concern, one becomes much more detached from success or failure* and much less ego-involved in the cause. But that does not mean that one loses all concern, which some non-meditators involved in social causes fear, nor that one demonstrates detachment through lack of concern, as some Buddhists demand. Rather, as *prajna* develops, one sees more clearly what needs to be done and how to do it. *Prajna* and detachment actually develop together as one practices Buddhist spiritual disciplines. Thus, at the same time as one sees more clearly what needs to be done, one's ego-involvement in the project is decreasing. Detachment and decreasing ego-involvement provide a reservoir of strength and humor that can help protect from heartbreak and burnout, thus protecting and strengthening one's ability to stay with a cause, despite setbacks, for the long term.

Finally, this ethic of non-harming and self-cultivation, when combined with feminist values and vision, provides a powerful feminist critique of conventional Buddhist patriarchy. Quite simply, once we see how harmful patriarchal systems are to women, and to men as well, the ethic of non-harming puts a stop to such conventions and practices, if one takes that ethic seriously. The argument is completely clear, given the Buddhist emphasis on non-harming as the basis for all ethical conduct and the feminist demonstration of the harm wrought by male dominance. Furthermore, I believe Buddhists long ago conceded that patriarchal systems are harmful, at least to women. That is why they provided methods to overcome female birth in the next life, the only solution they saw to the problem. What the classical analysis did not provide is the realization that male dominance is not that beneficial to men either. Even more important, what classical Buddhism failed to imagine is that there are any viable alternatives to male dominance and patriarchy. Additionally, the classical Buddhist resources, even though they were aware that the conventions of patriarchal society were harmful to women, lacked a tradition of and rationale for criticiz-

---

* This dilemma is exactly the problem raised by the famous Hindu scripture, the *Bhagadvad Gita*. It too suggests that action with detachment from the results of one's acts is the most appropriate course.

ing, changing, and reforming social institutions. But feminism, as a mode of the prophetic voice, includes both the vision for a less harmful social order and the will to voice criticisms and work for change. Clearly, according to the ethic of non-harming, the traditional values of Buddhism are more in line with feminist Buddhism than with conventional Buddhism.

SAMADHI AND SELF-DEVELOPMENT

Buddhist meditation disciplines are powerful techniques for self-cultivation and self-development. A major emphasis of first-turning teachings is that to dismantle ego and undercut its pain-producing habitual tendencies, ongoing disciplines of meditation and contemplation are essential. In the simple and basic practices of mindfulness and awareness,[16] one is taught how to experience thoughts without repressing them, judging them, or acting them out. One is taught to observe and notice, to increase awareness, to become much more familiar with one's thought patterns and habitual tendencies without immediately trying to fix them or change them. The purpose of such self-cultivation through meditation practice is the individual liberation discussed above. Many Western Buddhists, also familiar with various therapies and self-help endeavors, easily interpret individual liberation as the slow growth in self-esteem and self-approval that comes from knowing one's self quite well. Many of the Asian teachers most familiar with the Western milieu encourage this interpretation.

For women whose egos have been shaped by patriarchy, and whose sense of self has been seriously damaged, whether by internalizing or by fighting its values, this process can be powerfully healing on two levels. Nothing so distorts women's sense of self under patriarchy as the self-hatred that many women feel towards themselves for being female. Or if the feeling is not self-hatred, its counterpart is frustration that one is being shortchanged and denied one's potential because one is female. Even in that case, the woman still tends to blame herself for not being right, to feel immense anger and frustration at her lot. Such feelings lead to a poisoned and a poisonous life, but they are difficult to avoid under patriarchy. It is clear from materials quoted in the historical chapters that women have had similar feelings throughout Buddhist history.

I will never forget the immense relief I felt when I finally realized there was nothing wrong with me because I am female, but that what was wrong was patriarchy and its denial of women. In my case that transformative experience did not come through the agency of either feminism or Buddhism, for neither were yet available to me. But Buddhist meditation disciplines have strengthened that relief and release immeasurably. Once again, the combination of Buddhism and feminism reinforce and strengthen each other. As a feminist, I do not want from Buddhism techniques for avoiding female rebirth in the future. I want techniques for developing individual liberation and self-acceptance now and the courage and skill to keep up the battle, even with Buddhism, now and in the future. I have not been disappointed.

Part of the package I had not bargained for. Like many feminists, I was quite enmeshed in my anger, which seemed like a protection, like a necessary way of coping and being, given male-dominated academia and religions. In Buddhist terms, I had created an ego out of feminist anger, and I wanted to protect it. I had no idea that seriously practicing basic mindfulness-awareness practices would challenge that ego. It was somewhat disorienting when that solid ego began to dissolve a bit, when I found anger less personally satisfying than I had previously. For a while I thought I was losing my bearings as a feminist. But then I began to realize that something else was happening. The cloudy, murky emotion of anger was beginning to transmute. The energy was still there and still the same energy, but it was expressing itself much more frequently as analytical clarity, without the turbulent emotionalism upon which I had relied.* Though I was surprised at first, it is not too surprising that I became a much more effective spokesperson for feminism when I spoke gently, softly, and clearly, but without any decrease in strength of conviction, which came more and more naturally. Not too surprisingly, I also had more energy with which to continue to struggle through conceptual puzzles regarding how to express feminist knowing and being, and more humor with which to continue the sometimes seemingly hopeless battles with institutions, both Buddhist and academic.

Perhaps I am simply saying the Buddhist meditation is a powerful ally and source of strength and growth for a feminist. A feminist who is also a Buddhist meditator will never be content with the Buddhist status quo—and she will have the strength to seek to change Buddhism rather than to change her female birth!

---

* These comments describe the process of the transmutation of anger into "Mirror-like Wisdom." In Vajrayana Buddhism, anger is one of the five root *klesha*-s and its transmuted, enlightened manifestation is Mirror-like Wisdom. For a clear discussion of transmutation in general and this particular transmutation, see Trungpa, *Cutting through Spiritual Materialism*, pp. 224–30. For a personal discussion, see Rita M. Gross, "Feminism from the Perspective of Buddhist Practice," *Buddhist-Christian Studies* I (1981), pp. 73–82.

12

Gender and Emptiness:
Feminist Comments on the Mahayana

The earliest, best-known, and most widespread Mahayana teachings are a philosophical concept—*shunyata*—and an ethical precept—the Bodhisattva path. Here we are considering them as teachings of the second turning, following the system that sees some of the later Mahayana concepts as yet another complete revolution of the wheel of *dharma*, a classification scheme not agreed upon even by all Mahayanists. Mythically, the Buddha himself taught the doctrine of emptiness at Rajagriha on Vulture Peak Mountain to a congregation of both Bodhisattvas and *arahants*, as narrated in Prajnaparamita literature, especially the Heart Sutra, the most famous and widely used succinct summary of Mahayana teachings.[1] In the "three turnings" organizational framework, the second-turning teachings are particularly associated with the Madyamika school of Mahayana philosophy, while the third-turning teachings are particularly associated with the school often called the Yogacara school. However, the concepts of emptiness and the Bodhisattva path are also centrally important to all Mahayanists.

The second-turning refers especially to a specific emphasis on and interpretation of emptiness. The interpretation of emptiness to be discussed in this chapter emphasizes "what *shunyata* is *not*." This interpretation is the foundation for understanding that "*shunyata is not nothing*"[2] in subsequent sections of this feminist analysis of key Buddhist concepts. Furthermore, in the context of this chapter, the philosophical outlook and the ethical precept are interdependent with each other: because emptiness is, the bodhisattva path is possible.

SHUNYATA, TWO TRUTHS, AND GENDER:
THE CLASSIC BUDDHIST ARGUMENT

Even more than the term "egolessness," the term *shunyata*, "emptiness," confuses both outsider and insider. Buddhist texts themselves warn of the ease with which the concept can be misunderstood and of the extremely serious consequences of such misunderstanding. Like many another Buddhist concept that posits what it not, rather than what is, non-Buddhists have persistently attributed to it a negativity that is foreign to the concept itself. The concept has proved interesting and elusive to Westerners, especially those who look to Buddhism as a possible source of philosophical and spiritual inspiration for dealing with certain difficult issues in Western thought.[3] Perhaps no other Buddhist concept has attracted similar attention or proved more interesting to such seekers.

As we have seen, the concept of emptiness has already been directly and explicitly connected with the issue of gender by Buddhists. It is the only Buddhist concept to have been used in classical Buddhist texts to criticize Buddhist practices of gender discrimination. Buddhists long ago saw that, logically, the fact of emptiness makes gender discriminations, like all other discriminations, inappropriate.

Though arguments and analyses regarding *shunyata* can become incredibly complex and, therefore, confusing, if one keeps returning to the basics, much of the complexity and confusion can be defused. It is simplest to see that, from the Mahayana perspective, *shunyata* is the logical outcome of thoroughly understanding egolessness and interdependent co-arising. When things are said to be empty, the important question is "empty of what?" The answer is that they are empty of, or lack "own-being," inherent existence. They do not exist in and of themselves, but only relative to their matrix, dependent on causes and conditions. For Mahayana Buddhism, such emptiness is thoroughgoing and pervasive. Nothing escapes it to exist inherently, in its own right, independent of its matrix, not subject to causes and conditions. There is no exempted, privileged corner somewhere, whether a Supreme Being or an eternal Soul, or even Buddhist *nirvana*, that is not completely and thoroughly characterized by *shunyata*.

Mahayanists have always emphasized that emptiness is nothing but thoroughgoing egolessness. The early Buddhist analysis primarily focused on the first object of reification, the thing most likely to be taken as really existing, substantially, inherently, and eternally by those who absolutize conventional psychological reactions—the Self or Soul. That reified ego was examined, broken down into its component parts, and found to be lacking any metaphysical glue that held those parts together, which means that ego does not exist. Instead of focusing only on ego itself, Mahayana analysis also focuses on the constituents of ego, which in the Mahayana analysis, are comprised of just basic space, openness, all-pervasive egolessness, *shunyata*. Mahayanists claim that earlier Buddhist analysis stopped too soon; it understood clearly the egolessness of ego, but did not thoroughly comprehend the egolessness of the components of ego; instead it reified them. The Mahayanists claim that even at the subtle level of analysis involved in discerning the component parts of ego, we do not find "ultimate realities at all but only mental constructions."[4] One finds no fixed reference points, but only empty, interdependent, relatively existing fluidity.

Mahayanists claim that fully understanding the doctrine of interdependent co-arising, which can be seen as the central doctrine of early Buddhism, compels one to the conclusion of all-pervading emptiness. "To be dependent means to be devoid of self-nature or own-being (*svabhava*). What is devoid of self-nature is said to be empty (*sunya*). Conditionality and emptiness are the same thing."[5] Therefore, the most famous line of Nagarjuna's root text on the Madyamika: "*Pratityasamutpada* is *shunyata*."* According to Mahayana analysis, *nothing*, including the unconditioned elements posited by earlier Buddhist analysis, escapes this verdict. They exist only as mental constructs and only in relation to the conditioned elements; they do not exist as ultimate realities, since they are imaginable or thinkable only in relation to the conditioned elements. The unconditioned elements, including *nirvana*, are unthinkable by themselves; they are thinkable only in relation to, and therefore dependent upon, conditioned elements. Therefore, such asserted unconditioned elements cannot exist as genuinely unconditioned, but only as empty, conditioned interdependent, relative elements. This is the logic behind the assertions that so often baffle students of Buddhism and that so infuriated advocates of the earlier Buddhist systems—that *samsara* and *nirvana* can be equated, and that the Four Noble Truths are not absolutes.

Mahayanists see this analysis as the Middle Way, so important to all Buddhist endeavors, between eternalism and nihilism, between granting ultimacy either to assertions or to negations. But they also see this middle way as a razor's edge, from which it is easy to fall into either extreme. Falling into the extreme of nihilism was always considered to be the more dangerous pitfall. To emphasize this point, Mahanyanists warned of the "poison of *shunyata*," which they compare to a snake seized by the wrong end; it can easily wound a person fatally. Probably the most common version of the poison of *shunyata* is belief that, since, everything is relative rather than ultimate, nothing really matters and one can do anything one wants. To see emptiness, however, cuts only one's habitual tendency towards fixated attachment to things as if they were ultimate, not their existence in relative terms. Some things are still more or less helpful or satisfying than other things, even in a world devoid of ultimates.

The other way of retreating from the razor's edge is probably more abstract and less likely, though it is a way of understanding emptiness that often allures Westerners. It is often assumed that emptiness is what everything is made of, that it is a kind of negative substance underlying the appearance of things. Such

---

* David J. Kalupahana, *Nagarjuna: The Philosophy of the Middle Way* (Albany, NY: SUNY Press, 1986), p. 339. "We state that whatever is dependent origination, that is emptiness."

assumptions sometimes underlie the equation of God and emptiness that is so popular in some comparisons of Buddhism and Christianity. But Mahayanists are careful to point out that emptiness should not itself be reified. *Everything* lacks own-being, including emptiness, which is a tool used to cut conceptual fixation, not an alternative concept out of which to build a worldview. It is important to realize not just emptiness, but the emptiness of emptiness.

Because this understanding of emptiness would undercut all assertions, Mahayanists also developed a tool, already known to early Indian Buddhism, for using and evaluating language more effectively. It was recognized that there are two levels of language, or more accurately, two levels of truth—absolute truth and relative truth. It was always conceded by Buddhists that conventional ways of speaking about persons and things are convenient and useful, relatively speaking. That all things are empty of own-being does not obviate their relative existence and the need to operate in the world of relative things. To believe otherwise would be to fall into the poison of *shunyata*. It also must be conceded that within the realm of relative truth, some analyses are more cogent and some actions more appropriate than others. The temptation is to fixate and reify. The constant reminder that relative truth is only relative truth, not absolute or ultimate, cuts that temptation. The level of absolute truth transcends verbalization or conceptualization. To say anything at all about it is already to return to the level of relative truth, according to Buddhism, which does not mean that one should never speak of Absolute Reality, but only that one should regard one's words as nothing more than tools and pointers. The difficulty of speaking about Truth accurately does not, for Buddhists, undercut the expectation that it is possible to experience intuition into Things-As-They-Are (*tathata*).

Fortunately, some implications of these concepts to the problem of gender are found in classic Buddhist texts from which I quoted extensively in the historical chapter on Mahayana Buddhism. Those arguments need only be summarized here.

The application is quite simple. "Male" and "female," like all other labels and designations, are empty and lack substantial reality. Therefore, they cannot be used in a rigid and fixed way to delimit people. In the classic Mahayana texts, this argument is used against those who hold to a belief that high levels of spiritual attainment and Buddhist understanding cannot be combined with a female body. As we have seen, girls and women demonstrate by their skill in presenting complex Buddhist concepts that women can attain high levels of accomplishment. They also demonstrate how fluid sexual identity can be, as they change their sex into the male sex, and sometimes back again. All this can happen because maleness and femaleness do not exist as fixed, inherently existing forms, but only as convenient designations and mere tokens. And finally, they argue decisively that gender traits cannot really be found; therefore, they cannot be used as a basis for discrimination or challenges to change one's body into a male body in order to prove that one's understanding is as deep as it appears to be.

The goddess of the *Vimalakirtinirdesa Sutra* says it best, in words that could be echoed by many a contemporary liberal or equal- rights feminist. After being taunted to change her sex, as genuine proof of the depth of her understanding of emptiness (as if having a penis helped one understand abstract concepts), she says: "I have been here for twelve years and have looked for the innate characteristics of the female sex and haven't been able to find them."[6] Many a woman, held back from her life choices and unable to find comfort or relevance in the female gender role, has made similar statements about the lack of inherent, essential traits of femininity, supposedly possessed by all women, by virtue of their female anatomy. These traits simply cannot be found, even in the quantified research of contemporary psychology. Furthermore, the attempt to limit and classify people on the basis of sex, to say that women can't do something or that men should behave in a certain way, is to make absolute determinations and discriminations on the basis of a relative, empty trait. Or one could say that such judgments and limitations absolutize the relative. In either case, conventional social arrangements, including those common to Buddhist institutions contradict the essential Mahayana teaching of emptiness.

Though not explicitly citing the theory of the two truths, these texts also utilize that concept. After changing herself into a man and her interlocutor into a woman, the goddess says to him (who is now temporarily "her"), "Just as you are not really a woman but appear to be female in form, all women also only appear to be female in form but are not really women. Therefore, the Buddha said all are not really men or women."[7] In terms of the two truths, the level of convention and appearance is the level of gender roles and stereotypes, but at the level of absolute truth, "all are not really men or women." Notice that, consonant with the unspeakability of absolute truth, the text does not try to say what people really are beyond maleness and femaleness, but it does state clearly that they are not *really*, but only apparently, men or women.

The conclusions to be drawn are obvious and were drawn in theory in the Buddhist texts, though the practical applications of those conclusions have never been integrated into Buddhist institutions and everyday life. You cannot predict, on the basis of gender, who is likely to be able to comprehend and practice "the dharma which is neither male nor female."[8] The whole apparatus of preselecting people for roles on the basis of their gender, of forcing people to fit gender roles, and of limiting their options on the basis of gender would become inadmissible if the emptiness and relativity of maleness and femaleness were to be taken seriously.

Strong as these traditional arguments from emptiness, the assertions that the "*dharma* is neither male nor female" and that maleness and femaleness do not really exist, may be, they are not sufficient to undercut patriarchal conventions. These assertions are certainly useful and accurate. But they do not really break free of the androcentrism that so pervades Buddhist thought. The Buddhist statement that "the *dharma* is neither male nor female" is strikingly similar to the Christian Pauline statement that "in Christ there is neither male nor female," a statement that, however often quoted, has not kept Christianity from developing male dominance, any more than its Buddhist parallel has been effective in ridding Buddhism of male dominance. It is important to ascertain why.

In both cases, the statement about the irrelevance of gender is made in an androcentric context. Given that context, those statements are only superficially gender neutral. In fact, they always mean, "You can make it, even if you are female." They never mean, "You can make it even if you are male." Often the sex-neutral language hides the fact that women become acceptable only by transcending their femaleness and becoming "manly." They are supposedly given the opportunity to match the human norm, but that human norm is collapsed into the male ideal. Men are rarely, if ever, expected to become "unmanly" to the extent that women are expected to become "unfeminine" in order to achieve the same level of spiritual attainment, though, to be fair, it must be admitted that men must transcend their culture's version of the macho male. The point is, however, that the ideal "spiritual person," for both Buddhism and Christianity, is not androgynous or neutral, and certainly is not feminine; it is male, and the qualities that make a person spiritual are conflated with the qualities that make a person male, while the qualities that make a person overtly female are shunned as spiritual ideals by both traditions.* Therefore, concepts of sex-neutrality as a corrective to androcentrism are never sufficient because the neutral ideal is in fact much more male than female. As a result, both Buddhism and Christianity waver between a male-defined sex-neutrality that a few women might be able to achieve and an outright favoring of biological males. Clearly, these two options are not sufficient. When we discuss emptiness further in connection with the third-turning and its intuition that emptiness is not nothing, we will discover other dimensions of emptiness on which to base a vision of post-patriarchal Buddhism.

---

* Rosemary Ruether has demonstrated that this kind of thinking is commonplace in Christianity. "Misogyny and Virginal Feminism in the Fathers of the Church," Rosemary Ruether, ed., *Religion and Sexism: Images of Women in the Jewish and Christian Traditions* (New York: Simon and Schuster, 1974), pp. 150–83. At the level of popular culture, one need only remember the old prefeminist compliment: "You think like a man!"

Despite the ways in which insight into emptiness cuts clinging and fixation, people unsympathetic to prophetic criticism of the status quo, attempt, on the basis of the idea of emptiness, to defuse feminist objections to the conventional ways of proceeding and to undermine feminist visions for transformation. The same objections and arguments are brought against any kind of prophetic movement toward social activism in Buddhism. Sometimes, it is argued, all supposed injustice only occurs at the relative level. Since only relative problems are involved, things are not so urgent and "it doesn't really matter." We can just let things slide or remain as they are, rather than seek to rectify them, because "in emptiness, injustice and inappropriate social institutions don't really exist." Such thinking is very common, even on the part of Buddhist women, who though aware of sexism within Buddhist institutions, do not want to become existentially involved in dealing with that sexism. However, such complacency participates in the "poison of *shunyata*," in allegiance to nothingness, rather than being an expression of emptiness. Because things are not absolute but only relative does not make them irrelevant or non-existent.

Some also argue that, after all, at the relative level there are relative differences between men and women. Gender roles and stereotypes are just convenient designations or ways of handling those differences. Since that is the case, one need not worry seriously about their appropriateness, they say. One then has to ask why, if these gender roles and stereotypes are merely convenient relative conventions, they are insisted upon so absolutely and so rigidly, and why they are so carefully socialized into people. Can such rigidity really be nothing more than a merely convenient relative designation? If they really are non-ultimates, as those making this version of the argument for the status quo claim, non-adherence to conventional norms and limits for women and men should arouse no threat. Finally, when convenient arrangements become harmful, as they have with patriarchal gender-relations, then it is time to remember the basic ethic of non-harming. What is "convenient" for some may be quite oppressive for others. Real limits exist as to how much convenient conventions and non-harming can be combined.

However, one possible criticism that could be directed at feminism, or other movements of social reform, must be taken seriously. Just as one can make an ego out of feminism, or any other position, so one can absolutize feminism or any other cause. To do so would be to fall off the razor's edge into the extreme of affirmation, less dangerous than the extreme of negation, but still a deviation from emptiness. Nevertheless, taking an issue seriously is not tantamount to absolutizing it. Therefore, one cannot simply dismiss social action movements by citing this potential pitfall; to do so would be in fall into the other extreme, "the poison of *shunyata*." Instead, constant spiritual discipline is important to maintain humor, gentleness, and a light touch, so that one does not absolutize what one takes seriously.

FEMINIST ETHICS AND THE BODHISATTVA PATH

Mahayana Buddhism stresses two ideals—wisdom and compassion—which should be developed in tandem, parallel with and interdependent upon each other. They are considered to be equally essential for spiritual maturity. Both of them grow out of foundations already established in the *hinayana*, according to the three-*yana* perspective being employed in this discussion. Mahayana Buddhism of the second-turning primarily discusses wisdom as insight into emptiness—emptiness as what is not. All Mahayana Buddhists discuss compassion in terms of the discovery of *bodhicitta*, experientially translated as "enlightened heart," but traditionally translated as the "thought of enlightenment," and the consequent practice of the Bodhisattva path. In many versions of Mahayana Buddhism, the development of compassion through practicing the disciplines of a bodhisattva is actually more immediately important than grasping the meaning of emptiness, though in the long run, they are interdependent, often compared to one's right and left hands.

In stories already discussed in the chapter on roles and images of women in Mahayana Buddhism, we see how important is the discovery, or rousing, of the thought of enlightenment. Once this experience is firmly established, one is on the Bodhisattva path toward the full enlightenment of a Buddha. Therefore, for a Mahayanist, no other experience is more central than the discovery of *bodhicitta*, which is celebrated joyously in Mahayana texts and constantly aroused in Mahayana liturgies. In this experience, one intuits self-existing spontaneous compassion in the core of one's being. This compassion is not dutiful nor based on fear and need. It is utterly uncompelled and unstrategized and, therefore, completely genuine. Not based on hope of rewards and returned favors, such genuine compassion is accompanied by feelings of joy and freedom because one feels that one has recovered one's true nature, previously obscured by ego and attachment. This experience is so inspiring that one is motivated to pursue enlightenment, not merely for one's self, but for all beings, which is the essence of the famous Bodhisattva vow. Often understood as a "future Buddha," a Bodhisattva develops altruism, deep and widespread concern for others, to the point that self-interest is no longer the motivating force behind actions. Compassion takes its place.

In the three-*yana* perspective, such an awakening is the inevitable consequence of proper self-cultivation through meditation and contemplation, since they result in developing a healthy, sane sense of self relatively free of ego and negative habitual tendencies. This is because, in Buddhist perspective, human nature, beneath the constructions of ego, is basically good.[9] Though it has been much less explicitly noted, experiencing that basic good nature also means experiencing one's sane, enlightened self as fundamentally relational rather than essentially autonomous. When *bodhicitta* is experienced and allegiance to it is expressed through the Bodhisattva vow, one is affirming one's connections with others as fundamental and basic. They become the reference point of one's life, not in a co-dependent, but in a compassionate way. One sees one's life as fundamentally and inextricably interlinked with all other lives. One cares about them. In this caring, emotions are cultivated and trained, not repressed or endured. It is assumed that properly developed and cultivated emotions are as fundamental to a sane, healthy person as is a trained and cultivated intellect, and that both are equally trainable and tameable. Furthermore, the person who acknowledges and treasures this interconnectedness, and who contemplates and develops the emotions that enable one to contribute well and wisely to the relational matrix of life, is the lauded and valued person.[10] A person who has these qualities is considered to be mature and developed. They are the whole point of spiritual discipline.

The Mahayana ideal of the Bodhisattva path is strikingly consonant with much recent feminist ethical thinking. Carol Gilligan is best known for articulating the view that women tend to see life as fundamentally relational and, as a result, solve ethical problems differently from men.[11] The role of the emotions in being and knowing is also evaluated positively by many feminists, who criticize the conventional intellectual tradition for its dichotomizing of intellect and emotions and its denigration of the emotions. The possibilities opened up and clarified by these suggestions are among the most provocative, profound and relevant of the contributions yet made by feminist thinking. Clearly, the ethics of feminism and of Mahayana Buddhism have more in common with each other than either has with the ethic of individual autonomy and self-sufficiency favored by the dominant androcentric culture. But what of the similarity between feminist and Mahayana Buddhist ethics?

For myself, I am comforted and inspired by the profound sympathy between Mahayana ethics and what I regard as some of the most important insights of feminism. My own criticisms, as usual, center much more on the gap between Buddhist ideals and the way in which Buddhism manifests in the world. Women can and should feel affirmed in their mode of being, relating, and caring by the Mahayana emphasis on the centrality of such experiences to genuine spirituality. Feminists could well take the fact that Mahayana Buddhism gives such prominence to these emotions and experiences as outside confirmation of their conclusions and as a resource for continued development of these themes. Once again, the fact that Buddhism has such a well-developed repertoire of meditative and contemplative techniques for helping people develop their relational, compassionate selves should not be overlooked by feminists, who have the same goal.

Sometimes, however, feminists see a potential pitfall with this ethic as a relevant ethic for women. They say that the message of the centrality of compassion is a message women have heard all too often and all too well in patriarchal culture. Internalizing this ethic, women are given, and take, most of the responsibility for nurturing others, without much compensation, or much chance of being nurtured themselves. These critics would say that women need much more to learn to take care of themselves than to hear another religion telling them to take care of everyone else. This criticism shares something with the criticism discussed in the last chapter, that women need more, not less ego; in neither case do the critics understand Buddhism very well.

This criticism can be countered by two refutations. One the one hand, many feminists themselves would counter that patriarchal culture needs to be feminized by coming to value relationship appropriately; the problem of women as the unnurtured nurturers is not solved by having women also become autonomous and isolated, like men, but rather by feminizing men and the culture as a whole. Women should not give up what is sane and healthy about their modes of being and knowing, simply because it is not rewarded and affirmed by the general culture. The more important refutation, however, would recognize that many women do care in unwise and unhealthy ways. They need something besides another authority telling them to care more and be more compassionate. That, however, is not the Buddhist message. As we have seen, for Buddhism, the development of compassion is not the first message or agenda for spiritual development. The first step is non-harming, which includes learning to overcome self-destructive ego patterns, such as loving too much* or caring unwisely, in unhealthy ways. Caring, by itself, is not enough. One needs to learn to care with the detached and all-encompassing compassion of a bodhisattva; in order to be able to do that, one first needs to needs to learn non-harming and to develop some understanding of egolessness and emptiness. Caring, without the proper preparation of self-development, and not accompanied by clarity and wisdom, is often very destructive, both of self and other.

The term "compassion" is absolutely central in the traditional understanding of Mahayana ethics. However, the emphasis on "relationality" may not be so central to the traditional Buddhist understanding of compassion. In my own case, I have become much more aware of how interlinked are the practice of

---

* An enormous popular self-help literature has grown up around this theme, most notably the highly popular book *Women Who Love Too Much*.

compassion and the primacy of relationality since my own life experiences and feminist thinking have forced this awareness upon me. But I was not taught by Buddhists to value relationality, as an integral component of compassion. Now I see the two—relationship and compassion—as inextricable in Buddhist materials. Once I did not, and thought of compassion more as an attribute that I might possess than as the fruition of my utter interrelatedness with the world. I do not know if the fault lay with the inadequacy of my former understanding of Buddhist materials or if feminist thinking has added a nuance to Buddhist understandings of compassion that was slighted earlier. My suspicions favor the later hypothesis.

Finally, I wish to link feminist ethics and the Bodhisattva path much more definitively with the need for Buddhism to develop its prophetic dimension. Even more than the ethic of non-harming, the bodhisattva ethic of compassion and universal concern for all beings cries out for the development of a social ethic that includes prophetic social criticism and vision. Buddhism is sometimes accused of not having a social ethic. That is not really the case, since both first-turning teachings and the Bodhisattva path contain many guidelines for human interactions. What Buddhism has lacked, as I have said previously, is the will to direct significant amounts of communal energy into social concerns and reconstructions. But when one takes on universal liberation, rather than individual liberation alone, as one does when one takes the Bodhisattva vow, the time has come to go beyond individual rectitude to the communal efforts that effect large-scale social changes. When one realizes how unliberating, how oppressive, economically, politically, psychologically, and spiritually, are some of the dominant forms of social organization and authority, it is hard to imagine being serious about liberation or the bodhisattva path without being involved in social action at some level. The ethics and vision of the bodhisattva path strike me as the most relevant arena into which to introduce such prophetic discourse in Buddhism.

To apply these comments more specifically to gender issues, it is difficult indeed to reconcile patriarchal religious institutions with the serious practice of the bodhisattva path. Yet it has been done repeatedly, as we saw in the overview of Buddhist history; nuns were subjugated to monks; their order was allowed to disappear in many parts of the Buddhist world; women were actively discouraged from taking up serious spiritual discipline; women were taught to look down upon their specific form of the precious human body. No religion, of course, could be utterly free of individuals who did not live up to its vision. But I have always been puzzled by the generations of Buddhists who have taken the bodhisattva vow with utmost sincerity and yet have also practiced, promoted, and justified gender hierarchy and gender privilege in Buddhism. The gap between the vision and the practice of Buddhism nowhere seems wider. Some-one who has taken the bodhisattva vow should not promote gender inequality, whether by direct action or by passively accepting the status quo.

13

Gender and Buddha-Nature: Feminist Comments on Third-Turning Teachings and on the Vajrayana

The teachings specific to the third turning are considered part of the Mahayana when the three-*yana* system is superimposed upon the three turnings. Many of these third-turning teachings, such as the *trikaya*, the three manifestations of Buddhahood, and *tathagatagarbha*, Buddha-nature, have become part of the general Mahayana conceptual framework. However, the philosophical concepts associated with the so-called Yogacara or Vijnaptimatrata school, a philosophical alternative to the Madyamika school, have not become so widespread. According to Ray, these two schools can be regarded as "equally ultimate in their philosophical formulations, but they differ in their idioms."

Soteriologically, however, he claims that "the third turning, owing to the predominance of kataphatic language, has been taken to refer to a higher, more balanced understanding of *sunyata*,"[1] at least according to schools of Buddhism that classify the teachings of Buddhism into the three turnings. This is because the third-turning teachings and interpretations are said to understand *shunyata* in a fuller and more religiously adequate way than does the second turning. Again following Ray, the second turning teaches us to understand the emptiness of words and concepts, even if they occur in relevant "spiritual" teachings. After that recognition, "then reality begins to show itself in a different way, as charged with power and meaning." Some well-put sentences summarize the differences:

> Whereas for the second turning *sunyata* is explicitly presented mainly as the non-being of our verbal and conceptual versions of reality, for the third turning *sunyata* is explicitly presented mainly as the fullness of the Buddha's wisdom and compassion. When the dualistic life based on words and concepts has been abandoned, one does not fall into a void, an abyss, a nothingness. One meets face to face with that which is ultimately so.[2]

Whether or not one agrees with this soteriological ranking of the Yogacara and Madyamika schools, one must acknowledge their rather different styles of expression. It is also impossible to imagine that their historical order or their order of development on the spiritual path could be reversed. Only having discovered emptiness as what is not could one discover emptiness that is not nothing, that is *tathata*—Things-As-They-Are, Suchness, Thusness, to list a few of the awkward English translations of that term. What is the difference between *shunyata* and *tathata* besides the fact that one is "empty" and the other "full?" They are two sides of the same coin, but it is important to examine both sides carefully. With the second turning, we learn that "form is emptiness" but we need to learn as well that "emptiness is form,"* from the third turning. Those who utilize this method of systematizing Mahayana teachings regard the content of the third turning as essential because one needs the fullness and richness beyond *shunyata* as the basis of spiritual life. Having deconstructed the world of conceptual absolutes through intuiting emptiness, one needs to reconstruct, through skillful means, a non-absolute world, with which one may dance. This is the task taken up by Vajrayana Buddhism, which grows out of and is closely related with the third turning.

PREGNANT WITH BUDDHA: *TATHAGATAGARBHA* AND GENDER

The argument that the third turning develops significant insights beyond those found in the second turning is strengthened when third-turning teachings are applied to gender issues. The second-turning interpretation of *shunyata* undercuts gender bias by showing the non-existence of essential feminine or masculine characteristics. The third-turning teachings about *tathagatagarbha*, in explaining what is there beyond emptiness, give even greater strength to feminist criticisms of Buddhist gender practices and to feminist interpretations of Buddhism.

The term *tathagatagarbha*[3] is often translated as Buddha-nature, though this is not a literal translation. More literal translations, which have been avoided thus far, would be "tathagata-womb" or "tathagata-embryo." *Tathagata* is a title for Buddha and "*garbha*" connotes both "womb" and "embryo." Therefore, this term posits an embryo of Buddhahood or a womb containing Buddhahood. The obvious positive feminine and uterine symbolism of the term should not be overlooked, though that feminine symbolism may explain why scholars have preferred the more bland and neuter "Buddha-nature." This term is used to refer to indwelling Buddhahood, which is the inherent potential of all sentient beings, in some interpretations, of all that is, including the physical universe.

---

* This sentence is from the most important statement in the "Heart Sutra": "Form is emptiness; emptiness is form; form is no other than emptiness; emptiness is no other than form." Commentaries on this statement often indicate that emptiness cannot be regarded as the final word in Buddhist thought, though it is an essential component within Buddhist thought.

Several things should be understood about this Buddha-embryo. Despite the positive "full" style of language used about Buddha-nature, it is not a Self or Soul, according to those who propose this language. Those inclined to see the second-turning teachings, couched in a much more negative style of language, as the highest truth, have often made this criticism about some of the interpretations of *tathagatagarbha*.[4] Rather than being a Self, Soul, or Essence, it is that which one discovers in the experience of egolessness, when *shunyata* is thoroughly intuited. According to these teachings, one discovers that one is Buddha and has always been so, though that wisdom was veiled and obscured previously. When the veils and obscurations are removed, what remains is intrinsic, indwelling, innate Buddhahood. However, even before the veils are removed, Buddhahood is still there as seed. All the metaphors—seed, embryo, womb—suggest both growth potential and something obscured by or hidden in its container, but fully intact nevertheless. That is why the literal translations of Buddha-embryo, or womb containing Buddha are so much more evocative than "Buddha-nature." These translations also acknowledge that, in this case, the Buddhist tradition has explicitly compared the process of developing enlightened qualities with the processes of pregnancy and gestation, which are especially drawn from women's experience.

Using modern terminology, this trait has also been called "the enlightened gene," which indicates that it is something intrinsic and fundamental to one's make-up, not an adventitious extra. Furthermore, this one element, this one "gene" among the many in one's make-up is enlightened. Because this enlightened gene is already there, unborn, unceasing, and non-dwelling, not subject to causes and conditions, one can become Buddha completely. Were it not there, one could never become Buddha, no matter how hard one tried. Compared to this most basic and fundamental trait of everything that is, all other traits are superficial and irrelevant. And, finally, this Buddha-embryo is generic and common, not personal. It is not to be conflated in any way with personal identity and has no individuality. Certainly it has no gender and is not different in women then in men. Such a statement would be incomprehensible, and has never, to my knowledge, been made in any Buddhist text, important or minor. In fact, the opposite point is always made. Even if a being falls into extremely low forms of existence through evil deeds and negative karma, nevertheless, inherent, indwelling Buddha-nature continues to characterize that being as its basic nature.

Tathagatagarbha theory has always struck me as providing a remarkably strong basis for feminist interpretations and criticisms of Buddhism. Perhaps it is no coincidence that Queen Shrimaladevi, whom we met in the chapter on Mahayana Buddhist attitudes toward women, a mature woman who does not change her female sex to prove her competence as a teacher, is a teacher of *tathagatagarbha* theory. First, we should recognize this theory's more obvious, and perhaps superficial, implications regarding gender issues. When the actual meaning of the term is taken into account, the biological processes of gestation and pregnancy are valorized as the most apt metaphor for the existence and effects of indwelling inherent Buddhahood. It is self-contradictory to valorize these processes symbolically but at the same time to diminish and denigrate those among human beings who are most intimately involved with them.*

More critically, *tathagatagarbha* theory implies that since all beings are fundamentally characterized by Buddha-nature, women and men, equally, are fundamentally Buddha, beneath adventitious secondary and superficial gender traits. This doctrine would be extremely difficult to use in any attempt to justify gender hierarchy. When brought it bear on gender issues, the only compelling conclusion is that *tathagatagarbha* theory is gender-neutral and gender-blind. All *beings* are characterized by the enlightened gene. It is not stronger or more vigorous and dominant in men, weaker and more recessive in women.

That all sentient beings, certainly all men and women, equally have inherent potential for enlightenment provides an extremely strong criticism of existing Buddhist institutions. If women and men have the same basic endowment, the same potential for enlightenment, then their vastly different achievements, as recorded throughout Buddhist history, can only be due to inadequate institutions, to institutions that promote, encourage, and expect men to achieve higher levels of insight and realization. Some might try to justify the status quo by arguing that it is a woman's karma to live with religious institutions that discriminate against her, that do not provide her inherent Buddha-embryo with the same nourishment that is given to one growing in a male body. That attempted explanation, by way of women's less fortunate karma, is simply another manifestation of the inadequate institutions and lowered expectations limiting women. The "explanation" is itself one building block within the self-perpetuating, socially created patriarchal institutions that attempt to justify continued oppression of women, not a genuine explanation that stands apart from the system that is being explained.

Also important is the way in which second- and third-turning teachings work together, building upon one another with both negative and positive arguments against gender privilege and for egalitarian gender arrangements. On the one hand, because all phenomena are empty and lack inherent existence,

---

* Despite the contradiction involved, such symbolic valorization of birth, combined with sociological denigration of literal birth-givers, is not uncommon in world religions. In many religious contexts, the valuable birth is one's second birth, one's ritual rebirth, which may be seen as reversing the negativities of birth from a female body. Sometimes the symbolism becomes so divorced from its basis in physical birth that many people do not even realize that rebirth is occurring.

intrinsic maleness and femaleness cannot be found. Therefore women and men should not be defined by gender traits nor limited by gender roles and stereotypes. On the other hand, the intrinsic nature of all people, without regard for gender, is their potential for Buddhahood. Therefore, it is not appropriate to place institutional obstacles, such as formal subordination, lower expectations, or discouragement from the life of study and practice, in the path of either gender. Unfortunately, Buddhist texts have not emphasized, or even noted, how these key Mahayana concepts, especially in conjunction with each other, undercut the current Buddhist norms and practices regarding gender. Furthermore, taken together, the concepts of emptiness and Buddha-nature provide a very firm basis to argue that gender equality is a normative, rather than an optional position, for Buddhists. If gender equality is normative, then actively working to undercut gender hierarchy and privilege is a required ethical norm for all Buddhists, not merely a marginal position for a few feminists. It becomes a matter, not merely that Bodhisattvas should not perpetuate gender inequities, but that, as part of their Bodhisattva activity, they should promote the vision of a Buddhist world that is not based on gender privilege and gender oppression.

THINGS-AS-THEY-ARE AND THINGS THAT WE LET HAPPEN: SUCHNESS AND SOCIETY

The concept of Buddha-nature, given greater or lesser emphasis, is common to most forms of Mahayana Buddhism, despite its specific locus in third-turning teachings. However, the complex theories of mind and perception concerning the *alayavijnana*, or storehouse consciousness, and the doctrine that what is, is "mind-only,"[5] have remained more a specialized focus of third-turning teachings and the Cittamatra or Yogacara schools. I will not attempt to explain these complex concepts fully, but only point out some important implications of these theories for gender issues.

In very general terms, according to the Cittamatra school, what we have to work with is mind and its perceptions, which are defiled by the *klesa*-s (conflicting, negative emotions) in unenlightened people and purified in enlightened people, with some mix of these perceptions, depending on level of spiritual development, in most people. There is no point in talking about an objective reality apart from these perceptions, which is why the school is often called the "mind-only" school. The basis for perceptions is the *alaya* consciousness, and the other levels of consciousness that result in defiled perceptions, as well as the contents stored in the *alaya*, including personal karma, general karma, and *tathagatagarbha*.*

---

* For this reason, the alaya has sometimes been compared to the Collective Unconscious of Jungian psychology.

To explain how this all works, the Cittamatra school posits three levels of "truth," or ways things manifest and are perceived: the imagined level, the relative level, and the perfected level. These three have also been called the "three aspects," a translation of the three *svabhava*-s.[6] The first level, the imagined, constructed, or conceptualized level, is the level of dualistic consciousness, which falsely posits an objectively existing object perceived by a separately existing consciousness. This is the kind of perception experienced by everyday, unenlightened consciousness. "It is how things appear to us, the realm of subject-object duality. These things do not actually exist at all, things are not really like that."[7] The relative or dependent level or aspect perceives things according to interdependent co-arising. "It is that *which* appears, in opposition to the *way* it appears, which is the first Aspect, the conceptualized aspect."[8] Finally, there is the Perfected Aspect or level.

It is the "Suchness" or "Thusness" (*tathata*), the true nature of things which is discovered . . . through meditation we come to know that our flow of perceptions, of experiences really lacks the fixed enduring subjects and objects which we have constructed out of it. There is only the flow of experiences. The perfected aspect is, therefore, the fact of non-duality, there is neither subject nor object but only a single flow.[9]

If we apply these three levels to ways of perceiving gender, some interesting suggestions are forthcoming. The mental rigidity that assumes that people must conform to gender roles and stereotypes, demands that they be limited by them, and punishes those who do not conform, is obviously perception according to the first aspect, the imagined, conceptualized, constructed aspect. But "things are not really like that."[10] The relative aspect would be the basis for seeing that some people are males and some are females, but that seeing would be devoid of the fixed conclusions about those relatively accurate perceptions that characterize mind operating conventionally under the imagined aspect. This suggestion is quite similar to the comment made in connection with the first-turning teaching of egolessness, that someone who was egoless would "be aware of sex but would have transcended the need to rely on gender."[11] Finally, perceiving through the perfected aspect would involve seeing "the true nature of things." One would not especially see persons or males and females, but Buddha-nature. Seeing Buddha-nature is nothing but seeing egolessness or seeing emptiness fully, from the other side. But, given third-turning language, in which one sees that this woman, this man, *is* Buddha, intrinsically, to see femaleness instead, and to erect barriers and limitations on that basis, is unwarranted. Clearly, many features of the conventional Buddhist outlook, institutional set-up, and ways of dealing with gender actually encourage people to remain stuck in the first aspect, the aspect of imagined, constructed, conceptualized reality, whenever the topic of gender arises.

Under the perfected aspect, one sees Things-As-They-Are. One sees thusness or suchness, alternative translations of *tathata*. The primary meaning of thusness is, as we have seen above, to see things in a non-dualistic manner, to see the ever-flowing stream of events without reification, without imposing a subject-object dichotomy on them. Perhaps one could also say that to see suchness is to see things as a Buddha would see them. Such seeing also means accurately seeing what is, rather than the usual projections and preconceptions that color phenomena. It has already been suggested that vis-à-vis gender, that would involve seeing *tathagatagarbha* rather than persons or gender. Even prior to the realization of such seeing, however, it is important to minimize the tendencies to act as if one's imaginary constructions were actually Things-As-They-Are. Therefore, social institutions based on the notion that every person possesses *tathagatagarbha* would be much more conducive to spiritual transformation, to one's actual realization of suchness, than are the current social institutions of the Buddhist world, which rely heavily on fixed and rigid gender constructions contrived on the basis of the imaginary aspect and which encourage people to remain at that level of perception.

Finally, it is important not to degrade thusness or suchness by confusing Things-As-They-Are with the things that have been constructed to preserve self-interest and ego, with social conventions. Buddhist sometimes do that in their attempts to avoid feminist criticisms of the existing order. Once in Japan, when I gave a talk on Buddhism and feminism, one of the women respondents suggested, if I understood her correctly, that it might be feasible for me, as a Westerner to rebel so against the status quo, but Asians feel it is important to accept things as they are and to accommodate themselves to given conditions. That is, of course, impeccable advise. It does no good whatsoever to engage in wishful thinking, longing for conditions that one cannot have. That statement is almost a paraphrase of the first two noble truths, which tell us that we suffer because we desire what we cannot have—perfect security, permanence, and bliss. But Things-As-They-Are, to which we must give in, involves suffering, impermanence, and egolessness, and also emptiness and suchness. It *does not* involve war, poverty, oppression, sexism, and patriarchy—situations created by ego, by fixed mind, by projections, and by the imagined, conceptualized aspect of perceptions. Sometimes a person can do nothing to avoid such situations and must learn how to live through them with dignity, without losing one's cheerfulness and incipient Buddhahood. But that is very different from regarding those conditions as Things-As-They-Are.

This confusion is another manifestation of a tendency that has been pointed out in a number of other contexts. It is akin to a confusion of absolute and relative truths, and to the tendency to absolutize the relative, that can be so problematic. It also bears some resemblance to the argument that women's difficulties are due to their karma, not to the self-interests of a patriarchal system which benefits from and is put at ease by the conventional gender arrangements. This acceptance flourishes more readily in conventional Buddhist thought because of its frequent uncritical passivity regarding socially-created oppressive conditions. Once again, the contributions that the prophetic voice, if wisely modulated, could make to Buddhist thought are obvious. But the issue is not one-sided. The accommodation and acceptance emphasized by traditional Buddhism also contain a necessary message. One of my papers, largely stemming from my increasing tranquillity born of meditation, suggested that a very useful distinction for feminist thought would be between the sufferings inherent in the human condition and those dependent on patriarchal distortions.[12] Feminists, I suggested, sometimes blur the two, which is not helpful. These comments make the same suggestion—now directed primarily at a Buddhist tendency to under-react to the same conditions to which feminists may over-react. The razor's edge of the middle path is narrow.

SUCHNESS AND SACRED OUTLOOK: FROM THE THIRD TURNING TO VAJRAYANA

One of the major arguments made by those who advocate classifying Buddhist teachings into the three turnings is that, once emptiness is firmly established in the second turning, the flip side of the coin—suchness—allows a rich and full basis for the religious life. As is so often emphasized, emptiness, thoroughly understood, is not nothing; it is the basis for appreciating phenomena without reifying them. Phenomena are no longer seen as seductive elements that engender unwholesome reactions of clinging and fixation, but as primordially pure, vivid, non-dual Suchness. As such they need not be avoided, but can be appreciated, celebrated, and liberated. All elements of ordinary phenomenal existence can be seen in this sacred manner, which means that everything can be included in spiritual discipline. Called "developing sacred outlook," this attitude explains the Vajrayana technique of regarding all beings as Buddha, all sound as *mantra*, all phenomena as manifesting the union of bliss and emptiness.[13] Therefore, the human body, emotions, and sexuality, previously regarded as quite antithetical to serious spiritual practice, can now be integrated within sacred outlook and spiritual discipline because they can be utilized as vehicles for spiritual transformation, both in everyday life, and in ritual, liturgy, and symbol.

The subtlety of teachings about suchness is important to the religious, spiritual life in another, equally important, way. The language, style, and doctrinal intuitions that acknowledge empty phenomena, rather than merely emphasizing their emptiness, make possible liturgy, visualization, devotion, and other ritual aspects of the Vajrayana approach to Buddhism. Many phenomena arise out of emptiness in luminous, sacred purity. They can include deities—beings whose existence consists of symbol and mythology, whose presence is evoked through liturgy, visualization, and ritual, and whose effect is to promote realization through the practitioner's identification with this empty luminous being. These possibilities are the most important implications contained in teachings of suchness and Buddha-nature. The empty universe is replete with non-reified fullness, which can be invoked, and to which one can relate. The concept of suchness gives rise to the incredibly rich mythological and symbolic universe familiar to all Mahayana and Vajrayana Buddhists. In that mythological universe, ritual, praise, devotion, supplication, and other types of second-person language of address and relationship are quite common, but the familiarity of second-person language of address does not lead knowledgable practitioners to suppose that independently existing beings respond to being addressed. The effect is rather on the practitioner—and it can be quite powerful.

These two features of third-turning teachings form the basis for Vajrayana attitudes and approaches to the phenomenal world, as well as to the mythological, liturgical, and ritual world, that are so important if one is to understand Vajrayana Buddhism accurately. Thus, they are the foundation upon which is built the following comments, which select aspects of Vajrayana experience that have especially important implications for gender issues.

SUCHNESS AND PRIMAL EXPERIENCES: BODY, SEXUALITY, EMOTIONS

In Vajrayana Buddhism, primal experiences that are often regarded as obstacles on the spiritual path, and that are often associated negatively with women in androcentric thought systems, are differently evaluated and utilized. The body, sexuality, and emotions are not necessarily dualistic obstacles which must be denied and renounced. Seen properly, that is, through the lens of emptiness and suchness, they arise primordially pure and neutral. Approached with an attitude of egoistic, dualistic grasping and fixation, they become powerful traps; approached with the perspective of non-duality, they are part of the matrix of suchness, powerful, but neutral, rather than positive or negative. Because these primal experiences have so often been evaluated so negatively in spiritual disciplines, and then have been projected as experiences especially connected with or aroused by women, these alternative evaluations found in Vajrayana Buddhism are important.

To some extent, the Vajrayana evaluation of and approach to these primal experiences has already been discussed in the chapter on roles and images of women in Vajrayana Buddhism. But the presentation of the basic concepts was sketchy and feminist evaluation of the concepts was minimal. In any case, these concepts are so different from familiar materials that some repetition is probably helpful to understanding them.

Vajrayana Buddhism, and Buddhism in general, regard the human body as the vehicle through which enlightenment is attained. The "precious human birth" is the most conducive state for such attainment, and, for Buddhism, being human is inconceivable apart from being embodied. The body, along with speech and mind, is one of the "three gates" to the phenomenal world. As such, it is one of the major avenues of communication with, and manifestation in, the world. Though the body, like all other components of personality, must be disciplined, especially in early stages of the path of spiritual development, anti-body attitudes and regimens or a body-spirit dualism are completely foreign to Buddhism. Furthermore, in Vajrayana Buddhism, the body is the foundation upon which an elaborate esoteric "subtle physiology"* is built. One visualizes, and eventually experiences, this subtle body within the manifest body. Without the manifest body, such visualizations and experiences would be difficult, if not impossible.

It is quite possible, however, that such valorization of the body could valorize only a generic or androcentric male body and could be combined with fear or hatred of female bodies. At least in terms of Vajrayana symbolism and ritual, this does not occur, however. Female bodies are explicitly and graphically venerated. Because female *yidam*-s and *dakini*-s are so central to Vajrayana mythology and symbolism, and because iconography is so prominent, visual representations of the female body are frequent in sacred art and ritual. These females are naked or semi-naked, as are their male counterparts, and their female characteristics are not minimized or muted. In some ritual liturgies, these females are venerated or propitiated. But in major *sadhana*-s, these females are anthropomorphic, or perhaps we should say, gynemorphic, representations of enlightenment, with whom one identifies during a meditation of visualizing one's self as the female *yidam*. Both men and women do this meditation of visualizing their own identification with the enlightened female. In so doing, they take on her form, detail by detail, including her specifically female breasts and womb. For women, who have so often been treated as sex objects, or whose bodies, especially their specifically female organs, have been negatively

---

* Buddhist materials on the subtle body are quite esoteric and confined to the oral commentarial tradition. Accurate published sources are few and far between. Some comments, difficult to understand by themselves, are found in Snellgrove, *Indo-Tibetan Buddhism*, pp. 288–94.

regarded by religious systems, such meditations are healing and reassuring. For men, who have been socialized to believe that their maleness makes them more worthy, such meditations must be humbling and transformative.

Religious and spiritual understandings of sexuality are often closely linked with attitudes toward the body, for obvious reasons. Despite the strong emphasis placed on monastic celibacy, Buddhism has never regarded sex as inherently negative and antispiritual. But only in Vajrayana Buddhism is sexuality graphically and explicitly used as a positive religious symbol, and only in this form of Buddhism are there intimations that sexual experience itself may be helpful in one's spiritual development. As a symbol, sexuality is the most powerful representation of non-duality, of the subtle state beyond either duality or unity, which is so important for Buddhist realization. Full discussion of sexual symbolism will be more appropriate in the next section of this chapter. Many stories about sexual experience as a method on the spiritual path have already been discussed in the chapter on roles and images of women in Vajrayana Buddhism. For women, used to being told that they are oversexed sexual temptresses, such stories and symbols are reassuring. For anyone who regards sex as shameful and embarrassing, it must be quite challenging to see profound religious truths communicated through sexual symbolism. Since people who have negative attitudes regarding sexuality are also often misogynist, such symbolism can also encode messages countering misogyny.

Emotions are more basic than either the body or sexuality, and more difficult to integrate into realization. Because they are so powerful and can lead to such destructive results, many traditions, including some elements within Buddhism, regard emotions primarily as something to be tamed and transcended. Vajrayana Buddhism has a much more sophisticated position regarding emotions. Emotions are or arise from energy, which is itself powerful and neutral; it can manifest in either destructive or enlightened ways, depending on the degree of insight with which the energy is experienced. But emotion itself always contains tremendous wisdom, even if that wisdom is clouded and obscured by its deluded counterpart.*

Therefore, emotions are to be dealt with, not by denying them, overlooking their validity, or banishing them, but by harkening to their wisdom. This is done through the process of transmutation,[14] in which the emotion-energy is welcomed rather than rejected and the energy is worked with to release its wisdom. For women, who are so often accused of being "too emotional" and who *know*

---

* In Vajrayana Buddhism, such wisdom is talked about in terms of the five Buddha families, the five root *klesha*-s, and the five enlightened wisdoms. Properly channeled, the *klesha* transmutes into its corresponding wisdom, utilizing the same energy in enlightened rather than deluded ways. See Trungpa, *Cutting through Spiritual Materialism*, pp. 224–30; Trungpa, *Journey without Goal: The Tantric Wisdom of the Budda* (Boulder: Prajna Press, 1981), pp. 77–87.

that emotions contain deep truth that alienated and dysfunctional patriarchal systems wish to ignore, this sophisticated account of emotions is a welcome resource. Especially important and useful is the wealth of practical information contained in discussions of the five Buddha families on how to tame the negative aspects of the various emotions without losing the energy of emotion.

However, it must be acknowledged that traditional Vajrayana commentaries on these primal experiences as spiritual tools did not include discussions of how they might be used by women or by men to counter negative conventional attitudes and practices regarding gender. This is probably because, as has been said a number of times, previously very few Buddhists realized how undharmic the conventional attitudes and practices regarding gender really are. Probably even fewer imagined alternatives. That they are not already part of the commentarial literature does not lessen the cogency of these feminist comments.

MASCULINE AND FEMININE PRINCIPLES IN NON-DUAL PERSPECTIVE

Non-duality has been emphasized as the core experience of the perfected aspect or level of perception and, consequently, as fundamental to the experience of suchness. "Non-duality" means overcoming the subject-object duality in which an independent object is posited by the perceiving ego. Rather, there is just the continuity and flux of experience without dualistic overlay.

Though non-duality is discussed in these contexts primarily as the corrective to dualistic perceptions and fixations, it is also important to contrast non-duality with monism, the outlook that many adhere to in an attempt to find the reality behind apparent diversity and duality. Monism collapses the diversity of phenomena into an underlying, non-empirical, invisible "real" substratum; the diverse phenomena are relegated to the realm of illusion. With monism, one goes beyond the diverse phenomena to their purported underlying, common reality, which is true and valuable. Thus, for example, one may emphasize "common humanity," beneath gender, race, and class diversities, and thought to be more basic, elemental, and important than the traits of diversity.

The approach of non-duality is subtly different. Phenomena do not disappear into an underlying unity simply because their dualistic existence as reified entities is denied and transcended. Phenomena remain as they are—sharp, clear, vivid, specific, detailed. Or, perhaps more accurately, we could say that they are seen for the first time as they are—sharp, vivid, clear, specific, and detailed. But specificity is no longer used to limit and restrict phenomena, to divide and classify them. No longer is anything extraneous imposed on them. In an instant, the whole picture is intuited. The vivid and specific phenomena dance in basic primordial space; both vivid phenomena and the entire environment are perceived simultaneously. Phenomena are both vivid in their specificity and integrated within the Whole Space. In non-duality, specificity does not entail dualistic reified independent existence, nor is it lost beneath the alleged real monistic unifying principle. Non-duality is thus the middle path between the extremes of dualism and monism. Seen in this way, suchness and non-duality entail each other.

To apply this understanding of non-duality to gender is quite radical and illuminating. It will guide much of the post-patriarchal androgynous reconstruction of Buddhism, found in the final section of this book. Now, I will explore the extent to which, under the metaphor of masculine and feminine principles, Vajrayana Buddhism provides some models for a non-dualistic approach to gender. The guideline that will be used in this discussion seeks and looks for a balance of feminine and masculine principles in the phenomenal world. The terms "balance" and "phenomenal world" are the key terms in that guideline.

Such a balance is found, for the most part, in the symbolism surrounding the feminine and masculine principles. In symbolism, ritual, and iconography, both their vivid specificity and their mutuality within the whole space are emphasized and appreciated simultaneously. Both the specificity and the mutuality are extensively elaborated conceptually, iconographically, and ritually through meditation and liturgy. But, as already emphasized in the chapter on roles and images of women in Vajrayana Buddhism, there has been little sustained translation of these symbols into social reality. Nevertheless, the symbols may be the most useful resource of current Buddhism for a feminist revalorization of Buddhism.

When discussing and describing, first the philosophy, and then the iconography and ritual associated with the feminine and masculine principles, several difficult questions must be addressed. The masculine and feminine principles are associated with a whole host of additional dichotomies. In fact the world of experience is consistently classified into associated pairs. Why is this particular symbolic scheme chosen? How is such dichotomizing different from duality? Finally, even if it is psychologically and symbolically useful to dichotomize the world, why assign some qualities to a so-called masculine principle and others to the feminine principle?

The feminine and masculine principles of Vajrayana Buddhism are an elaboration and personification of a familiar, important, and basic Mahayana pair—wisdom and compassion, both of which are practiced and perfected by the Bodhisattva. Wisdom became associated with the feminine already in Mahayana Buddhism, partly by virtue of the feminine gender of the word *prajna*, and partly because such wisdom is the source, the "mother" from which a Buddha is born. The indispensable partner of wisdom in Mahayana Buddhism is compassion, which, perhaps by default, became associated with the masculine principle.

But why dichotomize experience? Why analyze things in terms of two principles, rather than three or four or half a dozen? These questions can be discussed on two levels. First, contemplative traditions worldwide encourage reflection on experience by means of simple and brief lists into which the myriad details of kaleidoscopic daily events can be subsumed. In Buddhism, one finds not only the twoness of masculine and feminine principles but also basic classification systems that operate in threes, fours, fives, and sixes, with the classification of things into the five Buddha families being almost as important for Vajrayana Buddhism as are the masculine and feminine principles. All these categories are *upaya*, skillful methods that are of great practical help in self-development. The exercise of contemplating one's experience in terms of a chosen and appropriate set of categories is a very illuminating technique of spiritual cultivation.

Why focus on a set of two? The experience of twoness is one of the most basic of all human experiences. First is the fundamental psychological fact of the experience of self and other, which is so basic and often so problematic. Second, language and thinking operate by means of differentiation and dichotomy because they cannot grasp non-duality fully. Finally, duality is most clearly transcended in the mutuality of the couple or the parent and child.

Some might question whether such dichotomizing does not reinforce dualistic perceptions. The two, masculine and feminine, however, are not an oppositional duality; they are a non-dual pair, a dyadic unity. The two are specific and vivid phenomena arising in the matrix of non-duality. One does not identify with one of them against the other, as is done in dualistic thinking. Rather, one regards the two as interdependent, complementary aspects of the Whole, aspects which cannot be collapsed into monistic unity any more than they can be brought into real opposition. Furthermore, one identifies with and develops *both* elements of the pair, regarding the image as an *upaya* for contemplating how to develop and balance divergent elements of experience. The mere presence of two elements is not always evidence of dualistic, hierarchical thinking. The two could be experienced non-dually rather than dualistically, which is the aim and intent of this symbolism in Vajrayana Buddhism.

Sometimes I have heard the objection that, while it might be useful or even necessary to dichotomize experience, it definitely is not helpful to conflate the two principles with the sexual dichotomy. Usually the reason given is the fear that, inevitably, women will be associated with the feminine principle and men with the masculine principle, to the long-term detriment of both men and women. Better simply to call them the "A" principle and the "Z" principle, some have claimed. Given that most, if not all, culturally familiar examples of gender-linked symbolic principles do expect men to be representatives of masculinity and women of femininity, there are some grounds for that fear. However, in Vajrayana Buddhism, both men and women who do the more esoteric practices work to develop both principles, precisely because they are not dualistic opposites, but distinctive complements within a non-dual matrix. The problem is not with how these practices are taught to those who do the meditational exercises, but with social conventions that conspire to keep women away from them, as has historically happened in Vajrayana Buddhist societies.

Furthermore, in a religious symbol system, there are real advantages to associating one pole of a dyadic unity with femaleness and the other with maleness. If one were dealing only with abstract philosophical concepts, it would be adequate simply to call them the "A" and "Z" principles. But symbolism, especially anthropomorphic symbolism, communicates religious insights much more effectively than abstract philosophical language, which is why it is so omnipresent in religious symbol systems. When dyadic principles are expressed through symbols, they almost inevitably evoke sexual symbolism. The familiar sexual couple of Vajrayana Buddhism has the further advantage of working with the primal experience of sexuality and valorizing it spiritually, rather than banishing it from such discourse. Finally, nothing so graphically and powerfully communicates non-duality as the symbol of the anthropomorphic sexual couple. They are neither two nor one, neither completely separated dualistically, nor completely fused monistically. Rather, they are non-dually two-in-one, distinct and vivid, yet complementary elements within the whole matrix. Their sexual complementarity also connotes an additional meaning; their passion suggests mutuality between masculine and feminine, between women and men.

The foundational non-duality is that between wisdom and compassion, already important to Mahayana Buddhism and associated respectively with the feminine and masculine. In Vajrayana Buddhism this most elemental dyad takes on another, more abstract set of meanings. Now the most basic dyadic unity is that between space and activity, between accommodation and that which arises in space, between emptiness and form. The masculine pole becomes primarily associated, not only with compassion, but also with *upaya*, a term with many meanings including "method" and "skillful means." It is the activity, arising out of wisdom, that accomplishes what needs to be accomplished, the appropriate action to be effective in the situation. At the same time as the symbolism becomes more abstract, it also becomes more pervasive, so that many elements in everyday experience and in spiritual discipline connote the masculine or the feminine principles and their dyadic unity. The sun and the moon, vowels and consonants, red and white, left and right, ritual bell and ritual scepter (*vajra* or *dorje*), liquor and meat, all connote, respectively, feminine and masculine. In each case, together they co-operate to manifest the Whole. Since in iconography and ritual, many pairs are used simultaneously (the left hand holds the bell and the right the scepter, for example), the whole symbol system becomes dense and multilayered.

Unless such a set of symbols is truly complementary, mutual, non-hierarchical, and precisely balanced, however, it would become a powerful tool for reinforcing gender inequities. Imbalance would be most obvious in two ways. First, is could be possible for either the masculine or the feminine principle to be subtly dominant, while the other is merely its extension, functioning only as its consort. Second, it could be that at some level, human beings are limited by the symbolism associated with either the masculine or the feminine principles. In this case, for example, could there be a subtle bias that, normatively, men should be more active and women more accommodating? Since most other examples of such symbol systems are imbalanced in one or both ways, I have sympathy with skeptical feminists who expect such schemes always to work against women.

In my own case, I began my reflections on this topic almost allergic to such systems, because of repeated negative experiences with concepts about and symbols of masculinity and femininity. Femininity, as I first experienced it in my socialization to convention, was nothing but a demand to deny my intelligence and integrity. No wonder I wanted to near nothing about feminine traits or symbolism and thought that "humanity" was a much more promising ideal than "femininity." Only much later was I able to see that the problem against which I was rebelling was not the sheer *presence* of a feminine principle, but a *lack of balance* between masculine and feminine principles. The "feminine" was the loser in a hierarchal dualism, while masculinity was the realm of prestige, value, and goodness.

Conventional Western monotheism was the first arena in which I encountered imbalance of feminine and masculine principles. Such a claim may seem strange, because usually it is thought that monotheism is characterized by its lack of a feminine principle, and by the solitary power and being of the one deity who, unlike his competitors for the loyalty of ancient Israelites, has no consort and is supposed to transcend gender altogether. Nevertheless, for monotheism, "he," and all its variants, is commonplace, while all variations of "she," including female religious leadership, is anathema. Therefore, the supposed gender transcendence is not a transcendence of gender at all, but a divinization of the maleness at the expense of a demonization of femaleness. Because of its emphasis on the uniqueness and singularity of the deity, monotheism attempts to reduce dualities to oneness. It accomplishes this by the attempted elimination of part of the duality. Therefore, in Western religious mythology, officially there is no feminine principle. Nevertheless, it frequently appears as a shadow, a demonic other, or a seducer, and, much less frequently, as a positive element in esoteric or mystical religion. It is difficult, if not impossible, to eliminate totally a feminine principle; in the process of attempting to eliminate it, however, it is easily trivialized, demonized, or diminished.

Furthermore, monotheism is unsuccessful in its attempt to purge itself of multiplicity, distinctiveness, and differentiation in its pursuit of unity, as is shown by the omnipresent problem of God and his attributes, solved in Christianity through the doctrine of the Trinity. This failure, more than anything else, convinces me of the importance of openly taking on duality, differentiation, and distinctiveness, including the sexual polarity of masculine and feminine principles, in religious symbol systems.

However, merely recognizing the need to acknowledge the feminine pole of experience is insufficient. Balance could still be seriously lacking, as I believe it is in the Western system that most seriously tries to integrate some feminine elements into itself—Jungian psychology. Jungian thought has come in for its share of feminist criticisms and attempted reconstructions.[15] Jung's system is completely inadequate at balancing the masculine and feminine principles, despite his calls for a revalorization of the feminine "unconscious." In his system, consciousness, which is associated with light and goodness, is male, while the frightening, dark unconscious, with which it is so difficult to form a proper relationship, is female. Furthermore, men are more likely to be able to achieve androgyny than women, who always are ill at ease in the male realm of consciousness and more at ease in the dark feminine unconscious.[16] Given the importance of Jungian thought for Western techniques of spiritual cultivation that seek to go beyond the narrowness and rigidity of conventional religion, its lack of balance between the masculine and feminine principles is disappointing.

Frustrated with such demonization or diminution of the feminine principle in most of the Western religious heritage, many feminists have turned to variations of the feminist spirituality movement to find a strong, dynamic, positive example of the feminine principle.[17] The only Western religion that avowedly and openly emphasizes a feminine principle, the feminist spirituality movement does very well in its self-assigned task of valorizing the feminine principle. However, it does not, at present, present a *balance* of feminine and masculine principles either. For completely understandable reasons, given the situation of women in Western patriarchy, many women involved in feminist constructions of the goddess and the feminine principle ignore or downplay the masculine principle. Others regard maleness as *the* problem, so inherently deficient as to be unworkable, even intrinsically evil.[18] Such thinkers would undoubtedly regard my guideline of seeking a balance of masculine and feminine principles in the phenomenal world as hopelessly misguided and naive.

Having found the major culturally familiar examples of masculine and feminine principles wanting, one might well wonder whether the Vajrayana Buddhist example could be more satisfactory. Is it less hierarchical, sufficiently non-hierarchical not to minimize either principle? Is there sufficient recognition that specific individuals need not mirror and manifest the principle whose sex they share?

About the latter question, I am quite certain of a positive answer. Women and men both equally strive to develop both wisdom and compassion, accommodation and activity. An enlightened being will manifest both qualities and enlightenment is not different in a man or a woman. Therefore, it would be ludicrous to claim that women will be more spacious, men more active, in their enlightened manifestation. On the path, men and women both are given practices, including visualizations, in which they identify with both the feminine and the masculine principles, and with both simultaneously. Even without the input of such practices, it is not my impression that Vajrayana Buddhism expects men to be more active and compassionate, while women are to be more accommodating and wise, nor is that regarded as an ideal toward which individuals should strive. Individuals simply cannot be that closely linked with the qualities of the feminine or masculine principles exclusively. Rather, they should seek to embody them both fully, and already do to some extent, even before reaching a high level of realization.

The question of hierarchy between the masculine and feminine principles is more difficult and subtle. Sheer female presence is not enough to overcome an androcentric hierarchy between masculine and feminine. In fact, in an androcentric portrayal of gender relations, the presence of a female could be detrimental, lulling some into assuming that egalitarian mutuality is being expressed. This happens frequently in culturally familiar situations in which some version of him and "his" consort dominates. The politician and his wife, or the minister and his wife, are perhaps the most common examples of such a practice. For me, the most graphic demonstration of how subtle and unconscious such presuppositions are in our society is the metal greeting card placed on the spacecraft, Mariners 10 and 11, sent out from our planet to civilizations in other solar systems of our galaxy, or even other galaxies. Intended to provide basic information about our planet, the card includes a simple line drawing of a nude couple, standing side by side. One's eye is drawn first to him, by virtue of his central placement within the overall design. He is looking straight ahead, facing the viewer, one arm raised, as if in greeting. She is off to the side, slightly turned towards the man, looking aside, toward the man, not straight into whatever world faces her.[19] To me, the message is quite obvious, but many would not notice what we are saying about gender relationships in our society by sending this design into outer space. Some of my friends, who admired the design, became upset and angry with me when I pointed out the message.

What of space and activity as they relate in Vajrayana Buddhism? Are they more balanced? When discussed as ideas that explain the interplay of experience, they are quite balanced. However, when the principles are portrayed iconographically as the sexual couple, or described verbally in ritual texts, sometimes, some androcentrism occurs.[20] These iconographic and verbal oversights do not undo the basic balance of the two principles as symbols standing for non-dual reality and could be corrected relatively easily, in those instances when they do occur. However, to date, there has been no recognition of these oversights and no attempt to correct them.

To demonstrate that feminine and masculine principles really are complementary and non-hierarchical, we first discuss the meaning of spaciousness or accommodation in this symbol system and then its relationship with compassionate skillful activity. A feminist untrained in meditation might jump to the conclusion that the feminine principle is passive, accommodating and enabling the more important masculine principle. But space, as understood in Buddhist meditation, is not passive, and accommodation is not at all the same as passivity in the Western sense. Space is the absolutely indispensable vibrant matrix for everything that is. Only the untrained ignore it. The wise realize that once one is familiar and comfortable with the energy of basic space, anything else is possible, but before that nothing is really possible. Furthermore, learning to recognize space, to do nothing, to develop wisdom (*prajna*) is the harder part of spiritual training. Once unobstructed space—vision unclouded by conventionality and discursiveness—is developd, then appropriate skillful and compassionate activity arises spontaneously and blissfully, whereas before such vision is developd, activity is usually futile and misdirected. Thus, wisdom provides the ground for compassionate and skillful activity, which completes the dyadic unity. Without such compassion, wisdom is too cold and hard, even destructive. But together, like the right and left sides of the body, they can co-operate to do what needs to be done.

But why should space and wisdom be associated with the feminine principle and compassionate activity with the masculine principle? Couldn't they be reversed? Logically, they could, for in some symbol systems they are reversed and Western gender stereotypes would often reverse them. I believe the association arises from the fact that female bodies have space within them that accommodates both their sexual partners and their unborn children, for the same reason that in the *I Ching*, broken lines are female and unbroken lines are male. The feminine principle is both partner and mother. As partners, the masculine and feminine are coeval and complementary, just as wisdom and compassion together constitute enlightened being. But as mother, the feminine principle is prior. A mother and a child cannot be coeval and complementary. Space is that in which form arises, not vice versa, and wisdom gives rise to compassionate, skillful activity, not vice versa. For these reasons, space and wisdom are associated with the feminine rather than with the masculine principle. But men and women are not limited in the same way. The more mature spiritually a woman or a man is, the more she will manifest *both*.

Given this symbolic and conceptual balance of feminine and masculine principles, it is unfortunate that sometimes iconography and liturgical texts give the impression that the focus is more on the male figure. As already pointed out, sometimes it is hard even to disentangle the female from the male in two-dimensional *thangkha* paintings. Some liturgical texts that describe the visualized sexual couple also focus on him, despite the instructions, given in the oral commentaries, that the meditator is to visualize herself as both of them, not him with an extension, or another ritual implement that happens to be his consort. Clearly, such portrayals do reflect androcentrism on the part of the artist or author involved. In other icons or texts, such problems do not occur. It is clear to me which artists I will patronize and what I would specify for a *thangkha* I would commission. Changing the wording of certain liturgical texts presents no more ultimate a problem. One would be changing only words, not meaning, so that the words more closely conform to the meaning.

This last chapter on Buddhism as currently constituted will end with some reflections on the meditation practices connected with Vajrayogini, an important female *yidam*, or anthropomorphic representation of enlightenment and the feminine principle. To say that I have found my formal introduction to her during my initiation into her *mandala* and my many years of practicing her *sadhana* illuminating, energizing, and empowering is an understatement at best.[21] How much of that experience is due to my having grown up female in a culture without powerful and positive female religious symbols and spiritual models? Can one ascertain that? Does it matter? Are not even traditional Buddhist cultures patriarchal enough at present that a woman who is no longer male identified would have similar psychological and spiritual experiences?

What about men who practice the same self-visualization and relate with a female *yidam* in the same way? I wish I could answer that question more fully and scientifically. Perhaps someday someone will construct appropriate questionnaires and do quantitative research on attitudinal changes among male and female practitioners of such spiritual disciplines. I have only my impressions and a surmise. Women find the female *yidam* confirming and comforting, while men often find her challenging. In any case, it is uncanny to me that the first major *yidam* for the aspirant, at least in some Tibetan Buddhist denominations, is a female *yidam*, whether one is a man or a woman. For psyches raised in a male dominant culture in which women are denigrated to some extent, which is the case whether the practitioner is an Asian or a Westerner, I could not imagine a more appropriate or powerful corrective and healing agent. That, of course, is *not* the traditional explanation for the order in which these practices are given to the aspirant, which does not undo its effectiveness.

For me, this *upaya*, this skillful method of initiating me into a meditation-liturgy connected with a female *yidam*, restored the balance of masculine and feminine principles in a way that nothing else could have. It not only restored the feminine in the dyadic unity; *it also restored the masculine.* Due to excessive over-masculinization of the religious milieu, I had reached a point in which, even in Buddhist liturgies, I could hardly bear another set of male pronouns and images. Due to deprivation and frustration, I dropped them or changed them, at least on occasion, as I had learned to do previously in other religious contexts. Now, with balance restored, I am quite comfortable with liturgies involving male *yidam*-s, which is fortunate, since such meditation-liturgies are also important in the overall program of developing both wisdom and compassion.

To receive such gifts within a community of both women and men, to engage in meditation-rituals, feasts, and fire-offerings invoking these *yidam*-s with both male and female companions is another good fortune. To me, such a situation is much more fortunate, sane, and balanced than a situation in which one feels one has to withdraw into a separatist community to find such integrity and wholeness. And these spiritual practices are old and well-tested, existing in the context of an unbroken spiritual lineage that is very long. Re-inventing the wheel spiritually is difficult and dangerous, not a task I am eager to take on when it can be avoided.*

My enthusiasm has an critical edge, however. I am fortunate to have received what I have received. As a Western, feminist woman, I have been far more thoroughly trained in Buddhist thought and meditation than was possible

---

* These comments are formulated with the example of feminist spirituality in the background. Much as I admire and feel a kinship with that movement, I also find it unfortunate to set up single-sex communities and I question the spiritual depth of many of the practices that have been "remembered, or failing that, invented."

for the vast majority of Asian Buddhist women throughout most of Buddhist history. In many cases, they still do not have available to them, simply because they are women, what has become available to me. It is not enough for a religious tradition to have all the right ideas about the balance of feminine and masculine principles in the phenomenal world. To translate such ideas into social realities requires another whole level of vision.

IV

THE *DHARMA* IS BOTH FEMALE AND MALE:

Toward an Androgynous
Reconstruction of Buddhism

14

Verdicts and Judgments:
Looking Backward; Looking Forward

Two major tasks in the feminist revalorization of Buddhism have now been completed. Buddhist history has been surveyed to see what are the precedents for women's roles, images, and life experiences in Buddhism. The implications of major Buddhist teachings for gender issues have also been discussed. Now it is time to summarize our findings and to look toward the post-patriarchal future. What verdict can we derive, overall, regarding Buddhist attitudes toward gender as we have watched the unfolding of the historical record and analyzed major teachings of the three turnings to glean what they imply about proper, *dharmic* ways of dealing with human sexual differentiation? Can we explain *why* the record is as it is, why it contradicts in so many ways the implications we derived from the analysis of Buddhist teachings? Are there any grounds to imagine or hope that significant reconstruction could occur in the Buddhist future? What major guidelines are appropriate for the reconstructions deriving from a feminist critique of Buddhism?

VERDICT: INTOLERABLE CONTRADICTION BETWEEN
VIEW AND PRACTICE

Overall, the view of Buddhism, as expressed in major teachings of each of the three turnings, is that "the dharma is neither male nor female."[1] This view is expressed explicitly in texts presenting second-turning teachings of emptiness and implied in the first-turning teachings of egolessness and the third- turning teachings regarding Buddha-nature. None of the major teachings of Buddhism supports gender inequity or gender hierarchy. Instead, if one tries to link these core teachings with questions about how best to think about and deal with human sexual differentiation, one must conclude that the Buddhist worldview and ethic are more consistent with gender equality than gender inequity, more consistent with flexibility and non-fixation regarding gender roles and stereotypes than with rigid, unalterable gender-specific norms and behaviors. Therefore, I am convinced that the only possible conclusion one can derive is that, at least in terms of worldview and major teachings, Buddhism is remarkable free of gender bias.

If life consisted solely of view, of theory and implications of theory, Buddhism would present something of an ideal. A feminist interpreter of Buddhism can make a strong case that the core of the tradition is without gender bias, whatever the practical record may reveal, and that sexist practices are in actual contradiction with the essential core teachings of the tradition. In fact, I would argue that since Buddhists, unlike feminists in other traditions, do not have to deconstruct any core teachings, they can make that case more confidently and completely than can feminists associated with any other major tradition.

However, with the exception of the teachings about emptiness, the Buddhist tradition itself has not made any connections, positive or negative, between its major *dharma* teachings and the practices it advocated or condoned surrounding gender. Instead, when Buddhists tried to explain and justify their gender practices, they relied upon the pan-Indian and pre-Buddhist idea of karma, interpreting this general statement regarding cause and effect into a claim that women's difficult situations were the result of negative karma and previous misdeeds. Therefore, they did not need to press specifically Buddhist teachings into service to support male dominance in Buddhist institutions. These teachings remain untainted by arguments using them to justify patriarchy and androcentrism. On the other hand, Buddhists could have used their major doctrines self-critically, against the gender institutions they inherited from surrounding cultures and willingly maintained, but they did not, with the exception of the idea of emptiness.

The Buddhist historical record, however, does not accord well with the possibilities inherent in the Buddhist teachings. Despite a strong basis for gender equality in key Buddhist teachings, Buddhism's record on gender equality is not significantly better than that of any other religion. Despite the implications of its key core teachings regarding gender, Buddhists in all periods and schools of Buddhist history limited women sharply. The attitudes toward women prevalent throughout Buddhist history were always ambiguous and contradictory, with the more normative attitude—that women are as fully capable as are men of achieving Buddhism's highest goals—being less popular than the attitude that women are less capable than men. Even Vajrayana Buddhism, with its explicit and weighty *samaya* obligation not to denigrate women, "who are the symbol of wisdom and *shunyata*, showing both,"[2] could not avoid or undo a belief about women's unfortunate situation that was so strong that the very word for woman in the Tibetan language literally means "low birth."[3]

Given the way women were treated, such beliefs may have seemed quite empirical and reasonable—that old circle of self-justification for the status quo, in which it is argued that the way things are proves that they should be that way. Since women do not achieve much, generally speaking, they must have inferior karma, which justifies keeping them in institutional set-ups that limit them severely. In historical forms of Buddhism, this vicious circle operated by socializing women to believe that their spiritual capacities were limited and that their proper sphere was the relatively disvalued realm of reproduction and domestic labor. Buddhism, as an intellectual and spiritual system, however, was not preserved and transmitted in lay institutions but in the great monasteries and universities. Women were discouraged from even dreaming of entering that realm, from the beginnings of Buddhism to the present day. The monasteries and educational institutions that do exist for women achieve that life option against the odds, and are usually poorly funded and understaffed, which means that educational opportunities for women are especially limited. Without thorough training in the Buddhist intellectual tradition, it is difficult for a woman to become a leader or to have any impact on the development of Buddhist tradition. She has few resources with which to rise above the circle of low expectations leading to lowered achievements, which limits her ability to gain a critical perspective on her situation. Even if she does become a highly regarded meditator, chances are high that she will have few students, even fewer male students, and that she will not be able to make the impact on her tradition that would be made by a male of similar attainments.

Therefore, after considering the history of Buddhist attitudes and practices surrounding gender in conjunction with an analysis of the implications of key Buddhist doctrines for gender issues, the verdict is that a massive and irreconcilable conflict between view and practice exists in Buddhism. To resolve that intolerable contradiction something must change. Minimally, the practices must be brought more in line with the view. When that happens, the view will also be enriched, in ways that would make it impossible for the practice ever to become so out of line.

LOOKING BACKWARD: EXPLAINING BUDDHIST PATRIARCHY

Because the view in Buddhism is so strongly non-sexist, Buddhists have less excuse for their androcentrism and male-dominance than do other religions which might, conceivably, claim that they are carrying out certain explicit standards revealed by a deity or mirroring socially the models of their mythology. Nevertheless, we can explain *why* Buddhists have historically constructed their institutions and attitudes surrounding gender as they have.

And we can do so utilizing explanations that are less unpalatable than simple prejudice, ill-will, and self-interest on the part of Buddhist men. Such factors may explain their desire to *continue* male dominance in the present, but they do not explain the genesis of these attitudes and institutions in the Buddhist past.

Buddhism emerged and has existed within an intellectual, social, economic, and cultural environment that was not sympathetic or conducive to gender equality. By the time Buddhism emerged into history, pre-patriarchal society and religion had long since been overtaken by male-dominant institutions, to the extent that most people probably assumed patriarchy was inherent in human biology. And, clearly, Buddhism accommodated itself to that environment rather than questioning it or standing against it.

The most important element in this explanation of Buddhist male dominance is the conclusion of feminist historical analysis that patriarchy is indeed a *historical* phenomena, dependent on certain causes and conditions, not an immutable fact of human biology, though many conservative commentators try to make that case, especially in popular anti-feminist literature[4] and in sociobiology.[5] To see patriarchy as a historical phenomenon that arises when certain conditions are present and disappears when they are absent accords well with basic Buddhist teachings. In the Buddhist teaching of interdependent co-arising, everything in our field of experience is seen as dependent on causes and conditions, rather than existing absolutely and eternally, which is precisely the claim feminist history makes about patriarchal social and religious forms. Thus, for Buddhists to argue against feminist reforms because such reforms would involve changing custom, long-standing traditions, and even precedents set down by the historical Buddha, is quite ironic. Not only are those forms dependent variables whose presence or absence is subject to causes and conditions. Additionally, they, like everything else in our experience, should be understood to be subject to all-pervasive impermanence. For a religion that so strongly posits impermanence as the basic fact of existence to exempt its own forms from that reality is highly inappropriate.

It may be more controversial to fix the exact causes and conditions that give rise to male dominance. What upset the balance and harmony of pre-patriarchal situations such as that of Chatal Huyuk, Old Europe and other pre-patriarchal societies?[6] It is more important to know that such societies existed than to know exactly what caused their demise. Simply knowing that they existed relatively late in human prehistory is sufficient to establish that patriarchy emerged relatively late in history and is not a condition of all human experience. It is also helpful to know that some less complex societies have preserved much less patriarchal, perhaps even completely non-patriarchal social forms into the present.*

Rather than locating its causes and conditions in one factor, it is more adequate to find the causes and conditions of patriarchy in a complex mix of economic, technological, social, and intellectual factors. The emergence of warfare as a major problem and preoccupation is one of the factors in the rise of male dominance—or at least one sees the co-emergence of a growing cult of war and an increasing male dominance.[†] As war becomes more of a problem and a preoccupation, the prestige of warriors increases. At the same time social stratification, urban crowding, and craft specialization made social hierarchies and subservience ever more commonplace. Additionally, the new technology of intensive agriculture, with its reliance on large draft animals, plows, complex irrigation systems, and labor-intensive grain crops wrested control of the economy away from women, who were less adapted to agricultural labor than they had been to horticulture. Finally, it is likely that these changing conditions pressed women into ever heavier reproductive responsibilities, as more children became desirable to have and possible to feed. Pregnancy, lactation, and early child care consumed more and more of a woman's life energies, under conditions of high infant and maternal death rates and a short lifespan. No wonder these changes were accompanied by a growing ideology of male superiority and dominance, which was reflected religiously and mythically in the worship of male deities who came to dominate the pantheons in which powerful independent goddesses had once played a significant role.[7] In extreme cases, they even totally overpowered the goddess and sought to root out her memory; at the same time women were eclipsed, made completely dependent socially and economically, and excluded from major religious expressions.

By the sixth century B.C.E., when Buddhism developed, the memory of pre-patriarchal society had been erased. Warfare, intensive agriculture, highly stratified societies with strong social and economic hierarchies, and male dominance socially and religiously, had become the expected norms. Buddhism, as we have seen, did not really participate in that society, but it did not seek to criticize and reform it either. Instead, its elite withdrew from that society into the countercultural monastic *sangha*, but they structured their own alterna-

---

* A generalization learned from the cross-cultural study of women is that foraging and horticultural societies usually are not as hierarchical as are societies that practice intensive agriculture.

[†] Gimbutas, "Women and Culture in Goddess Oriented Old Europe," pp. 29–31. In his culminating work on Mesopotamia, Thorkild Jacobsen arrives at similar conclusions, though he himself makes no connection between the rise of warfare and the rise of male dominance. Thorkild Jacobsen, *The Treasures of Darkness: A History of Mesopotamian Religion* (New Haven: Yale University Press, 1976), 77–78.

tive society by incorporating into it the same values and norms regarding male dominance, while rejecting for themselves, but not for society in general, virtually all the other current conventions and norms, including militarism, agricultural labor, hierarchy of social caste, and economic self-sufficiency. For its non-monastic larger *sangha*, Buddhism relied upon prevailing Hindu and Confucian social codes, with their strongly defined gender roles in which women and men were seen as complementary, though not of equal importance. These social norms, already entrenched in pre-Buddhist culture in India and in East Asia, included a clearly defined "woman's place." That "place" was one of formal subordination to males, whether father, husband, or son. Furthermore, that "place" was understood to involve family life, marriage, and reproduction, first and foremost. By and large Buddhists seem to have preferred that women stay in that "place" and not seek refuge in the monastic *sangha*.

Why was Buddhism so accommodating to its social environment, especially regarding gender arrangements? For on this issue alone, it accepted the prevailing conventions, not only for the wider lay society but also for its countercultural alternative society. And it did so despite developing its own *dharma* that is remarkably free of gender bias. This is an extremely tough puzzle to solve, more difficult than the emergence of patriarchy itself. But I believe two interlocking factors *may* explain Buddhist conventionality and conservatism on this issue. First is the fact that male dominance was already there as the norm for gender relations and second is the fact that Buddhism did not attempt to reconstruct or reform society because it saw withdrawal, rather than reconstruction, as the only feasible relationship with the larger society.

Had Buddhism been fortunate enough to enter history in an egalitarian rather than a patriarchal society, it would just as happily have accommodated itself to that situation. But in no case did it take as its task how best to structure society in the world, because the kind of liberation sought by Buddhists, especially in early Indian Buddhism, was not the result of justice and righteousness but of mindfulness, awareness, detachment, and tranquillity. As I have discussed earlier, Buddhism simply lacked a prophetic voice. Liberation was thought to be fostered, not by just social forms, but by renunciation. Therefore, the issue of better or worse social forms was of little consequence to Buddhists. They did not condemn warfare; they simply disallowed it for monks because a soldier could not maintain the mental state that brought liberation. Economic exploitation was not condemned; monks simply renounced economic self-sufficiency because greed and attachment were too likely to accompany economic activity. Gender hierarchy was not seen as harmful spiritually to those who practiced it in the same way that warfare or greed were seen as spiritually harmful and unliberating. Gender hierarchy, technically, did not prohibit

women from achieving the Buddhist goal of spiritual liberation; it only structured the institutions within which they pursued that goal. To see the debilitating
effects of conventional gender arrangements and the loss that Buddhism suffered because there were so few women teachers would have entailed the kind
of social self-scrutiny and self-criticism that simply was not part of the Buddhist
outlook. So, since social reform was the not the arena for liberation anyway, and
since prevailing codes for gender relationships were not thought to be spiritually harmful, no matter how unpleasant they might be, Buddhists had little
incentive to bring their vision and their practice regarding gender into align-
ment with each other.

LOOKING FORWARD: AUSPICIOUS COINCIDENCE

If things have remained at this level in Buddhism for 2,500 years, one may well
wonder if it is not sheer folly to think that changes might be possible at this
point. In so far as change is possible in Buddhist practices regarding gender
arrangements, they will not spontaneously self-generate from within Buddhism. It is not likely that those in positions of power and authority in Buddhism
will suddenly notice, on their own, the massive intolerable contradiction between view and practice that has prevailed for so long and rush to bring the
practice into line with the view.

Rather, historical tendencies and trends larger than Buddhism, affecting all
traditional religions to some extent, will force themselves upon Buddhism.
Some Buddhists, most of them marginalized people with little authority in
Buddhist hierarchies, will make a case that Buddhism has the internal resources
to meet the challenge, and that Buddhism will be truer to itself and its vision for
doing so. At that point, an interesting crisis will eventuate. Will those with
traditional authority to effect large-scale changes in Buddhist institutions do
anything? Or will they hope that the storm will blow over? Probably, as in
Christianity, the responses will be mixed and some denominations will respond
more adequately than others. At this point Buddhist feminists will face the
second level of difficulty in reconstructing Buddhism. Having already determined that the Buddhist worldview is workable and reformable, we will then
have to find out if it is possible to work with the hierarchical authorities of the
Buddhist world. Many a feminist eventually abandons her attempts to reform
her tradition, not because of problems with its symbol system and worldview,
but because trying to work for change within its institutional structures brings
too much burnout, heartache, frustration, and loneliness.

Two major contemporary historical forces could have a major impact on
Buddhist views and practices regarding gender. Together, they present a significant challenge and promise. First, the causes and conditions that sustained

patriarchy as plausible and tolerable are finally exhausting themselves. Second, Buddhism is no longer developing in intellectual and spiritual isolation, but is undergoing mutual transformation through its encounter with the prophetic voices of Western religions and feminism. Its encounter with the latter in particular can be seen as an auspicious coincidence—a magically appropriate, profoundly transformative encounter which could midwife enlightenment.

The causes and conditions that sustained patriarchy for so long are disappearing, at least in some parts of the world. That they may not be declining everywhere is cause for worry, but at least this form of social organization and value system is no longer taken for granted as the only possibility everywhere. Though feminist thought has eloquently defended women's humanity and detailed the psychological and spiritual harm patriarchy has wrought on both women and men, I do not expect a sudden arising of conscience and compassion, a change of heart and attitude, sufficient to undermine patriarchy. It has always been psychologically and spiritually harmful, but its harm was less noticed earlier. Rather, certain major changes in the technologies of both production and reproduction have made patriarchal gender roles obsolete and dysfunctional. For society in general, these practical liabilities are much more powerful inducements to go beyond patriarchy than are the arguments from justice and reason.

Patriarchal gender roles involve a specific way of structuring both economic production and human reproduction. Under intensive agriculture, women became increasingly separated from control over economic production, though in most instances their labor was still required at some points in the process. They became increasingly specialized in, limited to, and defined by their reproductive role, which meant that their input into politics and religion was also curtailed. Their realm of power and influence was within the household and extended family, the realm of so-called private life. Men meanwhile were increasingly cut off from those realms to specialize in military, economic, religious, and political affairs in the so-called public realm.

These gender specializations increased, at least in fantasy and ideal, after industrialization. Women were given the role of consumer, but their reproductive responsibilities were structured so as to make it almost impossible for them to take part in productive economic activities, making them more economically vulnerable and dependent than at any point in history. As work moved out of the ever smaller household into factories and offices without childcare, women could no longer combine their reproductive labor with participation, at some level, in the productive tasks of the economy, as they had always done previously, whether in foraging, horticultural, or agricultural economies. Thus, an extreme of male specialization in economic production and female confinement to dependent domestic consumption and reproduction was reached, at least as the ideal that the upwardly mobile strove to attain.

Perhaps the very extremes to which the situation had developed caused something of a reversal. For strong intellectual and moral objections to such male dominance began almost as soon as this system became dominant.* However, this patriarchal extreme has been more effectively challenged by significant changes in both the productive and the reproductive realms.

People used to justify the patriarchal division of labor in terms of men's greater average physical strength, which made them more suited to agricultural and industrial labor. But the nature of labor has changed drastically, requiring not physical strength, but training, skill, and intelligence—traits that are not sex specific. Very few jobs, even in the military, can today be creditably linked with the physical endowments of one sex. Gender roles in the productive realm have become more dysfunctional and less useful, less tied to the biological capacities of each sex, than they have ever been in human history. The kinds of economic specializations that were found in foraging, horticultural, and agricultural societies all made a certain amount of sense, given male and female biology. In today's technological environment, to insist that women should specialize in nurturance and reproduction, taking a back seat professionally and economically to men, makes no sense on any grounds, biological, technological, or psychological. Therefore, it becomes almost impossible to maintain the traditional gender roles, no matter how much paranoia and nostalgia some reactionaries conjure up.

At the same time, the reproductive realm has been changing equally, if not more drastically. Many of the conditions that earlier led Buddhists and others to consider female birth a misery to be endured have now been altered. At the most basic level, unless a women overbreeds in complete irresponsibility and insensitivity to global overpopulation, she can no longer occupy herself with reproduction for her lifespan, no matter how hard she tries to be "traditional." She lives too long for that. Even if women specialize in child-rearing for a time, that would take up a short part of the entire lifespan. The existence of birth control, much lower infant and maternal mortality rates, and a vastly increased lifespan means that women cannot focus their whole lives on reproduction, even if their society continues to idealize outmoded models. Since women are intelligent and creative human beings, it should be no surprise that, in this

---

* By the end of the eighteenth century, literature that could be called "feminist" without anachronism was being written. Mary Wollstonecraft's *A Vindication of the Rights of Women* was first published in 1792.

situation, they take up active roles, and even leadership positions, in politics, religion, and economics. Since these activities do not require male anatomy to be successfully pursued, the dysfunctionality of the old gender roles is demonstrated on yet another level.

These causes and conditions for the demise of patriarchy are more apparent in Western societies than in the Asian homeland of Buddhism. But they have already impacted Buddhism to some extent because Buddhism, like all other major religions, is no longer intellectually and spiritually isolated. Buddhism's growing involvement in global intellectual and spiritual developments affects it in other ways besides these technological causes and conditions. Buddhism is ever more subjected to the prophetic voice, to the idea that religions might criticize and shape societies, not just accept them as they are, or withdraw from them. The argument that one cannot really withdraw from situations, but is always involved in outcomes, whether one's participation is active or passive, a more active interpretation of the central Buddhist idea of interdependent co-arising, links well with the prophetic call for judgment, criticism, and responsibility. Therefore, Buddhists are involved in social reconstruction, peace work, animal rights movements, and environmental movements to a degree that was probably unthinkable earlier.

The feminist reconstruction participates in that prophetic set of concerns. For the first time, Buddhists are hearing that patriarchal gender arrangements are not just unpleasant for women, but spiritually harmful to both perpetrators and victims. For the Buddhist elite to participate in sexist discrimination has the same negative effects as would participation in warfare or exploitative economic activities. Conventional gender arrangements are being discussed as discriminatory choices, not as inevitabilities of human biology. The word "oppression" is coming into the vocabulary, making the appeal to women's negative karma less cogent. The old understanding of Mahayana Buddhists that one individual could not be liberated apart from the liberation of the whole interdependent matrix of existence is now being applied to social issues, like women's position in Buddhism, not just to spiritual well-being.

All these new currents in Buddhism owe something to Buddhism's immersion in the global network of ideas and influences, but the Buddhist feminist concerns are especially dependent on Western feminism and are taken most seriously by Western Buddhists. The most powerful agent promoting post-patriarchal Buddhism is the auspicious coincidence of feminism and Buddhism in the West. That Western Buddhists should have so quickly moved into leadership on this issue, which is so critical for Buddhism's future, is due to an auspicious coincidence of two independent streams of influence.

"Auspicious coincidence" is a Buddhist term used in a number of contexts, especially in Tibetan Buddhism. The term is connected with subtle teachings about *karma*, the law of cause and effect as commonly understood in Asian traditions. According to these teachings, events are never random, but happen because of previous causes and conditions that set in motion the factors necessary for their arising. But not all events involve "auspicious coincidence." In an "auspicious coincidence," two lines of cause and effect intersect (coincide) in ways that are "auspicious" (producing positive results) because conditions are somehow "ripe." This phrase, often used to describe the meeting of spiritual teacher (guru) and disciple, is about "coincidence" in the literal sense—that things coincide or happen at the same time, not the frequent popular sense that coinciding is random or inexplicable. That coincidence, happening "in the fullness of time," brings together two lines of cause and effect whose interaction proves to be highly charged, provocative, and productive.

The "coincidence" of Buddhism and feminism in the West may well be such an "auspicious coincidence" capable of producing significant results. Consider first what has coincided. Western Buddhism is a very recent phenomenon. Large numbers of Euro-Americans have taken up serious involvement with Buddhism only in the last twenty to thirty years. Buddhism could become a spiritual possibility for Westerners, rather than an academic hobby or esoteric mind-game, only after the arrival of Asian Buddhist teachers who were willing to work with Westerns students. They did not come in any numbers until the late sixties and early seventies,[8] a time when the countercultural movement meant that Westerners were far more open to such influences. The Westerners who began to meditate did not, however, follow conventional gender roles. To some extent, virtually all of them had been affected and changed by feminism, which was already an important cultural movement. Women simply assumed that, if serious Buddhist practice was beneficial, then it would be beneficial for them. The Asian models were totally ignored, to the extent that it has been suggested that the single biggest difference between Asian and Western Buddhism is the active and equal involvement of women in all aspects of Buddhist practice.

The timing could not have been more critical. Had the teachers arrived ten years earlier, probably women would have been enablers, doing all the childcare and holding bake sales to raise funds for a new shrine hall, while men meditated and studied. That, after all, was the Asian model, as well as the postwar American model. But because the Westerners who were attracted to Buddhism were also at least moderately sympathetic to feminism's goals, a whole new model of Buddhist practice regarding gender spontaneously and naturally burst into being, without intention and theory, at first. The Asian teachers, wisely and perhaps without full understanding of the revolution in which they were participating, taught their female and male students in the same manner, rather than trying to convince the women that they should fill their gender roles and hope for better karma next time.

Something new came into being in this situation. Western Buddhists were in the enviable position of not owing allegiance to any form of patriarchy, despite their having grown up in one culture that had strong patriarchal standards and their growing involvement in a religion from another culture with different, but equally strong, patriarchal standards. For Buddhists, the religious underpinnings of Western patriarchy are no longer relevant in any way. But at the same time, Western Buddhists are free of all the Asian cultural patriarchal baggage. This freedom is partly due to the fact that Buddhist teachers are careful about the distinction between cultural habits and the *dharma*. They do not want their students to become Tibetans or Japanese, but Buddhists. Most of them agree that discrimination against women is a cultural prejudice, not a Buddhist teaching.

To participate in an instance of auspicious coincidence is, of course, not just a matter of good fortune and basking in well-being. With the good fortune and well-being come trust and responsibility. After the magical meeting, the tasks and assignments are transmitted. Western Buddhists are in the position to model and to theorize sane gender arrangements that would finally manifest, in everyday reality, what the Buddhist *dharma* has said explicitly and implicitly for so long.

With too much ignoring or too much complacency, however, this auspicious situation could easily be sabotaged. In the second generation of Western Buddhism, the current visible presence of women could become dim memory. Historically similar situations present an ominous model. In the first generation of a new religious movement or in other frontier situations, women frequently step out of conventional roles into positions of equality and leadership. In subsequent generations, this situation reverses itself and older patterns of gender hierarchy and male dominance reassert themselves. Scholars have made such a case for the beginnings of three major world religions—Buddhism, Christianity, and Islam—as well as many new movements within these and other religions. One could even note, in support of such a thesis, that in the Western "frontier" states of the United States, women obtained the right to vote some years before that right was generally secured by constitutional amendment. For the case of Christianity, I believe that feminist scholars have established incontrovertibly that early Christianity did indeed provide women with a new-found dignity and equality that was soon withdrawn. The case has been less well established for Buddhism, but there is good evidence that such a pattern of new opportunities for women in new situations, followed by a later reversion to patriarchal conventions, occurred several times in the history of Buddhism. With too much ignoring of patriarchy and history, with too much complacency, too much taking Western women's current level of participation in Buddhism for granted, Western Buddhism could manifest merely another instance of that old pattern rather than the results of the auspicious coincidence of Buddhism and feminism.

THE JUDGMENT: ANDROGYNOUS VISION IN BUDDHISM

The verdict derived from consideration of Buddhist historical models and from analysis of the key concepts of Buddhism is that currently, there is an intolerable contradiction between view and practice. To overcome that contradiction, the first line of reconstruction is to reform Buddhist practices surrounding gender. The guideline for such reconstruction is quite simple. It is important to *mandate* and *institutionalize gender equality*, to build it into the very fabric of Buddhist life and institutions completely, in a thoroughgoing fashion.

To mandate gender equality means to regard it as of utmost importance, as a normative obligation for all Buddhists. It could be included in the eightfold path, under the category of right action, which includes all the other ethical and interpersonal norms and the lists of behaviors that one should avoid. It could even be included within the first, and most grave precept, of not harming beings. Once we realize how badly sexism harms both perpetrators and victims, how much it cuts them off from their basic goodness, such a locus for the mandate is not at all extreme.

To institutionalize gender equality means to pay attention to details of community life and organization, as well as to messages being sent out about the relative standing of the various groups within the community. Are all the head teachers men? Do women lead the chanting as often as men? Who sits on the governing bodies? Who does the childcare? Are there female gurus? Are nuns supported as well as monks are? Are the nuns subjected to any diminished status or demeaning rules of behavior? Does everyone have the same opportunity for education and for advanced training in meditation? Or is one sex routinely taking on gender-related tasks that keep them from such education or training in meditation? If gender equality is mandated in the basic ethical guidelines of the tradition, then it will be important to correct any institutional non-compliance, whether deliberate or inadvertent.

These guidelines are aimed specifically at correcting the *practices* of gender discrimination and hierarchy. Buddhist view, the verbal, philosophical formulations of Buddhist *dharma*, is not directly challenged or augmented by mandating and institutionalizing gender equality.

However, the insistence that the Buddhist *dharma*, as it currently exists, must be applied equally to women and men requires something different from what has prevailed throughout Buddhist history. This solution to gender issues is totally different from eliminating painful female birth. The Pure Land being envisioned here will be peopled by both women and men, rather than by men only. This will be an androgynous Pure Land. The view that has prevailed throughout Buddhist history has not produced such an androgynous Pure Land, either in fact or in vision.

What changes when we switch from imagining a Pure Land without painful female birth to a Pure Land inhabited by both women and men who practice Buddhism equally without liability? The vision of an androgynous Pure Land grows out of a subtle but profound shift in consciousness from androcentrism to androgyny. When this transformation occurs, we think of women as human beings, not as objects to be classified, labelled, and limited by male constructed worldviews. To be committed to mandating and institutionalizing gender equality, one must already have experienced this shift in consciousness to some degree. This androgynous consciousness is not incompatible with the core teachings that have prevailed throughout Buddhist history, but those traditional views were formulated with an androcentric rather than with an androgynous mindset. Therefore, while the view found already in Buddhism is not inaccurate, it is undoubtedly incomplete. As we live with newly androgynous Buddhist institutions, we will find the familiar, non-sexist view being augmented and expanded.

Because the term "androgyny" is ambiguous and can be used with a number of meanings, it is important to define its meaning more carefully. As stated in the methodological appendix on feminism, the meaning of "androgyny," as the term is being used in this book, is "both male and female." As scholarly method, model of humanity, and mode of consciousness, it contrasts with "androcentrism" or male-centered consciousness. But it also contrasts significantly with sex-neutral models and ideals, in which something is said to be "neither male nor female." Androgyny affirms both male and female, whatever those labels may involve, while the sex-neutral model denies them both. Both styles of language and thought are useful and appropriate in different contexts. But the sex-neutral model is not sufficient to overcome and undo androcentrism, as we have already seen. Since it is said classically that "the *dharma* is neither male nor female," but not that "the *dharma* is both male and female," these claims need to be carefully spelled out.

We must start with the reality that androcentrism is and has been the prevalent model of humanity and mode of consciousness in Buddhism. Next we must concede the inadequacy, inaccuracy and incompleteness of that mode and model, as delineated in feminist theory. Then we ask what best replaces and overcomes androcentrism and its concomitant social form—male dominance. Most contemporary feminist theory claims that one cannot successfully move from an androcentric to a sex-neutral and sex-blind mode of consciousness or social forms. The attempt to do so will only result in more subtle forms of androcentrism. Instead, one must take seriously the fact that, in present androcentric religion and society, gender roles are very prevalent and people have been thoroughly soaked and socialized in them, to the point that it is accurate to speak of "women's culture" as something distinctly different from men's culture, though women and men also inhabit a common cultural universe. To take these separate cultures seriously means that one must first dive into women's culture to learn what it is about *before* one can hope to speak of "common humanity" that is neither male nor female.

However, there is great resistance on many fronts to spending time and energy to explore "women's reality"[9] specifically and explicitly. There is even more resistance to taking it seriously as a norm for humanity, as an ideal, as a view containing valuable wisdom not found in the general culture or in men's culture. People are often more comfortable with neuter than with androgynous ideals. This can be very clearly demonstrated quite easily. In some versions of monotheism, it is now quite common to make liturgical reforms to bypass the conventionality of referring to the deity only with male pronouns and images. Two options are possible. One can neutralize or neuterize the deity, or one can androgynize the deity. "God the Father" could become "God the Mother and Father," or it could become "God the Parent," even "God the Caregiver." "Father-Mother God" is the least heard option. I have long contended that all the change from "Father" to "parent" accomplishes to make the androcentrism more subtle, whereas "Mother-Father God" forces the awareness that women are dignified, worthy human beings.

In patriarchy, being female is such a shameful condition that many find it impossible to affirm femaleness, even when they really do abhor patriarchy. They would rather leap to an abstract common humanity. But precisely because femaleness has been so degraded, it must be explored and valorized to achieve a genuinely post-patriarchal mode of consciousness and form of society.

Classical Buddhist texts have long claimed that "the *dharma* is neither male nor female," a slogan that was used against those who discriminated against women and denigrated their *dharmic* abilities. The entire corpus of Buddhist teachings can be included under this slogan, for Buddhism does not have any explicitly androcentric doctrines. All this has not kept Buddhism from serious institutional patriarchy. This happened, I believe, because Buddhist doctrine to date has not affirmed women as females, but only as generic humans, while men are affirmed as both males and as generic humans. Buddhist thought has wavered between androcentrism and sex-neuter ideals, but there has been little genuinely androgynous thinking in Buddhism.

However, some Buddhist materials contain a resource in which one can readily ground such thinking. The third-turning teaching of non-dual Suchness and its closely associated Vajrayana concept of feminine and masculine principles provide a base that readily accommodates fully androgynous thinking. The plurality and diversity of phenomenal experience are appreciated without falling into either dualism or monism. Hierarchy is not imposed on the diversity and the masculine and feminine principles are not conflated with men or women. All that we found lacking was the direct translation of symbol into social reality, so that women and men might become androgynous rather than being confined to limiting female and male gender roles.

Starting with the present reality of strong gender roles, which limit both women and men significantly, androgynous thinking takes women's experience seriously, as seriously as it takes the world-construction and the experiences of men. Furthermore, when constructing ideals and norms, it takes the concerns and needs traditionally associated with women as seriously as it takes those associated with men. That is to say, androgynous thinking takes women as human beings, fully and completely, without reference to the question of whether they are very similar to men or very different from them. For men are no longer taken as the norm for humanity and women are no longer measured by how closely they conform to that male norm, falsely called the human norm. Out of these experiences, concerns, and world-constructions of both females and males, we can construct some fully human, humane, sane world—an androgynous Pure Land. The people who live in the Pure Land will be both women and men—each one of them living out some unique style of androgyny.

15

Androgynous Institutions: Issues for Lay, Monastic, and Yogic Practitioners

The feminist reconstruction of Buddhism begins with suggestions regarding everyday practices and institutional forms for two reasons. First, they are much more seriously deficient than is Buddhist theory about gender. Second, such obvious problems are more easily noticed than the subtle omissions to Buddhist doctrines that result from androcentrism. Therefore, any androgynous adjustments or additions to the Buddhist teachings would suggest themselves only after or in conjunction with serious changes in the institutional format. Usually, male dominance in the social or ritual spheres is more obvious and more objectionable than subtly androcentric intellectual, doctrinal formulations; thus it is much more likely to noticed, critiqued, and reconstructed first. This model also holds for Christian feminism. People agitated first for the ordination of women, and even today accept it far more readily than they insist on female god-language, even though male god-language is probably the cause of the problem and the male priesthood the effect.

At first, reconstruction of Buddhist institutions seems simple. Women have been excluded from the game and kept on the sidelines as cheerleaders. So let's allow women to join in the game. Let's open the meditation halls, classrooms, and monasteries equally to women. Women need and want equal rights to be human, to do the same things men have always done. At this point, it is usually assumed that the rules of the game are appropriate as they stand, that the problem has been that women were not allowed to play. Such liberal, or equal-rights feminism is the first rebellious move away from patriarchy. The opposition to it usually states that women are intrinsically different and really cannot play by the same rules.

Women who succeed at playing the men's game often come to share some of the antifeminist belief that women do indeed do things differently. But rather than concluding that women should, therefore, retire from the public life of the classroom, boardroom, and meditation hall, to return to the bedroom and the kitchen, they begin to critique and rewrite the rules of the game that is played out in the public sphere. The rules of the game, having been written by men, are male rules reflecting men's values in a patriarchal, gender-role ridden culture. They are not necessarily very complete, humane, or sane, as they stand. Rewriting the rules involves not just changing the formal guidelines of the game, though that is an important step; it eventually includes reconceptualizing why people play the game, how to construct game plans, and what is the point or purpose of the game. This more radical feminist critique and reconstruction is far more creative and liberating than the first stage of simply letting women do the things men have always done and become just like men. That is because equal-rights feminism is still somewhat androcentric, whereas radical or transformative feminism calls for androgynization of the entire game and all its players.

To rewrite the rules from an androgynous perspective within Buddhism will involve first rethinking the various options and styles of involvement with Buddhism. All three major lifestyles of Buddhism—monastic, lay, and yogic—as currently practiced are seriously lacking from a feminist point of view. The most favored members of the community are the monks, who alone fully involve themselves in all dimensions of Buddhist practice. Nuns have a decidedly secondary position within the monastic elite. Lay people are looked to mainly for economic support. In their everyday lives, laypeople follow prevailing male-dominant gender roles and stereotypes, which further limits nuns. In Tantric forms of Buddhism, the third option for style of involvement in Buddhist practice, the *yogi-yogini* lifestyle, which is neither strictly monastic or lay, is important. This option will be appealing to contemporary Buddhist feminists, but not with its traditional tendency to focus on the *yogi*, while ignoring the *yogini*.

OVERCOMING MUTUAL INCOMPETENCE:
ANDROGYNOUS LAY BUDDHISM

The androgynous reconstruction of lay Buddhism must take into account two rather different problems. The first is that Buddhism offers very weak models for meaningful lay Buddhist life and must forge new paths in the West and in the modern world, even without reference to the questions and issues raised by feminism. The second set of issues concerns creating styles of lay Buddhist life that accord with a feminist vision of androgyny beyond the unsatisfactory mutual incompetence fostered by patriarchal gender roles.

Classical Buddhism was the religion and lifestyle of its monastic elite. They not only kept the simple ethical code of Buddhism, but also pursued its philosophical and meditational disciplines, thought to be essential to attaining enlightenment. The laity, by contrast, were taught and observed the lay version of the ethical precepts, but were not expected to have the time, interest, or will power to pursue Buddhist meditation and philosophy seriously. Buddhism, as a lay tradition, is faced with serious structural problems. Valuing neither pious devotion to deities, unquestioning adherence to doctrines, nor faithful performance of ritual as an effective means to release, one is left with a serious question. What is Buddhist observance for the non-renunciate householder in a tradition that regards deep personal transformation resulting from protracted meditation and study as the only means to release?

Classical Buddhism worked out an answer to this question that promoted a deeply symbiotic relationship between the lay and monastic communities and that provided a means for lay Buddhists to work towards their own eventual enlightenment. Called the "two accumulations," this solution thought of the whole process of spiritual attainment as quite long, occurring in different stages. To be free, one needed to accumulate sufficient merit and sufficient wisdom. Merit was earned mainly through generosity and brought one to the life situation in which freedom-granting accumulation of wisdom, gained through study and meditation, would be possible. The most effective method of accumulating merit was generosity to those already engaged full time in the accumulation of wisdom. Thus, lay Buddhists could participate meaningfully in the perpetuation of their tradition, while at the same time promoting their own future spiritual well-being.

In this system, laywomen, if they controlled their own resources, were not at any disadvantage to laymen. Buddhist literature contains accounts of highly admired generous laywomen, such as Vishakha,[1] who sometimes were more committed to Buddhism than were their husbands. In cases in which the household as a whole was committed to the support of monks, the laywomen, who managed food and other household resources, were the actual donors who, day by day, ladled out food into the monks' begging bowls. Women were at a disadvantage only in situations in which they did not control resources and their husbands or fathers disapproved of the monks. Such stories also occur in Buddhist literature and are prominent in the account of Nangsa Obum.[2]

However, this system also presumes the existence of a large body of Buddhists who have both financial resources and the wish to delay their own intensive involvement in Buddhist study and practice. As such, it is a highly unlikely model for Western Buddhists. Not too many wealthy Westerners are becoming Buddhists. Furthermore, most people who take on Buddhism as their religion of choice, whether wealthy or not, are primarily interested in it as a full-scale discipline of study, practice, and ethics for themselves—though most of them do not want to become monks or nuns in the process of taking on commitments to serious Buddhist study and practice. If they could support someone in monastic practice, they would, but few have such resources available. Virtually everyone contributes to the maintenance of meditation centers, but they also use these centers extensively themselves and a large portion of their financial support to the institutions is in the form of fees they pay to attend programs.

Thus a very different model of non-monastic lay Buddhism is being created among Western Buddhists. In this model, for lay, as for monastic practitioners, the heart of their involvement in Buddhism is a commitment to the practice of meditation and the study of Buddhist teachings. They may not do such disciplines as intensively as do monks and nuns, but they do them frequently, and, at intermittent intervals, quite intensively. This model is largely dependent on the needs of Western Buddhists, but I think it is also much more adequate than the classic symbiotic model. In the model of lay meditators at the heart of the Buddhist community, a much more complete version of Buddhism is being followed by the average Buddhist. For, while generosity is central to Buddhist values, no one would claim that it is sufficient for the full practice of Buddhism. For that, study and practice are also required in all versions of Buddhism with the exception of East Asian Pure Land Buddhism. This model perhaps also accords with the needs of contemporary people in general, since lay meditation has also become quite important in Buddhist revivals in several Asian countries.[3] For women, this model of lay Buddhist life can work very well; many Western Buddhist laywomen who use this method of combining worldly pursuits with serious Buddhist practice have been able to pursue more advanced meditation practices and philosophical studies than do Buddhist nuns in many Asian contexts.

However, this model of lay Buddhist life also brings up certain issues that intersect with central feminist concerns. The young people first attracted to Buddhism in the sixties and seventies were childless and marginally employed, for the most part. Ten years later they had both children and careers. Meditation centers, probably for the first time in Buddhist history, were struggling to provide childcare for meditators attending intensive meditation sessions. The Western women who became Buddhists became *Buddhists*, not enablers of Buddhist men. When the women insist on practicing Buddhism as fully as do the men, and when lay Buddhists with families and careers insist that the heart of their involvement in Buddhism is meditation and study, not just donating to others who meditate and study, vast changes are required. Fortunately, feminist thought had already considered related problems in great depth.

Much of the most practical feminist thought deals with an evaluation of patriarchal gender roles and with proposals for more attractive, equitable, and humane alternatives. Both the critique and the proposed alternative are summarized quite well in the suggestion that it is desirable to avoid mutual incompetence. With the extreme of male specialization in production and economic activities and female specialization in reproduction and caretaking that were the stereotypical ideal, a state of rather advanced mutual incompetence has been achieved in all patriarchal religions and societies. Extremely strong, rigid, and fixed gender roles always result in caricatures, half-humans who are emotionally stunted and inept at many essential life tasks.

The alternative is not to banish all specialization, for people do have special abilities that warrant fostering. But specializations would not be expected to follow gender lines, since psychological measurements show overlapping curves delineating male and female test results in all areas. Men may, on the average, have higher test scores in certain areas and women in others. But many women will have great ability at a skill for which men have higher average scores than women. The reverse is also true. This fact is ignored by those who encourage conformity to gender stereotypes by citing averages garnered from test results as their justification.

To avoid the mutual incompetence fostered by rigid gender roles, some basic competencies should be expected of all human beings, rather than being assigned along gender lines. All people should be able and willing to take some responsibility for their livelihood, rather than being dependent on others completely, as some women have believed is their right. And all people should be able and willing to nurture themselves and others emotionally and psychologically, rather than regarding it as their right to remain "relational retards," to quote a friend's characterization of many men. Furthermore, these expectations beyond mutual incompetence are not merely unwelcome obligations thrust upon the unwilling victim by social reformers. They are integral to becoming fully human, to realizing one's innate potential to be both competent and nurturing, which is the only way to live up to the opportunities that come with the "precious human birth."[4]

More explicitly, the well-known feminist suggestion that women share in the burdens and joys of livelihood and that men share in the burdens and joys of housework and childcare is the agenda for going beyond mutual incompetence toward androgyny. As already discussed, the prevailing patriarchal ways of constructing both production and reproduction, and linking them with gender have already become obsolete and dysfunctional. But, to date, in moving from mutual incompetence toward androgyny, women have made considerably more progress than have men. Both women and men seem to be more eager for and comfortable with women moving into male roles and specializations than vice versa. Women have taken on the responsibilities for livelihood and self-sufficiency to a considerably greater degree than men have taken on responsibility for housework and childcare *or for emotional maturity and communication skills.* Once again, the shame associated with femaleness in patriarchal culture makes many people of both sexes reluctant to encourage men to become more womanly, though encouraging women to be more manly is frequently regarded as good advice.

In the Buddhist world, this was brought home to me very clearly in a small, but indicative example. I once taught a course on Buddhism and feminism to a mainly Japanese/American Buddhist congregation. The men, who became quite enthusiastic at a certain point, eagerly told me that they had decided they wanted to initiate a rule that every other congregation president should be a woman. At the time we were feasting on a wonderful meal that the women had prepared in the temple kitchen. I suggested that it was a very good idea, but that it needed to be balanced by a requirement that men do some of the work in the temple kitchen, so that the women could, indeed, sit on the board without becoming overworked. The men's faces fell dramatically and drastically.

In the context of lay Buddhist practice, responsibilities for both livelihood and reproduction, the stereotypical male and female specializations, must be structured in a way that is compatible with and fosters serious lay Buddhist practice. For lay Buddhists to be seriously involved with the accumulation of wisdom, not only the accumulation of merit, means that the priority is given to one's Buddhist practice, whatever that comes to mean, not to one's livelihood and domestic involvements. The feminist critique of conventional ways of handling both livelihood and domestic life meshes well with Buddhist concerns to balance and limit these activities sufficiently to be able to engage in serious Buddhist practice.

To some, the primary feminist approach to the workplace is its demand for equal opportunity at all levels of employment, and its advocacy that women be economically competent, rather than continuing to rely on men for their maintenance. Indeed, these are important concerns, the former in the interests of promoting justice, and the latter in the interests of promoting human wholeness and psychological well-being. Feminist assessments of livelihood recognize that it is dangerous for women when they are discriminated against in the workplace, because they are then vulnerable economically and psychologically, and also that most human beings develop a sense of vocation beyond their own domestic nest if they are not confined to their immediate environment. Though less clearly recognized, this agenda also frees men from the unfair and unreasonable expectations sometimes placed upon them to provide others with economic support.

However, that is only the first agenda in the feminist discussion of livelihood and the workplace. Congruent with the more radical feminist insight that women ultimately want, not just to play the men's game using their rules, but to help write more humane and sane rules, feminists want not only access to the workplace but a better working environment once there. Though there are many facets to this desire for a more humane, less alienating work environment, one of the most important, and most relevant to Buddhists, concerns the unreasonable time demands commonplace in many professions. One constantly hears of the difficulties of working mothers trying to balance demanding, time-intensive careers with their desire to spend time with their children. This visible and often discussed problem is only the tip of the iceberg, however. Work is scheduled and structured in a way to make it inimical to self-development, psychological growth, and long term well-being. This generalization is more, rather than less true, in more rewarding, creative, and prestigious livelihoods. The experience of parents wanting to spend more time with children and finding it difficult to do so, due to work demands, only highlights the situation faced by everyone who wants both to contribute meaningfully through livelihood and to lead a meaningful life. When workdays readily creep up to twelve hours in length, insufficient time is left for becoming fully human through friendship, family time, artistic endeavors, exercise, and spiritual discipline. This is a doubly insane situation, for not only are people with careers prohibited from developing their full humanity, but many other people are shunted into work situations in which their potential is underutilized, and yet others are unemployed.

For the lay Buddhist meditator, this situation presents serious obstacles. Traditionally, one of the reasons lay people were not expected to practice meditation very seriously is precisely because of overwhelming time demands thought to be unavoidable in their domestic and economic lives. Being a lay Buddhist meditator is unquestionably much more demanding and time-intensive than being a lay member of most other religions. The model of lay Buddhist meditators being developed in both Western and Asian forms of Buddhism seeks to find a middle path between the traditional choices of being either a monk with plenty of time for spiritual discipline or a layperson with very little time for it. The encouragement to become a workaholic that is so pervasive in contemporary society is certainly a major negative factor against the development of this new model. To deal with this situation, one could imagine a new dimension to guidance on "right livelihood." Not only does right livelihood involve supporting one's self by means of a socially useful job. One could also understand that right livelihood should include a sense of balance and proportion that integrates work into the rest of life and avoids workaholism.

For lay Buddhist meditators, it is also important to spread the concern for livelihood between the sexes, rather than to link gender with responsibility for livelihood. The positive dimensions of livelihood, its satisfactions and relevance, can be an important dimension of lay Buddhist practice. When livelihood is satisfying and enhances one's practice, female as well as male meditators need the opportunity for such a positive relationship with livelihood. In so far as livelihood can become all-consuming and burdensome, it is even more important for the sexes to share livelihood responsibility. Job sharing, or at least sharing the task of earning sufficient income, is a reasonable solution to the need both to have a livelihood and to have major blocks of time away from it. Feminists often advocate such arrangements, but many employers are less than eager to make them available. For Buddhists, who want to be able to spend significant amounts of time in spiritual discipline, such an option would be appealing. Otherwise, the person who takes responsibility for livelihood is likely to end up with insufficient time for self-development and spiritual discipline, while the stay-at-home partner may not be so burdened and, in many cases, finds it much easier to blend spiritual discipline into the daily routine.

The other major human occupation that has been assigned following gender lines and that has been thought to be too distracting and time-consuming to be combined with serious meditation practice is the round of domestic, nurturing, reproductive responsibilities. Since women have been so completely defined by and limited to their reproductive roles, and since it is so difficult to combine contemporary methods of securing livelihood with ability to give childcare, restructuring the parental occupation is a very high priority. To do so, it is helpful to survey both Buddhist and feminist perspectives on parenthood and motherhood. Then we will be in a better position to suggest some restructurings of domestic and parenting activities that avoid both mutual incompetence and the overburdening that makes serious lay Buddhist practice so difficult.

Buddhist attitudes toward mothers (who were almost solely responsible for childcare in the contexts in which the classic texts were written) are complex and differ with the context. The literal mother is not a spiritually valued model; if anything she is regarded as someone whose spiritual development is likely to be minimal. Motherhood is not idealized, as in some religious traditions. If anything, the sufferings attendant on motherhood are one of the things that makes female rebirth undesirable. Motherhood as a symbol is more highly regarded, as we have already seen in the discussion of Prajanparamita as "Mother of all the Buddhas" and Vajrayogini as the "Co-emergent Mother." This ambiguity regarding motherhood is not untypical of androcentric evaluations of motherhood. On the other hand, at least Buddhists do not idealize the self-sacrificing, over-burdened mother as The Woman Who Is Fulfilling Her True Potential, a Paragon of Female Virtue, to be emulated by all women, the mother to whom every son and husband is entitled by rights of masculine privilege.

A widespread Buddhist assessment of motherhood is that motherhood inevitably brings attachment, which always brings grief quickly behind it, and which is the emotion that traps one in endless *samsara*. A mother cannot avoid attachment, but attachment is a negative, unproductive, pain-filled attitude, to be replaced by detached joy and equanimity. In the *Therigatha*, mothers frequently became nuns after being grief-stricken by the death of children. In so doing, they make the transition from attachment to detachment, from motherhood to the spiritual life, from suffering to joy and equanimity.

The quality of attachment is the negative aspect of motherhood, not the care and concern for another involved in mothering, for such concern, when detached rather than attached, is highly prized, especially in Mahayana Buddhism. Diana Paul has very clearly delineated the difference:

> In similar ways the Bodhisattva strongly and intensely identifies with all living beings as a mother identifies with her child. Yet the Bodhisattva, unlike the mother, remains free and detached from living beings through the wisdom of Emptiness. The mother does not view the world as empty. She is in a never-ending cycle of attachment. The conflict between the mother's role and the spiritually free and detached individual is resolved by the Bodhisattva.[5]

The text which she analyzes in her chapter on motherhood speaks of a young monk who remembers his past lives. In each of four previous lives, he died very young and now remembers his mothers' intense grief. He then narrates how grief-stricken his mother in his present life became when he left home to study the path. His resolution to this problem is in keeping with Bodhisattva vows: "Now, because I am liberated, I remember my five mothers [from former lifetimes] who were unable to be free because they grieved over me. I vow that they all will finally end [their grief]."[6]

In these traditional contexts, one finds little, if any, celebration of the joys of parenthood, probably because family life is of relatively low value to these monastic authors. The more immediate and pressing question of the possibility of a detached style of parenthood, based on the practice of mindfulness, meditation, and spiritual discipline, is not discussed, to my knowledge, in any classical sources. Such possibilities are, however, critically important for post-patriarchal Buddhism.

In other contexts, one is encouraged to regard one's mother positively because of all that she suffered on one's behalf, and most especially because she took care of her helpless infant. In the important Mahayana meditation of "taking and sending,"[7] otherwise known as "exchanging oneself with others," one encourages one's feelings of kindness and one's ability to extend kindness to others by first remembering one's mother, to whom, more than anyone else, one should be kind and generous because of her caretaking. I have heard teachers be quite adamant that it doesn't matter if you think she did things wrong or was cruel—"she still took care of you when you were helpless." Traditional religions tend to side with parents against children in requiring respect and reverence unconditionally. Some Buddhist teachers would probably say that, no matter what else they did, or neglected to do, your parents gave you the precious human body, so veneration is appropriate and anger or criticism is inappropriate.

Interestingly, in these various considerations of human mothers, they are never taken as models of compassion or proper dedication to others' well-being. Rather, the meditator pities his mother because of her attached grief over him, or she regards the mother as the easiest and most natural object of her compassion and generosity, almost a lubricant to intensify and expand the compassion which she, as a Bodhisattva, wants to feel, in a detached manner, toward all beings. In countless Mahayana contexts, after one arouses compassion by thinking of one's own mother, all her sufferings, and one's eagerness to ease her burden, one then reflects that, in the ceaseless round of rebirth into *samsaric* existence, all beings have, at one time or another, been one's mother and suffered for oneself. The "mother sentient beings" are constantly in the Mahayanist's awareness, not as models of compassion, but as models of the recipients of compassion.

Mothers are models in classical Buddhism only when they are embodiments of the feminine principle of wisdom, which gives birth to Buddhahood. This valorization is double-edged. On the one hand, it recognizes the utter primacy of birth-giving and nurturing as the foundation of life. To have positive maternal symbols at some level in a religious symbol system can help valorize parenthood and provide models for humans. A person can, for example, recognize that one does not have to be a literal mother to mother both projects and people. And perhaps literal parents could model themselves more upon the principle of even-minded wisdom that gives birth to Buddhahood, and less upon the model of attached, *samsaric* styles of parenthood. On the other hand, embodiments of feminine wisdom give birth to Buddhahood, not to screaming infants who try one's patience, disrupt one's meditation practice, and produce dirty diapers. Not much has yet been said about handling that result of birth-giving in the context of being a lay Buddhist meditator!

Feminist considerations of motherhood are quite different from Buddhist evaluations and are highly varied, ranging from Shulamith Firestone's early call to free women through the development of artificial wombs[8] to endorsements of maternity as the most noble human activity, a model for solving other difficult human problems.[9] Of these, the discussions by Nancy Chodorow and Dorothy Dinnerstein[10] of the dynamic that occurs when women are given sole responsibility for early childcare, are most relevant for a reconstruction of androgynous parenthood for lay Buddhist meditators. According to both of them, "much of what is wrong with men and women as individuals (and us as a society) . . . is traceable to the fact that women do all the mothering."[11] They both are convinced that "the oppression of women originates in the female monopoly on mothering."[12] Both of them also see dual parenting as the way to end the oppression of women as well as to raise saner, more whole people who are not caught up in the dysfunctionalities of gender roles.

They explain how women's monopoly on early childcare produces all these negative effects and how dual parenting would assuage the situation, not in terms of the fairness of sharing the joys and the burdens of motherhood, but in terms of pre-oedipal consequences for an infant raised only by a female. Such child-rearing practices give the infant lifelong negative attitudes about women, whether the infant is a boy or a girl.

Since Dinnerstein's analysis is more directly relevant to Buddhism, I will focus more on it. According to her, the infant experiences its caregiver as its mode of introduction to ". . . an unreliable and unpredictable universe."

> Mother is the source of pleasure and pain for the infant, who is never certain whether his or her physical or psychological needs will be met. As a result, the infant grows up feeling very ambivalent toward mother figures (women) and what they represent (the material/physical universe).[13]

Men, when grown, do not want to re-experience such utter dependence on another and seek to control both women and nature. Women, when grown, seek to be controlled by men, trying to keep their own maternal power in check. This situation leads to the conventional gender arrangements that are so dysfunctional and mutually destructive. But, most important, especially for Buddhists, women's control over childrearing is responsible for "our subsequent tendency to blame mother/woman for everything wrong with the human condition, especially the fact that we are limited beings destined to fail and ultimately to die."[14]

This situation, Dinnerstein argues, can be rectified by dual parenting. Then, because men share equally in the task of nurturing infants and introducing them to the frustrations of being human, grown infants will no longer be able to scapegoat and blame women alone for the human condition. Therefore, the major reason for dual parenting is not to free women to participate more fully in culture or to allow men to experience the satisfactions of parenthood, though these are useful side effects. The critical need served by dual parenting is freeing the next generation from the unconscious, pre-oedipal hatred and fear of women that makes mutually satisfying relations between the sexes, as well as full humanity, so difficult for both women and men to achieve.

In post-patriarchal Buddhism, parenthood will need to be constructed quite differently than it has been in conventional society, Buddhist or non-Buddhist. Building parenthood on the foundation of serious lay meditation practice means that parenthood should be undertaken much more deliberately, mindfully, and seriously than has usually been the case previously. Then there may be some possibility for parents to become at least somewhat detached in their parenting. Dual parenting, in both literal and extended meanings, would be chosen for many reasons, including the ones outlined by Dinnerstein. And Buddhist meditation centers would routinely offer childcare in conjunction with meditation training.

For lay Buddhists to take the accumulation of wisdom through meditation practice as a central expression of their Buddhist identity should change their structuring of reproduction very dramatically. First, and most important, having children at all should become a mature choice, not a product of chance. People whose basic mental and spiritual discipline is the development of mindfulness and awareness should not slide into reproduction mindlessly. Doing so could easily be construed as a violation of the major precept to avoid sexual misconduct. Rather, being aware of one's likely behaviors ahead of time and being prepared with birth control should be routine practice for lay Buddhist meditators, a refreshing change from practices advocated in some religious traditions.

Furthermore, introducing some real egolessness and detachment into the childrearing process would greatly improve the experience for both parents and children. The percentage of children conceived and raised primarily as an extension of their parents' egos, and the emotional abuse inherent in such a situation are astounding. Egoless parents would not conceive children out of habitual responses to societal pressure and then regard the children as extensions of themselves, whose purpose is to fulfill the parents' needs and expectations. Some ability to regard children as beings whose karmic potentialities bring them temporarily into close relationships with oneself, rather than as possessions or objects to be shaped into the desired result, would eliminate some of the painful attachment, leading to grief, that is usually associated with motherhood in classical Buddhist texts.

Though this call for a more detached, egoless style of parenting applies to both men and women to some extent, I believe it would seriously and positively undercut one of the most unattractive aspects of femininity, as it is constructed by patriarchy. This is the tendency, socialized into all women and believed by many, that they can always flee to maternity to find something to do with their lives. Because men do not have this easy biological resolution of the quest for meaning and relevance in one's life, deep resentments between the sexes are fostered. Women who find in maternity the meaning they cannot find in their own lives often fall into an extreme of attached parenting, living through their children.

The burdens placed on children when they are extensions of parents' egos are immense and can require many years of spiritual discipline to overcome. That such burdens were inflicted and carried in classical Buddhist cultures, not just in non-Buddhist societies, is demonstrated by the repeated theme in Buddhist biographical literature of parents who object strenuously to the child's desire not to marry and continue the family line, but to take up the religious life. But such Buddhist parents were undoubtedly not the lay Buddhist meditators being developed in contemporary forms of Buddhism—a further point in favor of developing a whole new model of lay Buddhism.

Egoless and mindful decisions to take on parenthood should also have profoundly positive effects on several other issues. In the context of egolessness and the Bodhisattva vow, the primary issue surrounding children should become a concern for the quality of life available to the children that are reborn, rather than the mindless pro-natalism that fuels so many public policies and private prejudices. Adoption should be a widely favored option of egoless, detached parents who have taken the bodhisattva vow, whether or not they can conceive their own children. Especially for those who do not readily conceive, adoption rather than medical extremes should be a routine option. There are already plenty of children in the world—too many for the safety of Earth. Recognizing that, mindful and detached, egoless parents would limit their reproduction. Recognizing the hazards of overpopulation, reproductive choices are not made solely on the basis of private ability to support another child or desires for one. Limiting one's own reproduction to care for children properly and fully could well be considered part of the most basic precept of non-harming. Everyone loses from excessive reproduction, from the planet, to crowded, undernourished, poverty-stricken people, to children who do not receive sufficient attention from their parents, to the parents who are too consumed with childcare to take care of themselves emotionally and spiritually.

Parents who are lay Buddhist meditators need to structure their parenting so that it is not in conflict with their own disciplines of meditation and study. This means that dual parenting, extended parenting, and communal childcare networks are essential. Formal institutions of the Buddhist world must be involved in this extended childcare. First-generation Western Buddhists are struggling with questions of how to educate their children about Buddhism and how to raise Buddhist children in a non-Buddhist environment. This is not an issue that can be dealt with family by family. As "monasteries," i.e. places dedicated to spiritual discipline, become at least in part meditation centers frequented by lay Buddhists, childcare and children's education become concerns of Buddhist centers in a way that has probably not happened previously. Buddhist lay meditator parents usually do not want to break their spiritual discipline entirely during the years that they have young children. The old solution of having women deal with the children until they are old enough to be able to manage at Buddhist ceremonies and meditation sessions is not appropriate in feminist perspective, which insists that women be accorded the privileges and responsibilities that go with the "precious human birth," rather than being treated as a servant class. Therefore, Western Buddhist institutions currently are experimenting with how best to meet the needs of lay Buddhist meditators with children.[15]

Concerning routine daily childcare, some restructuring, including significant primary childcare from fathers and other forms of extended childcare, is necessary, even on non-Buddhist grounds. The expected style of parenting in some Western societies has reached an extreme, even for male-dominant societies. Even in patriarchal societies, it is unusual to isolate one women with her children, cutting her off from other women, the adult world in general, participation in household economic production and other cultural activities. Some form of communal caretaking from members of an extended family, servants, and neighborhood networks is far more common. (Of course, the frequent practice of pressing young girls into heavy childcare responsibilities is not a feasible alternative.) Some extended childcare provides relief from too much and too constant contact with one's own children, some interaction with other adults, and a mechanism for participation in ongoing adult economic and cultural activities. This cross-cultural information is important for setting the furor over childcare that rages in our society into perspective.

Dual parenting usually means that fathers should also take primary responsibility for early childcare. That suggestion, however, presupposes a two-parent family, which is not the situation in which many women and children find themselves. These mothers also need relief from being the major caregiver, perhaps even more than women in two-parent families. Men who may not be living with their children's mother still need to be involved in primary caregiving and children not living with their own father still need a male caregiver if the kind of problems pointed out by Dinnerstein are to be avoided. This suggests that some breakdown in the conventional privatization of the family and a greater reliance on extended communal care networks, including communal living arrangements, especially among single parents, would be useful.

Arguments for extended networks for routine, daily childcare, including significant primary involvement from fathers, or from men in general, can be made on two levels. First, one should recognize considerations of fairness and of promoting human wholeness beyond mutual incompetence. Childcare is rather time-intensive and absorbing. Parents routinely complain of the difficulty of getting anything done that involves concentration and withdrawal, such as meditation practice or study. Mothers who are lay Buddhist meditators need and deserve time for their own spiritual discipline. And in situations in which mothers commonly do have employment outside the home, fairness would dictate that they receive significant help from their partners in parenting, the stereotypical female specialization, just as they are providing help with the stereotypical male specialization, providing economic support. Such arrangements would ease one of the greatest sources of frustration among contemporary women. On the other hand, those who argue that childcare is so rewarding and satisfying that women are foolish to want to do anything else cannot, in good conscience, make it difficult for men to participate in such a rewarding and renewing experience. That would be another form of gender privilege, something that is consistently undermined by Buddhist doctrine and humane social arrangements.

Finally, the post-Freudian feminist psychoanalytic analysis of Dorothy Dinnerstein has great relevance in the Buddhist context. As she, and many others reconstruct it, infancy and early childhood are not especially easy experiences for the infant. It is a time of discovering limits and frustrations and experiencing the beginning of long-lasting resentment against those conditions. In Buddhist terms, the infant or young child is discovering and being introduced to the inevitably *samsaric* character of human existence. *Nothing* a parent does, no quality of care, no matter how appropriate and loving, can alter or change this basic fact, which is very disturbing to both parent and child. Some parents, like Siddartha Gautama's father, struggle to keep their children from experiencing *samsara*, seeming to believe that if they are loving and available enough, their children will avoid finitude and limitation. Some grown children have a hard time disentangling what their parents did to them, which may indeed have been abusive, from their inevitable immersion in limitation and finitude, frustration and dissatisfaction.

In this drama of blame and guilt, mothers often come in for more resentment than fathers. I believe Dinnerstein is right when she postulates that this is because, in a culture that places on women alone primary responsibility for childcare, women preside over all the incidents of frustration and limitation that initiate us into the human condition, and are subconsciously blamed for those inevitabilities. Succinctly, in Buddhist terms, she is arguing that, in conventional patriarchal culture, women, more than men, introduce us to *samsara*, and are, on some level, blamed for it in a way that men are not, even if the child later learns that such suffering is inevitable and results from karma accrued in past lives. This blame takes one form in persistent religious symbolism and mythology that sees women as intrinsically evil and that blames women for the human fall from primordial innocence and bliss. Buddhism, as we have seen, does include this motif, though it is less dominant and normative than in many other religions. Nevertheless, in Buddhism, women are feared and resented in a way that men never are. This resentment may well be linked to our resentment and fear of the whole *samsaric* mess to which we are introduced by our primary caregivers—who happen, unfortunately, to be almost exclusively women.

For Buddhism, however, unlike Dinnerstein, introduction to *samsara* is not the only message we learn. Only the first two of the Four Noble Truths talk about *samsara*. The last two talk about release, freedom, and spiritual discipline. But the gurus and religious teachers who introduce us the those disciplines and to the possibility of *nirvana* are almost always men. This division of labor is very difficult and unbalanced. Women are informally, but rather systematically excluded from religious leadership and from teaching roles in Buddhism, but they alone are left with the task of introducing their children to *samsara*. Meanwhile, men are freed both to pursue *nirvana* for themselves and to teach the methods promoting freedom to others. Perhaps, subconsciously, women have been excluded from teaching roles *because* of their conventional associations with our initiation into limited and frustrating *samsaric* human existence. Rather an unpleasant and vicious circle!

For Buddhism a great deal is at stake in breaking this vicious circle. Probably the point at which the links can be severed is with large-scale serious involvement of laywomen in Buddhist meditation and with massive reforms regarding philosophical and meditative training for nuns. From that point, reconstruction can occur in two directions. Such women will take on teaching roles in Buddhism, whether inside or outside the recognized structures of authority, thereby breaking the male near-monopoly on the introduction of spiritual discipline and *nirvana*. And some men will, for various reasons, take on their fair share on childcare, thus breaking the female monopoly on the introduction of the next generation to *samsara*. Breaking these two monopolies, which make women primary childcare givers and men primary Buddhist teachers, will begin to undo all the extra and unnecessary negativity and pain brought to *samsara* by those monopolies.

MONASTICISM AFTER PATRIARCHY:
RECONSTRUCTING THE HEART OF TRADITIONAL BUDDHISM

Traditional Buddhism's heavy reliance on its monastic institutions, which are preponderantly male at present, is responsible, more than anything else, for the superficial impression that Buddhism is a highly patriarchal religion. This male dominance, almost male monopoly, at the heart of traditional Buddhism also produces that familiar ache experienced so often by every religious feminist— of being on the outside looking in. Most recently, I leafed through a beautifully illustrated book called *Living Buddhism*.[16] My partner commented, "There sure aren't many pictures of women," and there it was again—that stab in the heart that angers and saddens all at once.

The androgynous reconstruction of monastic institutions is the least threatening or revolutionary part of the feminist agenda for post-patriarchal Buddhism. The reforms simply would bring women fully, without prejudice or discrimination, into the heart of traditional Buddhism, its monasteries and educational institutions, which have been primarily responsible for preserving and transmitting Buddhism. The modifications to what is already in place would not be nearly as massive as those required for lay Buddhism. Furthermore, in some cases, historical precedents favor the reformers, not the present conservative holders of power and authority.

Because the required reforms are so undisruptive and have such great continuity with traditional Buddhism, the opposition of some Buddhist leaders to any of the reforms and the slow pace of the male hierarchs in all Buddhist sects, are extremely discouraging. If someone with the prestige of the Dalai Lama were simply to declare that recent Buddhist ways of dealing with nuns are inappropriate and un-Buddhist, and to insist that his order, at least, take direct action to correct the situation, that would be a tremendously beneficial development.* Declarations of support and sympathy, while the situation is investigated further, are not nearly so helpful. One has to wonder what there is to investigate! It is difficult to imagine that the issue could be controversial. Rather, the present situation should be a matter of extreme embarrassment to the Buddhist establishment.

The slowness with which even the most sympathetic male authorities act on issues such as re-establishing the nuns' order and educating and supporting nuns adequately and equally has the effect of making me mistrust them on other matters, including their ability as spiritual advisors. If they can't be adequate on something as simple and straightforward as restoring the nuns' order or treating nuns fairly, one has to wonder how they can be trusted on much more complex and subtle questions, such as whether certain symbols or practices might be androcentric and damaging to women. The unfortunate, but perhaps saluatory, réaction is a certain skepticism, a feeling that it is safer to check everything out for myself rather than to have blind and total trust in the hierarchy. Such an

---

* Karma Lekshe Tsomo, ed., *Sakyadhita: Daughters of the Buddha* (Ithaca, NY: Snow Lion, 1988), pp. 267–76, published an interview with the Dalai Lama on this issue. While one gains the impression from this interview that, while he personally is quite sympathetic to the reintroduction of the nuns' ordination into Tibetan Buddhism, he is also quite cautious about in his statements about how to effect this reform.

attitude may somewhat compromise the recommendation that devotion to the guru is essential in Vajrayana Buddhism, but under the circumstances, there is no alternative.

Some feminists might wonder why reconstructing the monastic institutions should be important to Buddhist women. Nunship, whether of the Buddhist or the Christian variety, is not the most popular or best understood option for women among contemporary feminists. They often see it as highly patriarchal and as rather repressive, because of the centrality of celibacy to monastic discipline. While it is true that current forms of Buddhist monasticism are male-dominated, post-patriarchal reconstruction would change that. And whatever place repression of sexuality may have in Christian nunship, that is not the central concern for Buddhist nuns. Celibacy in Buddhist monasticism is a means rather than an end.

One can make a rather strong case for the attractiveness of the nuns' lifestyle, especially in post-patriarchal Buddhism. Even in patriarchal Buddhism becoming a nun was often a woman's best refuge from harsh and abusive domestic situations. Contrary to outsiders' impressions of the limitations of being a nun, most nuns stress the freedom inherent in their lifestyle. Freed of energy-draining, conflict-ridden family relationships, they can develop themselves fully and be available freely and as needed to provide service and support. The emphasis is not on losing an immediate family and a primary relationship, but on taking on a much wider, more inclusive network of relationships that will be healthier and less prone to conflict. Furthermore, nuns live in a supportive community of like-minded and like-spirited companions. Such a community can be very attractive to those living in a society in which alienation and loneliness are the widespread norm. Nuns live a lifestyle dedicated to study and spiritual discipline (though in some contemporary still-patriarchal contexts, these are sub-standard). The opportunity to pursue these goals single-mindedly in a community dedicated to such vocations sometimes seems almost utopian. Finally, especially in Western Buddhism, in which monastics may have to undertake some of their own support, nuns may be able to develop and perfect their competence in arts, crafts, and other skills in a supportive community environment.

The question of how important nunship is for Buddhist women is integrally connected with the question of the role that monastic institutions will play in contemporary and future Buddhism. While some would argue that the history of Buddhism reveals a gradual decline in the centrality of monastic institutions, others argue that the existence of a strong core of monastic practitioners is and always has been essential for the health of Buddhism. Monasticism is so central to Southeast Asian, Tibetan, and Chinese forms of Buddhism that it is difficult to imagine any rapid changes away from monasticism in them. The question of the role of monasticism in Western Buddhism intrigues many observers. The vast majority of Western Buddhists have not taken monastic vows and do not expect to do so. However, monastic-like meditation centers are absolutely critical to Western Buddhism. Most people may not take long-term monastic vows, but places for monastic retreats are essential for lay Buddhist meditators. Many envision the development of a situation somewhat akin to that common-place in contemporary Theravadin Buddhism, in which virtually everyone (every male, that is) takes monastic vows temporarily. However, these periods of retreat would be viewed, not as a rite of passage for youths, but as something available at any point in life, and would be available to women as well as to men.

Post-patriarchal monasticism does require some reconstruction from the present monastic practices. Some of these changes are nothing but restorations of what has been lost. Others would disrupt long-standing Buddhist practices that are male-dominant and disadvantageous to women. But none of them involves any major renovations to the basic structure and style of the monastic life.

The first, very obvious, reform is the restitution of full ordination for nuns in Theravadin and Tibetan Buddhism, in which it has been lost and has not been available for over a thousand years. Without this restoration, women are confined to perpetual novice status, in the Tibetan case, or to the status of "lay nuns," who receive no formal ordination ceremony at all, and wear white or other non-monastic colors, in Theravadin countries. Since the nuns' order, albeit with reservations and male hierarchy, was part of early Buddhism, it is hard to imagine opposition on Buddhist grounds. Even if no nuns' orders existed anywhere in the Buddhist world, it would be possible to reconstruct the order, if those in positions of authority cared enough about the quality of women's involvement in Buddhism. But the full ordination, including the ordination lineages and ceremonies, has survived in Chinese and Korean forms of Bud-dhism. In an age of international travel, receiving the ordination from these lineages presents no problems. In fact in 1988, a Chinese monastery in North America offered the nuns's ordination to a large number of women from all over the Buddhist world.

The reactions vary. Women, mainly Westerners, who practice following Tibetan lineages have received no opposition to their participation in these ordinations and some encouragement from the male hierarchy. Their status as fully ordained nuns has not been officially recognized, however, nor has the ordination been offered in Tibetan monasteries in India or Nepal, which means that very few Tibetan women can receive the ordination, due to lack of funds to travel to a place where it is offered.

The official word about these ordinations is that they are under investigation to determine whether the ordination lineages are genuine and acceptable to the Tibetan Buddhist authorities. Given the urgency of the issue, such reactions and policies seem timid and unnecessary. Such recourse to legalism, which is not the religious concern usually dominant in Buddhism, and least of all, in Tibetan Buddhism, makes me suspicious that a smokescreen is being used to delay rectifying the denigration and objectification of women that occurs when there is any question about their abilities and rights to the monastic lifestyle. I doubt such caution would be employed if the issue concerned something of such vital importance to the male monastics. In fact, the monks' ordination has also been lost several times in various Buddhist countries throughout Buddhist history, but such lengthy investigations of the authenticity of the ordination lineage were not pursued when monks' ordination again became available. One also wonders what will happen if it is determined that the ordination lineages are invalid. Will women then be denied status as fully ordained nuns perpetually, despite the historical model of early Indian Buddhism?

The situation in Theravadin countries is even more stark. Most of the monastic authorities are adamant in their opposition to recognizing nuns in Theravadin Buddhism, in large part because they are unwilling to recognize Mahayana ordination lineages as valid, even though those lineages derived historically from the same sources as their own ordination lineages. They are equally unwilling to initiate the original group of ten fully ordained nuns who could then carry on the ordinations in the manner laid out in the *vinaya*, or rules of monastic discipline. One of the reasons given against either method of reinstating the nuns' order is that, since some Theravadin Buddhists would not accept its validity, reinstating the order would cause a schism in Theravadin Buddhism.[17] This argument is strikingly like that used by some members of the Church of England against women's ordination—it would make eventual reunion with Rome more difficult! In both cases, the objectification and dehumanization of women is so extreme that males with power are willing to continue to victimize women, condemning them to perpetual inferiority, to protect their possible future unity with other males. One has to wonder about such priorities! Meanwhile, women from some Theravadin countries who defy the monastic authorities and receive the ordination abroad are forbidden by the government to wear robes of monastic colors, rather than the white robes of lay nuns, when they return home to their own country.[18]

Even if the nuns' ordination were restored, that would not fully constitute an androgynous reconstruction of monasticism. The extant monastic institutions exhibit considerable male dominance, both formally and informally. The formal dominance is expressed in the eight special rules, while the informal dominance is evidenced in the widespread low levels of support that nuns receive. These two interlocking forms of male dominance have greatly disadvantaged the nuns' order historically and are probably largely responsible for its disappearance from so many parts of the Buddhist world.

The informal male dominance in Buddhist monasticism stems from popular gender stereotypes in androcentric and patriarchal societies and is partly due to the androcentrism of the lay Buddhist matrix in which the monastic institutions exist. Overcoming androcentric lay Buddhism is thus inextricably linked with the creation of post-patriarchal monastic Buddhism. The basic change requires overcoming a subtle embarrassment about the nuns's order, a reaction consonant with the shame associated, in patriarchal cultures, with being female. This embarrassment is evident first in recruitment mechanisms for the nuns' order. Often, even in the world of the *Therigatha*, it is a place for rejects from the androcentric marriage market—widows, old women, bereaved women—in a way that the men's order is not a place for rejects from the marriage market. (In fairness, it must be noted that, at least in Tibet, monasteries could be the place for extra sons who would cut into the family inheritance too greatly.) Conversely, women who have a genuine vocation for the monastic life often find their wishes blocked if they, like Yeshe Tsogyel, are viewed as desirable objects in the androcentric marriage market. In neither case is family honor enhanced when a female enters the monastery, as it is when a male enters the monastery.

The embarrassment also expresses itself in the lower level of economic support given nuns historically and in many groups within contemporary Buddhism. Finally, facilities for academic and meditation training for nuns also frequently lag well behind those for monks.[19] Again we have a vicious circle. Poorly supported nuns are poorly educated and do not become renowned spiritual leaders. But renowned leaders are precisely the monastics who attract large followings and generous economic support. Given this low prestige and low levels of support from its own community, it is more understandable that parents may not view nunship as an ideal life choice for their daughters.

The point at which the cycle can be broken is with the establishment of monastic communities in which women are educated seriously, both academically and in terms of advanced meditation programs, with the intent that they become teachers when they complete their training. Several such centers are in existence or being planned among Tibetans in exile.* Several very brave Theravadin women have also established such centers in Sri Lanka and

---

* No one deserves more credit in this enterprise than the American born nun Karma Lekshe Tsomo, who practices in the Tibetan Buddhist manner.

Thailand.* In North America, Buddhist women from the various sects are also working on such centers and such projects.[20]

Formal subordination of nuns to monks is also part of the traditional monastic organization. The eight special rules were a concession to the prevailing gender hierarchy of ancient India. They obviously have no relevance in post-patriarchal androgynous Buddhism, since their sole function is to subordinate all nuns to each and every monk. They involve a completely artificial gender hierarchy which has often inhibited nuns from functioning as religious authorities and teachers in Buddhism in general.[21] Whatever hierarchy is necessary and appropriate in post-patriarchal Buddhism should be a hierarchy based on length of monastic standing and, even more, on accomplishments and abilities, which have little to do with gender. Men would then salute their female seniors in age and accomplishment, the practice that the Buddha objected to because not even heretical sects permitted women to be saluted by men.[22] Since Buddhists have never worried about conventionality and being like everyone else in matters of doctrine, and, in fact, prided themselves on proclaiming truth, even if it goes "against the grain," it is painful to know that on this one issue, Buddhists have been so utterly conventional. It is time to go against the grain on this point too, since the humanity of half the Buddhist world is at stake.

The interactions of nuns and monks need to be reconsidered on one further important question. How much should the men's and women's orders be segregated for daily activities, study, and practice? How much common life should the two orders engage in together? The *vinaya* rules limit quite severely the extent to which nuns and monks can interact on a regular basis for everyday activities. In the stories surrounding the formulation of these rules, most of the ordinances that separate the two orders resulted from gossip on the part of the laity that monks and nuns carried on sexual encounters under the pretext of meeting for joint religious ceremonies. In one case, the Buddha had to reformulate a rule a number of times to eliminate any possible bases for such suspicions.[23] For reconstructing post-patriarchal Buddhism, such reasoning is hardly sufficient. Instead, it should be asked what kind of and how much interaction between the nuns and the monks would best facilitate the spiritual and intellectual development of both.

Regarding this question, arguments familiar from feminist debate will emerge. Sometimes, it is argued, quite persuasively, that women need the safety

---

* A German-born woman who lived much of her adult life in the United States, Ayya Khema practices in the Theravada tradition and has established a nunnery on an island in Sri Lanka. Voramai Kabilsingh, a Thai woman, was the first Theravadin woman to obtain the full ordination from Chinese ordination lineages. She started Thailand's only monastery run by and for women, in Nakhonpathom. See Chatsumarn Kabilsingh, *Thai Women in Buddhism* (Berkeley: Parallax Press, 1991).

of their own assemblies, in which they will not be under subtle pressure to defer to men, and in which they would have to make decisions, learn to lead, and to manage their own affairs. If the nuns' order were truly autonomous, as it was not under the *vinaya* and the eight special rules, these benefits would happen of necessity.

Against this position is the argument that a completely segregated and separate group is more easily marginalized and ghettoized, as sometimes happens to the women studies perspective in academic institutions. Unless the women's institutions have real power, they will then be financed on "soft money" and leftovers, which happened to the nuns throughout Buddhist history. It must also be asked whether "separate but equal" facilities can ever be a realistic possibility. The idea has a poor track record, especially when the parallel institutions serve two groups, one of whom has historically dominated over the other. Why, to solve the problems of insufficient education and meditation training for nuns, should it be necessary to construct a whole parallel set of facilities and institutions when excellent ones already exist for men only? The current problems could probably be solved much more quickly and inexpensively if nuns simply trained with monks in the same classrooms and retreat centers, not as second-class inhabitants occupying the backs of those spaces, but as full-fledged equal members of the monastery.

As with so many other issues, the recommended middle path requires a "both-and," rather than an "either-or" answer. Same-sex gatherings can be healing and relaxing. They are especially useful for airing intensely personal issues and for gaining self-confidence in new undertakings, such as leading a liturgy. There is every reason to continue to have some assemblies that are sex-segregated. But same-sex assemblies, when they are the required and usual mode, usually involve great inequities of power, prestige, and training, especially when they reduplicate each other. For a same-sex gathering to have validity and to be helpful rather than harmful, there needs to be some substantive reason for sex segregation that has to do with the nature of the activities undertaken. If the only reason to have separate-sex assemblies is to keep the sexes apart, presumably to inhibit sexual attraction, usually the institution will be disadvantageous to women. There are, after all, only so many great teachers in each monastery. If that teacher has to lecture to the monks, and then walk across town to give the same lecture to the nuns at a separate facility whose only purpose is keep the women and the men apart, the lectures to the nuns will probably cease after a while.

The issue of real or alleged sexual attractions between the monks and nuns has been seriously overplayed as a reason to maintain sex-segregated and male-dominated religious institutions, not only in Buddhism, but in many other contexts.* At the simplest level, much less drastic methods than separating the sexes could be invoked. I remember the Theravadin monk arguing for the desirability of separate meditation sessions for laywomen and laymen because of an experience with an underclad female meditator who exposed herself, inadvertently or on purpose, while she sat in meditation. It's overkill to build separate meditation facilities to cope with such problems. Institute a sensible dress code, and apply it to men also, who have been known to dangle inappropriately when dressed in track shorts in a hot meditation hall.

Interestingly, that story and my response to it brings up a point that is *never* discussed in androcentric contexts—men as sexually attractive or disturbing objects to women. Perhaps men also need to learn to curb their self-display. Usually, unlike women, men are allowed to wear what is comfortable, rather than what is modest, even if such attire might be sexually alluring to women or distracting to them. Once again, we see how sexuality is projected onto women by androcentric commentators, who do not own or take responsibility for their own sexuality.

It is difficult to avoid the conclusion that frequently the motivation behind male preference for sex-segregated monasteries is a projection of male sexual urges onto women and the men's desire to have their celibacy protected at any costs. Often, it seems to me that male celibacy is bought at the cost of women's religious lives, since nothing is done to assure women of genuinely equal segregated facilities. That cost is too high. In any cost-benefit analysis, the loss to women throughout Buddhist history due to sex segregation in monastic institutions, starting with the loss of nuns' ordination itself far outweighs anything that may have been gained by the men.

Perhaps there would be more infractions of the rules of celibacy if monks and nuns had more routine contact for daily activities, study, and meditation, but that is less problematic than the present situation. On the other hand, if monks and nuns studied and meditated together, which is by far the most practical solution to the problem of providing training for both of them, the quality of the celibacy would be higher and more genuine. It would be based more on personal taming and less on an artificial separation. Celibacy that can be maintained only by sex segregation is rather shallow.

Another casualty of too much sex segregation is barely mentioned in these debates. Human beings of "neighboring sexes"[24] can have meaningful and mutually helpful friendships. Such friendships are totally discounted in an-

---

* This same argument has been used for centuries in orthodox Judaism to maintain a seating arrangement which places women in a balcony or behind the men, behind a curtain, so that men will not be distracted by the sight of women while they are praying. Thus, clearly, not only monastic religions victimize women with the argument.

drocentric thinking in which women are understood primarily as sexual beings and as sex objects. Sex segregation intensifies that kind of thinking. If the only time that men and women encounter each other is for sexual purposes, it is not too surprising that people start to think about sex as soon as they are in mixed company. If they learn to encounter each other as human beings, fellow monastics and meditators, such conditioned responses start to diminish. That, in turn, undercuts the argument that women must be kept away so that the men are not disturbed by temptations to break their vows of celibacy. The casualty of the loss of genuine androgynous friendship between women and men is too high a cost to continue to pay. Human beings are of two sexes. To live the spiritual life as if that were not a basic truth of relative existence, to live with contact only with one of the sexes, is artificial, unhealthy, and insane. It produces warped, neurotic people.

Western rather than Asian monasteries are the more likely pioneering places for this innovation. One such place is Gampo Abby, in Nova Scotia, which houses both nuns and monks who engage in a rigorous course of joint training and who work together to improve their facility. Though the titular head of the monastery is a Tibetan monk, the senior resident monastic, both in length of service and in authority, is an American nun who is widely respected for her teaching skills.[25]

PIONEERS AND PROPHETESSES: *YOGINI*-S AND POST-PATRIARCHAL BUDDHISM

In Indian and Tibetan Buddhism, *yogi*-s and *yogini*-s lived a lifestyle that was neither monastic nor lay. They were more single-mindedly devoted to spiritual discipline and self-development than was the average layperson and they abhorred the conventions of society, especially its social hierarchies and puritanical behavior code. Though they devoted their lives to spiritual discipline and realization, they did not live by monastic codes either. They preferred caves to monasteries and took part in many activities forbidden by the monastic code. Many of them had partners with whom they shared their lives of spiritual searching; often their spiritual disciplines were unconventional, neither known about nor approved of by the monks of the day.[26]

This model of a practitioner who is neither monk nor lay is relevant and attractive for contemporary Western Buddhists who are simultaneously taking on Buddhism as a religion of choice and, by choice and necessity, creating new models of Buddhism. It provides a model for being Buddhist that is quite open-ended in its specific details, yet demonstrates heroic commitment to spiritual development and to the development of Buddhism in directions that are relevant for the time. It is also the style of being Buddhist in which women fared the best, though the literature records them in androcentric fashion.[27]

In the contemporary Buddhist world, especially in Western Buddhism, the *yogini* and the lay meditator may sometimes seem to blur into one model. Indeed, some of the inspiration for the model of the contemporary lay meditator is the *yogi* tradition, in which people in many walks of life, some with major professional and household responsibilities, still took on long-term, intensive meditation practice. If the contemporary *yogini* is different from the lay meditator, it is in the intensity of her quest and the unconventionality of her results. On both counts, she might well be regarded as extreme, even by fellow lay meditators or nuns. They will proceed more slowly, cautiously, and rationally; she will test the boundaries of the tradition and her own limits and horizons more recklessly. They will probably not question the forms given to them; she may well explore their hidden corners, finding unacceptable evidence of androcentrism and patriarchy in them. She will assume responsibility as an innovative leader and teacher in her community.

One can expect most of the innovations and rethinkings that will lead to post-patriarchal Buddhism to come from the ranks of the contemporary *yogini*-s. They are the unconventional visionaries who have the courage and the energy to create a universe, uncharted and forbidden in patriarchy, beyond androcentrism. They are the pioneers who have the imagination somehow to "name reality"* that is unconditioned by patriarchal thought-forms. They are the prophets who cannot rest with the comforts and conveniences of oppressive conventions, even if they are persecuted and rejected for their daring. They are the restless seers, longing for spiritual wholeness and depth, who test and try all the forms to find which ones contain gold, who may even discover a new seam of gold in the post-patriarchal wilderness.

These *yogini*-s often have a very difficult time. Even a religious tradition that goes "against the grain" itself, wants its followers, especially its women, to stick with the patterns it has laid out. Even if the *yogi*-s and *yogini*-s of the past are glorified, those of the present are not. Perhaps that goes with the territory and cannot be helped. In any case, the backlash against the post-patriarchal *yogini* probably comes more from the patriarchy than from Buddhism, insofar as they can be disentangled at this point in time. For these *yogini*-s are not only intense and zealous; they think past patriarchy and in so doing destroy its power little by little. But they pay a price for their courage and honesty. Gerda Lerner in *The Creation of Patriarchy* has put it most succinctly and best:

> Even those of us already defining ourselves as feminist thinkers and engaged
> in the process of critiquing traditional systems of ideas are still held back by

---

* This phrase has become a slogan used to explain the vision of feminist philosophy. It originates with Mary Daly, who also stated that under patriarchy, the power of naming had been stolen from women.

unacknowledged restraints embedded deeply within our psyches. Emergent woman faces a challenge to her very definition of self. How can her daring thought—naming the hitherto unnamed, asking the questions defined by all authorities as "non-existent"—how can such thought co-exist with her life as a woman? In stepping out of the constructs of patriarchal thought, she faces, as Mary Daly put it, "existential nothingness." And more immediately, she fears the threat of loss of communication with, approval by, and love from the man (or the men) in her life. Withdrawal of love and the designation of thinking women as "deviant" have historically been the means of discouraging women's intellectual work. . . . No thinking man has ever been threatened in his self-definition and his love life as the price for his thinking.[28]

When the feminist thinker is exploring the centrality of community and relationship to sane human being, as are so many current feminist thinkers in their new naming of reality beyond patriarchy, the poignancy of that loss of love is extreme.

Perhaps Gerda Lerner is only saying in a sophisticated way what many a bright female high school student has discovered and over which she has agonized—her contemporaries don't like smart girls. As a result, many of them learn to hide their brilliance, but a few don't or won't. Perhaps Gerda Lerner is only rephrasing, in a sophisticated fashion, a sociological stereotype that holds cross-culturally in patriarchal societies: women should "marry up" and men want to "marry down." He should be taller and make more money. Otherwise he feels emasculated. If she is too bright, he is intimidated. Commonly, it is expected that he should be better educated and better known. People feel sorry for the husband of a famous woman but they regard it as normal for a famous man to have a wife of lesser accomplishments. If there is an age difference, it is much more acceptable for him to be older; people talk about a younger man with an older women. For men to "marry down" on at least some criteria maintains patriarchy; it also assures that the brightest, most capable, most deserving women produced by a patriarchal society will be the most often rejected. That, too, maintains patriarchal power, as Gerda Lerner so eloquently points out.

One thinks of the example of Margaret Mead and Gregory Bateson. No slouch himself, he divorced her because he felt he couldn't keep up with her. She mourned the relationship the rest of her life and died with his picture in her hospital room.[29] From the other side of the world, comes the example of an unnamed young Thai woman who lived for some years as white-clad lay Buddhist nun, an unusual undertaking for a young woman. No longer living as a nun, she is more serious in her observance of Buddhism than most young people of either sex. She is scorned by her contemporaries and by older people alike.[30]

The men with whom the feminist *yogini* often loses communication, approval, and love take many forms. Frequently, they include teachers and other respected authority figures; they withdraw their support and approval when she goes beyond certain orthodoxies of thinking. Even more frequently they take the form of colleagues in the institutions in which she must work. These colleagues in academic, religious, economic, and professional institutions are often brutal to the most innovative women who work with them. And, very frequently the men take the form of desired friends and lovers, who often prefer more conventional women. Surviving such treatment makes the feminist *yogini* tenacious—and more insightful than ever if she does not go crazy.

Working both within and beyond the limits of Buddhism as currently constituted, these feminist *yogini*-s have already made a deep, though unacknowledged, impact on Buddhism. In the future, their influence will grow with greater articulation of post-patriarchal Buddhism. Because of their energy and insight, the auspicious coincidence of Buddhism and feminism in the West is occurring. Without them, the reforms currently under way in the training of women lay meditators and nuns would not have begun. Given these basic reforms in the education and training of laywomen and nuns and the continued input of feminist *yogini*-s, the next major step in the development of post-patriarchal Buddhism could occur. The androgynization of Buddhist patterns of everyday life and institutions will produce the one thing that Buddhism has always lacked—large numbers of thoroughly trained, well-practiced and articulate female Buddhist teachers—laywomen, nuns, and *yogini*-s—*who are not male-identified.*

The great challenge for Buddhism is to welcome such women rather than ostracizing them. One hopes that the situation current in Christianity, in which many feminist *yogini*-s teach and write, largely unsupported by the church hierarchy, while the male hierarchs ignore and denigrate them, will not be the course of events in Buddhism. Ideally, such feminist *yogini*-s, when they are spiritually developed, should be recognized as gurus and entrusted with major responsibilities for the fuller articulation of post-patriarchal Buddhism.

The presence of female gurus, which currently is the major piece still missing from post-patriarchal androgynous Buddhism, will be a most radical development for Buddhism. Previously, female gurus have been rare, and may well have been male-identified, rather than androgynous in their consciousness. Therefore, the presence of significant numbers of such female gurus would radically transform Buddhism in ways that go far beyond sheer affirmative action and equal opportunity issues. In fact, because of the importance of the guru in some forms of Buddhism, this development will be as transformative for non-theistic Buddhism as is the development of female language and imagery for deity in the theistic religions currently caught up in male monotheism.

In some forms of Buddhism, the guru or spiritual director is of supreme importance. Regarded as the beacon who can light the way out confusion and suffering, the guru is as important as, even more important than, the Buddha, the *dharma*, and the *sangha*, as a source of refuge. The lineage of such gurus, going back at least mythically to the Buddha, and the conviction of direct transmission down that lineage to one's own guru and then to oneself is central to Vajrayana[31] and to Zen Buddhism.

Devotion is the proper attitude with which to regard this wondrous guru. The importance of these gurus is explicitly recognized in Buddhist meditation liturgies and religious art. Daily chants include an invocation to and a recitation of the lineage of gurus, from one's own guru back to sect founders and the Buddha. Gurus, like *yidam*-s and Buddhas, are frequently the subject of Buddhist religious art. The lineage is sometimes portrayed in the form of a lineage tree, a great tree in whose branches sit all the gurus of the lineage, surrounded by the Buddhas, Bodhisattvas, *yidam*-s, and protectors, with the sacred books also supported by the tree. Prostrations are done before this lineage tree containing all the objects of refuge. Given the centrality of the guru in the spiritual life of the student and the intensity of the devotion that is cultivated and recommended, it is accurate to suggest that, in the forms of Buddhism that regard the guru so highly, the guru is a non-theistic, functional equivalent of the deity of theistic religions.

That such gurus and teachers are almost always men is thoroughly androcentric and completely disempowering for women in the same way as is the male monopoly on images of deity in monotheism. The lack of female presence in the lineage supplications, on the limbs of the refuge tree,* and on the teaching throne from which living teachers teach reinforces and drives home the shame of being female in patriarchy. It is living proof that Buddhist institutions do not respect and nurture the Buddha-embryo present in women in the same way that they nurture the Buddha-embryo present in men. Therefore, the deliberate cultivation of female gurus and teachers is the most critical agenda for achieving a genuinely post-patriarchal Buddhism. This is equally true for those forms of Buddhism that do not revere the guru so formally, for the teacher is always central to the transmission of Buddhism from generation to generation.

The presence of female gurus would complete Mahayana Buddha theory in a powerfully transformative way. Mahayanists, who saw Buddhahood in much more encompassing terms than did earlier Buddhist schools, developed

---

* Yeshe Tsogyel is found on the Nyingma lineage tree and is supplicated in lineage chants, the only exception to this generalization of which I am aware.

the *trikaya* concept to explain Buddhahood. According to this teaching, Buddhahood manifests in three levels, or "three bodies," the literal translation of "*trikaya*." The *dharmakaya* is impersonal and pervasive, another way of understanding both emptiness and suchness, and available and present as the omnipresent Buddha-embryo. The *sambhogakaya*, or "glorified body" is anthropomorphic, but visible only to highly developed meditators. It is, however, made visible to more ordinary practitioners through initiation and visualization techniques. Much Vajrayana Buddhist art portrays such *sambhogakaya* Buddhas as *yidam*-s. The *nirmanakaya* or appearance body is fully human, Buddhahood manifested and expressed in the life and teachings of an enlightened being. Siddartha Gautama is the best-known *nirmanakaya* Buddha, but, according to some understandings of *trikaya* theory, others are present in our world throughout history. In fact, anyone who really matures the Buddha-embryo is a *nirmanakaya* Buddha, which is why the gurus are recognized as "living Buddhas."

According to Buddhist theory, as we have already seen, *dharmakaya* as *tathagatagarbha* is present for all human beings without respect for gender. Female manifestations of the *sambhogakaya* are found in the form of Vajrayogini and other anthropomorphic representations of the feminine principle. One would expect *nirmanakaya* manifestations of Buddhahood to be likewise androgynous, occurring routinely in both female and male forms. But the female *nirmamakayas* have rarely been recognized as such, and, when recognized, have not usually been given the teaching authority of their male counterparts. Only Yeshe Tsogyel[32] is regularly invoked in lineage chants and portrayed in the lineage tree of only *some* Tibetan Buddhist lineages. Such imbalance at the *nirmanakaya* level can only be explained by persistent pervasive androcentrism and patriarchy.

Completing Mahayana Buddha-theory through cultivating the presence and teaching authority of female *nirmanakaya*-s would have a more powerful impact in ending definitively the shame associated with being female in patriarchal culture and undoing the scapegoating of women for *samsaric* existence than would any other act or symbol. Seeing a woman on the guru's throne, teaching the *dharma* and granting initiations and blessings, would be powerfully transformative for both men and women. For men, the experience of devotion to a *female* guru, accompanied by all the longing and yearning that characterizes non-theistic guru-devotion, would undo the negative habitual patterns, learned in early childhood under patriarchal childrearing practices, that scapegoat women for the limitations and finitude of life. Here would be a woman undoing *samsara* for the male by her teaching presence. For women, this presence will be affirming, empowering, and encouraging in a way that nothing else can be. At last Buddhist women will have the same kind of role model that Buddhist men have always had! For both genders, it will be definitively, incontrovertibly clear that there is no shame in being female, that it's okay to be a woman.

Completing Buddhist theory as currently expressed is not the only blessing that comes with the presence of female teachers. Sometimes it is imagined that things will end when women regularly take on the teaching role in Buddhism. It is thought that these women will continue to present the same messages verbally that the male teachers have always presented, that only their form and presence will be different. That they will present *only* the same messages seems unlikely, however. It seems unlikely that males speaking out of patriarchal conditions have said everything that needs to be said about liberation. It seems unlikely that when women finally participate in Buddhist speech, they will not add to the sum total of Buddhist wisdom about liberation. Certainly the example of Christianity, in which feminist analysis is far more developed than in Buddhism, strongly suggests that the androgynous voice does not merely amplify what had always been said, but adds to it significantly. And this androgynous voice *will* be articulated, whether or not the Buddhist authorities recognize it as the wisdom of the Buddha.

16

Androgynous View: New Concerns in Verbalizing the *Dharma*

To add to what has already been said in Buddhist tradition, rather than merely to amplify its volume, is to suggest the agenda for an androgynous reconceptualization of Buddhism. To date, very little, if any such reconceptualization has been attempted. Therefore, beginnings will necessarily be modest, tentative, and somewhat idiosyncratic.

First, it must be explained, in Buddhist terms, not just feminist terms, why the speech of the feminist *yogini*-s will add to the sum total of Buddhist wisdom that already exists. Buddhist texts often state that the liberated state is beyond gender, not obtainable in either a male body or a female body. If that is true, and I believe that it is, what could women possibly say or understand that is not already part of the teachings?

The *dharma* is not only beyond gender; *it is also beyond words*. Words and doctrines, for Buddhism, "have utility rather than truth; . . . their importance lies in the effects they have upon those who believe in them."[1] This means that for Buddhism, doctrines are really a part of *upaya*, or skillful means, not *prajna* or intuitive, often non-verbal wisdom. This point has been made over and over in Buddhist texts, but because this assessment of the truth-value of doctrines is so different from the familiar Western perspective, it is often forgotten, if, indeed, it is even *heard*. That *all* verbal doctrines are in the realm of relative, not absolute, truth provides the means to understand how the speech of feminist *yogini*-s could add to the sum total of *dharmic* wisdom.

The words of *dharma*-texts we now have are men's words. In a society that constitutes itself by means of strong gender roles and in which only men articulate the religious experience and its vision of liberation, religious speech will grow out of male experience. The more rigid are gender roles, the more impossible it is for a member of either sex to speak adequately for the whole human experience. Clearly these conditions have prevailed in Buddhism. The men who wrote Buddhist *dharma* texts lived in patriarchal, not androgynous, societies and had little access to women's experiences. Therefore, it is quite likely that their words are *incomplete*, however *accurate* they may be. An accurate but incomplete set of words is actually dangerous—a point familiar to Buddhist analysis with its constant concern to balance wisdom and compassion in order to avoid harm. On the other hand, at least Buddhism begins with words that, despite their incompleteness, are accurate, even from a feminist point of view. Androgynous speech in Buddhism does not have to be preceded by a deconstruction of androcentric doctrines.

This early attempt at Buddhist androgynous reconceptualization will focus on three areas of concern, all of which are interrelated in that they focus on issues of the connection between "spirituality" and "ordinary" communal or domestic life. In many classic formulations of Buddhism, communal life and domestic existence, to an even greater degree, are seen as irrelevant, or even antithetical to spirituality.

The most basic reconceptualization involves deeper appreciation of the absolute centrality of the *sangha*, the Buddhist community and the third of the Three Refuges to Buddhist life—a reconceptualization drawing its inspiration from experience and from widespread recent feminist thought exploring the thesis that relationship is as critical to identity as are individuation and separation. Deriving from this central insight into the absolute centrality of the *sangha* are two subsidiary questions. Ordinary, everyday domestic life, which has never received much attention in formal Buddhist thought, needs to be addressed much more directly as a *Buddhist* problem, rather than merely a secular or a lay one. Finally, I will raise some questions about the basic nature of spirituality and the purposes of spiritual discipline in the light of feminist-androgynous analysis, criticism, and reconstruction of Buddhism.

"I GO FOR REFUGE TO THE SANGHA":
RELATIONSHIP AND ENLIGHTENMENT

The interplay of Buddhism and feminism in my life has convinced me that relationship and community are far more central in Buddhism and far more crucial to achieving Buddhism's goal of liberation from suffering than is commonly perceived, either by Buddhists or non-Buddhists. By now, it should be clear that every major Buddhist teaching reinforces the view that interdependence and relationality are the reality of our lives and that individual autonomy is a fiction, one of ego's tricks. This discussion of relationship and enlightenment could be connected with any major teaching of the three *yana*-s. I choose to connect it with the refuge of *sangha* because nothing is more basic in Buddhism than going to the Three Jewels for refuge. To appreciate what is at stake in this thesis about the *sangha*, it is necessary to have some understanding of traditional definitions and perceptions of the *sangha*.

The most basic categories in Buddhism are the Three Jewels, also known as the Three Refuges—the Buddha, the *dharma*, and the *sangha*. They are so basic that the transition from being a non-Buddhist to becoming a Buddhist is made by "going for refuge to the Three Jewels." The act of going for refuge to the Three Jewels is also so basic that it is found universally in all forms of Buddhism—one of the few features found in all forms of this far-flung and geographically separated religion.

The practice of "going for refuge" is especially poignant given Buddhism's non-theism. Many religions promise help and comfort from unseen but powerful forces; Buddhism usually proclaims that there is no external saviour and no remote possibility of vicarious enlightenment. But Buddhists do have the Three Refuges as models, inspirations, and guides. The meaning of these Three Refuges is commonly explained by saying that the Buddha is the example of human potential, the *dharma* is trustworthy teaching, and the *sangha* is the companionship and feedback of fellow travellers on the path to freedom.

Thus, it would seem that Buddhism, at least in its vision, recognizes the centrality of community to the task of achieving well-being and liberation. Nevertheless, Buddhism, as currently constituted and usually interpreted, does not manifest that vision. Both outsiders and insiders usually present the *sangha* as a poor third and devote significantly more energy to presentations of the Buddha and the *dharma*. In textbooks on Buddhism, its various philosophical schools are described in some detail, but Buddhist ethics are often barely mentioned and few descriptions of Buddhist communal life are found. These emphases may not result entirely from the common overemphasis of academic religious studies on matters of belief and creed; Buddhists themselves often seem to take *sangha* for granted in a way that the other two refuges are not. Lavish Buddhist art in all Buddhist countries attests to the centrality of various Buddhas; an immense literature explores innumerable philosophical nuances of the *dharma*; millions of hours are spent in meditation practices; popular devotional practices bring these concerns to the general population.

Though everyone takes refuge in the *sangha* as well, very little attention is devoted to exploring the meaning of this refuge. Rarely does one find explicit statements interpreting the *sangha* as the matrix necessary for the accomplishment of Buddhist concerns, especially freedom. What one does find instead are encomiums to aloneness, from early texts to the present day. The "Rhinoceros Discourse" of early Buddhism recommends as the refrain to each of its forty-one verses, "Let one walk alone like a rhinoceros." This refrain follows comments on the evils and dangers of family, society, and friendship, and the benefits of caring about nothing and for no one.[2] Not unexpectedly, the *yogi* and poet of Tibet, Mila Repa, also praises his solitude.

> I have lost my taste for crowds
> to gain my freedom in solitude
> have given up bother
> to be happy in loneliness[3]

A current Buddhist newspaper, read while preparing these pages, gives similar counsel from one of the most highly regarded living Tibetan Buddhist meditation masters, Dilgo Khyentse, Rinpoche. "We . . should be satisfied with such dwelling places as mountain caves and solitary hermitages. . . . the thought of the dharma leads . . to a solitary life. . . . We should, as much as possible adopt this frame of mind as our own." [4]

The purpose of such aloneness is to promote detachment. But, like celibacy enforced by the absence of women, detachment dependent on being alone may be a trivial achievement. The state of mind finally cultivated and achieved may have little to do with detachment, but be based simply on habitual remoteness and emotional dryness; the effect on those from whom one is removed may be unwarranted and counterproductive emotional distress. Such glorifications of aloneness and loneliness seem quite counter to the foundational Buddhist practice of going for refuge to the *sangha*, which should instead lead one to expect both to *be* a companion and to *be able* to find *dharmic*, detached companionship in the sangha. Why else would the *sangha* be a refuge equal to that provided by the Buddha and the *dharma*?

The situation is familiar to feminist theologians. The categories of the tradition are full and provocative, but important meanings of those categories have been overlooked, underplayed, or ignored by androcentric interpreters. Why is the *sangha* one of the three refuges? Surely not to be taken for granted in the pursuit to understand *dharma* and to emulate Buddha, and surely not to be ignored in favor of individualistic self-reliance, but because *sangha* is the essential matrix for the Buddha and the *dharma*. If the *sangha* is unhealthy and unsupportive, very few people will successfully emulate the Buddha or understand the *dharma*. Therefore, one would expect to find keen appreciation of the *sangha*, not "poor third" status for it. One would also expect detailed instructions and explicit emphasis on how to be a companion of the way—a *sangha* member—and one should be able to expect such companionship from one's fellow travellers. These have not, however, been emphasized in the Buddhist world. Feminist analysis can easily explain this curious omission and fill in the missing elements.

As one might expect, the Buddhist texts that come closest to providing some basis for valuing friendship and companionship over aloneness and loneliness are found in Mahayana contexts. Gampopa's training manual, *The Jewel Ornament of Liberation*, is both a promising and a disappointing resource in this regard. In his discussion of the first *paramita* central to the discipline and training of a Bodhisattva, the practice of generosity, he explores three categories of giving, the three most basic things that people need and that one concerned for general well-being would want to provide. They are material goods, fearlessness (also translated as psychological comfort), and the *dharma* teachings themselves. This list seems promising, for it recognizes that there must a context or container in which the *dharma* teachings can be heard and received, that physical and psychological needs must also be recognized, that one cannot practice the *dharma* in a vacuum or while overwhelmed by unmet but legitimate physical and emotional needs. When one reads that among the gifts that are permissible and sometimes appropriate are wife and children, who are listed along with food, drink, clothing and vehicles,[5] suspicions begin to arise.

The discussion of the gift of fearlessness is quite disappointing. It is extremely brief, whereas discussions of the gifts of material goods and the *dharma* are lengthy and elaborate. The gift on fearlessness is described by a single statement, which is proved by a quotation, saying exactly the same thing, from another text. Giving psychological comfort involves giving refuge to those threatened by "robbers, diseases, wild animals, and floods."[6]

These examples make the gift of fearlessness sound like an extension of filling material needs, rather than helping someone deal with depression, anxiety, loneliness, or victimization, truly psychological traumas. Yet these emotional conditions present as many obstacles to the realized life as do robbers, diseases, wild animals, and floods, and are far more common and widespread. Interestingly, voluminous contemporary oral commentaries on the three gifts to be given in the practice of generosity are almost as unconvincing and sketchy in their discussions of the gift of psychological comfort. Most discussions of helping, or of giving the gift of fearlessness, remain at the level of outer, physical and material needs, ignoring, with embarrassed silence, the inner level of psychological comfort. It is much more difficult, because it is so close to home, to discuss the need for and the nature of a proper psychological environment for spirituality. Furthermore, it is part of the masculinist bias, which still dominates most public arenas of discussion, to be uncomfortable with open discussions of vulnerability, emotions, and the need for psychological comfort. So the topic is often glossed over, as in Gampopa's text.

Buddhists unsympathetic to my reconceptualization might, at this point, object that the *sangha* really consists only of its monastic members, who are dedicated to a life of renunciation that has nothing to do with issues such as loneliness and companionship. The purpose of the *sangha* is to facilitate freedom from the world, *not* to provide a community of comfort and support. Therefore, the proper attitude toward the *sangha* is reverence for world renouncers rather than concern for communal well-being. Lay Buddhists should be regarded as secondary members whose main function is to revere the monastic community and support it economically. How they cope with their emotional well-being is not a Buddhist concern. Such commentators might also contend that the *sangha*, meaning the (male) monastic community, already does receive significant and sufficient attention. Monks are given privileged status all over the Buddhist world. This attitude, it would be claimed, is the normative Buddhist attitude toward the *sangha*—an attitude which is fully sufficient and adequate.

The response would be that such an extreme of limiting the "real *sangha*" to the monastic *sangha* is, at best, a caricature of early Indian or Theravadin forms of Buddhism. To disregard the laity so totally is inaccurate, as well as spiritually inadequate. Furthermore, declaring that issues of psychological comfort, of community, of emotional wholeness are irrelevant or non-Buddhist is simply part of the masculinist ignoring that is being reconstructed. Some have also expressed the fear that emphasizing the *sangha* as psychological matrix for enlightenment would somehow be dangerous and misleading. Even some who have been sympathetic to certain aspects of my feminist discussions of Buddhism are quite uncomfortable with this suggested reconceptualization. They seem to fear that, if Buddhists really worked to make their *sangha* a community of support that sustained people emotionally and provided a matrix of psychological comfort, then somehow the environment would not be tough enough, that we would be trying to circumvent the first noble truth of all-pervasive suffering. I would suggest again the fine distinction, enhanced by the development of *prajna*, between suffering that is constitutive of existence, and suffering that is really quite superfluous. The suffering born of inadequate communal support systems is of the latter, not the former variety. Furthermore, it detracts seriously from one's spiritual development, to the point that it becomes difficult to deal appropriately with the former kind of suffering.

Perhaps if we looked more closely at the definition of psychological comfort that I propose, we could see its necessity more clearly. The essence of psychological comfort is, in my experience, communication—direct, straightforward, open, intense, and regular, ongoing communication. Such communication includes and demands attention to emotions and willingness to communicate emotionally as well as intellectually. Interpersonal warmth is one of the most important ingredients that leads to fearlessness and psychological comfort. Physical, as well as verbal, contact is often an important element in such communication. When such communication is stable and ongoing, psychological trauma and disorientation readily give way to some level of sanity.

Without it, a crisis is prolonged and intensified, and everyday loneliness prevents one from being as effective or as insightful as one could be.

It is important to acknowledge that such communication is not to be confused with some magic potion that would make suffering, anxiety, or depression disappear, to be replaced by bliss. The bittersweet edge of ultimate aloneness cannot be cut. Rather, communication makes the inevitable stresses and traumas bearable. It provides the necessary measure of relief that allows one to continue to deal with stress and suffering. The need for companionship, despite ultimate aloneness, could be compared to a more familiar topic in Buddhism. The first noble truth states that life is permeated with suffering. But this truth has never led Buddhists to seek out suffering deliberately, or to feel that they needed to provide it for others. Rather, one always tries to alleviate suffering. Similar practices regarding alienation and aloneness need to become much more explicit and important to Buddhists. Just as there is sufficient suffering, so there is sufficient aloneness; just as Buddhists seek to alleviate, rather than to increase, the suffering of others, so they should seek to alleviate the loneliness of others. For inappropriate loneliness and lack of in-depth communication is among the most devastating and destructive of all forms of suffering.

My own route to this conclusion was lengthy. I first needed to absorb myself as thoroughly as possible in Buddhism as it was being taught to me, or as I perceived it being taught. I heard a great deal about Buddhism as a "lonely journey," which was the emphasis of the explanatory comments given at the ceremony at which I went for refuge to the Buddha, the *dharma*, and the *sangha*.

> Taking refuge in the Buddha means that we .. proclaim .. that there is no saviour. . . . Very genuinely, very basically, we are 100 per cent alone. This is the inspiration of the Buddha. "We take refuge in the *sangha*" is the final statement of being alone. . . . Taking refuge in the *sangha* means that nobody is depending on anybody else. Buddha, *dharma, sangha*, which adds up to one lonely journey.[7]

Having coped with being utterly alone for most of my life by romanticizing loneliness, that interpretation suited me fine at the time. Such romanticization of aloneness is, I now believe, a common, though unconscious strategy in our hypermasculine and highly alienated culture.

I listened attentively to great teachers as living exemplars of the Buddha, studied a great deal, and meditated in exemplary fashion, which seemed to be the recommended Buddhist way of dealing with the enigma of existence. Sometimes I complained of feeling lonely, but all my Buddhist friends told me that that's what the Buddhist way of non-theism is all about.

264 BUDDHISM AFTER PATRIARCHY

Years later, with the wisdom of hindsight, I feel that another message, which most of us missed, was also being beamed to us by our Buddhist teachers, but we were missing it, still are missing it, because it doesn't accord with the values of a highly alienated, masculinist, and individualistic culture. We were also being told:

> "We take refuge in the Sangha as companionship. That means we have a lot of friends, fellow refugees, who are confused, as we are, and are working along the same guidelines as we are. . . . They provide feedback, they bounce things back on you. Your friends in the sangha provide a continual reference point which creates a continual learning process. . . .
>
> The companionship within the sangha is a kind of clean friendship—without expectation, without demand, but at the same time fulfilling.
>
> The sangha acts as the source of the learning situation as much as the spiritual friend or the teacher does. . . . Without that sangha, we have no reference point. We are thrown back into the big samsaric soup and we have no idea who we are or what we are. We are lost.[8]

For some time, I didn't notice that clear message, nor, in fairness, did anyone around me emphasize or manifest that message. Instead, I began to experience intensely that there can be too much aloneness—that while aloneness is integral to human experience and spiritual development, it can be overdone. I also began to notice more clearly the extreme contrast between the personal ineffectiveness accompanying too much aloneness and the sane joy of proper communal and relational existence, of genuine friendship and closeness, of true *sangha* experience. With these in place, it was so much more possible to be a decent person and to study or meditate effectively! I was discovering existentially what I had not been taught explicitly. *The Three Jewels are completely interdependent; without the sangha, there is no Buddha and no dharma.* The *sangha* as community, as source of psychological comfort, is the indispensable matrix of spiritual existence. It is not something to be taken for granted, a poor third, to be ignored while one focuses on self-reliance and non-theism.

At the same time, I was slowly beginning to agree with two basic theses of more recent feminist thought. I became ever more willing to concede that there are real and profound differences between men's and women's cultures. I do not regard these differences as inevitable or biologically based; if they are, in fact, based in biology, I see little cause for optimism regarding the human future. A friend of mine once put the difference between women's and men's cultures succinctly, perhaps in an over-simplified and certainly very harsh fashion. "Men achieve identity through separation and women through relationship, which creates a lot of hell," a colloquial, one-sentence version of the work of Carol

Gilligan.[9] This hell is compounded by the fact that we live in a hypermasculine society, a society in which alienation, loneliness, and lack of community have reached dangerous levels, but are still tolerated and even encouraged, a society in which violence and separation receive more support and approval than nurturance and relationship.

In patriarchal thought, similar differences between men and women are also posited. In that context, they are interpreted in a fashion negative to women, and are used to keep women in their very limited, private roles. Evaluated by less patriarchal standards, it becomes clear that these stereotypical women's values and concerns are, *and always have been*, essential to the well-being and survival of the species. Because they are so healthy and normative for humanity, one of the greatest needs of our time is for these values to enter the realms of public discourse rather than to be privatized and minimized. Stereotypical "feminine values" need to become the basis of public life and community; otherwise the rate of acceleration towards oblivion will only increase. So much that is wrong with the society, both on the macro- and the micro-levels, is clearly the result of too much separation, not enough relationship. In this situation, the values of female culture need to become much more normative and universal. They are so profoundly human, humane, healing, and enlightening; in many ways and contexts, they are more worthy and more helpful than the masculine values of isolation and aloneness.

My suggested reconceptualization is simply to fill the profound and provocative category "*sangha*" with the feminist values of community, nurturance, communication, relationship, and friendship. To emphasize these values is to recognize how critical they are, *and always have been*, as matrix and container for emulation of the Buddha and for meditative or philosophical pursuits of the *dharma*.

Looking backward, we can now easily explain the common perception that the *sangha* is less essential than the Buddha and the *dharma*. At the same time, we can also appreciate that the *sangha* as matrix of psychological support has always been important, though its importance has largely gone unrecognized. Men, speaking out of the traditional Buddhist masculinist culture, have written most Buddhist texts and been far more numerous as teachers. So they said less about *sangha* than about philosophy, meditation practice, or devotion, and when they did speak of *sangha*, they tended to emphasize its loneliness more than its relationality. American Buddhists, also brought up in a masculinist culture, imbibe that bias until it is possible to develop deeper insights about the proper relationship between relationship and isolation. What pushes those insights is the experience of too much separation, not enough relationship, in a context in which one can discover the positive, feminist evaluation of stereotypical feminine values and women's culture.

But why would men reared in a masculinist culture emphasize the joys of being alone, the values of self-reliance and separation, to the exclusion of recognizing the values of relationship and community? Feminist theory again suggests an answer, though there is no consensus on the answer. In so far as this answer is correct, and I believe it has a great deal of cogency, it strongly recommends an important restructuring of parenting activity consonant with, in fact mandated by, understanding post-patriarchy as freedom from gender roles, a restructuring already discussed in the chapter on androgynous lay Buddhist institutions. A great deal has been written in a variety of contexts about the difficulty of the male experience of growing up, about his difficulties in separating from rather than identifying with his mother, and his consequent reluctance ever again to trust and be vulnerable to intense feelings of connection. A great deal has also been written in a variety of contexts about the need for such separation to achieve masculinity.[10] The result is a masculine personality structure that feels better with autonomy than with relationship. Since men have held power for so long, that results in a society that glorifies self-reliance and does not value or reward nurturative activities or personality traits. Many point out how this value system brings us to the brink of disaster through constant warfare and ecological destruction. According to post-Freudian feminist psychologists, those dynamics and outcomes are what result from the patriarchal practice of assuming that parenting, especially of infants and young children, should be almost solely the responsibility of females. With less patriarchal, more androgynous parenting practices, the exaggerated need to glorify self-reliance and aloneness may well disappear.

In the meantime, it is important to emphasize that even though the men who formulated Buddhist tradition to date did not emphasize the *sangha* as a nurturing matrix of psychological health, as container for Buddhist meditation and philosophy, nevertheless, the *sangha* did function as such for them. Without proper nurturing, these men would not have renounced conventional life to enter the positive and valued role of monk and world renouncer; they would have renounced the world of convention to become sociopaths, destructive social deviants. Even more important is the comradeship, support, and encouragement, often unacknowledged and uncelebrated, of like-minded companions in the *sangha*.[11] The Buddha, after all, did not send his world-renouncer monks into solitary retreat to work out their spiritual attainments utterly alone. He established an alternative *community* for them, and suggested periods of solitary retreat as an intermittent technique. That the Buddha established a monastic, communal order rather than an order of anchorites, strongly suggests that he really did think that the *sangha* as companionship on the spiritual path is vital.

The feminist or androgynous reconceptualization turns on the realization that human beings simply do not do well in the absence of deeply satisfying, supportive, and comforting human relationships. It recognizes that unavoidable human aloneness is no excuse for unfriendliness, alienation, or deliberate isolation. The best statement of this position, the best definition of *sangha* according to this reconceptualization that I have ever found comes from the writings of a great contemporary teacher of Buddhism, a teacher very familiar with Western thought, including some aspects of feminism. "You are willing to work with your loneliness in a group. The *sangha* is thousands of people being alone together, working with their own loneliness."[12] The phrase "alone together" captures vividly exactly what is at stake. Both are fundamental to our experience. Both must be acknowledged and worked with on the spiritual path. Prevailing masculinist cultural values have emphasized aloneness exclusively and excessively. The feminist restructuring would recognize that interdependence is also a fundamental human truth, to be ignored only at great peril. When *sangha* really functions as people working "alone together," rather than fundamentally alone, then people can study and practice Buddhism far more effectively.

These comments should lead to a further recognition. Though "*sangha*-ship," or being a communicative and supportive *sangha* member is critical, it is by no means "natural," especially for people trained in a masculinist culture. Therefore, one must train for it as surely as one trains to understand the teachings and to develop the mind of awareness and freedom. Buddhism needs to develop disciplines surrounding being a *sangha* member and take them seriously, emphasizing these disciplines in the same way that disciplines of meditation and philosophy are emphasized. To take refuge in the *sangha* should mean to join a community of people sensitive to the importance of communication and companionship. And those who aspire to take refuge in the *sangha* should aspire to be such companions and friends.

Given that Buddhism is non-theistic, this understanding of *sangha* is even more urgent. The appeal of theism, which is sometimes appealing even to Buddhists, is the faith it provides that there is a caring Ultimate Other with whom relationship is always possible, who will always be faithful, even when human companions are faithless. To Buddhists, such a hypothesis, no matter how attractive, seems unrealistic. However, this Buddhist contemplation of the strengths of theism should engender one sobering implication. Since people do need to be in relationship, to be taken care of and to care, and since a non-theist cannot imagine an Ultimate Other with whom that relationship is possible, there's no one left to do it but ourselves, each other, the *sangha*. After all, according to non-theism, no one is going to save us; we have to do it ourselves.

Previously I had thought of that basic teaching in terms of the individual's quest for enlightenment. Now it seems as important to realize that to save ourselves by ourselves, it is necessary to create the social, communal, and companionate matrix of a society in which friendship and relationship are taken as categories of the utmost spiritual importance.

I would like to conclude this reconceptualization by linking it with several central and basic concepts in classical Buddhism. Interdependent co-arising (*pratityasamutpada*), a central concept as old as Buddhism, explains the dense, completely interconnected web of causality in which everything is linked with everything else. Though often used to illustrate how one *samsaric* experience inevitably leads to another, unless one breaks the link between feeling and desire, one can also contemplate how, because of the truth of interdependence, one's acts really do affect others and their acts also affect oneself. Isolation is impossible and words and deeds really do matter. They don't just have negative karmic effects for oneself later. They hurt, or they help. Relatively speaking, the sanity or insanity of us all is dependent on how we treat each other, because we are interdependent beings, not isolated monads. Whether the *sangha* manifests as a matrix of psychological comfort or as an alienated glorifier of loneliness makes a great difference, at least on the relative level. Such a realization makes very immediate all the emphases in Mahayana Buddhism on kindness, gentleness, and compassion. They are not only demands on me; they are also what I need to receive from my fellow wayfarers to be able to wake up.

This reconceptualization can aptly be summarized and concluded by a revision of one of the basic lists found in some schools of Buddhism. To grasp the significance of this revision, it must be remembered that in an educational system and a culture that relies heavily upon oral tradition and memorization, as did most of the premodern Buddhist world, such lists encode much information as well as fundamental values. One such list is called the "Three Wheels that promote the *dharma*," which are traditionally listed as study, practice, and livelihood. The idea of this list is to include all the basics necessary to a balanced lifestyle in which one can practice Buddhism in a well-rounded, rather than a one-sided fashion. Thus, livelihood is included as a wheel of *dharma* because of the necessity of a proper economic basis for the Buddhist way of life. One cannot study the *dharma* or practice meditation lacking an economic base. This recognition is laudatory and realistic. However, it seems self-evident to me that the three wheels are, in fact, *relationship*, livelihood, and study *cum* practice. Study and practice are really one pursuit, not two, which together constitute spiritual discipline. And the psychological basis for them is at least as crucial as the traditionally recognized economic basis. It is natural and appropriate to invest the same energy and intensity in friendships as in work or spiritual discipline. It is also normal to expect reciprocity in that energy. Only a dysfunctional *sangha* or society would value work and spiritual discipline while ignoring or minimizing the value of relationship and friendship.

SACRED OUTLOOK AND EVERYDAY LIFE

The relationship between spirituality and so-called "ordinary existence" or "everyday life" is a complex and difficult issue for many religious traditions. The solutions are complex and varied among different religious traditions and within Buddhism. They range from collapsing and interfusing the two realms to setting them at odds against each other.

As we have seen, in Buddhism, they have often been seen as antithetical to each other and Buddhism often demonstrates little interest in "ordinary" life, at least when ordinary life is seen as the householder lifestyle, involved in domestic and livelihood issues. However, in Buddhism after patriarchy, which will be informed by feminist values and androgynous institutions, rethinking that traditional evaluation of ordinary life will be inevitable.

Nothing less radical than a transvaluation of values is required. Everyday activities, such as carrying out one's livelihood and taking care of one's immediate environment and family, need to be evaluated as an alternative, not an inferior, lifestyle to monasticism. For this to happen, the tasks of the householder must be re-evaluated as arenas in which the basic attitudes of mindfulness and detachment can be practiced. In turn, for that re-evaluation to be accurate, these two lifestyles need to be seen much less as alternatives opposed to each other and more as alternating phases of one's life, whose values interfuse and inform each other. When that happens, ordinary everyday domestic life will be seen much more directly as a *Buddhist* rather than merely a secular or a lay problem. We have already looked at the practical issues of institutional form that facilitate this transvaluation of values. Those practical changes entail conceptual changes as well.

Some religions, particularly those with no monastic tradition, have explored in depth how to infuse everyday life with spiritual significance. In these contexts, renunciation of ordinary existence is not the recommended method for attaining spiritual depth. Instead, looking contemplatively into the depths of the ordinary phenomenal world, one experiences its sacredness. Rather than leading one away from the Real, these phenomenal forms conduct one into its very presence. Since this evaluation is so antithetical to some Buddhist emphases, and so promising for the feminist-androgynous revalorization of ordinary life and concerns, we might look more closely at several examples of this mode of spirituality.

Classical Judaism, with its minute and intimate code for daily domestic living, provides an example of the sacralization or spiritualization of everyday behaviors. From getting up and dressing, to cooking food and eating properly, to praying at the appropriate times of the day, to noticing new clothing or unusual weather, to retiring again at night, there is a continual effort to infuse one's daily experience and activities with sacred awareness, and to connect directly with the spiritual forces that sustain life. Every seven days, this awareness intensifies in the celebration of the Sabbath[13] but there are no retreat centers or monasteries into which one could retire temporarily or permanently. One does not need to get away from the daily routine to experience spiritual awareness, but to bring more awareness of their spiritual dimensions into daily activities. Though encrusted in a strict and precise legal code, for which Jewish meditative disciplines are often mistaken by both Jews and non-Jews, each precisely delineated ritual behavior is accompanied by an intention (*kavvanah*) that reminds the person keeping the commandment *why*, in terms of spiritual awareness, this act is to be done now. If the intention is not remembered or understood, the act becomes empty formalism, but by contemplating the intentional matrix in which the commanded act is contained, this mundane everyday task becomes an instant of sacred awareness and connection with the spiritual energy sustaining life.

Without relying on a sacred law code to determine their activities, some native American groups cultivate a similar all-encompassing awareness of the spiritual meanings laced through daily events and ordinary activities. Lame Deer's explanation of the pot of boiling soup is unsurpassed. He suggests that to the white outsider, the pot probably doesn't have a message:

> But I'm an Indian. I think about ordinary, common things like this pot. The bubbling water comes from the rain cloud. It represents the sky. The fire comes from the sun which warms us all—men, animals, trees. The meat stands for the four-legged creatures, our animal brothers, who gave of themselves so that we should live. The steam is living breath. It was water; now it goes up to the sky, becomes a cloud again. These things are sacred. . . . We Sioux spend a lot of time thinking about everyday things, which in our mind are mixed up with the spiritual. We see in the world around us many symbols that teach us the meaning of life.[14]

Clearly, in this case, the ordinary and the spiritual interpenetrate rather than oppose each other.

The classical Buddhist approach seems, at least superficially, to be almost the opposite. Buddhist texts are more likely to declare that the ordinary household life is counterproductive spiritually: "The household life is a confined and dusty path; wandering forth is the open air. It is not easy for a householder to practice the religious life, completely pure and fulfilled in its entirety and polished like mother-of-pearl. Then let me cut my hair and beard, put on the yellow robes and wander forth from home to homelessness."[15]

Throughout its history, Buddhism's institutional structure has stressed a dichotomy between monastics and laypeople. This format has afforded Buddhism certain strengths. Its traditions have been maintained with great vigor and authenticity by its core of completely dedicated practitioners. Its monks could more easily carry Buddhism across cultural frontiers than is usually possible for non-monastic religions. But, in other ways, this focus on the monastic *sangha* as the true carrier of the religion has also been its greatest weakness. It has led to a relative lack of attention to lay members, which, in turn, means that Buddhism does not survive persecution or disfavor well, since the laity have usually already turned elsewhere for some of their spiritual needs.

Though the classic pattern has important alternatives in Tibet and Japan, the usual expectation has been that lay Buddhists would provide economic support to the monastic *sangha* in exchange for minimal ritual and expository services, but serious involvement in philosophical studies and meditation practice were not easily available to or generally expected of the laity. In contemporary Buddhism, not only in North America, but also in Asia, this model is being challenged by movements of serious lay practice and study. Many variations are found, but the usual pattern involves short but disciplined regular periods of study and practice interspersed with periods of "retreat" for full-time study and practice, during which normal patterns of household life are set aside.

This development involves a potentially vast transformation of Buddhism, in which monastic practitioners are no longer regarded as the best, or the only serious, practitioners of Buddhism. Western Buddhism, in which the vast majority of Buddhists are both serious practitioners and lay people heavily involved in family and career concerns, may well be the most fertile ground for this development. Interestingly, Western Buddhism is also the only form of Buddhism subject to significant feminist influence and the most likely vanguard of Buddhism after patriarchy. Most teachers of Western Buddhists, who are still Asians in this first generation, are not encouraging the majority of their students to take monastic vows, but are encouraging their lay students to be serious full-fledged, full-time Buddhist practitioners. Monastic situations are often regarded as temporary retreats in which very complex studies and practices occur; these periods of monastic living are seen as training for everyday life as well.

Clear analysis of what this development entails is important. The traditional Buddhist skepticism of the spiritual value of domestic concerns, both familial and economic, could remain. The development of serious lay Buddhist practice does not necessarily mean a transvaluation of values in which activities that were formerly held in low esteem are accorded value. It means only that lay people now attempt to make time for practices usually engaged in only by monastics, and that their efforts are being supported and encouraged. However, if enough lay Buddhists participate long and seriously in such an endeavor, and *especially if significant numbers of them are women*, such a transformation is inevitable. The everyday life of career and family will come to be regarded as Buddhist practice, rather than as the parentheses within which such practice occurs, a vast transformation of values. This vast transformation and enlargement of Buddhist concerns is far more radical than simply encouraging lay people to engage in extensive study and practice. The traditional hierarchy between the spiritual and the ordinary is being erased and the lines between them become blurred. Housework vs. meditation, business vs. study, childcare vs. retreat, marriage vs. celibacy, all the dichotomies and hierarchies that once seemed so clear, vanish. Such a re-evaluation enormously enlarges the canon of Buddhist concerns. It also introduces new tensions which can be difficult to resolve.

Before exploring this transvaluation of values further, let us look at the Buddhist hesitancy to follow the models, set up by traditional Judaism or by Lame Deer, of collapsing the ordinary and the spiritual. In my opinion, certain resources for doing precisely the same thing have been lying dormant within the Buddhist tradition—and they are found precisely within the rationale for valuing the life of renunciation. The Buddhist fear would be that a person practicing the kind of rituals recommended by Judaism or the kind of contemplation of symbolic meanings recommended by Lame Deer could still be attached to the very things that are the basis for sacred awareness in the midst of daily life. And so long as there is attachment, there is no true freedom. Furthermore, one can easily mistake a spiritual high that may accompany ritual or religious experience for detachment, insight, and release. Ordinary life is too seductive, the Buddhist might respond. It is safer, surer, and more productive of true freedom to cut one's ties with ordinary life for an unconventional lifestyle that leaves few hooks on which attachments could form. The very things that promote sacred awareness could promote attachment instead.

The link between *things* and *attachment* is extremely subtle according to Buddhism. Unfortunately, there is no guarantee about how to break this link; one can become attached to virtually anything, including the routines of monastic life. In breaking this link, clearly, the *attachment* is what must be overcome; things themselves are blameless. One renounces *attachment* because that, rather than any particular *thing*, is the problem. The basic transformation sought in Buddhist disciplines is a change of attitude, of heart and mind, because fundamentally attitudes, not conditions and things, are the cause of suffering. The foundation practice is to overcome attachment; the monastic lifestyle is only an *upaya* to that end, not something of intrinsic worth and value apart from that end. Like the raft of the Buddha's teachings,* when it has done its job, it can be left on the shore.

The point of Buddhist spiritual discipline is to cut attachment, to enhance awareness, to promote freedom. In the long run, the point of Buddhist spiritual discipline is also to increase appreciation of Suchness (*tathata*). After cutting attachment and intuiting emptiness, at least according to third-turning teachings, one encounters the vivid, brilliant world of phenomena without projection, the phenomenal world of Things-As-They-Are. Then one no longer needs to renounce anything or to cultivate a specific special lifestyle. Everything can be appreciated; everything is experienced in a matrix of clarity and detachment. For this reason, Vajrayana Buddhism encourages people to think of our world as a sacred world and encourages the cultivation of "sacred outlook."[16] Lame Deer's pot of soup strikes me as a perfect example of viewing the world with "sacred outlook" beyond attachment. If a pot of soup can be so viewed, why not one's livelihood, one's vacuum cleaner, one's garden, or one's children?

Buddhism itself, thus *does* possess the conceptual resources to go beyond the view that the ordinary world, ordinary things, and everyday experiences, cannot be apprehended with mindfulness, awareness, and detachment. In fact, many forms of Buddhism, most explicitly certain aspects of Vajrayana and Zen Buddhism, regard this state of luminous everyday awareness as the culmination of spiritual discipline.[†] What is less clear in the traditional literature is how often this consciousness is thought to be experienced by anyone other than old men at the end of a monastic career. But the form of serious lay Buddhist practice and the transvaluation of values that comes with it will make more explicit that Buddhist monks do not have a monopoly on this level of spiritual development. Everyday activities surrounding livelihood and domestic life, if interfused with disciplines of mindfulness and awareness, can also promote this level of development.

---

* Rahula, *What the Budda Taught,* p. 11. The text reads, "O bhikkus, even this view, which is so pure, and so clear, if you cling to it, if you fondle it, if you treasure it, then you do not understand that the teaching is like a raft, which is for crossing over, and not for getting hold of."

† Vajrayana Buddhism talks of this stage as the "old dog" state, attained when one fully understands that nothing needs to be renounced or pursued. Trungpa, *Cutting through Spiritual Materialism*, p. 243. In Zen Buddhism, the same insight is expressed in the Ten Oxherding Pictures, which describe the spiritual journey. Finally, the seeker realizes that from the very beginning, all things exist in intrinsic purity. Kapleau, *Three Pillars of Zen*, pp. 310-11.

The earliest model for this pursuit of calm clarity in the midst of daily life occurs in the *Therigatha*. The commentary which tells the life story of the author of the very first verse, an unknown nun, narrates that first she became a lay disciple. After hearing Prajapati speak, she desired to leave the world, but her husband would not consent:

> So she went on preforming her duties, reflecting on the sweetness of the doctrine, and living devoted to insight. Then one day in the kitchen, while the curry was cooking, a mighty flame of fire shot up, and burnt all the food with much crackling. She, watching it, made it a basis for rapt meditation on the utter impermanence of all things. Thereby she was established in the Fruition of the Path of No-Return.[17]

When she refused to wear jewels after this experience, her husband finally relented and let her become a nun. Thus, her story illustrates the possibilities of practicing mindfulness in household life, but not the transvaluation of values attendant on feminist reconceptualization of the whole issue. Though she attained a high level of development while living as a householder, she still became a nun eventually. In the value system of early Indian Buddhism, any other outcome was incongruent.

In the context of lay Buddhist meditation, the phases of her life might well be reversed. Lay Buddhists, in their attempt to interfuse the values of monastic and householder lifestyles, might well engage in a period of intensive training *before* taking on the duties and potential distractions of the householder life, which would mean they would be far better equipped to handle its allures without succumbing to utter attachment and completely *samsaric* consciousness. Such a life plan has never been widely available to women in the Buddhist world; they were always married off as soon as they could become pregnant and reproduce, as is the case in patriarchal societies around the world. Men in some Buddhist countries more routinely experienced a period of monastic training before settling down to marry and pursue a career. But the purpose of that monastic period is often to fulfill a debt to one's ancestors and complete one's transition into manhood, rather than to take the values of monasticism back into domestic life. Furthermore, in the model of lay Buddhist meditators, the intensive training period is not confined to youth. Throughout the life cycle, one would return for further periods of intensive practice, interspersed within one's career and one's family responsibilities.

The feminist-androgynous transvaluation of values grows out of conflicts that can occur when people try to combine the monastic and the householder lifestyles. As one person put it: "We often talk about practice and everyday life as opposites. We feel that zazen is 'pure' practice, while work or everyday life is 'applied' practice. And in both spiritual and scientific circles, the 'pure' activity is more prestigious than the applied side of it."[18] These conflicts have probably been most poignantly articulated by parents, women, for the most part, who were involved seriously in formal lay Buddhist meditation practice before they become parents with the major responsibility for childcare. On the one hand, there simply is no time for the demanding discipline of formal Buddhist meditation practice, and there are constant interruptions when one does make the attempt. On the other hand, people often report feelings of deep conflict. They intuitively feel that their childcare activities are *spiritually* significant, are a kind of meditation practice, but they find little validation of that point of view in retreat manuals and other traditional Buddhist texts. To continue with the comments quoted above:

> I have to admit that the strongest teacher I have ever known is my son, Joshua. When he was just a newborn, he opened my eyes to the meaning of practice. Just going to Joshua when he cried, just cleaning up his messes, moving from one thing to another, I experienced being present each moment. "This is beginner's mind," I said to myself. For the first time I understood what Suzuki Roshi had been talking about. . . .
>
> I had been sitting for seven years before my son was born. The year before his birth I did little zazen, but the year before that I spent at Tassajara (San Francisco Zen Center's training monastery). I was struck by how similar my year at Tassajara and my first few years of mothering felt, but I assumed that the monastery was where practice really took place. I assumed that my feeling that what I was doing with my child was practice must be some kind of misunderstanding. My doubt and my confusion grew.[19]

People in this situation also often experience guilt over "not practicing" and "not being serious about Buddhism." Though the example is most dramatic for childrearing, it is important, in the long run, to remember that these same conflicts can arise regarding a broad range of "ordinary" domestic and work-related concerns of both women and men.

This situation obviously invites feminist reconceptualization, but the task is trickier and more subtle than it may at first appear. The standard feminist observation and critique that Buddhism, like all the male-created and male-dominated religions, has little understanding of or advice relevant to women's life cycles, bodies, or reproductive experiences is appropriate. These topics are rarely discussed in classic sources, and if they are, the discussion is remote and of little use, obviously coming from someone who has no direct experience of them. They are rarely evaluated positively or as of direct spiritual significance. Because of the paucity of traditional resources on such topics, many people feel that it is useless to ask the traditional Buddhist authorities for guidance. One would do better to ask one's grandmother and to trust oneself, in the view of one frustrated mother: "I am personally reluctant to open this matter to patriarchal advice. What would Dogen Zenji, who never got laid, never got married, never had kids, never had a 'job' possibly know about the difficulties that come along with all these life choices?"[20]

When those concerned to fuse their traditional Buddhist disciplines with their householder tasks of livelihood and childcare speak to these questions, they call for a revalorization of these experiences, stressing their dignity as well as their spiritual potential. The issues are usually put in terms of parenting because mothers have felt the most left out. A Buddhist with significant experience of both monastic life and motherhood expressed her longing and her frustrations:

> One might argue that women should have a spiritual path in which they do not have to remove themselves from their life rhythms in order to practice. I agree with that theoretically, and I would like to see more teachings given which really help in dealing with relationships and childrearing in a positive way.... The possibilities are endless, but I have never heard a male teacher discussing these possibilities. This is natural since these experiences do not generally fall upon men, and I think it is the duty of women who are spiritually awake to make connections between their lives and the teachings.[21]

Though I have heard rare male teachers with relevant things to say on these topics, her feeling of being without guidance and having to figure it out for ourselves is generally correct. Furthermore, while I agree in general with her point, the issue is not confined to women and motherhood. In post-patriarchal Buddhism, it is as important that women not be the sole childcare givers as it is that childcare be revalorized and included in the realm of spiritual discipline. Furthermore, the *whole round* of domestic and economic activities, not just childcare, must be included in this transvaluation of values. This revalorization should encompass and include not only parenting but the entire round of domestic and worldly activities usually left behind by "serious Buddhists" and devalued even by some lay Buddhists, who see study and practice as their "real" Buddhist activity.

Nevertheless, the childcare issue remains central. From the point of view of the parent, it has never been systematically and seriously integrated into discussions of the *dharma*. The parent-child relationship, which does play a significant role in some Mahayana contemplations of compassion, deals with the experience from the child's point of view, of evaluating his mother as extremely compassionate because she took care of him in a fashion similar to his inspiration to care for all sentient beings as a bodhisattva. But that set of contemplations *does not* valorize parenting as a spiritual discipline from the parents' point of view. This revalorization could only be done by people with actual experience as primary care-giving parents who are also Buddhist teachers. These people, most of them women, are only now beginning to articulate their experience and reflections—indicative of how much we have to learn from a feminist reconceptualization of Buddhism.

That childcare has never been revalorized, in Buddhist terms, from the parents' point of view, is somewhat embarrassing when we contrast it with what has happened to many stereotypically male activities over the years. In Zen Buddhism, daily physical work has become a critical part of meditation training. Cooking, cleaning, gardening, building and maintaining the monastery, are all done with precise mindfulness and are regarded as central to overall training. Notoriously, Zen Buddhism even lent its hand to disciplining warriors in Japan, using meditation training to aid their skill as warriors. Tibetan monasteries also had military components in some cases. If the stereotypical male pursuits of agriculture and militarism, two activities strictly forbidden in the *vinaya*, can be revalorized, one wonders why childrearing has not been. The answer, of course, is that few childrearers (mothers) had a chance for complete training or a chance to become Buddhist teachers. That childcare has not been revalorized is doubly embarrassing when one realizes that not only male work, but also sexuality, another activity that early Indian Buddhist did not see as conducive to realization, has been revalorized in Vajrayana Buddhism, both as symbol and as experience. Only the experiences traditionally central to women's lives have been left out. They had to wait for post-patriarchal Buddhism to be included.

In this confusion about "real" practice and the tasks of daily life, another observation is important. Classically, Buddhism has stressed the differences between the life of a monastic and the life of a householder. But perhaps they are not so different. Monastics by no means spend all their time in study and meditation. They clean their quarters and wash dishes; they wash and mend their robes; they keep records; they eat their meals, and they sleep. In some monastic contexts, they also cook, and work on the grounds and in the garden. In still other monastic contexts, monks occupy themselves with endless ritual housekeeping, maintaining the shrines properly, making all the required offerings, and making the numerous and complex temporary ritual objects, such as *torma*s* and sand paintings. In short, they engage in all sorts of mundane, everyday activities. In the case of the monastic, these activities are all bases for mindfulness and awareness; in the case of the householder, they are invitations to mindlessness and distraction. Or so it

---

* A *torma* is a representation of a *yidam* made from roasted barley flour and butter, decorated with butter wheels and paints. They are very precisely shaped and detailed. Making them is time-consuming and difficult.

has been traditionally viewed. But in a transvaluation of values that regards both domestic life and monastic life as potentially the realm of spiritual discipline and sacred outlook, these assumptions do not hold. As Fran Tribe has written: "We think that a monk working in the temple garden is practicing, but it is harder to see that a lay person taking care of his or her own garden may be practicing, too. True practice does not live in any institution; it lives in the innermost part of each of us."[22] The issue it not whether one is in a monastery or a meditation hall, doing formal meditation practice, or in an office or a nursery, doing "applied" meditation practice. The issue is whether some level of awareness and clarity is fused with one's activities, wherever they are done.

The container for "true practice," whether it occurs in the meditation hall or the so-called "ordinary world," is the basic Buddhist mindfulness discipline, taught with many subtle variations.[23] This is the training that allows one eventually to be able to maintain awareness, whether in one's own garden or the monastery garden. Because the basic form of meditation does not cultivate trance states and withdrawal from the phenomenal world into alternate states of consciousness (though such meditations are also practiced in Buddhism), Buddhism after patriarchy is well equipped to help people bridge the dichotomy of "practice" and "everyday life." True practice really is being here, aware, with "just this,"* whether "just this" is one's everyday occupation or one's seat in the meditation hall.

To maintain both kinds of true practice is a complex and subtle balancing act, however. The feminist appreciates the potential valorization of everyday activity inherent in this approach to spiritual discipline and attainment. The Buddhist insists that true mindfulness and awareness are critical to avoid attachment and distraction and insists that for most people, it is wishful thinking to hope for that state of mind without the container and basis of ongoing formal meditation practice and periodic intensive retreats.

The feminist reconceptualization calls for seeing "ordinary" activities as sacred—as spiritually significant. This call is an important challenge to the conventional religions, especially to those, including Buddhism, that have a long tradition of seeing spiritual discipline as otherworldly and anti-worldly, as promoting freedom from the world. The feminist call is for nothing less that finding freedom within the world, within domestic concerns, within emotions, within sexuality, within parenthood, within career. This vision goes far beyond simply encouraging householders to make time in their lives for traditional study and practices.

---

* Francis Cook, at the 1986 sessions of the Cobb-Abe Buddhist-Christian Theological encounter, mystified many with his claim that his cat represented ultimate reality for a Buddhist, since the cat was "just this." *Buddhist-Christian Studies* IX (1989), pp. 127–42.

While this feminist reconceptualization certainly has compelling merit, some care and caution is required in its endorsement. Buddhism has traditionally been suspicious of ordinary, conventional, worldly life for good reason. Often and easily, it becomes petty, trivial, distracting, and indulgent. Even people who take care to live contemplative and introspective lives in the midst of worldly activity often feel that they have become distracted and caught up in trivial or indulgent reactions and pursuits; how much more easily would an ordinary life unsuffused with awareness and introspection become petty, unattractive, and undesirable. The point is not that ordinary activities are necessarily sacred but that they can be sacred when done with the proper mental and spiritual attitude. The corresponding, equally significant point is that one can easily loose that mind of clarity, awareness, and mindfulness.

The vision of Buddhism as freedom within the world is that one can be free not only in a monastery, but also in an office or a nursery. If one loses one's freedom in the nursery or office and becomes petty, trivial, unmindful, and unclear, one is not experiencing the sacred in everyday activities, but merely *samsaric* attachment and pettiness. While it sounds attractive to see the sacred in ordinary everyday activities, in dirty diapers and busy schedules, actually being able to do that, rather than simply becoming distracted and petty, is not easy. It fact, such an ability is often claimed to be the acme of spiritual attainment, of true freedom. But it is not attained overnight or without significant spiritual practice, simply by declaring its desirability. There is inevitable tension connected with this enlargement and revalorization of Buddhist concerns. On the one hand, it is attractive not to dichotomize experience into important spiritual concerns and unimportant worldly concerns, but to see these two arenas of life as interpenetrating and indistinguishable. On the other hand, it is easy, while attempting to unify one's life, simply to fall into mere unaware, worldly attitudes.

Two questions might occur to an outsider. Why is it important to maintain clarity? Return to basic Buddhist principles. Without clarity and insight, one will fall into attachment and ignorance, which inevitably bring suffering in their wake. Is it any easier to maintain awareness and detachment in a monastic than in a household environment? The answer is an unqualified "yes," based on my experiences of many periods of retreat into quasi-monastic environments for intensive study and meditation. All-pervasive discipline, a strict schedule, lack of interruptions, and focused attention to meditation practice, all conspire to enhance clarity, insight, and awareness.

However, the Buddhist and feminist concerned with spirituality as freedom within the world sees perpetual retreat into such protected environments as rather limited and artificial, violating the balance sought in the Three Wheels principle discussed earlier. Dichotomizing one's life into important spiritual and unimportant ordinary activities is similarly unattractive. A whole, balanced lifestyle, in which all its parts are valued as important to overall spiritual well-being, without ever degenerating into mere conventional worldliness, is much more the ideal. For this lifestyle, we really have no models; to create such models is one of the tasks of post-patriarchal Buddhism seen as freedom within the world.

Thus, I suggest balancing on the razor's edge—a familiar Buddhist metaphor for the life of spiritual discipline. While affirming the sacred potential of ordinary domestic householder concerns, one must also hold firmly to the Buddhist dissatisfaction with conventional attitudes and approaches to them. To maintain this balance, to maintain both the feminist sense of the potential sacredness of everyday work and the Buddhist call for detachment and equanimity, ongoing meditative discipline, sometimes intensely formal, sometimes unstructured, is necessary. That ongoing attitude of awareness will itself be the protection we need to keep us in balance and out of extreme behavior, whether the extreme behavior would take the form of a continual need to be in retreat from "worldly activities" or the temptation to lose and bury oneself in excessive involvement with career or family, by becoming a workaholic or by reproducing excessively.

SPIRITUAL DISCIPLINE: VISION AND TRANSCENDENCE IN REMAKING THE WORLD

The most difficult issue remains. Post-patriarchal androgynous Buddhism will continue to be centered in spiritual transformation through spiritual discipline. But will they be the *same* spiritual disciplines? Will the conceptualization of appropriate and helpful spiritual transformation and the fruits and outcomes of spiritual discipline remain the *same*? Or will some of these disciplines and fruitions be tried in the fire of feminist experience and be found wanting, found unduly macho and androcentric? Given that the practices and goals currently defined as appropriate spiritual discipline came from men alone, rather than from the entire Buddhist community, there are no guarantees. Since spiritual discipline is so subtle and since self-deception is so easy, these questions are provoking—either way. Since self-deception is always a threat, the current male-created program of spiritual discipline really could be missing something vital. Since self-deception is always a threat, feminist criticisms and reconstructions could be quite off the mark. No question in reconstruction of post-patriarchal Buddhism is more overwhelming.

One guideline from classical Buddhism can, I believe, be trusted and become something of test for other recommendations. That guideline is to seek the middle path of balance and wholeness in lifestyle and values. To seek the middle path means avoiding falling into one extreme or another. Instead, one finds the methods to blend both options if both offer spiritual meaning, and, equally, to reject them both, if all they offer is a half-truth. But what are the extremes regarding spiritual discipline that one seeks to blend or avoid? In earlier sections of this reconstruction, we worked with extremes. The extremes of gender role specialization and the mutual incompetence fostered by them have been rejected in favor of finding balance and wholeness through blending the previously separated roles into a well-rounded androgynous lifestyle. Regarding religious lifestyles, we similarly rejected the extreme of casting people into the role of being either a merit-making lay person or a monk primarily involved in the accumulation of wisdom. Rather, time and space for serious spiritual practice are factored into a lifestyle of lay Buddhist meditation, with the monastic alternative available equally to both women and men for whom it is appropriate.

Now we must ask the same questions of spiritual discipline and find the same balance. When does spiritual discipline function to sharpen perception and insight and when does it become a macho endurance contest? When does it act as a buffer against experience and when does it clarify and intensify experience? What kinds of spiritual disciplines promote gentle sanity and which have the potential to desensitize a person to basic emotional realities? For that matter, why is one pursuing spiritual discipline? To escape into another realm of consciousness and being, or to experience fully and vividly the complexity and ambiguity of the present situation? Is meditation practice the most, even the only valuable human activity, the only spiritual discipline conducive to enlightenment and clear seeing into Things-As-They-Are, as traditional Buddhist texts would often have us believe? Among the various kinds of meditation, are some more relevant to human wholeness and integrity than others?

Sometimes I become rather impatient with some of the models and heroes presented to me by my tradition, not because they are men, but because they seem extreme. Do I really want to emulate these guys! Does my skepticism have anything to do with a valid feminist critique, or is it simply due to laziness and resistance? Though nothing is more important to me than clear seeing, than seeing Things-As-They-Are, in classic Buddhist terms, I find it difficult to appreciate some of the methods utilized by some who are acclaimed as having achieved that goal. Long periods of isolation are routine in Tibetan Buddhism and Zen monks do lengthy periods of continuous zazen. What can Mila Repa's isolation in his cave, turning green from his diet of nettles,[24] have to do with enlightenment? What about Naropa, forcing his equally *dharmic* wife Niguma to take the blame for the dissolution of their marriage, forcing her to tell his parents that their separation resulted from the inevitable faults of women, rather than from their mutual desire to renounce the domestic life?[25] What about Siddartha Gautama, abandoning his wife and new-born child? Nor am I am attracted when I read of contemporary Western women, studying under Tibetan teachers, one of whom routinely goes into long periods of solitary meditation in a Tibetan cave, which cannot even be reached for much of the year because it is snowbound, and the other who was in a retreat hut in New York state for twelve years. Are such practices necessary? Are they even helpful to anyone? Why are they often praised and admired? Why do so many people seem to think that to realize one's innate enlightened humanity, such anti-human disciplines are helpful? What about seemingly less extreme measures? What about the shorter solitary retreats and the time and expense involved in significant periods of intensive meditation practice?

What about the emphasis, so prevalent in Tibetan Vajrayana Buddhism, that regards the whole point of all this intensive meditation practice as preparation for death? Does it make sense to practice spiritual disciplines in order to attempt to root out attraction to life because the whole point of life to end the cycle of becoming? Is death the major event of life, for which one must be prepared at all costs? At *all* costs, including twelve years in a cave? Including denial of the primacy of human relationships, even for those who long to transcend triviality and conventionality to see clearly into Things-As-They-Are? Is life so counterproductive that one must so rigorously struggle to make one's energies flow in contrary directions? Is death so intractable without a lifetime spent in intensive wariness?

These lines of questioning, especially when combined with feminist skepticism, are deeply troubling. Because the patriarchs have been wrong about so much, and because they hang onto their sexism so desperately, even after its demonic nature is pointed out to them, resisting even the most uncontroversial and fair-minded reforms, such as reinstitution of the nuns' ordination, healthy skepticism about anything they say is warranted. One cannot simply trust that the leaders have everything right, that they've picked good and healthy models for us, that we do have to go to such extremes as they recommend to be fully human. Because patriarchal religions will not rid themselves of their patriarchy, a feminist who wishes to remain within that tradition must take nothing on faith and test everything. Ultimately, this includes the beloved heart of Buddhist life—its emphasis on meditative and spiritual disciplines, an emphasis which sometimes seems extreme and one-sided. At some moments one questions whether the demanding meditations actually help one live well and truthfully, or whether they get in the way. Maybe they are simply the creations of patriarchs who use them to control life and distance themselves from others!

Maybe that is why Buddhism sometimes seems to glorify aloneness and be deficient in its emphasis on relationship. Clearly, such reflections are frightening to one who has deeply invested in Buddhism.

What is the exact content of these restless questions? I am not questioning whether meditation is or has been very pleasurable—sometimes peaceful, sometimes exhilarating—as well as at least seemingly beneficial. In fact, the various meditations are so conducive to the feeling that one has finally come closer to seeing into the depth of things that one *is* tempted to say, as I have sometimes done after periods of intensive meditation, "*this* is the real world!" Then one can almost believe that those who spend most of their time in meditation caves, as so many heroes of the tradition have done, are, in fact, the only ones who really see Things-As-They-Are. But if that were true, then all the attempts to create a balanced lifestyle that accommodates both "spiritual" and "ordinary" concerns as being of one flavor would obviously be an impossible waste of time. This conclusion I am not willing to make, initiating another whole cycle of questions about what is the point of meditation.

Clearly, however, two common assertions of the tradition are highly questionable in my view. Helpful as meditation may be to some people, I doubt that it is as indispensably necessary as is sometimes claimed. More important, I doubt that one should pursue meditation as single-mindedly and as exclusively, to the exclusion of other pursuits, as did many of the heroes of the tradition.

These questions reflect a deeper tension found in all religious traditions and between the religions and feminism. All religions, not only world-denying traditions, but also the supposedly world-affirming traditions, have a deep impulse to remake people, to declare that the human condition, unrefined and unreworked by religious disciplines, initiations, or confessions, simply does not make it. It is filled with original sin, completely consumed by suffering, lacking esoteric knowledge, or even a properly shaped penis. Without the intervention of time-consuming, expensive, painful, and *seemingly unnatural* religious disciplines, we human beings, as we are, are quite hopeless. But religion can cope, can wash away original sin, show the path beyond suffering, fill one with proper knowledge, or reshape the body properly. Spiritual disciplines designed to achieve these goals abound.

Feminists tend to be quite suspicious of such claims. This suspicion is due to the evaluation, found in most religions, that women are even worse off than men, that women are the cause of these negative conditions, that women are less capable of being repaired by religious disciplines, and, in some cases, that women should be forbidden even to approach the religious disciplines that repair the human situation. Obviously, these strongly anti-female claims, so common in world religions, are unequivocally rejected by feminism. More important, feminism's rejection of anti-female teachings and practices predisposes it to be suspicious of other negative evaluations common to religions. Often feminists say that the tendency of religions to find life deeply unsatisfactory is a patriarchal value, and that the more accurate and feminist assessment is to find life, including its dark aspects and its limitations, joyful and satisfactory. Thus, for example, Starhawk, the well-known and articulate spokesperson for feminist wicca, writes, specifically contrasting Buddhism and wicca:

> Witchcraft does not maintain, like the First Truth of Buddhism, that "All life is suffering." On the contrary, life is a thing of wonder. The Buddha is said to have gained this insight after his encounter with old age, disease and death. In the Craft, old age is a natural and highly valued part of the cycle of life, the time of greatest wisdom and understanding. Disease, of course, causes misery but it is not something to be inevitably suffered: The practice of the Craft was always connected with the healing arts, with herbalism and mid-wifery. Nor is death fearful: It is simply the dissolution of the physical form that allows the spirit to prepare for a new life. Suffering certainly exists in life—it is part of learning. But escape from the Wheel of Birth and Death is not the optimal cure, any more than hara kiri is the best cure for menstrual cramps. When suffering is the result of the social order or human injustice, the Craft encourages active work to relieve it. Where suffering is a natural part of the cycle of birth and decay, it is relieved by understanding and acceptance, by a willing giving over to both the dark and the light in turn.[26]

Some of the contrast between Buddhism and feminist wicca as outlined by Starhawk could equally aptly be read as the contrast between Buddhism interpreted as the quest for freedom from the world and Buddhism interpreted as the quest for freedom within the world.[27] Given feminist distrust of dualistic, otherworldly spiritualities, feminist Buddhism would sound more like what Starhawk outlines as the position of the Craft. According to such an interpretation of Buddhism, spiritual disciplines seek, not to free us from the "dark" aspects of life, but to enable us to find our ease in them, which will enable us to appreciate them. Thus, at a certain level, it could be claimed that feminism simply expresses the alternative attitude, also espoused by most religions in their more accepting modes. Though often lost in the barrage of rhetoric regarding the unsatisfactoriness of life, this alternative assessment is, in fact the deeper, more normative attitude, especially in Buddhism.

All the confusions and defilements that cause so much suffering are not our original true human nature at all, but a veil, a secondary overlay, according to Buddhism. In this assessment, the spiritual need is to be able to accept and settle into our human goodness and our human potential. Life conditions are fundamentally sane and satisfactory, but we have a difficult time seeing that they are. The point of spiritual discipline is to be able to let ourselves be fully human. But how can years of solitary retreat effect that goal? Granted that the *point* of Buddhist disciplines is freedom within the world, does the traditional *program* of Buddhist meditations led toward or away from that goal? We are back to the original question.

Spiritual disciplines espouse two seemingly contradictory views. We are told, both that our original nature is fundamentally good or inherently enlightened and, at the same time, that we are not fully in touch with that goodness and enlightenment. Regarding this set of seeming extremes, the challenge is to hold *both* of them always to heart. Without both, one will fall into either trivial superficial spiritual materialisms of the "love and light" variety, or one will fall into rigid and depressing dualistic otherworldliness. And I believe that, in terms of attitude toward spiritual transformation, holding both these attitudes is the *essential* challenge.

This set of attitudes can also be contrasted as transcendence and immanence, as the orientation toward sky and light versus the orientation toward earth and darkness, that has fueled so such competition and antagonism between spiritualities. This also often reads as the script for the conflict between patriarchal world-denying spiritualities of longing, dissatisfaction, quest, and transcendence, on the one hand, and feminist spiritualities of acceptance, joy, community, and cycles, on the other.[28] Settling with either extreme brings imbalance and one-sidedness in the long run.

Both classical Buddhism and the milieu in which most Westerners who become involved with Buddhism matured, emphasize the transcendent impulse, the side of spiritual experience that longs for cleansing and remaking, the side of spiritual experience that declares that there has to be more to being alive than repeating the same old miseries of conventional existence from generation to generation. This is the spirituality that compelled a poverty-stricken farmgirl like myself to leave home, to seek to understand and be transformed, to reject as inadequate the conventions laid out for me because of my gender and class. Like a moth attracted to the flame, some people simply cannot bear to live the conventional existence, unreflectingly repeating the patterns of the ages. A life dictated by the female gender role, and, to a lesser extent, a life dictated by the male gender role, warrant the evaluation that those who immerse themselves in such lives lead lives of quiet desperation.

In the spiritual impulse to leave behind such lives are intertwined, I believe, both vision and unwisdom based on pain. This volatile combination leads people not only to renounce conventionality to seek a heaven-oriented transcendence, but also to glorify renunciation, aloneness, and self-sufficiency, to become alienated from much that is deeply sane about earth-oriented immanence. Feminist spirituality provides the countervailing weight, the skepticism that there is anything special to attain, the tranquillity and acceptance that are discussed by Buddhists as the ultimate goal and fruition of years of spiritual discipline. Feminist spirituality also provides a way for that message to be heard more clearly, sooner. But, by itself, I believe that this message is equally one-sided, because it does not sufficiently encourage people to vision and discontent. Today, spiritual vision and discontent are necessary, as they have always been, to propel us to stop being content with things-as-they-are-conventionally, and to seek things-as-they-are-in-reality. In finding things as they are, we will find the sanity and deep peace of earth intermingled with the yearning of heaven.

In affirming these feminist first impressions that the human situation is fundamentally good and should not be rejected by dualistic, anti-worldly spiritual values, only half the problem is solved. The question remains as to what kinds of spiritual disciplines are most effective and conducive to enabling the blend and balance of spiritual values being recommended here. At the beginning, any kind of spiritual discipline seems counterproductive and boring or irrelevant. But eventually, the necessity of some kind of difficult, "against the grain" discipline that enables us to return to and rest in the fundamental goodness becomes obvious. Without such discipline, few people transcend trivial, conventional, repetitive styles of immanence for those grounded in deep peace. The question is not "Whether discipline?" but "What kind of discipline?" Sorting out excesses, many of them due to patriarchal limitations, from genuinely sane, balanced approaches will be difficult. This will be another major task of Buddhism after patriarchy.

In general, the same kind of balance sought for in other arenas of post-patriarchal reconceptualization would hold here. Lifelong, regular spiritual discipline is obviously important, but it should not be regarded as the only thing worthwhile, "the one thing needful" in life, and the demands of one's spiritual discipline should not incapacitate one regarding other dimensions of a whole, complete lifestyle. Nothing can substitute for the long-term training and processing that results from years of practicing regularly the disciplines of mindfulness and awareness that are the heart of Buddhist meditation. On the other hand, sometimes formal meditation practices, especially of the variety that stresses visualization and projecting a visualized reality upon the empirical world at hand can lead away from being fully engaged in the present experiences. Resorting to them can be an escape or coping device, rather than an engagement of the present.

As I wrote this section of this chapter, these questions, with which I have struggled for so long, became even more vividly clear to me. Within fifteen pages of the end of this manuscript, I found my heart companion, who had cheered me on in this difficult task, dead. Very suddenly, very abruptly, without warning, he was dead in our house. We only had three years together, but those three years confirmed the truth of the chapter on relationship and enlightenment, found earlier in this section and drafted before he came into my life. I seized the experience while it was at hand, since he was twenty-two years older than me; Buddhist friends, young males of the age and temperament that the classic tradition idealizes, fretted that I had sold out on my intense commitment to Buddhist practice. I said, "This is my practice now. This is my life." The experience transformed me as much as Buddhist practice, but without Buddhist practice, I would not have known how to use this opportunity to be transformed.

When he died, Buddhists pressured me to practice formally to deal with the experience. But I felt, and stuck to my feelings, that moment by moment, I was practicing—I was fully present. And I felt intensely that any formal practice, whether of mindfulness or of visualization, would distance me from what was happening immediately, which was my practice. I have never felt more aware and alive to my experience, which was one of piercing hollowness and emptiness, yet fullness. I am also certain that without the years of formal Buddhist training, I could never have withstood so much and would have shut it down somehow. At a certain point, it was time to do the formal Buddhist practices surrounding death. They too, done not out of desperation to get through the experience but out of the fullness of training, were intense and immediate, enhancing awareness and vivid presence.

From that experience, I believe several principles can be deduced. The first is that there is no substitute for formal training in meditation, which will often feel "unnatural," or "against the grain." Such disciplines cannot be rejected as the products of a male or dualistic style of spirituality simply because they can be boring and difficult. A meditation practice that grounds people more presently and fully in experience, a meditation discipline without gimmicks, hyperbole, and promises of bliss, is indispensable for dealing with the myriad stresses that a feminist woman, or anyone else for that matter, will face. These basic formless practices of mindfulness and awareness can easily be integrated into one's ongoing life and, after some intensive experience with them, they readily inform one's life beyond formal practice. The more esoteric practices associated with Vajrayana Buddhism, which are quite time-consuming and which involve visualizing an alternate reality, do produce expanded states of consciousness. But to do them seriously also requires setting aside other concerns. I am uncertain to what extent they will be integrated into a post-patriarchal Buddhism that seeks balance and wholeness. Finally, an important part of the practice of spiritual discipline should be to use it skillfully, as a tool rather than a prison, so that one is not so compulsively meditating that one misses one's life. Spiritual disciplines should not be used to deaden or distance oneself from the vibrancy of the moment.

The final important post-patriarchal question concerning spiritual discipline asks "For what purpose?" What do we hope will result from the practice of spiritual discipline? What changes will it effect? Freedom from rebirth and communication with unseen beings, often currently the hoped-for results, do not seem to be relevant. In fact, the whole orientation of practicing a spiritual discipline to be prepared for death will probably not survive into post-patriarchal Buddhism. If a spiritual discipline promotes wholeness and balance, tranquillity and deep peace, that will be sufficient. And communication with one's fellow human beings will also be sufficient. If spiritual discipline results in a sense of the presence of other realms, that would be an additional bonus, but would not overshadow the desire to develop enough sensitivity to communicate with and comfort the people with whom one lives. One can also question the relevance of exalted, euphoric states of consciousness or esoteric knowledge and understanding. They can be exhilarating, and, properly used, may deepen one's appreciation of one's life and the world, but when they are pursued instead of one's immediate connections with earth and one's fellow human beings, they are counterproductive.

Rather, the point of such discipline is basic psychological grounding, deep sanity, and peace with ourselves. Out of that grows the caring for community and for each other that is so important for spiritual insight and well-being. Additionally, our sensitivity to, appreciation of, and desire to care for our earth will shine forth. Spiritual discipline will no longer encourage us to seek to leave her behind for a better world or to superimpose another purer, visualized world upon her. The tradition speaks of becoming deities (*yidam*-s) and living in the palace of the deities through our spiritual discipline. For that to happen properly, we will indeed see ourselves and each other as valuable, divine beings whom we cherish and for whom we care. We will not need to leave our world behind to visualize the palace of the deities in her place. When we look out our windows, we will see the palace of the deities. When we comfort each other, we will converse with the deities. To become sane, to live in community with each other and our earth, is to experience freedom within the world—the mutual goal of feminism and of (post-patriarchal) Buddhism.

METHODOLOGICAL APPENDICES

APPENDIX A
HERE I STAND: FEMINISM AS ACADEMIC
METHOD AND AS SOCIAL VISION

In comparison with other books on Buddhism, the innovation of this study is that it uses both feminism and women studies as methods. Many books on the history of Buddhism are found on library shelves; none of them includes a systematic or detailed discussion of women's participation in that history. Many books discuss and analyze the philosophical worldview of Buddhism, but those books almost never analyze the implications of this worldview for gender-related activities and roles. A smaller number of books considers the input Buddhism might have in the contemporary world, seeking to reconstruct outmoded aspects of Buddhism or to bring a Buddhist perspective to contemporary issues when relevant.[1] Surprisingly, except for a few volumes devoted specifically to the topic of women and Buddhism,[2] books on Buddhism and contemporary issues contain little commentary on gender-related issues. This ignoring of women and gender-related topics is unfortunately common in the cross-cultural and comparative study of religion. Therefore, the compelling justification for this book is not that it is another study in the history of religions or Buddhism, but that it is a rare study in the history of religions and Buddhism that is thoroughly grounded in women studies and in feminism.

Since this book includes both discussions of Buddhist history and reconstructions of Buddhist values and institutions, this appendix includes considerations of feminism both as academic method, i.e. the women studies perspective, and as social vision, i.e. the perspective of feminist philosophy. The women studies perspective is more relevant to historical discussions while the perspective of feminist philosophy is more relevant to the post-patriarchal reconstruction of Buddhism. Though the values and insights of these two perspectives are intertwined and closely linked, they are not identical. The women studies perspective is less radical, claiming only that scholars *must* include women in their data base if they wish to claim that they are discussing humanity (rather than human males). Feminist philosophy in its many varieties proposes reconstructions of current religions and societies to render them more just and equitable to women, and thereby, also to men.

FEMINISM AS ACADEMIC METHOD:
THE WOMEN STUDIES PERSPECTIVE

In 1967, when I first decided to write a paper on women in religion, I had no idea that I stumbled onto the concern that would occupy much of my scholarly and personal life, nor did I realize that I had located the most serious blindspot of contemporary scholarship, not only in religion, but also in all humanistic and social scientific disciplines. I only knew that I had decided on this paper topic because I felt frustrated and blocked as a woman seriously involved in current Western religions and I wanted to find out if "things are as bad everywhere." Therefore, for a required graduate course in primitive religions, I decided to write a paper on the role of women in Australian and Melanesian religions.

Researching and writing that paper was difficult and absorbing. Data were almost impossible to find, but the scholars all told me that in these religions, men are regarded as sacred while women are regarded as profane and unclean and had no significant religious life.[3] On the surface, it seems I should have concluded that "things were that bad (or even worse) everywhere." Nevertheless, I couldn't help but notice that the actual data of Australian and Melanesian religions recounted myths in which women originally held power and taught men all the religious rituals; only later, according to these myths, did men steal power and knowledge from the women. The actual data also included numerous rituals in which men imitated female physiological processes, even though they also excluded women from participation in those rituals. Something seemed not quite to add up.

I concluded in my paper that indeed women did have a religious life, that they were important in the symbol system of men's separate religion, and that the conventional scholarly hypothesis that these data indicated that men are sacred while women are profane was somehow inadequate. Women clearly seemed to be evaluated as sacred, though different than men.[4]

That paper turned into more that I bargained for or dreamed possible. Its effects are still very much with me in my identity as an outspoken feminist scholar and theologian. Were it not for that paper, I doubt that *Unspoken Worlds: Women's Religious Lives*[5] would have been written. And I probably would have had a much smoother ride through graduate school.

When Mircea Eliade, for whom I had written the paper, returned it to me, he strongly urged me to continue these explorations into my doctoral dissertation. His rationale, so vividly remembered all these years, "You're seeing things in these materials that I, as a man, would probably not see." My immediate response is also etched in my memory. "No, I want to do my dissertation on something important." But he countered that, as I could see from the research I had done, very little had been written on the topic and, therefore, further scholarship would be helpful. Somehow, I did end up deciding to continue studying something about women and religion for my doctoral work. In those days, women studies as a field and focus was non-existent and categories regarding women and religion were extremely vague; therefore, one could be studying something amorphous and ill-defined as women and religion.

At the dissertation stage, my initial paper turned into a critique of conventional history of religions methodology—a sacrosanct topic at the University of Chicago. That move led both to difficulties with my faculty mentors, which nearly resulted in my being unwillingly exited from the Divinity School, and to my career as a feminist scholar. These events all stemmed, not from my decision to continue studying "women and religion," but from my asking a question of feminist methodology: why had women and religion *not* been studied very much or very well previously. That question led me to further methodological considerations and to the claim that, while the history of religions was quite concerned with *homo religiosus*, it did not seem to be much concerned with *femina religiosa*. That question, though it did not yet articulate the essential feminist critique of conventional scholarship, was threatening enough to garner the reply that an intelligent graduate student should understand that the masculine covered and included the feminine, thereby obviating the need for any specific attention to women's religious lives. Though not without serious opposition, I eventually did receive a doctorate for the first dissertation in women studies in religion to be accepted by any major graduate institution.[6]

The reason for retelling these stories is not because I am the protagonist in them but because they illustrate so well the major issues and themes in the study of women and religion. Typically, in women studies, the link between experience and scholarship is openly acknowledged, despite a bias that scholarship should be "objective." Discipline lines are blurred, as is the distinction between so-called descriptive and so-called prescriptive studies; feminist scholarship is often deliberately synthetic. Finally, risks are taken in this kind of scholarship. Especially when we were graduate students and young scholars, those of us who first articulated the voice of feminist scholarship took enormous risks; even though many of are now better established, we still routinely write articles that make us feel vulnerable and exposed.

Experiences of alienation and frustration regarding my own religious heritage led me to explore religion in a wider context. Then I felt a strong but inarticulate reaction that somehow conventional scholarship had not really looked at women accurately and adequately. These experiences of frustration with my own religion and with scholarship on religion ultimately resulted in a basic paradigm shift in my thinking. Eventually, I realized that I was so frustrated by scholarship on women and religion and it seemed so inadequate because such scholarship resulted from an androcentric model of humanity in the scholars' minds. It became clear that when I responded that I wanted to do my dissertation on something important, not women, I, too, had been utilizing an androcentric model of humanity. After many months, perhaps even years of conceptual struggle, it became clear that a fundamental paradigm shift was called for. A better, more accurate and complete model of humanity was desperately needed by all scholars. We needed to exorcise the androcentric model of humanity from our consciousness and replace it thoroughly and completely, once and for all, with an androgynous model of humanity. That paradigm shift I now regard as the most essential issue in the study of women and religion, as well as the significant challenge and contribution of the women studies perspective. This challenge and contribution affect all humanistic and social scientific disciplines as profoundly as they affect religious studies.

The fundamental challenge and potential of women studies in religion, as in other fields, is its delineation and critique of androcentrism. The tasks of laying bare the fundamental unconscious preconceptions of androcentrism, demonstrating their inadequacy, and providing a more adequate alternative are the most important and central contributions of the women studies perspective to the field of religious studies and comparative religions. These are also the implications of feminism for most other disciplines.

Both the essential promise of women studies to induce a paradigm shift in scholarship, and the necessity of a phase during which the women studies perspective manifests as a separate focus researching lost or suppressed data on religion, are results of the prevailing conventional mindset of most scholars. That mindset utilizes an androcentric, one-sex model of humanity. The women and religion movement criticizes that model of humanity as inadequate and offers instead a two-sex, androgynous model of humanity. All these terms need to be defined.

Definitions of androcentrism could easily be multiplied. While abstract discussions are important, a simple example has great power. How many times has one read or heard the equivalent of the following statement: "the Egyptians allow (or don't allow) women to . . ."? The structure is so commonplace that even today many of my students have no clue about what is wrong with such a statement. For both those who make such statements and for those who hear them without wincing, "Egyptians" are men. Egyptian women are objects acted upon by real Egyptians, but are not themselves "Egyptians." What, in more analytical terms is behind this long-standing habitual pattern of speech? The androcentric model of humanity has three central characteristics which, when stated bluntly, suffice to demonstrate both the nature and the inadequacy of androcentrism.

First of all, in androcentric thought, the male norm and the human norm are collapsed and become identical. In fact, recognition that maleness is but one facet of human experience is minimal or non-existent. As de Beauvoir states:

> In the midst of an abstract discussion it is vexing to hear a man say: "You think thus and so because you are a woman," but I know that my only defense is to reply: "I think thus and so because it is true," thereby removing my subjective self from the argument. It would be out of the question to reply: "And you think the contrary because you are a man," for it is understood that the fact of being a man is no peculiarity. A man is in the right in being a man; it is the woman who is in the wrong. It amounts to this: just as for the ancients there was an absolute vertical with reference to which the oblique was defined, so there is an absolute human type, the masculine. Woman has ovaries, a uterus; these peculiarities imprison her in her subjectivity, circumscribe her within the limits of her own nature. It is often said that she thinks with her glands. Man superbly ignores the fact that his anatomy also includes glands, such as the testicles, and that they secrete hormones. He thinks of his body as a direct and normal connection with the world, which he believes he apprehends objectively, whereas he regards the body of woman as a hindrance, a prison, weighted down by everything peculiar to it.[7]

Thus in androcentric thinking maleness is normal; in addition, it is the norm. Any awareness of a distinction between maleness and humanity is clouded over and femaleness is viewed as an exception to the norm.

The second major characteristic of androcentrism follows directly from the first. If the male norm and the human norm are identical, it follows that the generic masculine habit of thought, language, and research will be assumed to be adequate. So we might say that scholarship dependent on the androcentric model of humanity utilizes generic masculine language. As a result, research about the religions of other times and places as well as about our own religious situation deals mainly with the lives and thinking of males. It seems unproblematic to include only a few stray comments about women's religious lives as a footnote or a short chapter towards the end of the book. The generic masculine habit of language, thought, and research is so pre-reflective and so strong that many scholars are genuinely unaware that one has studied only part of a religious situation if one has studied only the religious lives and thoughts of men. The need to present a full account of women and religion thoroughly integrated into the account of men and religion simply is not perceived. The generic masculine covers the feminine, as I was told by my mentors when I first questioned the completeness of current understandings of "homo religiosus."

The problem, of course, is that it really doesn't, which brings up the third, and perhaps most problematic aspect of androcentrism. The third constituent of the androcentric outlook is its attempt to deal with the fact that, since men and women are taught to be different in all cultures, the generic masculine simply does not cover the feminine. The generic masculine would work only in a religious-cultural situation where there were no sex roles, either explicit or implicit. That situation, of course, does not exist, not even in modern Christianity or Judaism, to say nothing of the religio-cultural situations of other times and places. Therefore, women "per se" must sometimes be mentioned in accounts of religion. At this point, adherents of the androcentric model of humanity have reached a logical impasse. Their solution to this impasse is the most devastating component of the androcentric outlook. Because they differ from the male (presumably human) norm, women must be mentioned, at least in a cursory fashion. But because they deviate from these norms when women, "per se," are mentioned, androcentric thinking deals with them only as an object exterior to "mankind," needing to be explained and fitted in somewhere, having the same epistemological and ontological status as trees, unicorns, deities, and other objects that must be discussed to make experience intelligible. Therefore, in most accounts of religion, males are presented as religious subjects, as namers of reality, while females are presented only in relation to the males being studied, only as objects being named by the males being studied, only as they appear to the males being studied.

As a corrective to this situation, a basic re-orientation of the scholar's consciousness is called for. We need a basic paradigm shift from models of humanity and modes of research and thought that perceive males at the center and females on the edges to modes that perceive both females and males at the center and reflect the essential "femaleness-maleness" of androgynous humanity. That would be a "two-sex" model of humanity, as opposed to a "one-sex" model of humanity.

The most important aspect of what I have called "androgynous methodology" or the "androgynous model of humanity" is this characteristic of being a "two-sexed" or "bisexual" model of humanity. This concept required clarification, for what I have in mind when I speak of androgynous models or methods differs considerably from both conventional notions of androcentric "mankind" and from the unisexual and sex-neutral meaning of androgyny that is popular at the present time.

What I mean by androgyny as a two-sex model of humanity and why such a model of humanity is mandatory, should be clear from what has already been stated. First, to present the matter colloquially and informally, we may look at the alternative to stating that "the Egyptians allow women . . ." A scholar who really understands the inadequacies of the androcentric model of humanity and the need for a more accurate two-sexed model of humanity would write that ". . . in Egyptian society men do "X" and women do "Y", or perhaps, in some cases, she might write that ". . . Egyptian men allow Egyptian women to . . . ," thereby recognizing both that Egyptian men have patriarchal control over the society and that Egyptian women are nevertheless Egyptian human beings, not an extra-human species.

Thus, as scholars, very simply, we are in need of a model of humanity that accurately reflects two basic facts. First, biologically, for the most part humans are of one sex or the other, with little overlap at the most obvious level. Second, and even more important, the two-sexed biology of the human species is augmented and enhanced rather than minimized by culture, society, and religion, so that today in all cultures, there is more stress on behaviors proper to and limited to one or the other sex than would be required by basic biology. As a result, men's and women's lives are more separate and different from each other than is biologically dictated. No scholarship prior to the current women studies movement has come close to dealing adequately with the sheer massive unyielding presence of such sex-role differentiation in all religio-cultural situations, which is the major reason why all previous scholarship and theology failed so abysmally to understand women and religion. Clearly, a model of humanity is needed that compels recognition that humans come in two sexes and that both sexes are human, at the same time as it forbids placing one sex in the center and the other on the periphery. Androgyny as a two-sex model of humanity, as the notion that humanity is both female and male, meets those requirements, while traditional androcentrism and a sex-neutral model of humanity both fail completely. (By way of brief definition, a sex-neutral model of humanity is one that minimizes sexual differentiation, that regards distinct maleness and femaleness as irrelevant, and that urges pursuit of a "common humanity." While one could debate the utility of such a model of humanity as a prescription for the future, it is obviously quite useless as a guide to descriptions of the past or present.)

When this model of humanity and these methodological guidelines are applied to virtually any subject in the humanities or social sciences, massive changes in scholarship result. What one studies, how one studies it, what results one finds in their materials, the analyses one finds cogent, and the overarching theories that one accepts as good basic tools with which to understand the world all change. It is not too extravagant to say that internalizing this model of humanity results in a transformation of consciousness so profound that, not just one's scholarship, but everyday habits of language and perception change. The insecurity many feel in the face of such basic change probably explains why the women studies perspective has not been universally adopted, since one could not fault it for lack of relevance and common sense. Once one makes the change from an androcentric to an androgynous model of humanity, it is hard to believe that anyone could ever imagine doing adequate scholarship and theorizing from a point of view that objectifies women as non-human.

The minimal requirement of the women studies perspective is that scholarship must always treat women as human subjects who must be studied as thoroughly, as critically, and as empathetically as are men. It is important to recognize that this scholarly feminism is just that—feminism as an academic method. Feminism as academic method does not inherently entail any social philosophy regarding what women's position in society should be. It only entails a requirement to study women thoroughly and completely. Thus, it is possible that a scholar could do exemplary androgynous scholarship while at the same time holding a personal philosophy of male dominance or even misogyny. Examples of such scholars are rare or non-existent, but the distinction is important. To construct a feminist vision of society is a different task from doing feminist scholarship that is gender-balanced.

FEMINISM AS SOCIAL VISION:
THE PERSPECTIVE OF FEMINIST PHILOSOPHY

In this study of Buddhism, feminism as social vision is also important, for I seek not merely to present a gender-balanced historical record of Buddhism but to construct a vision of Buddhism after patriarchy, a Buddhism in accord with feminism as social vision. This feminist philosophy is grounded in the results of feminist scholarship in history, sociology, and psychology, as well as religion. Just as feminist scholarship critiques "androcentrism" as the basic problem with previous scholarship, so feminist social philosophy has focused on "patriarchy" as the fundamental problem. "Patriarchy" has become feminist shorthand for the anti-vision that has fueled much of society and religion for the past several thousand years and led to the mindset in which the androcentric model of humanity not only found acceptance, but reigned without conceptual alternatives. For more than twenty years, feminists have discussed the creation, outlines, and inadequacies of patriarchy vehemently and vibrantly. With even greater vigor, they have discussed the vision of a post-patriarchal world. Since these discussions should be quite familiar, I will only summarize the conclusions that are most important to a post-patriarchal vision of human life and society.

The most important and encouraging conclusion of feminist scholarship is that patriarchy is the cultural creation of a certain epoch in human history, not an inevitable necessity of human biology.[8] The importance of this claim is that whatever is created is subject to decay and dissolution—a point commonplace in Buddhism. With this realization, the advice to generations of rebellious daughters who were told, "You can't do anything about *that*," is overcome. One *can* do something about patriarchy, though the task is immense.

Well before feminists felt confident of the case that patriarchy emerged relatively late in human history, feminists were very clear in their critique of patriarchy. The early literature of feminism was an outcry of pain; people certainly did want to do something about patriarchy. After years of refining analyses, one could summarize the critique as the claim that patriarchy is "without redeeming social value," that it is clearly linked with the most destructive forces in human history, and that it causes harm to all people, including men, though not as obviously, directly, or extremely as it does to women.

What about patriarchy makes it such an offensive system to its critics? Most feminists would outline the problems in a similar fashion. Patriarchy turns on the many ramifications of the literal meaning of its name—"rule by fathers." Two elements dominate the discussion: on the one hand, patriarchy is a system in which rulership, *power over*, is quite central; on the other hand, by definition, men have power over women. The variety and oppressiveness of men's power over women was the first element of the complex to be thoroughly recognized and described. Men received preferential treatment, monopolizing or dominating all the roles and pursuits that society valued and rewarded, so that inequality became one of the first patriarchal demons to be named. Furthermore, men literally ruled over women, setting the rules and limits by which and within which they were expected to operate. Women who did not conform, and many who did, could be subjected to another form of male dominance— physical coercion.

Among the most sophisticated and influential abstract formulations of the power patriarchy gives men over women are de Beauvoir's concept of the objectification of women[9] and Mary Daly's description of how "the power of naming had been stolen from women."[10] With deepening analysis of patriarchy, many focused not merely on the way in which men hold power over women as the problem, but also on the centrality of having *power over* others in patriarchal society. Many see male power over females as the basic model of all forms of social hierarchy and oppression. From this conclusion, many analysts move on to link patriarchy with militarism and with ecologically dangerous use of the environment. This conclusion is based on the fact that all these policies share an attitude of glorifying and approving *power over* as inevitable and appropriate.

Though these familiar analyses of patriarchy are cogent and relevant, I believe that they do not sufficiently clarify the fundamental aspiration of modern feminism. The most basic vision of the contemporary feminist movement is not equality or total lack of hierarchy, though these goals are aspects of the vision. Much more fundamental is the vision of *freedom from gender roles*. On this vision depend all other aspects of the various feminist programs. Unfortunately, many feminist analyses do not arrive at this simple, foundational level of understanding what is the source of pain and suffering in current gender arrangements, and what is most essential in the program to overcome that pain. If people are forced to fit themselves into their social place on the basis of their physiological sex, then there will be suffering and injustice even in a situation of "gender equality"—whatever that might mean.

The difference between freedom from gender roles and gender equality is profound. Any concept of gender equality presupposes the continued existence of gender roles and all the imprisoning implied in such conditions. In early liberal, as opposed to radical feminism, equality usually meant that women should be able to do the things men had always done, and, sometimes, that men should be forced to do the things that women had always done. This definition depends on the fact that the male role (rather than men) is preferred to the female role. A frequently cited alternative meaning of "equality" is that what women do should be regarded as of "equal value" with what men do—a version of separate-but-equal thinking which is so often advocated as a conservative alternative to patriarchy.

Neither version of equality quite escapes the prison of gender roles. Claiming that the female role is distinctive, but of equal rather than of inferior value, does not even attempt to escape that prison, since it is assumed that only women can fulfill the female role. To give women access to men's roles, which often requires an attempt to get men into women's roles as well, comes much closer to conceptualizing the basic truth that gender roles are the problem to be overcome. Nevertheless, sexual identity and social roles are still collapsed conceptually. But sometimes it would be desirable for men to fill the female role and vice versa. In other words, under certain circumstances, crossovers between sexual identity and social roles could be desirable. However, whenever sexual identity and social roles are conflated, even subtly, the result is a kind of "anatomy-is-destiny" thinking. But if anatomy *is* destiny, then there may be no hope for post-patriarchal vision of life outside the prison of gender roles.

On the other hand, if it is clearly conceptualized that the vision is not merely allowing or encouraging crossovers between one's sexual identity and one's social role (thought of as normally sex-linked), but a definitive breaking of links between sexual identity and social roles, then a social order beyond patriarchy is inevitable. Patriarchy depends, in the final analysis, on fixed gender roles. No gender roles—no one with automatic access to any role or with automatic power over another because of her physiological sex.

Seeing the essential problem as gender roles and the essential vision as freedom from gender roles also puts the feminist critique of patriarchy as "power over" in another light. The abuse of power is certainly a major human problem and patriarchy is rife with abuse of power. But one of the most abusive aspects of patriarchal power is men's *automatic*, rather than earned or deserved, power over women. Though one wants to guard against and be wary of abuse of power, a totally egalitarian society in which no one has more influence or prestige, or even wealth, than anyone else, seems quite impossible. The issue is not abolishing hierarchy, which is impossible, but establishing *proper hierarchy*. This is a complex and difficult topic, which cannot be fully explicated in this context, but it is important to state that proper hierarchy is not the same thing as what feminists mean by "domination" or "power over" in their critique of the patriarchal use of power. It connotes the proper use of power that has been properly earned, a topic not much explored in feminist thought—a serious omission, in my view. But if the essence of post-patriarchal vision is freedom from gender roles, then there is no possibility of men automatically receiving any power, prestige, influence, or position simply because of their sex. Though following this guideline would not, by itself, guarantee proper hierarchy, it would abolish the worst abuses of patriarchal power.

To see the essential problem of patriarchy as the very existence of gender roles and post-patriarchy as freedom from gender roles is both radical and visionary. Some may well feel that a world without gender roles is even more visionary than a world without relationships of domination and submission. Some may well feel that the goal should be finding and institutionalizing more equitable and just gender roles. It is clear, however, that virtually every feminist critique of patriarchy and every feminist agenda for the future really derives from an unstated assumption that sex is not a relevant criterion for awarding roles or value. Furthermore, any set of gender roles whatsoever will be a prison for some who do not readily fit them. As someone who feels that one of the greatest sources of suffering in her life has been the prison of gender roles, I am reluctant to see any place for them in a visionary post-patriarchal future.

Nevertheless, though there is little if any universality regarding gender roles, all known cultures have some gender roles. (The rigidity of gender roles varies significantly cross-culturally.) Such information is not especially encouraging to the vision of post-patriarchy as freedom from gender roles. One might conclude that since the sexual distinction is so obvious, it inevitably will serve as a basic method of organizing society. But before we concede that point, it is important to analyze how sex differences have been used to generate the gender roles now organizing society. After this analysis, we may conclude that, while past technologies made gender roles unavoidable, under current conditions, gender roles may well have become dysfunctional.

Gender roles are essentially strategies for organizing reproduction and, to a lesser extent, production. The ways in which production and reproduction are organized depend in large part on the mode of subsistence utilized by the society, as well as on the reproductive needs of the society. Under conditions in which reproduction necessarily consumed vast quantities of human energy (short lifespan, high infant-mortality rate, high maternal death rate, and lack of birth control), much was predetermined for both women and men. Furthermore, the technologies available for producing life's economic necessities were matched with the physical and reproductive endowments of each sex. The results were the gender roles that some take as eternal necessities. But these gender roles really are adaptations to specific technologies, modes of production and reproductive demands. For, example, premodern agriculture was the dominant subsistence mode for most of humanity during historical times, including the cultures in which both patriarchy and the great world religions arose. The gender roles adaptive to intensive agriculture favor high rates of fertility and the specialization of men in production and women in reproduction. Not only were women already heavily involved in reproduction; the physical demands specific to agricultural production were not easily combined with pregnancy and lactation. This is the pattern of gender roles that many in our society take for granted, but it was not typical of pre-agricultural societies, a vastly longer period of human history.

The conditions that made the gender roles of agricultural societies adaptive no longer prevail. For human reproduction to continue to consume the same proportion of human energy in the future as it has in the past will result in uncalculable tragedy for the planet and all its inhabitants. Modern industrial and post-industrial economies do not make the same intense physical demands as did traditional agriculture. Very few aspects of modern production depend upon or demand male anatomy or strength. These two conditions combined make traditional gender roles completely irrelevant, since there is no basis for the traditional assumption that women should be largely confined to reproduction and men to production. No relevant basis for new gender roles is readily apparent. Nevertheless, we are very far from a post-patriarchal society free of gender roles. Archaic gender-role expectations and outmoded educational, employment, and childrearing policies based on those gender roles continue to imprison everyone, at least to some extent.

What might life free from gender roles be like? In some ways, one's sex is important and in other ways not at all. In some ways, it remains necessary to rely on traditional concepts of masculinity and femininity, at least in the short run, and in other ways they are already irrelevant. I think of my own life as participating in a post-patriarchal mode of existence. I am a female; I do not fill the female gender role or the male gender role; I believe that my psychology and lifestyle are both traditionally feminine and traditionally masculine. Thus, my own experience provides me with some of the guidelines for a post-patriarchal future free of gender roles. Sexual identity remains clear. Sexual differentiation is so obvious and so basic that it seems impossible to ignore or deny one's sex. But one's sex implies nothing inevitable about one's reproductive decisions, one's economic and social roles, or even one's basic psychological traits and tendencies.

Nevertheless, because we have inherited a whole repertoire of traits and qualities that are conventionally labeled "masculine" and "feminine," most thoughtful people would probably want to combine those traits into an "androgynous" personality and lifestyle as well as to strive to create a more androgynous society. To call this person and this society that are free of gender roles "androgynous" may seem confusing, since androgyny implies a combination of masculinity and femininity. However, the *concepts* of "masculinity" and "femininity" are not themselves problematic or imprisoning; what imprisons is the expectation that women should be feminine and men should be masculine. In fact the symbols of "femininity" and "masculinity" may well remain useful to specify the poles within the rich dyadic unity that we all experience.

However, the society free from gender roles will be much more "feminine" than current patriarchal society. Why? Because in patriarchy, women are feminine and silent (the power of naming has been stolen from women) while men are masculine and articulate. Therefore, in patriarchy, most public policy and most religious thought is "masculine" and, as a result, quite incomplete, even destructive, due to its incompleteness. As women become more articulate so that women's experience of femininity becomes part of public discourse and public policy, society will become both more feminine and more androgynous. At that point individuals of both sexes will more easily become androgynous whole persons instead of "half-humans" trapped in female or male gender roles.

In conclusion, it is important to note what links these two arenas of feminist thought. Feminism as scholarly method is critical of the androcentric mindset. Feminism as social vision is critical of patriarchal culture. Androcentrism and patriarchy share the same attitude toward women. In both cases, women are objectified as non-human, are spoken about as if they were objects but not subjects, and are manipulated by others. In both cases, the end results are silence about, as well as the silence and the silencing of, women. Scholarship proceeds as if women did not exist, or if their existence is noted, they are treated as objects only. They are not allowed or encouraged to create language and culture, to "name reality"; the realities they do nevertheless name are not heard or recorded. The reality-constructions of non-entities are dismissed by those who do not see them as human subjects and those who assert dominance over them.

Just as both varieties of feminism share the same critique of androcentric scholarship and of patriarchal society, so they share the same corrective. The massive conspiracy of silence will be undone. Scholars will correct their model of humanity, gather their data anew, and reconceptualize their disciplines and their theories where necessary. Women's naming of reality will be heard, and more importantly, will be articulated *for the first time* in the case of most worldviews, religions, and theoretical systems.

APPENDIX B
RELIGIOUS EXPERIENCE AND THE STUDY OF RELIGION: THE HISTORY OF RELIGIONS

My methods of working with Buddhist materials as a feminist are set in the larger context of an understanding of what it means to study religion and to experience religion in the modern world. In fact, important as I believe it is to engage in the feminist revalorization of Buddhism, in some ways, this revalorization is only an example of the kind of scholarship done by what I call an engaged historian of religions. What I am engaged in is certainly not conventional Buddhist studies or conventional history of religions; it is an enterprise for which there are no real models, either in Buddhist thought or in Western scholarship, except perhaps Western feminist theology. But precisely because I am not working with Western materials, I am again working in territory without map or model. Because I am not following already well-laid-out methodological pathways, I wish to articulate the methodological vision that drives my work. That method is perhaps best summarized as the simultaneous or inseparable practice of theology and of the history of religions. Though not usually practiced by most contemporary students of religion, this method is the only method adequate for my task. I believe it also provides a fuller and more complete understanding of religion than most other methods.

At the present time, the single most important fact facing any student of religion or religious person is the enormous leap in knowledge about religion provided by the cross-cultural study of religion. The possibilities for serious reflection on the human religious heritage have been revolutionized in the past century, and especially in the past thirty years. An immense growth in our knowledge of religious data from all times and places and the growing sophistication of the social sciences are responsible for this quantum leap. This revolution of possibilities has been accompanied by a significant increase in the number of departments of religious studies in colleges and universities. No longer is serious reflection on religion solely the business of seminaries and male seminarians preparing to propagate their own version of religion to their own membership. Undergraduates frequently enroll in neutral courses in religious studies taught by well-trained scholars whose religious allegiances are not germane to their teaching agendas. Not surprisingly, both students and teachers of this new discipline, the academic study of religion, are no longer predominately male; religion is, after all, a serious *human* question and pursuit.

What is called for, however, is not merely an increasingly large file of data about religion, but also serious reflection about religion. The study of religion should be understood as the cross-cultural and comparative study of all religious perspectives found in human history and culture. The purpose of such study is to understand both religion as a human enterprise, and the various religions that have been practiced throughout human history, so that one can comment, in an informed, accurate, and empathetic manner, on the purpose and effect of religion in human life, past, present and future. Such commentary, evaluation, and assessment is an essential aspect of the study of religion, which is properly the cross-cultural study of religion, rather than the study of religion within a single cultural context.

Such an understanding of the study of religion is, however, not the norm for the field. Most scholars instead limit themselves to either the historical-descriptive studies of religion or to constructive-theological-normative concern with religion. Many scholars of religion fail to study religion widely, in its many contexts and varieties, though they make broad evaluative statements about religion. Many others fail to articulate any view about the purpose and effect of religion, though they may be veritable gold mines of information about a tradition. In other words, most scholars takes an "either-or" stance regarding theology and the history of religions, rather than engaging the simultaneous or inseparable practice of theology and the history of religions.

The task of a feminist revalorization of Buddhism could not be carried out under such limited methodologies. Nor do I believe that, in the long run, one can do justice to the phenomenon of religion by limiting oneself to one or the other approach. For these two reasons alone, I have come to advocate a "method of inseparability" regarding these two usually separated approaches to discourse about religion. I am thoroughly aware that my position about religious studies is a distinct minority in the field as a whole, and especially among those who call themselves historians of religion. This position is the result of years of training, study, reflection, and teaching about a wide array of topics within the discipline of religious studies. It is also the position that allows, as well as compels, me to do what I have set out to do—a feminist history, analysis and reconstruction of Buddhism. This brief appendix is not intended as a survey of the literature on such methodological issues, nor is it a fully argued delineation of this position. It should be viewed rather as position paper on how I proceed methodologically in this study.

SURVEY OF THE CURRENT SITUATION IN RELIGIOUS STUDIES

My own training in the field was based on this "either-or" approach to religious studies. An honors undergraduate student in philosophy, I opted out of graduate training in that field because the alternatives then in vogue in philosophy seemed sterile and limited. Philosophers were unwilling to include emotional life within their concerns or to consider issues of meaning and orientation vis-à-vis "the ultimate questions." The academic study of religion seemed to be a much more amenable discipline in which to puzzle out my youthful, but completely genuine commitment to study, understand, and teach about "what really matters," about what is deepest, most meaningful, and least superficial in life. I also felt, already as an undergraduate, that it was trivial and superficial to study such questions only as they had been asked and answered by one's own religious and cultural tradition. Armed with such visions, I enrolled in the History of Religions program at the University of Chicago, the best choice among available programs, both in my limited understanding at that time and in hindsight.

Clearly, my vision was to study religion comparatively and broadly, rather than to become an area specialist. My vision was also to ask basic questions about the nature and meaning of religion, rather than to remain at the more superficial, but more reliable, level of purely descriptive scholarship. To study the History of Religions at the University of Chicago under Mircea Eliade was to be able to ask such questions and to pursue such interests to a degree not possible under most other mentors. In fact the circle within which we were allowed to roam was so large that for a very long time, I did not see the limitations which I now reject in my own methodology.

To be a student of the history of religions was by definition also to be a student of some "non-Western" religious tradition. Though the history of religions methodology seemed to apply to so-called Western religions with equal cogency, few made the connections, except for Islam—a "foreign" Western religion. Now it is clear to me that the radical implications of history of religions method and theory concerning the non-absolute, historical, and relative nature of any symbol system were felt to be "too much" to be applied to Judaism and Christianity. A tacit territorial division left those religions to the domain of theologians, Biblical scholars, and church historians, who used very different, and much less radical methods, to study their data.

However, this division of labor regarding subject matter was the more superficial manifestation of a deeper limitation. As historians of religion, we were free to study the meaning of religion to *homo religiosus*, but, very clearly, we were not supposed to *be homo religiosus*. For many years, even today in many cases, nothing is more likely to be the kiss of death for a "serious" historian of religions than the suspicion of personal interest or involvement in the religion one studies professionally. Even any kind of evaluation or constructive use of the materials being studied brings suspicion. Lauding the practice of phenomenological "bracketing" (of our own presuppositions), which we studied relentlessly, we were allowed to speak through the eyes of the Hindu or the tribal person about her religious experience. We were allowed to discuss what religion meant to her in her context. But to discuss what religion meant to one of us, or to discuss what a religion could or should mean in our own context as citizens of the global village, was off limits. To raise such questions was (and still is, in many cases) to be called a "crypto-theologian," clearly an assessment lower than "misguided," or "feeble-minded."

Meanwhile, however, those on the other side of the great divide in the academic study of religion were equally limited in their training. Though allowed to be personally interested in the religion which they studied professionally and to make claims about religion's meaning or relevance, they were, and still are, usually excused from the rigorous and thoroughgoing training in cross-cultural, comparative studies in religion that would make their claims interesting, widely applicable, or generally useful. Philosophical or theological claims growing out of a narrow segment of human experience lack force or interest, since they are so limited, both in derivation and in applicability. Furthermore, any religious constructive claims not grounded thoroughly in the social sciences are merely apologetic claims based on received tradition. However, professional theologians and ethicists are significantly better grounded in Western social sciences than in the history of religions.

In recent years, theologians and ethicists have indicated a significantly increased interest in major world religions, to the extent that today most prominent theologians and ethicists are somewhat cognizant of some religion other than their own, or at least concede that one needs some cross-cultural knowledge to be a proficient theologian in the global village. Their interest often takes the form of participation in interreligious dialogue.* In such contexts, they express willingness to learn both about and from the traditions with which they are in dialogue. But such participation in dialogue does not begin to substitute for thorough training in the history of religions, which is apparent to the few professionally trained historians of religion in their midst.[1] Therefore, most theologians involved in dialogue do not accomplish the radical co-practice of theology and of the history of religions any more than do the historians of religion.

---

* The most prominent of these groups is the Buddhist-Christian Theological Encounter, better known as the Cobb-Abe group. Records of its proceedings are published in *Buddhist-Christian Studies*.

Thus, at present the academic study of religion is hopelessly divided into two subdisciplines that do not seriously engage each other, rather than being a unified and coherent discipline. This situation represents a significant loss for all concerned. Those scholars willing to comment upon and evaluate religion or specific religious ideas do so speaking out of and to the rather narrow audience of those within familiar cultural boundaries. Those scholars of religion who are widely trained in cross-cultural and comparative studies or deeply trained in some unfamiliar cultural situation are usually unwilling to make any comments about the materials that they have worked so diligently to understand. This division of labor will never produce the kind of discussion study of religion that was my vision when I entered the field as a graduate student. Therefore, I have abandoned my allegiance to one side or the other of this division within religious studies. I propose instead to combine, without confusing, these two approaches to the study of religion.

THE STUDY OF RELIGION AS THE SIMULTANEOUS PRACTICE OF THEOLOGY AND THE HISTORY OF RELIGIONS

For those who regard their domain as world-construction, normative comment on religion, or theology, the emergence of the cross-cultural comparative study of religion is the most significant event for these various traditions since they were founded. This claim is made because the history of religions has changed irrevocably and definitively what we know about religion. We now know a great deal about the historical processes religions undergo; we know that there is a basic model of religion that works more or less well for all religions from every time and place; we know how religious myths and symbols arise. Historical, comparative, phenomenological, sociological, and psychological accounts of religion illuminate all religions as was never possible when each religion, in isolation, and unclear about how the laws of cause and effect apply to religion, regarded itself as the uniquely relevant result of transcendent intervention into history.

Why must someone who speaks mainly as a theologian, from within a religion, incorporate the results of the cross-cultural, social-scientific study of religion into his work? Minimally, because they're there and can't be ignored without intellectual violence. Taking them seriously has a radically de-absolutizing effect on religious worldviews, which is probably why so many religious leaders do not utilize such material in their world-construction.

Yet to regard the de-absolutization of one's worldview as a negative discovery is a rather limited and spiritually immature response to the contemporary situation. Free of the impossible burden that they be universally relevant, as well as scientifically and historically true, symbols and myths can shine more preciously in their culturally conditioned matrices. When we learn to hear their claims and demands as symbols embedded in and growing out of a specific and relative context, when we truly learn to appreciate them as myths, then our symbols and myths can again speak to us and comfort us in a way that is impossible so long as we try to take them as unconditioned givens.

A position that incorporates the methods and results of the history of religions is much more satisfying, as a religious position, than one that attempts to ignore these dimensions of knowing. Furthermore, religious spokespersons who have mastered the comparative, cross-cultural and social-scientific study of religion have at their disposal a myriad of resources with which to think about problems that may be insufficiently addressed in their own tradition. For theologians, and others involved in world-constructive approaches to the study of religion, this constitutes a claim that the only way to be responsibly religious today is to incorporate the methods and results of cross-cultural studies into the religions. Some reasonable and reputable knowledge about the history of religions is the only reliable framework within which to make claims about or to suggest reforms appropriate to any specific religion.

Furthermore, when a traditional religious concept or practice conflicts with information or values that we cannot ignore without radical intellectual violence, then the religion should be changed or be abandoned. How much better to have informed change led by knowledgeable hierarchs than accommodation to uninformed or unethical "tradition."

On the other side of the great divide, the equally serious problems that characterize current practice of the history of religions could be significantly diminished by input from theology, just as theology is improved by input from the cross-cultural comparative study of religion. At the opposite end of the spectrum from the theologians, many historians of religion and area specialists strive to give the impression that they are utterly indifferent to the materials they study. They confine their passion to debating appropriate methods of study, or to analyses and conclusions *about* their data. As a result, their articles often have an intensely combative tone and a gamelike quality, as if the only concern were winning. Any caring for the materials under discussion or any sense of wonderment about their place in the scheme of things, even any glimmer of curiosity about the scheme of things, seems quite buried. Personal evaluations are eschewed because the scholar wants to give the impression, and perhaps often believes, that his work is value-free. In short, the work is very professional and competent, but also often quite dull and of questionable significance.

Much of the blame for this state of affairs in the history of religions can be attributed to the quest for neutrality and objectivity, which many seem to think prohibits any open value stance. However, the neutrality and objectivity of the historian of religions, though important, should not be construed as they so often are. One does not maintain neutrality and objectivity by non-allegiance to religious, symbolic, or value systems, because such a value-free stance is quite impossible. Rather, they are protected by probing exploration, self-consciousness about, and open declaration of one's *particular* evaluative stance as a scholar of religions.

My own conviction that scholarship *always* hides and includes a normative position, a worldview, and a set of values, stems from my discovery, as a graduate student and throughout my career, of the androcentric and patriarchal norms, worldview, and values of most scholarship. These unstated and unacknowledged values and points of view deeply color and predetermine, not only many of the conclusions derived by scholars, but also what data are even included in the materials to be analyzed. I am also deeply aware that my non-allegiance to those androcentric values and worldview definitively affects my choice of subject matter, my interests, and, to some extent, my analyses. To have been the first feminist historian of religion was a very radicalizing introduction to impossibility of objective and neutral scholarship in the history of religions—radicalizing not only through the experience of seeing how much androcentric scholarship had missed but also through the experience of receiving a great deal of hostility and ridicule from threatened, supposedly neutral, but highly androcentric scholars. From that experience I have learned much about how best to proceed in the study of religions; most of my other suggestions regarding values in the history of religions are founded on that experience.

However, feminism or androcentrism are not the only methodological stances or value systems a scholar projects onto his work. For some, agnosticism or another philosophical or religious view is entirely relevant to their scholarship. Certainly their academic lineages and camps color the work of all scholars. Every methodological stance includes values. I have long urged the practice of declaring such inclinations and interests openly as the only reliable form of objectivity and neutrality.

When such declarations are taken for granted because we concede that we all have some point of view about or some investment regarding our chosen field of study, we can move onto a far more important topic. We might begin to talk about the ethical *responsibilities* of the historian of religions, about being an "engaged scholar" in the cross-cultural comparative study of religion. We are in this strange business of studying religion widely and deeply, rather than within the confines of our own culture, because of some vision that cannot be completely denied or forgotten, and that vision entails responsibilities. Once we admit that even the most banal methodological point of view entails an evaluative stance, we should recognize that we have a responsibility to use our knowledge to promote community rather than disunity in the global village. After all, the virtue that recommends the history of religions approach is not only that is provides *more accurate* knowledge but that those who have this more accurate knowledge about "the other" are better equipped to live in a pluralistic world. There is little other reason for state universities to employ historians of religion to teach undergraduates about Hindu mythology, for example. Furthermore, I would contend that the major reason to spend one's life studying and teaching the history of religions is not merely for the pure accurate knowledge, but to increase empathy and respect, both in one's self and others, in a pluralistic world. If we admit this much, then we can go a step further. I often feel that historians of religion, who know so much about so many other cultures and religions, are especially obligated to comment upon, even to evaluate, that about which they know so much.

Such work clearly moves over the borderline from descriptive studies to world-construction. I was taught that, as a historian of religion, my job to study other peoples' world-constructions, but that world-constructive work was off limits to me. However, such a position and such a division of labor is naive. Only a specific world-construction allows us to pursue our discipline at all. The very existence of the cross-cultural comparative approach to religion is a value-laden choice and a rejection of previous approaches to religion. Furthermore, every one of us surely believes that this is the *superior* theory of and approach to studying religion than the culture-bound, and often imperialistic, methods of studying religion that our discipline rebelled against in its formative period. Some might claim that its superiority lies in the rigid prohibition of personal involvement in religion or world-construction. But such claims are self-defeating; we construct a world every time we construct a course in religion, especially an introductory course, or write an article "about" some phenomenon. So we might as well engage in our world-construction deliberately, self-consciously, and openly.

Once again, feminist experience was critical in bringing me to this position. To be a feminist *is* to disagree with the socially constructed world one has inherited and to attempt to construct an alternative world. As a feminist, I cannot help thinking constructively and ethically about my subject matter, which makes me less reluctant to admit to other world-constructive interests. I find it inappropriate to limit my constructive reflections only to feminist issues within my own society. Aside from promoting intellectual and spiritual schizophrenia, such an artificial division between critical reflective work and cross-cultural scholarship would be a serious abdication of responsibility.

A scholar and thinker whose practice is to blend, but not confuse, the formerly separated disciplines of history of religions and theology will manifest and embody certain important intellectual and spiritual stances in her work. This kind of scholarship can make important contributions to resolving many of the debates currently prevalent about methodologies appropriate to the cross-cultural, comparative study of religion.

First, such a scholar is indeed objective. As already discussed, that objectivity cannot mean that the scholar has no interest or involvement in her subject matter, but that she declares her methodologies and interests clearly. Additionally, the scholar's objectivity demands that he not function as an apologist in any way. This lack of apologetic fervor is the essence of the historian of religion's objectivity. Doing one's scholarship to promote one's own religious affiliation is unworthy. A scholar clearly has points of view, but she does not suppress negative information or highlight positive information concerning her evaluative or confessional stance. She consistently applies what I call "the unity of methodology rule"; according to this rule, the same standards are used to interpret and describe all positions and points of view, whether or not we find them palatable. We do not engage in hierarchic evaluations or rankings of religions. We do not use one standard when talking about "us" and another when talking about "them." We are more interested in accuracy than in promoting any specific religion or point of view. We have a deeper loyalty to honesty than to any specific religion or philosophy. Because we value such honesty, we do not pretend that we can present "the objective picture," which brings us what level of objectivity we can have. Without partisan apologetic loyalties, we state, "This is the point of view, the story out of which I work. These are the values central to me as a scholar of religion and these are my analyses and conclusions, derived in the following manner."

Second, promoting the development and protection of genuine objectivity even further is the most central and critical value necessary for any student of religion—empathy. Along with the ability of cross-cultural comparative studies of religion to de-absolutize any symbol system, the development of empathy for any symbol system creates a powerful tool for understanding. To quote the definition I use in my introductory classes, empathy involves "mentally entering into the spirit of a person or thing and developing appreciative understanding of that phenomenon." Any good scholar of religions should have developed the ability to speak in many voices, or from the point of view of many different outlooks and symbols. She should be able to speak convincingly from any of these positions and should be able to switch from one to another readily. She should also be able to translate between the voices or positions. And in all these vocalizations, her own voice should be quite hidden. The historian of religions who is competent in the requirement to be non-apologetic can present with great empathy points of view that she may find personally unappealing. It is difficult to overemphasize this need to develop skill in phenomenological bracketing as well as empathy in order to do good work in religious studies. It is also impossible to recount the number of failures to do so; lack of empathy is probably the most serious failing in most discussions of religion and most teaching methods in the field.

Eschewing apologetics and practicing empathy are widely recognized values for the cross-cultural student of religion and most practitioners of the discipline pay some attention to them. However, rather than regarding them as a sufficient orientation for the student of religion, I would advocate regarding them as the foundation necessary for bringing additional values, critical to the contemporary situation, into the study of religion. The most interesting students of religion will not only demonstrate skill in being non-apologetic and empathetic; they will also bring into their work values and orientations involving certain tasks in world-construction, utilizing their vast storehouse of knowledge. This task is new to the cross-cultural and comparative study of religion, since, as already discussed, most historians of religion have been reluctant to engage openly in world-construction.

In this world-constructive dimension of one's work, no task is more central that somehow finding, promoting, and fostering genuine pluralism in our world. To think and to act critically and constructively about this task is the third major value guiding the engaged historian of religions in her work. That we live in a world of competing, conflicting, multiple religious symbol-systems is news to no historian of religions. That the historian of religions has some responsibility to think constructively and ethically about that situation would be debated by many. But what else justifies the expenditure of time, resources, and energy on cross-cultural studies? Who else is in a better position to say something intelligent and helpful about the problems of living with diversity and pluralism? This is not the context in which to develop a philosophy of religious pluralism based on an engaged, ethically responsible, world-constructive history of religions. To define "genuine pluralism," to describe carefully the concomitant de-absolutizing of every specific symbol-system, and to delineate the resulting appreciation of one's own specificity, would go too far into another book.[2] But this history, analysis, and reconstruction of Buddhist attitudes toward gender is in harmony with that agenda.

Finally, to conclude this short commentary on the values important to the engaged historian of religions, I will make a suggestion that goes far beyond the usual agenda of conventional history of religions. An advanced task of the fully engaged historian of religions involves taking a critical stance against some values espoused in some of the symbol-systems one studies. Some traditional values studied by the comparative scholar may well undermine the dignity of some members of that religion, as do the patriarchal values common to many religions. Some traditional values of a religion studied by the comparativist may directly contradict the vision of genuine pluralism in a global village by promoting militancy or hostility toward "the others." Obviously, it is important to avoid ethnocentrism and colonialism when one takes up this difficult critical task of making such evaluations. Here again, the "unity of methodology" rule is very useful. Also, once again, being a feminist has taught me how to expand my vision for the cross-cultural comparative study of religion. To explain the worldview of patriarchy with empathy is a required assignment; to do scholarship that extends, perpetuates, legitimates, or justifies patriarchy is not acceptable. In order to meet that double assignment, one must not only describe but expose patriarchy, militarism, fundamentalism, or other deeply held but destructive traditional religious values. Not all the points of view that one can describe and understand deserve to survive. To describe the negative effects of some values in the symbol-systems one studies is essential to the task of the historian of religions.

It is important to note in this discussion of the values relevant to anyone who practices religious studies that the four values I have advocated are a seamless harmonious web. In particular, the practices of objectivity and empathy lead to rather than contradict the latter two values, promoting genuine pluralism and criticizing dysfunctional traditional values found in the religions. Objectivity leads one to see that the values which foster and promote pluralism are to be advocated; the practice of empathy allows one to criticize what one has first understood. The great fear and danger is that many give themselves permission to engage in critical world-construction without first engaging in objective and empathetic cross-cultural study. That problem is not remedied by disallowing or discouraging those who continuously engage in such studies from critical world-construction, for the world remains quite unfinished and incomplete without their input.

SOME CONCLUDING POSTSCRIPTS ON OLD METHODOLOGICAL ISSUES

I will conclude this orientation with a brief discussion of two other methodological problems that are much studied by historians of religions. Though I cannot argue the case for my conclusions in this context, my resolutions of these issues are important to the way I conduct this feminist history, analysis, and reconstruction of Buddhism.

One of the oldest debates in academic studies of religion involves the question of whether or not religion is *sui generis*, a non-reducible aspect of human life which must be studied on its own terms and deserves its own disciplinary framework. The competing point of view regards religion as an epiphenomenon of history, economics, sociology, or psychology, a dependent rather than an independent variable in human life, best studied from within the framework of one of the social sciences. One of the strongest arguments in favor of the latter point of view is the difficulty of finding any "essence" of religion that is readily demonstrable across cultural and temporal frontiers. Despite this difficulty, and despite the fact that religion cannot be accurately studied apart from the use of methods deriving from the social sciences, I prefer to regard religion as non-reducible to its cultural matrix, however much it is illuminated by close attention to that matrix. As for the non-reducible "essence of religion" that such a view implies—this is not the context for extended arguments. It seems quite clear to me that we can descriptively locate a non-reducible essence to religion, not in any intellectual, spiritual, or behavioral commonalities found in religion, but in the structures of religions and in the function of religion in human life. Simply put, all religions share, to an extent unique among human cultural creations, an attempt to provide meaning and orientation in a chaotic world. Thus, I locate the essence of religion in its impulse toward world-con-struction of great significance to those who live in these worlds. What lies behind or drives that impulse to find meaning and orientation, to construct a world in the face of chaos, is not a question that needs to be settled in order to study religion non-reductionistically.

A more recent debate in comparative studies of religion concerns the dynamic and possibly hostile interaction between "insiders" and "outsiders." The question of which approach provides the best approach to and the most accurate understandings of religion seems to me to pose a false dichotomy. Accurate and interesting accounts of religion are not forthcoming using one approach exclusively or in opposition to the other. The tools and insights of the outsider provide much that is absolutely essential to the study of religion. Without the outsider's breadth of knowledge, the whole comparative and cross-cultural dimension, so critical to contemporary understanding of religion, would be missing. The comparative mirror[3] would be lacking and understand-ing of religion would be much poorer without the de-absolutizing and relativ-izing knowledge brought by its use. The perspective of the outsider gives the student of religion vision and breadth. At the same time, this perspective is incomplete by itself.

The perspective of the insider provides a level of understanding not other-wise available that provides warmth and intimacy—a kind of depth not avail-able without direct experience of the phenomenon being studied. This comment should not be taken to mean that the scholar's qualifications must include card-carrying membership in a recognized form of religion; in fact, most such zealots are probably incapable of tempering their insider's understanding with a sufficient dose of the outsider's tools and methods. But without sympathy for the impulse toward religion and in-depth experience as a participant in some religious activities, one's work is likely to lack the heart and passion that come from intense curiosity and that make one's work useful and interesting, rather than merely technically accurate.

The history of religions, or the cross-cultural and comparative study of religion, thus constituted, is the largest and most comprehensive orienting framework within which this feminist revalorization of Buddhism is conducted. The combination of insider and outsider approaches and the combination of descriptive and normative world-constructive assignments called for in this appendix is essential to my task and my method throughout the book. If, at this point, one were to exclaim in exasperation that I have collapsed and muddied the distinction between studying religion and taking a religious point of view, I would reply that that is not the case at all. Rather, I believe that I am able to, and must, *do both*, knowing clearly which is being done when. One cannot otherwise function as a responsible, engaged scholar living and working in our chaotic world. Not only do I advocate such simultaneous work in theology and history of religion; I contend that it always occurs, in adequate or inadequate fashions, in all considerations of religion, so we might as well do it openly and thoroughly. The engaged study of religions, with its combination of dispassionate de-absolutized understandings and passionate existential commitment to just and humane values, is the single most powerful lens through which one can view religion.

NOTES

CHAPTER ONE: A FEMINIST REVALORIZATION OF BUDDHISM

1. Carol P. Christ, *Laughter of Aphrodite: Reflections on a Journey to the Goddess* (San Francisco: Harper and Row, 1987); and Christine Downing, *The Goddess: Mythological Images of the Feminine* (New York: Crossroad, 1981).

2. Eleanor McLaughlin, "The Christian Past: Does It Hold a Future for Women?" Carol P. Christ and Judith Plaskow, *Womanspirit Rising: A Feminist Reader in Religion* (San Francisco: Harper and Row, 1979), pp. 93–106.

3. Rita M. Gross, "The Study of Religion as Religious Experience," *Buddhist-Christian Studies* XI (1991), pp. 254–58.

4. See Rita M. Gross, "Studying Women and Religion: Conclusions after Twenty Years," *Women and World Religions: Contemporary Situations*, ed. Arvind Sharma and Katherine Young (Albany: SUNY Press, forthcoming).

CHAPTER TWO: ORIENTATIONS TO BUDDHISM

1. For more in-depth discussion of these basic teachings, I recommend Walpola Rahula, *What the Buddha Taught* (New York: Grove, 1974); Joseph Goldstein, *The Experience of Insight: A Natural Unfolding* (Santa Cruz: Unity Press, 1976); Chogyam Trungpa, *Cutting through Spiritual Materialism* (Boulder: Shambhala, 1978); and Osel Tendzin, *Buddha in the Palm of Your Hand* (Boulder: Shambhala, 1982).

2. See Richard H. Robinson and Willard L. Johnson, *The Buddhist Religion: An Historical Introduction*, 3rd edition (Belmont, CA: Wadsworth, 1982) for a good historical survey of Buddhism.

3. See Sandy Boucher, *Turning the Wheel: American Women Creating the New Buddhism* (San Francisco: Harper and Row, 1988) for a thorough discussion of these women.

CHAPTER THREE: WHAT IS AN ACCURATE AND USABLE PAST GOOD FOR?

1. Nancy Schuster Barnes, "Buddhism," *Women and World Religions*, ed. by Arvind Sharma (Albany, NY: SUNY Press, 1987), pp. 105–33.

2. Eleanor McLaughlin, "The Christian Past: Does It Hold Future for Women?" *Womanspirit Rising: A Feminist Reader in Religion*, ed. by Carol P. Christ and Judith Plaskow (San Francisco: Harper and Row, 1979), pp. 94–95.

3. *Ibid.*

4. *Ibid.*

5. Chogyam Trungpa, "Sacred Outlook: The Vajrayogini Shrine and Practice," *The Silk Route and the Diamond Path: Esoteric Buddhist Art on the Trans-Himalayan Trade Routes*, ed. by Deborah E. Klimberg-Salter (Los Angeles: UCLA Arts Council, 1982), pp. 231, 233.

CHAPTER FOUR: DAUGHTERS OF THE BUDDHA

1. Mrs. C.A.F. Rhys-Davids, tr., and K.R. Norman, tr., *Poems of Early Buddhist Nuns (Therigatha)* (Oxford: Pali Text Society, 1989).

2. This account is paraphrased and quoted from I.B. Horner, tr., *The Book of Discipline (Vinaya-Pitaka), Volume V (Cullavagga)*, (London: Routledge & Kegan Paul, 1975), Book X: 1.1-2.2 (pp. 352-57). See also I.B. Horner, *Women under Primitive Buddhism: Laywomen and Almswomen* (New York: E.P. Dutton and Co., 1930) pp. 102-04).

3. Horner, pp. 2-71; Nancy Auer Falk, "An Image of Woman in Old Buddhist Literature: the Daughters of Mara," *Women and Religion,* revised edition, ed. by Judith Plaskow and Joan Arnold Romero (Missoula, MT: Scholars' Press, 1974), p. 105.

4. Falk, "Daughters of Mara," pp. 105-06.

5. *Ibid.*, p. 106.

6. Kajiyama Yuichi, "Women in Buddhism," *Eastern Buddhist*, New Series, 15, no. 2 (1982), pp. 53-70.

7. Horner, *Women under Primitive Buddhism*, pp. 105-17.

8. *Ibid.*, p. 105.

9. Horner, pp. 124, 130, *Cullavagga*, x: 6.1-3, pp. 360-61.

10. Horner, pp. 154-55.

11. Horner, pp. 119-20. Karen Christina Lang, "Lord Death's Snare: Gender-Related Imagery in the Theragatha and Therigatha," *Journal of Feminist Studies in Religion* II, no. 2 (Fall 1986), p. 65. The order here given is that found in the Pali *Cullavagga.* For order given in a Sanskrit *vinaya,* see Diana Paul, *Women in Buddhism: Images of the Feminine in Mahayana Buddhism* (Berkeley: Asian Humanities Press, 1979), p. 103.

12. Nancy Auer Falk, "The Case of the Vanishing Nuns: The Fruits of Ambivalence in Ancient Indian Buddhism," *Unspoken Worlds: Women's Religious Lives*, ed. by Nancy Auer Falk and Rita M. Gross (Belmont, CA: Wadsworth, 1989), p. 159.

13. Falk, "The Case of the Vanishing Nuns," pp. 157-60.

14. Paul, *Women in Buddhism*, pp. 3-59.

15. Rhys-Davids and Norman, *Therigatha*, p. 19 (verses 23-24).

16. *Aguttaranikaya* iv. 8, 10, quoted by Cornelia Dimmitt Church "Temptress, Wife, Nun: Woman's Role in Early Buddhism," *Anima: An Experiential Journal*, 1, no. 2 (Spring 1975) p. 55.

17. E. J. Thomas, *The Life of the Buddha as Legend and History* (London: Routledge and Kegan Paul, 1949), p. 166; Horner, *Women under Primitive Buddhism*, p. 300.

18. Yuichi, "Women in Buddhism," *Eastern Buddhist 15, no. 2 (1982), pp. 53–70.*

19. Cornelia Dimmitt Church, "Temptress, Housewife, Nun," p. 55. She cites *Anguttaranikaya* I.15.

20. Horner, *Women under Primitive Buddhism*, p. 30; Falk, "The Daughters of Mara," p. 106.

21. Caroline A.F. Rhys-Davids, trs. & ed., *Stories of the Buddha: Being Selections from the Jataka* (New York: Dover, 1929), pp. 125-27, 136-42.

22. Edward Conze, *Buddhist Scriptures* (Baltimore: Penguin Classics, 1959), p. 31.

23. Horner, *Women under Primitive Buddhism*, pp. 28, 48.

24. Yuichi, "Women in Buddhism," pp. 61-62.

25. Rhys-Davids and Norman, *Therigatha*, p. 90 (verses 214-17).

26. Falk, "Daughters of Mara," pp. 107-09.

27. Paul, *Women in Buddhism*, pp. 3-59; Lang, "Lord Death's Snare," pp. 67-73.

28. Barnes, "Buddhism," p. 108.

29. *Dighanikaya*, xvi.5.9. Quoted in Church, "Temptress, Housewife, Nun," p. 53.

30. Lang, "Lord Death's Snare," p. 67.

31. I.B. Horner, *Women under Primitive Buddhism*, p. 155.

32. Rhys-Davids and Norman, *Therigatha*, pp. 67-68 (verses 139-42).

33. Church, "Temptress, Housewife, Nun," p. 55, citing *Anguttaranikaya*, v.6,5.

34. *Ibid.*, p. 55, citing *Anguttaranikaya* I i.1.

35. Horner, *Women under Primitive Buddhism*, p. 182.

36. Barnes, "Buddhism," p. 108.

37. Rhys-Davids and Norman, *Therigatha*, pp. 127-33 (verses 366-99).

38. Oral presentation by Miriam Levering.

39. Henry Clarke Warren, *Buddhism in Translation* (New York: Atheneum, 1968), pp. 77-81.

40. Falk, "Daughters of Mara," p. 110.

41. *Samyuttanikaya*, iii.2.6, cited by Falk, "Daughters of Mara," p. 105; Horner, *Women Under Primitive Buddhism*, p. 110.

42. Church, "Temptress, Housewife, Nun," p. 56, citing *Udana*, ii.10.

43. Horner, *Women under Primitive Buddhism* p. 104; see also Yuichi, "Women in Buddhism," p. 59.

44. Falk, "The Case of the Vanishing Nuns," pp. 162–63.

45. Henry Clark Warren, *Buddhism in Translation* (New York: Atheneum, 1986, reprint of 1896 edition)

46. Horner, *Women under Primitive Buddhism*, p. 352–53.

47. *Ibid.*, p. 137.

48. Warren *Buddhism in Translation*, pp. 451–81: see also Horner, *Women under Primitive Buddhism*, pp. 345–57.

49. Falk, "The Case of Vanishing Nuns," p. 164.

50. Two English translations of the *Therigatha* exist. Mrs. Rhys-Davids, tr., *Psalms of the Early Buddhists: I. Psalms of the Sisters* (London: Pali Text Society, 1909); K.R. Norman, tr., *The Elders' Verses: II Therigatha* (London: Pali Text Society, 1971). Without the introductions and notes, these two translations have been issued together by the Pali Text Society as *Poems of Early Buddhist Nuns (Therigatha)*.

51. Barbara Stoler Miller, "Ballads of Early Buddhist Nuns," *Zero*, vol. 5 (1981), p. 69.

52. Rhys-Davids and Norman, *Therigatha*, pp. 155–56.

53. *Ibid.*, verse 1; pp. 6–7.

54. *Ibid.*, pp. 88–89.

55. *Ibid.*, p. 90. (verses 215–17).

56. *Ibid.*, p. 39 (verse 66). See also Rhys-Davids, tr., *Psalms of the Early Buddhists II: Psalms of the Brethren*, (London: Pali Text Society, 1951), pp. 359–61.

CHAPTER FIVE: ROLES AND IMAGES OF WOMEN IN INDIAN MAHAYANA BUDDHISM

1. Quoted from Paul, *Women in Buddhism*, p. 230. This quote sets the tone for much of this chapter.

2. Paul Williams, *Mahayana Buddhism: The Doctrinal Foundations (London: Routledge, 1989), pp. 1–6.*

3. Williams, p. 5; David Snellgrove, *Indo-Tibetan Buddhism: Indian Buddhists and Their Tibetan Successors* (Boston: Shambhala, 1987), pp. 65–66.

4. *Ibid.*

5. Falk, "The Case of the Vanishing Nuns," p. 157.

6. *Ibid.*

7. Paul, *Women in Buddhism*, p. 82.

8. Janice D. Willis, "Nuns and Benefactresses: The Role of Women in the Development of Buddhism," *Women, Religion, and Social Change*, ed. by Yvonne Haddad and Ellison Banks Findley (Albany, NY: SUNY Press, 1985), p. 75.

9. Har Dayal, *The Bodhisattva Doctrine in Sanskrit Literature* (Dehli: Motilal Barnasidass, 1932, 1970 reprint), p. 224.

10. Nancy Schuster, "Striking a Balance: Women and Images of Women in Early Chinese Buddhism," *Women, Religion, and Social Change*, pp. 87–111.

11. *Ibid.*

12. Karma Lekshe Tsomo, ed., *Sakyadhita: Daughters of the Buddha* (Ithaca, NY: Snow Lion, 1988), p. 106.

13. Paul, *Women in Buddhism*, pp. 98–102.

14. Paula Richman, "The Portray Tamil Buddhist Text," *Gender and Religion: On the Complexity of Symbols*, ed. Caroline Bynum, Steven Harrell, and Paula Richman (Boston: Beacon Press, 1985), pp. 143–65.

15. *Ibid.*, p. 163, fn. 3.

16. Willis, "Nuns and Benefactresses," p. 69. A list of highly misogynist texts is given by Dayal, *The Bodhisattva Doctrine in Sanskrit Literature*, p. 224.

17. Paul, *Women in Buddhism*, p. 189. See Yuichi, "Women in Buddhism," for a detailed discussion of this list, its date of origin, and alternate versions of it.

18. Yuichi, "Women in Buddhism," p. 65.

19. Schuster, "Changing the Female Body: Wise Women and the Bodhisattva Career in some *Maharatnakuta* Sutras," *Journal of the International Association of Buddhist Studies* 4 (1981), p. 28. She is paraphrasing the *Diamond Sutra*'s argument.

20. Paul, *Women in Buddhism*, p. 308.

21. Schuster, "*Maharatnakuta* Sutras," p. 37.

22. Paul, *Women in Buddhism*, p. 176.

23. Steven Beyer, ed., *The Buddhist Experience: Sources and Interpretation* (Belmont, CA: Dickenson, 1974), p. 53.

24. Williams, *Mahayana Buddhism*, p. 245.

25. Paul, *Women in Buddhism*, pp. 169-70.

26. Paul, *Women in Buddhism*, p. 109, summarizes very important material on spiritual friends found in the *Avatamsaka Sutra*.

27. Paul, *Women in Buddhism*, pp. 107-65 for comments on "conventional" good friends. See pages 281-302 for her discussion of Shrimala.

28. *Anguttaranikaya*, quoted in Horner, *Women under Primitive Buddhism*, p. 291.

29. *Majjhimanikaya*, III, 65, 66, quoted by Horner, *Women under Primitive Buddhism*, p. 291.

30. Paul, *Women in Buddhism*, pp. 189-90. The previous summary and short quotations are from Schuster, "Changing the Female Body," pp. 42-43 and Paul, *Women in Buddhism*, pp. 187-90.

31. Miriam Levering, "The Dragon-Girl and the Abbess of Mo-Shan: Gender and Status in the Ch-an Buddhist Tradition," *Journal of the International Association of Buddhist Studies* 5, no. 1 (1982), esp. pp. 24-30.

32. See Paul, *Women in Buddhism*, pp. 208-09; Schuster, "Changing the Female Body, pp. 52-54.

33. Barnes, "Buddhism" in Sharma, ed. *Women in World Religions*, p. 259, note 10.

34. Williams, *Mahayana Buddhism*, p. 21.

35. Levering, "The Dragon Girl and the Abbess of Mo-Shan," pp. 27-30.

36. Paul, *Women in Buddhism*, p. 230.

37. *Ibid.*, p. 236.

38. *Ibid.*, pp. 292-301.

39. *Ibid.*, pp. 280-89.

40. *Ibid.*, pp. 284-85.

41. Paul, *Women in Buddhism*, pp. 259, 253. See also Paul, "KuanYin: Saviour and Saviours in Chinese Pure Land Buddhism," *Book of the Goddess: Past and Present*, ed. by Carl Olsen (New York: Crossroad, 1983), pp. 161-75; C. N. Tay, "Kuan-Yin: The Cult of Half Asia," *History of Religions* 16 (November 1976), pp. 147-77; John Chamberlayne, "The Development of Kuan Yin: Chinese Goddess of Mercy, " *Numen* 9 (January 1962), pp. 45-52.

42. Paul, *Women in Buddhism*, p. 258.

43. Joanna Rogers Macy, "Perfection of Wisdom: Mother of all Buddhas," *Beyond Androcentrism: New Essays on Women and Religion*, ed. by Rita M. Gross, (Missoula,

MT: Scholars' Press, 1977), p. 320. See also Edward Conze, "The Iconography of Prajnaparamita," *Thirty Years of Buddhist Studies: Selected Essays of Edward Conze* (Columbia, SC: University of South Carolina Press, 1968), pp. 243–60.

44. Macy, p. 315.

45. Ibid., p. 319.

46. *Perfection of Wisdom in 8000 Lines*, cited in *ibid.*, p. 318.

47. *Ibid.*, pp. 319–20.

48. *Ibid.*, p. 319.

49. Paul, *Women in Buddhism*, p. 236.

CHAPTER SIX: ROLES AND IMAGES OF WOMEN IN INDO-TIBETAN
VAJRAYANA BUDDHISM

1. David Snellgrove, *Indo-Tibetan Buddhism: Indian Buddhists and Their Tibetan Successors*, 2 vols. (Boston: Shambhala, 1987) is an exhaustive survey of the topic.

2. Barbara Aziz, "Moving Toward a Sociology of Tibet," *Feminine Ground: Essays on Women and Tibet*, ed. by Janice D. Willis (Ithaca, NY: Snow Lion, 1987), p. 79.

3. *Ibid.*, p. 81.

4. *Ibid.*

5. *Ibid.*

6. Karma Lekshe Tsomo, "Tibetan Nuns and Nunneries," *Feminine Ground*, p. 123.

7. Chogyam Trungpa, *Shambhala: The Sacred Path of the Warrior* (Boston: Shambhala, 1988), p. 94.

8. Snellgrove, *Indo-Tibetan Buddhism*, p. 113, quoting *Ratnagotravibhaga*.

9. Gampopa, *The Jewel Ornament of Liberation*, tr. by Herbert V. Guenther (Berkeley: Shambhala, 1971), p. 65.

10. *Ibid.*, pp. 92–93.

11. Tsultrim Allione, *Women of Wisdom* (London: Routledge and Kegan Paul, 1984), pp. 76–77.

12. Reginald A. Ray, "Accomplished Women in Tantric Buddhism of Medieval India and Tibet," *Unspoken Worlds*, pp. 192–93.

13. Keith Dowman, tr., *Sky Dancer: The Secret Life and Songs of the Lady Yeshe Tsogyel* (London: Routledge and Kegan Paul, 1984), p. 16.

14. Keith Dowman, tr., *Masters of Mahamudra: Songs and Histories of the Eighty-four Buddhist Siddhas* (Albany, NY: SUNY Press, 1985), p. 373.

15. Allione, *Women of Wisdom*, pp. 80–126.

16. *Ibid.*, pp. 114–15.

17. *Ibid.*, p. 225.

18. Anne Klein, "Primordial Purity and Everyday Life: Exalted Female Symbols and the Women of Tibet," *Immaculate and Powerful*, ed. by Clarissa W. Atkinson, Constance Buchanan, and Margaret R. Miles (Boston: Beacon, 1985), pp. 133–34; Beatrice D. Miller, "Views of Women's Roles in Buddhist Tibet," *Studies in the History of Buddhism*, ed. by A.K. Narain (Dehli: B.R. Publishing Co., 1980), pp. 155–61.

19. Allione, *Women of Wisdom*, pp. xix–xxxv, presents the distinctions. For an excellent discussion of Tibetan nuns, see Hanna Havnevik, *Tibetan Buddhist Nuns* (London: Norwegian University Press, n.d.).

20. Klein, *Immaculate and Powerful*, p. 120.

21. Tsomo, "Tibetan Nuns and Nunneries," *Feminine Ground: Essays on Women and Tibet*, ed. by Janice D. Willis (Ithaca, NY: Snow Lion, 1989), pp. 124–34.

22. *Ibid.*, 122.

23. *Ibid.*

24. *Ibid.*, p. 119.

25. Willis, "Tibetan Ani-s: The Nun's Life in Tibet," *Feminine Ground: Essays on Women and Tibet*, p. 101.

26. *Ibid.*, p. 105–09.

27. Allione, *Women of Wisdom*, pp. 236–57.

28. *Ibid.*, pp. 236-57. Klein, "Primordial Purity," pp. 115-18.

29. Allione, *Women of Wisdom*, p. 255.

30. K. Dhondup and Tashi Tsering, "Samdhing Dorjee Phagmo—Tibet's Only Female Incarnation," *Tibetan Review*, 14, no. 8 (1979), pp. 11–17.

31. Allione, *Women of Wisdom*, p. 64.

32. Willis, "Tibetan Ani-s," p. 109.

33. Levering, "The Dragon Girl and the Abbess of Mo-Shan," pp. 28.

34. Two translations exist: Dowman, *Masters of Mahamudra*; and James Robinson, *Buddha's Lions: The Lives of the Eighty-Four Siddhas* (Berkeley: Dharma Publishing, 1979).

35. Ray, "Accomplished Women," pp. 195–98.

36. Dowman, *Masters of Mahamudra*, pp. 68-69.

37. Two Translations exist: Dowman, *Sky Dancer*; and Tarthang Tulku, *Mother of Knowledge: The Enlightenment of Yeshe Tsogyel* (Berkeley: Dharma Publishing, 1983).

38. Glenn Mullin, *Selected works of the Dalai Lama II: The Tantric Yogas of Sister Niguma*, p. 24, and Snellgrove, *Indo-Tibetan Buddhism*, p. 500, contain stories of Niguma's transmission of the Six Yogas.

39. Herbert V. Guenther, tr., *The Life and Teaching of Naropa* (London: Oxford University Press, 1963), p. 18.

40. Chogyam Trungpa and Nalanda Translation Committee, *The Life of Marpa the Translator* (Boulder: Prajna Press, 1982).

41. Rita M. Gross, "Yeshe Tsogyel: Enlightened Consort, Great Teacher, Female Role Model," *Feminine Ground*, pp. 11-32.

42. Tarthang Tulku, *Mother of Knowledge*, pp. xi-xii.

43. Tulku, *Mother of Knowledge*, p. 5; Dowman, *Sky Dancer*, p. 3.

44. Tulku, *Mother of Knowledge*, p. 13.

45. Dowman, *Sky Dancer*, p. 10.

46. *Ibid.*, p. 16.

47. *Ibid.*, p. 44.

48. *Ibid.*, p. 78.

49. *Ibid.*, p. 125.

50. *Ibid.*, p. 135.

51. *Ibid.*, p. 146.

52. *Ibid.*, p. 150.

53. *Ibid.*, p. 186.

54. *Ibid.*, p. 147.

55. *Ibid.*, p. 150.

56. Allione, *Women of Wisdom*, pp. 143-87. For other, much shorter accounts of Machig Lapdron, which nevertheless focus almost completely on her period of distress and difficulty, rather than her accomplishments, see Ray, "Accomplished Women," p. 194 and Snellgrove, *Indo-Tibetan Buddhism*, pp. 468-69.

57. Allione, *Women of Wisdom*, p. 186.

58. *Snow Lion Newsletter and Catalogue* 3, no. 1 (Spring 1988), pp. 1-2.

59. Tarthang Tulku, *Mother of Knowledge*, p. 105.

60. *Ibid.*, p. 102.

61. Judith Hanson, tr., *The Torch of Certainty* (Boulder: Shambhala, 1977), p. 41.

62. Janice Dean Willis, *The Diamond Light: An Introduction to Tibetan Buddhist Meditations* (New York: Simon and Schuster, 1972), p. 103.

63. Marina Warner, *Alone of All Her Sex: The Myth and Cult of the Virgin Mary* (New York: Alfred A. Knopf, 1976), p. xvii.

64. Anne C. Klein, "Non-Dualism and the Great Bliss Queen: A Study in Tibetan Buddhist Ontology and Symbolism," *Journal of Feminist Studies in Religion* 1 (Spring 1985), pp. 73–76.

65. Allione, *Women of Wisdom*, p. 29; Chogyam Trungpa, "Sacred Outlook: The Vajrayogini Shrine and Practice," *The Silk Route and the Diamond Path: Esoteric Buddhist Art on the Trans-Himalayan Trade Routes*, ed. by Deborah E. Klimberg-Salter (Los Angeles: UCLA Art Council, 1982), p. 236.

66. Hanson, tr., *Torch of Certainty*, pp. 30-33.

67. Trungpa *Cutting through Spiritual Materialism*, pp. 220-30.

68. Snellgrove, *Indo-Tibetan Buddhism*, p. 268.

69. *Ibid.*, pp. 271–72.

70. *Ibid.*, p. 261.

71. *Ibid.*, pp. 287-88.

72. Trungpa and Nalanda Translation Committee, *The Rain of Wisdom* (Boulder: Shambhala, 1980), p. 145.

73. Snellgrove, *Indo-Tibetan Buddhism*, pp. 167–68.

74. Allione, *Women of Wisdom*, pp. 35–36.

75. Willis, "Dakini: Some Comments on its Nature and Meaning," *Feminine Ground*, pp. 57-75.

76. Guenther, *The Life and Teaching of Naropa*, p. ix, 24, 48.

77. Allione, *Women of Wisdom*, p. 17.

78. Dowman, *Sky-Dancer*, p. 71.

79. Beyer, *The Cult of Tara: Magic and Ritual in Tibet* (Berkeley: University of California Press, 1978), p. 55.

80. David Templeman, tr., *The Origin of Tara Tantra*, (Dharamsala, India: Library of Tibetan Works and Archives, 1981), pp. 11-12.

81. Martin Willson, *In Praise of Tara: Songs to the Saviouress* (London: Wisdom Publications, 1986), p. 125.

82. *Ibid.*

83. *Ibid.*, pp. 105-06.

84. *Ibid.*, p. 301.

85. *Ibid.*, pp. 190-93.

86. *Ibid.*, pp. 305-06.

87. *Ibid.*, pp. 191-93.

88. Allione, *Women of Wisdom*, p. 30; Trungpa, "Sacred Outlook," p. 234.

89. Allione, pp. 31-34 contains some discussion of some meanings that can be attributed to some her implements and aspects of her pose. See also Trungpa, "Sacred Outlook," pp. 238-40. Another description of her and the meaning of her implements, in her role as consort of Cakrasamvara, is found in Kazi Dawa-Samdup, *Sri Cakrasamvara-Tantra: A Buddhist Tantra* (New Dehli: Ditya Prakashan, 1987, original 1919), pp. 20-21.

90. Trungpa, "Sacred Outlook," pp. 238-40. Additional praises are given on these pages, as well as extensive commentary on their meanings, which are quite opaque without guidance.

CHAPTER EIGHT: RESOURCES FOR A BUDDHIST FEMINISM

1. Christ and Plaskow, *Womanspirit Rising*, pp. 131-92.

2. *Ibid.*, pp. 193-287.

3. Rosemary Ruether, *Women-Church: Theology and Practice* (San Francisco: Harper and Row, 1986).

4. Margot Adler, *Drawing Down the Moon: Witches, Druids, Goddess-Worshippers and Other Pagans in America Today* (Boston: Beacon, 1979); and Starhawk, *The Spiral Dance: A Rebirth of the Ancient Religion of the Great Goddess* (San Francisco: Harper and Row, 1979).

5. Robinson, *The Buddhist Religion*, pp. 18-20 and Trungpa, *Cutting through Spiritual Materialism*, pp. 131-43.

6. Hanson, tr., *Torch of Certainty*, pp. 29-35.

7. Gross, "Feminism from the Perspective of Buddhist Practice," *Buddhist Christian Studies* I (1980), pp. 73-82; and Gross, "Buddhism and Feminism: Toward Their Mutual Transformation," *Eastern Buddhist*, New Series, XIX, nos. 1 and 2 (Spring, Autumn, 1986), pp. 44-58, 62-74.

8. Gross, "Suffering, Feminist Theory, and Images of the Goddess," *Anima: An Experiential Journal* 13 (Fall Equinox 1896), pp. 39-46.

9. Gross, "Buddhism and Feminism," pp. 56-58.

10. Gross, "Feminism from the Perspective of Buddhist Practice."

CHAPTER NINE: PRESUPPOSITIONS OF THE BUDDHIST WORLDVIEW

1. A few of the most significant volumes include Ruether, *Sexism and God-Talk: Toward a Feminist Theology* (Boston: Beacon Press, 1983); Daly, *Beyond God the Father: Toward a Philosophy of Women's Liberation* (Boston: Beacon Press, 1973); Judith Plaskow, *Standing Again at Sinai: Judaism from a Feminist Perspective* (San Francisco: Harper and Row, 1990); Sallie McFague, *Models of God: Theology for an Ecological Nuclear Age* (Philadelphia: Fortress Press, 1987), and *Metaphorical Theology: Models of God in Religious Language* (Philadelphia: Fortress Press, 1982); and Carol P. Christ, *Laughter of Aphrodite: Reflections on a Journey to the Goddess*, (San Francisco: Harper and Row, 1987).

2. Daly, *Beyond God the Father*, p. 13.

3. Carol P. Christ, "Why Women Need the Goddess: Phenomonological, Psychological and Political Reflections," *Womenspirit Rising*, pp. 273-87.

4. Gross, "Female God-Language in a Jewish Context," *Womanspirit Rising*, pp. 167-173.

5. Gross, "Hindu Female Deities as a Resource in the Contemporary Rediscovery of the Goddess," *Journal of the American Academy of Religion*," XLVII (September 1978), pp. 269-291) and "Steps toward Feminine Imagery of Deity in Jewish Theology," *Judaism* 30:2 (Spring 1981), pp. 183-193.

6. *Anima: An Experiential Journal* 13 (Fall 1986), pp. 39-46.

7. " 'I will Never Forget to Visualize that Vajrayogini is my Body and Mind,' " *Journal of Feminist Studies in Religion* 3 (Spring 1987), pp. 77-89.

8. *Ibid.*, p. 79.

9. *Ibid.*, 87.

10. *Ibid.*

11. Rosemary Ruether, "MotherEarth and the Megamachine," *Womanspirit Rising*, pp. 43-52.

12. Guy Welbon, *The Buddhist Nirvana and its Western Interpreters* (Chicago: University of Chicago Press, 1968); Th. Tscherbatsky, *The Conception of Buddhist Nirvana* (London: Mouton and Co., 1965).

13. Shinryu Suzuki, *Zen Mind, Beginner's Mind* (New York: Tuttle, 1974), pp. 102-03.

14. Robert Bellah, "Religious Evolution," *Reader in Comparative Religion*, 3rd edition, ed. by Lessa and Vogt (New York: Harper and Row, 1972).

CHAPTER TEN: A FEMINIST ANALYSIS OF KEY BUDDHIST TERMS

1. Leonard Grob, Riffat Hassan, and Haim Gordon, *Women's and Men's Liberation: Testimonies of Spirit* (New York: Greenwood, 1991).

2. Gross, "The Three-Yana Journey in Tibetan Vajrayana Buddhism," *Buddhist-Christian Studies* VII (1987), pp. 87–104.

3. Snellgrove, *Indo-Tibetan Buddhism*, pp. 79–116; and Reginald A. Ray, "Response to John Cobb," *Buddhist-Christian Studies* VIII (1988), pp. 83–101.

4. Sandy Boucher, *Turning the Wheel: American Women Creating the New Buddhism* (San Francisco: Harper and Row, 1988).

5. Ray, "Response to John Cobb," p. 86.

6. Snellgrove, *Indo-Tibetan Buddhism*, pp. 94–116.

7. Ray, p. 87.

CHAPTER ELEVEN: GENDER AND EGOLESSNESS

1. Pages 130–2.

2. Anne Klein, "Finding a Self," *Shaping New Vision: Gender Values in American Culture*, ed. by Clarissa W. Atkinson, Constance H. Buchanan, and Margaret Miles (Ann Arbor: UMI Research Press, 1987), p. 195.

3. Gross, "Buddhism and Feminism," *Eastern Buddhist*, New Series, XIX (Spring 1986), pp. 49–50.

4. Rahula Walpola, *What the Buddha Taught* (New York: Grove Press, 1974), p. 51.

5. *Ibid.*, p. 26.

6. Chogyam Trungpa, *Cutting through Spiritual Materialism* (Berkeley: Shambhala, 1973), p. 122.

7. *Ibid.*, p. 122.

8. Rahula, p. 51.

9. Valerie Saiving, "The Human Situation: A Feminine Perspective," *Womanspirit Rising*, pp. 25–42.

10. For extended and varied examples of how women cope with patriarchal projections, see sections two and three of *Unspoken Worlds: Women's Religious Lives*, ed. by Nancy Auer Falk and Rita M. Gross (Belmont, Ca: Wadsworth, 1989).

11. Carol Gilligan, *In a Different Voice: Psychological Theory and Women's Development* (Cambridge: Harvard University Press, 1982), and Catherine Keller, *From a Broken Web: Separation, Sexism, and Self*, (Boston: Beacon, 1986).

12. Nancy Chodorow, *The Reproduction of Mothering: Psychoanalysis and the Sociology of Gender* (Berkeley: University of California Press, 1978); and Dorothy Dinnerstein, *The Mermaid and the Minotaur: Sexual Arrangements and Human Malaise* (New York: Harper, 1977).

13. For a clear discussion of this process, see Chogyam Trungpa, *Cutting through Spiritual Materialism*, p. 126.

14. Bhikkhu Khantipalo, *Banner of the Arhants: Buddhist Monks and Nuns from the Buddha's Time Till Now* (Kandy, Sri Lanka: Buddhist Publication Society, 1979), p. 132.

15. Gross, "The Three-Yana Journey," p. 91.

16. While all systems of Buddhist meditation recommend personal instruction, a number of sources give accurate information on basic Buddhist meditation techniques. See Chogyam Trungpa, *Shambhala: The Sacred Path of the Warrior* (Boston: Shambhala, 1988), pp. 35-41; Osel Tendzin, *Buddha in the Palm of Your Hand*, (Boulder: Shambhala, 1982), pp. 32-36; Rahula Walpola, *What the Buddha Taught*, pp. 67-75; Joseph Goldstein, *The Experience of Insight: A Natural Unfolding* (Santa Cruz: Unity Press, 1976), pp. 1-6; and Philip Kapleau, *Three Pillars of Zen* (Boston: Beacon Press, 1967), pp. 30-38.

CHAPTER TWELVE: GENDER AND EMPTINESS

1. The Heart Sutra has been translated many times. For two translations, see Edward Conze, *Buddhist Scriptures* (Middlesex, England: Penguin Books, 1959), pp. 162-64; and Dwight Goddard, *A Buddhist Bible* (Boston: Beacon Press, 1970), pp. 85-86. For a discussion of commentaries on the Heart Sutra, see Donald Lopez, Jr., *The Heart Sutra Explained: Indian and Tibetan Commentaries* (Albany, NY: SUNY Press, 1988).

2. Ray, "Response to Cobb," p. 87.

3. Gordon Kaufman, "God and Emptiness: An Experimental Study," *Buddhist-Christian Studies* IX (1989), pp. 175-87; and John Cobb, "Ultimate Reality: A Christian View," *Buddhist-Christian Studies* VII (1988), pp. 51-64.

4. Bhikshu Sangharakshita, *A Survey of Buddhism* (Boulder: Shambhala, 1980), p. 258.

5. *Ibid.*

6. Paul, *Women in Buddhism*, p. 230.

7. *Ibid.*, p. 230.

8. *Ibid.*, p. 236.

9. Chogyam Trungpa, *Shambhala: The Sacred Path of the Warrior*, pp. 29–34.

10. Ann Klein, "Gain or Drain?" Buddhist and Feminist Views on Compassion," *Women and Buddhism: A Special Issue of the Spring Wind Buddhist Cultural Forum* VI, nos. 1–3 (1986), pp. 105–16.

11. Carol Gilligan, *In a Different Voice*.

12. Ann Klein, "Gain or Drain?" pp. 108–15.

CHAPTER THIRTEEN: GENDER AND BUDDHA-NATURE

1. Ray, "Response to John Cobb," p. 86.

2. *Ibid.*, p. 87.

3. Two new books on this concept add significantly to the literature. Sallie B. King, *Buddha Nature* (Albany, NY: SUNY Press, 1991); and S. K. Hookham, *The Buddha Within: Tathagatagarbha Doctrine according to the Shentong Interpretation of the Ratnagotravibhaga* (Albany, NY: SUNY Press, 1991).

4. See Williams, *Mahayana Buddhism: The Doctrinal Foundations*, pp. 99–109, for a helpful summary of the arguments on both sides.

5. Williams, *Mahayana Buddhism*, pp. 77–95; and Sangharakshita, *A Survey of Buddhism*, pp. 353–68.

6. Snellgrove, *Indo-Tibetan Buddhism*, p. 95; Williams, *Mahayana Buddhism*, pp. 82–85.

7. Williams, *Mahayana Buddhism*, p. 83.

8. *Ibid.*, p. 83.

9. Williams, pp. 84–85.

10. *Ibid.* p. 83.

11. See above, p. 166.

12. Gross, "Suffering, Feminist Theory, and Images of Goddess."

13. John Blofeld, *The Tantric Mysticism of Tibet* (New York: Dutton, 1970), pp. 76–78.

14. *Ibid.*

15. Naomi Goldenberg, "Archetypal Symbolism and the Separation of Mind and Body—Reason Enough to Return to Freud?" *Journal of Feminist Studies in Religion* I, no. 1 (1985), pp. 55–72; *Changing of the Gods: Feminism and the End of Traditional Religion* (Boston: Beacon Press, 1979), pp. 54–64.

16. Erich Neumann, *The Origins and History of Consciousness* (New York: Pantheon Books, 1954), pp. 5–143.

334 BUDDHISM AFTER PATRIARCHY

17. Christ, *Laughter of Aphrodite*; Downing, *The Goddess*; Starhawk, *The Spiral Dance; A Rebirth of the Ancient Religion of the Great Goddess* (San Francisco: Harper and Row, 1979); Goldenberg, *The Changing of the Gods*; Margot Adler, *Drawing Down the Moon; Witches, Druids, Goddess-Worshippers, and Other Pagans in America Today* (Boston: Beacon, 1979.)

18. Mary Daly, *Gyn/Ecology: The Metaethics of Radical Feminism* (Boston: Beacon Press, 1978), pp. 252–55; Charlene Spretnek, ed., *The Politics of Women's Spirituality: Essays on the Rise of Spiritual Power within the Feminist Movement* (Garden City, NY: Anchor Books, 1982), pp. xv–xxi and 565–73.

19. *Smithsonian*, 1978, no. 9, p. 41 contains a plate of the card.

20. See above, pages 105–8.

21. Gross, "I Will Never Forget to Visualize that Vajrayogini is my Body and Mind" contains a fuller description and more complete reflections.

CHAPTER FOURTEEN: VERDICTS AND JUDGMENTS

1. Paul, *Women in Buddhism*, p. 236.

2. Williams, *The Diamond Light*, p. 103.

3. Aziz, "Moving Toward a Sociology of Tibet," p. 79.

4. For example, Lionel Tiger, *Men in Groups* (New York: Vintage Books, 1970).

5. The book that originated the debate is E. O. Wilson, *Sociobiology: The New Synthesis*, (Cambridge: Harvard University Press, 1975). A Feminist discussion is found in Marion Lowe, "Sociobiology and Sex Differences," *Signs: Journal of Women and Culture* IV (Autumn 1978), pp. 118–25.

6. Ann Barstow, "The Prehistoric Goddess," Carl Olsen, ed., *The Book of the Goddess* (New York: Crossroad, 1983), pp. 7–15; Marija Gimbutas, "Women and Culture in Goddess Oriented Old Europe," Charlene Spretnak, ed., *The Politics of Women's Spirituality* (Garden City, NY: Anchor Books, 1982), pp. 22–31; Elinor W. Gadon, *The Once and Future Goddess* (San Francisco: Harper and Row, 1989), pp. 1–107.

7. Gadon, pp. 108–88.

8. Rick Fields, *How the Swans Came to the Lake: A Narrative History of Buddhism in America*,(Boulder: Shambhala, 1981).

9. Ann Wilson Schaef, *Women's Reality* (Minneapolis: Winston Press, 1981).

CHAPTER FIFTEEN: ANDROGYNOUS INSTITUTIONS

1. See pages 49–51.

2. Pages 84–5.

3. George D. Bond, *The Buddhist Revival in Sri Lanka: Religious Tradition, Reinterpretation, and Response,* (Columbia: SC: University of South Carolina Press, 1988), pp. 130–298.

4. See page 194.

5. Paul, *Women in Buddhism*, p. 66.

6. *Ibid.*, p. 70.

7. Gampopa, *Jewel Ornament of Liberation*, pp. 92–94.

8. Shulamith Firestone, *The Dialectic of Sex: The Case for Feminist Revolution* (New York: Bantam Books, 1970).

9. Sara Ruddick, *Maternal Thinking: Toward a Politics of Peace* (New York: Ballantine Books, 1989).

10. See Rosemarie Tong, *Feminist Thought: A Comprehensive Introduction* (Boulder: Westview, 1989), pp. 149–61 for a good summary.

11. *Ibid.*, p. 149.

12. *Ibid.*, p. 156.

13. *Ibid.*, p. 150.

14. *Ibid.*, p. 152.

15. For a fuller account, see Boucher, *Turning The Wheel*, pp. 326–377.

16. Andrew Powell and Graham Harrison, *Living Buddhism* (New York: Harmony Books, 1989).

17. Khantipalo, *Banner of the Arahants*, p. 153.

18. Stephanie Kaza, "Thai Buddhist Women: An Interview with Dr. Chatsumarn Kabilsingh," *Buddhist Peace Fellowship Newsletter*, Summer, 1990, pp. 24–25.

19. For the Tibetan monasteries in exile, these points are well documented in Hanna Havnevik, *Tibetan Buddhist Nuns* (Oslo: Norwegian University Press, n.d.).

20. Boucher, *Turning the Wheel*, pp. 87–147.

21. Falk, "The Case of the Vanishing Nuns," pp. 158–60.

22. See page 37.

23. *Cullavagga* x.9.4. Horner, *Women under Primitive Buddhism*, pp. 130–33.

24. Dorothy Sayers, "The Human-Not-Quite-Human," *Are Women Human?* (Grand Rapids, MI: Eerdmans, 1971), p. 37.

25. Boucher, *Turning the Wheel*, pp. 93–99.

26. See pp. 87, 90 of this book for a summary. See also Ray, "Accomplished Women"; Dowman, *Masters of Mahamudra*; and Allione, *Women of Wisdom*, for some accounts.

27. See pp. 91-2.

28. Gerda Lerner, *The Creation of Patriarchy* (Oxford: Oxford University Press, 1986), pp. 226-27.

29. Jane Howard, "Margaret Mead, 'Self-Appointed Materfamilias to the World,'" *Smithsonian* XV (September, 1984), pp. 122, 12632.

30. Penny van Esterik, "Laywomen in Theravada Buddhism," *Women of Southeast Asia*, Penny van Esterik, ed., (De Kalb, IL: Northern Illinois University Press, 1982), pp. 65-68.

31. Trungpa, *Cutting through Spiritual Materialism*, pp. 31-50.

32. See pp. 93-8.

CHAPTER SIXTEEN: ANDROGYNOUS VIEW

1. Paul Griffiths, *Christianity through Non-Christian Eyes* (Maryknoll, NY: Orbis, 1990), p. 136.

2. Lucien Stryk, ed., *World of the Buddha: A Reader—From the Three Baskets to Modern Zen* (Garden City, NY: Anchor Books, 1969), pp. 219-23.

3. Stephen Beyer, ed., *The Buddhist Experience: Sources and Interpretations* (Encino, CA: Dickenson, 1974), p. 76.

4. Dilgo Khyentse, Rinpoche, "The Wish-Fulfilling Jewel," excerpted in *The Vajradhatu Sun* 12, no. 5 (June-July 1990), p. 3.

5. Gampopa, *Jewel Ornament of Liberation*, p. 155.

6. *Ibid.*, p. 157.

7. Tape recording, Refuge Vow Ceremony, Karma Dzong, Boulder, Colo, August 13, 1977.

8. Trungpa, "Taking Refuge," *Garuda V: Transcending Hesitation* (Boulder: Vajradhatu, 1977), p. 25

9. Carol Gilligan, *In a Different Voice: Psychological Theory and Women's Development* (Cambridge: Harvard University Press, 1982).

10. Among previously cited sources, Dinnerstein, Chodorow, and Keller.

11. For a study of the importance of friendship in monastic life in Christianity, see Brian Patrick McGuire, *Friendship and Community: The Monastic Experience 350–1250* (Kalamazoo, MI: Cistercian Publications, 1988).

12. Trungpa, "Taking Refuge," p. 25.

13. Abhraham Joshua Heschel, *The Sabbath* (New York: Shocken, 1951).

14. John Lame Deer and Richard Erdoes, *Lame Deer: Seeker of Visions* (New York: Simon and Schuster, 1972), pp. 108–09.

15. Beyer, ed., *The Buddhist Experience*, p. 82.

16. Trungpa, *Journey without Goal*, pp. 25–54. This view is part of the oral commentary of Vajrayana Buddhism and is developed at considerable length in various privately circulated manuscripts taken from those oral commentaries.

17. Rhys-Davids and Norman, translators, *Poems of the Early Buddhist Nuns*, pp. 6–7.

18. Fran Tribe, "Ordinary Practice," *Kahawai* V, no. 1 (Winter 1983), p. 4.

19. *Ibid.*, pp. 5–6.

20. Letter to the editor, Hathaway Barry, *Kahawai* IX, no. 1 (Winter-Spring 1987), p. 9.

21. Allione, *Women of Wisdom*, p. 19.

22. *Kahawai* 1, p. 4.

23. See p. 332, fn. 16.

24. Nalanda Translation Committee and Chogyam Trungpa, trs., *The Rain of Wisdom* (Boulder: Shambhala, 1981), p. 186.

25. See pp. 92–3.

26. Starhawk, *The Spiral Dance*, pp. 27–28.

27. See chapter 9, "Setting the Stage: Presuppositions of the Buddhist Worldview."

28. Ruether, "Mother-Earth and Megamachine," pp. 47–52.

APPENDIX A: FEMINISM AS ACADEMIC METHOD AND SOCIAL VISION

1. For example, Fred Eppsteiner, ed., *The Path of Compassion: Writings on Socially Engaged Buddhism* (Berkeley: Parallax Press, 1988); and Ken Jones, *The Social Face of Buddhism: An Approach to Political and Social Activism* (London: Wisdom Publications, 1989).

2. Sandy Boucher, *Turning the Wheel: American Women Creating the New Buddhism* (San Francisco: Harper and Row, 1988).

3. See Gross, "Tribal Religions: Aboriginal Australia," *Women in World Religions*, ed. by Arvind Sharma (Albany, NY: SUNY Press, 1987), pp. 41–42 for a summary of that literature and its refutation.

4. Gross, "Menstruation and Childbirth as Ritual and Religious Experience Among Native Australians," *Unspoken Worlds: Women's Religious Lives*, ed. by Nancy

Auer Falk and Rita M. Gross (Belmont CA: Wadsworth Press, 1989), pp. 257–66, and Rita M. Gross, "Tribal Religions: Aboriginal Australia," *Women in World Religions*, ed. by Arvind Sharma (Albany, NY: SUNY Press, 1987), pp. 37–58.

5. Nancy Auer Falk and Rita M. Gross, *Unspoken Worlds: Religious Lives* (Belmont CA: Wadsworth, 1989).

6. Gross, "Exclusion and Participation: The Role of Women in Australian Aboriginal Religion," Ph.D., University of Chicago, 1975.

7. de Beauvoir, *The Second Sex* (New York: Bantam Books, 1961), p. xv.

8. Lerner, *The Creation of Patriarchy* (New York: Oxford University Press, 1986).

9. de Beauvoir, *The Second Sex* (New York: Bantam Books, 1961).

10. Daly, *Beyond God the Father: Toward a Philosophy of Women's Liberation* (Boston: Beacon Press, 1973), p. 8.

APPENDIX B: RELIGIOUS EXPERIENCE AND THE STUDY OF RELIGION

1. See Gross, "The Study of Religion as Religious Experience," *Buddhist-Christian Studies* IX (1991), pp. 254–58.

2. Gross, "Religious Diversity: Some Implications for Monotheism," *Wisconsin Dialogue* 11 (1991), pp. 35–49.

3. William E. Paden, *Religious Worlds: The Comparative Study of Religion* (Boston: Beacon Press, 1988), pp. 164–68).

BIBLIOGRAPHY

BIBLIOGRAPHY

Abhayadatta. *Buddha's Lions: The Lives of the Eighty-Four Siddhas*, trs. by James B. Robinson. Berkeley: Dharma Publishing, 1979.

Adler, Margot. *Drawing Down the Moon: Witches, Druids, Goddess-Worshippers and Other Pagans in America Today*. Boston: Beacon Press, 1979.

Allione, Tsultrim. *Women of Wisdom*. London: Routledge and Kegan Paul, 1984.

AmaraSingham, Lorna Rhodes. "The Misery of the Embodied: Representations of Women in Sinhalese Myth." In *Women in Ritual and Symbolic Roles*. Ed. by Judith Hoch-Smith and Anita Spring. New York: Plenum Press, 1978, pp. 101-25.

Arguelles, Mirian and Jose. *The Feminine: Spacious as the Sky*. Boulder, CO: Shambhala, 1977.

Aryasurya. *Jatakamala (Once the Buddha was a Monkey)*, trs. by Khoroche, Peter. Chicago: University of Chicago Press, 1989.

Aziz, Barbara. "Moving Toward a Sociology of Tibet." In *Feminine Ground: Essays on Women and Tibet*. Ed. by Janice Dean Willis. Ithaca, NY: Snow Lion, 1987, pp. 76-95.

Barnes, Nancy Schuster. "Buddhism." In *Women in World Religions*. Ed. by Arvind Sharma. Albany: State University of New York Press, 1987, pp. 105-33.

Barstow, Ann. "The Prehistoric Goddess." In *The Book of the Goddess*. Ed. by Carl Olson. New York: Crossroad, 1983, pp. 7-15.

Barry, Hathaway. "Letter to the Editor." *Kahawaii* IX, no. 1 (1987), p. 9.

Bechert, Heinz, and Gombrich, Richard. *The World of Buddhism: Buddhist Monks and Nuns in Society and Culture*. New York: Facts on File Publications, 1984.

Beck, Charlotte Joko. *Everyday Zen: Love and Work*. San Francisco: Harper and Row, 1989.

Belenky, Mary Field, Clinchy, Blythe McVicker, Goldberger, Nancy Rule, and Tarule, Jill Mattuck. *Women's Ways of Knowing: The Development of Self, Voice, and Mind*. New York: Basic Books, Inc., 1986.

Bell, Sir Charles. *The Religion of Tibet*. Oxford: Clarendon Press, 1968.

Bellah, Robert. "Religious Evolution." In *Reader in Comparative Religion*, 3rd Edition. Ed. by William A. Lessa and Evan Z. Vogt. New York: Harper and Row, 1972, pp. 36-50.

341

Bernbaum, Edwin. *The Way to Shambhala: A Search for the Mythical Kingdom beyond the Himalayas.* Garden City, NY: Anchor Books, 1980.

Beyer, Stephen, ed. *The Buddhist Experience: Sources and Interpretations.* Encino, CA: Dickenson Publishing, 1974.

—–—. *The Cult of Tara: Magic and Ritual in Tibet.* Berkeley: University of California Press, 1978.

Bharati, Agehananda. *The Tantric Tradition.* London: Rider and Company, 1965.

Bhattacharya, N.N. *History of the Tantric Religion.* Dehli: Manohar, 1982.

Bianchi, Ugo. *The History of Religions.* Leiden: E.J. Brill, 1975.

Blofeld, John. *Bodhisattva of Compassion: The Mystical Tradition of Kuan Yin.* Boulder, CO: Shambhala, 1978.

—–—. *The Tantric Mysticism of Tibet.* New York: E.P. Dutton and Co., 1970.

Bode, Mabel. "Women Leaders of the Buddhist Reformation." *Journal of the Royal Asiatic Society of Great Britian and Ireland* 1893, pp. 517–66 and 763–98.

Bond, George D. *The Buddhist Revival in Sri Lanka: Religious Tradition, Reinterpretation, and Response.* Columbia, SC: University of South Carolina Press, 1988.

Boucher, Sandy. *Turning the Wheel: American Women Creating the New Buddhism.* San Francisco: Harper and Row, 1988.

Carter, John Ross. *The Threefold Refuge in Theravada Buddhist Tradition.* Chambersburg, PA: Wilson Books, 1982.

Chamberlayne, John H. "The Development of Kuan-Yin: Chinese Goddess of Mercy." *Numen* IX (January 1962), pp. 45–62.

Chang, Garma C.C., trs. *The Hundred Thousand Songs of Milarepa,* 2 vols. Boulder, CO: Shambhala, 1977.

Chodorow, Nancy. *The Reproduction of Mothering: Psychoanalysis and the Sociology of Gender.* Berkeley: University of California Press, 1978.

Christ, Carol P. and Plaskow, Judith, eds. *Womanspirit Rising: A Feminist Reader in Religion.* San Francisco: Harper and Row, 1979.

Christ, C.P. *Laughter of Aphrodite: Reflections on a Journey to the Goddess.* San Francisco: Harper and Row, 1987.

—–—. "Why Women Need the Goddess: Phenomenological, Psychological and Political Reflections." In *Womanspirit Rising.* Ed. By Carol P. Christ and Judith Plaskow. San Francisco: Harper and Row, 1979.

Church, Cornelia Dimmitt. "Temptress, Housewife, Nun: Women's Role in Early Buddhism." *Anima: An Experiental Journal* I:2 (Spring 1975), pp. 53–58.

Cobb, John B, Jr. *Beyond Dialogue: Toward a Mutual Transformation of Buddhism and Christianity*. Philadelphia: Fortress Press, 1982.

———. "Ultimate Reality: A Christian View." *Buddhist-Christian Studies* VII (1988), pp. 51–64.

Conze, Edward, Horner, I.B., Snellgrove, David, and Waley, Arthur, eds. *Buddhist Texts through the Ages*. New York: Harper and Row, 1964.

Conze, Edward. *Buddhism: Its Essence and Development*. New York: Harper and Row, 1959.

———, ed. *Buddhist Scriptures*. Middlesex, England: Penguin Books, 1959.

———. *Buddhist Thought in India*. Ann Arbor, MI: University of Michigan Press, 1967.

———. *The Prajnaparamita Literature*. The Hague, The Netherlands: Mouton, 1960.

———. "The Iconography of Prajnaparamita." In *Thirty Years of Buddhist Studies: Selected Essays by Edward Conze*. Columbia, SC: University of South Carolina Press, 1968.

Cook, Francis. "Just This: Buddhist Ultimate Reality." *Buddhist-Christian Studies* IX (1989), pp. 127–42.

Coomaraswamy, Ananda K. *Buddha and the Gospel of Buddhism*. New York: Harper and Row, 1964.

Corless, Roger. *The Vision of Buddhism: The Space under the Tree*. New York: Paragon, 1989.

Cowell, E.B., ed. *Buddhist Mahayana Texts*. New York: Dover Publications, 1969.

Daly, Mary. *Beyond God the Father: Toward a Philosophy of Women's Liberation*. Boston: Beacon Press, 1973.

———. *Gyn/Ecology: The Metaethics of Radical Feminism*. Boston: Beacon Press, 1978.

Dasgupta, Shashi Bhushan. *An Introduction to Tantric Buddhism*. Berkeley: Shambhala, 1974.

Davis, Winston. " 'Wherein There Is No Ecstacy.' " *Studies in Religion* XIII:4 (1984), pp. 393–400.

Dawa-Samdup, Kazi, ed. *Sri-Cakrasamvara-Tantra: A Buddhist Tantra*. Dehli: Aditya Prakashan, 1987.

Dawson, Lorne. "Neither Nerve Nor Ecstacy: Comment on the Wiebe-Davis Exchange." *Studies in Religion* XV:2 (1986), pp. 145–51.

Dayal, Har. *The Bodhisattva Doctrine in Buddhist Sanskrit Literature*. Dehli: Motilal Barnasidass, 1970.

de Bary, William Theodore, ed. *The Buddhist Tradition in India, China, and Japan*. New York: Vintage, 1972.

de Beauvoir, Simone. *The Second Sex*. New York: Bantam Books, 1961.

de Jong, J.W. "Notes on the *Bhiksuni-Vinaya* of the Mahasamghikas." in *Buddhist Studies in Honor of I.B. Horner*. Ed. by L. Cousins, A. Kunst, and K.R. Norman. Boston: D. Reidel Publishing Co., 1974.

Dhondup, K. and Tsering Tashi. "Samdhing Dorjee Phagmo—Tibet's Only Female Incarnation." *Tibetan Review* XIV:8 (1979), pp. 11–17.

Dinnerstein, Dorothy. *The Mermaid and the Minotaur: Sexual Arrangements and Human Malaise*. New York: Harper and Row, 1977.

Dowman, Keith, tr. *Masters of Mahamudra: Songs and Histories of the Eighty-four Buddhist Mahasiddhas*. Albany, NY: State University of New York Press, 1985.

———. *Sky Dancer: The Secret Life and Songs of the Lady Yeshe Tsogyel*. London: Routledge and Kegan Paul, 1984.

Downing, Christine. *The Goddess: Mythological Images of the Feminine*. New York: Crossroad, 1981.

Duley, Margot I. and Edwards, Mary I. *The Cross-Cultural Study of Women: A Comprehensive Guide*. New York: The Feminist Press, 1986.

Ekvall, Robert B. *Religious Observances in Tibet*. Chicago: University of Chicago Press, 1964.

Eliade, Mircea. *Yoga: Immortality and Freedom*. New York: Pantheon Books, 1958.

Eppsteiner, Fred, ed. *The Path of Compassion: Writings on Socially Engaged Buddhism*. Berkeley, CA: Parallax Press, 1988.

Falk, Nancy Auer and Gross, Rita M. *Unspoken Worlds: Women's Religious Lives*. Belmont, CA: Wadsworth, 1989.

Falk, Nancy Auer. "The Case of the Vanishing Nuns: The Fruits of Ambivalance in Ancient Indian Buddhism." In *Unspoken Worlds: Women's Religious Lives*. Ed. by Nancy Auer Falk and Rita M. Gross. Belmont, CA: Wadsworth, 1989.

———. "An Image of Women in Old Buddhist Literature," In *Women and Religion: Revised Edition*. Ed. by Judith Plaskow and Joan Arnold Romero. Missoula, MT: Scholars Press, 1974.

Fields, Rick. *How the Swans Came to the Lake: A Narrative History of Buddhism in America*. Boulder, CO: Shambhala, 1981.

Firestone, Shulamith. *The Dialectic of Sex: The Case for Feminist Revolution*. New York: Bantam Books, 1970.

Friedman, Lenore. *Meetings with Remarkable Women: Buddhist Teachers in America.* Boston: Shambhala, 1987.

Furer-Haimendorf, Christoph von. "A Nunnery in Nepal." *Kailash* III:2 (1976), pp. 121-54.

Gadon, Elinor W. *The Once and Future Goddess.* San Francisco: Harper and Row, 1989.

Gampopa. *The Jewel Ornament of Liberation*, trs. by Herbert V. Guenther. Berkeley: Shambhala, 1977.

Getty, Alice. *The Gods of Northern Buddhism.* Rutland, VT: Charles E. Tuttle Co., 1962.

Gilligan, Carol. *In A Different Voice: Psychological Theory and Women's Development.* Cambridge: Harvard University Press, 1982.

Gimbutas, Marija. "Woman and Culture in Goddess Oriented Old Europe." In *The Politics of Women's Spirituality.* Ed. by Charlene Spretnak. Garden City, NY: Anchor Books, 1982, pp. 22-31.

Goddard, Dwight, ed. *A Buddhist Bible.* Boston: Beacon Press, 1938.

Goldenberg, Naomi. "Archetypal Symbolism and the Separation of Mind and Body— Reason Enough to Return to Freud?" *Journal of Feminist Studies in Religion* I:1 (1985), pp. 55-72.

———. *Changing of the Gods: Feminism and the End of Traditional Religion.* Boston: Beacon Press, 1979.

Goldstein, Joseph. *The Experience of Insight: A Natural Unfolding.* Santa Cruz: Unity Press, 1976.

Govinda, Lama Anagarika. *The Way of the White Clouds: A Buddhist Pilgrim in Tibet.* Berkeley: Shambhala, 1970.

Griffiths, Paul. *Christianity Through Non-Christian Eyes.* Maryknoll, NY: Orbis, 1990.

Grob, Leonard, Hassan, Riffat, and Gordon, Haim, eds. *Women's and Men's Liberation: Testimonies of Spirit.* New York: Greenwood, 1991.

Gross, Rita M. "Buddhism After Patriarchy." In *After Patriarchy: Feminist Reconstructions of the World Religions.* Ed. by Paula Cooey, Bill Eakin, and Jay McDaniel. Maryknoll, NY: Orbis, 1991, pp. 65-86.

———. "Buddhism and Feminism: Toward Their Mutual Transformation." *Eastern Buddhist* (New Series) XIX: 1 & 2 (1986), pp. 44-58 and 62-74.

———. " 'The Dharma is Neither Male nor Female': Buddhism on Gender and Liberation." In *Women's and Men's Liberation: Testimonies of Spirit.* Ed. by Leonard Grob, Riffat Hassan, and Haim Gordon. New York: Greenwood Press, 1991.

———. "Female God Language in a Jewish Context." In *Womanspirit Rising*. Ed. by Carol P. Christ and Judith Plaskow. San Francico: Harper and Row, 1979, pp. 167-73.

———. "The Feminine Principle in Tibetan Vajrayaya Buddhism: Reflections of a Buddhist Feminist." *Journal of Transpersonal Psychology* XVI:2 (1984), pp. 179-92.

———. "Feminism From the Perspective of Buddhist Practice," *Buddhist-Christian Studies* I (1980), pp. 73-82.

———. "Hindu Female Deities as a Resource in the Contemporary Rediscovery of the Goddess." *Journal of the American Academy of Religion* XLVII:3 (1978), pp. 269-91.

———. " 'I Will Never Forget to Visualize the Vajrayogini is My Body and Mind.' " *Journal of Feminist Studies in Religion* III:1 (1987), pp. 77-89.

———. "Menstruation and Childbirth as Ritual and Religious Experience among Native Australians." In *Unspoken Worlds: Women's Religious Lives*. Ed. by Nancy Auer Falk and Rita M. Gross. Belmont, CA: Wadsworth, 1989, pp. 257-66.

———. "Religious Diversity: Some Implications for Monotheism." *Wisconsin Dialogue* XI (1991), pp. 35-49.

———. "Steps Toward Feminine Imagery of Deity in Jewish Theology." *Judaism* XXX:2 (1981), pp. 183-93.

———. "Studying Women and Religion: Conclusions after Twenty Years." In *Women and World Religions: Contemporary Issues*. Edited by Arvind Sharma. Albany, NY: State University of New York Press, forthcoming.

———. "The Study of Religion as Religious Experience." *Buddhist-Christian Studies* XI (1991), pp. 254-58.

———. "Suffering, Feminist Theory and Images of Goddess." *Anima: An Experiental Journal* XIII:1 (1986), pp. 39-46.

———. "The Three-Yana Journey in Tibetan Vajrayana Buddhism." *Buddhist-Christian Studies* VII (1987), pp. 87-104.

———. "Tribal Religions: Aboriginal Australia." In *Women in World Religions*. Ed. by Arvind Sharma. Albany, NY: State University of New York Press, 1987, pp. 37-58.

———. "Yeshe Tsogyel: Enlightened Consort, Great Teacher, Female Role Model." In *Feminine Ground: Essays on Women and Tibet*. Ed. by Janice Dean Willis. Ithaca, NY: Snow Lion, 1987, pp. 11-32.

Guenther, Herbert V., trs. *The Life and Teaching of Naropa*. London: Oxford University Press, 1963.

Hamilton, Clarence, ed. *Buddhism: A Religion of Infinite Compassion.* Indianapolis: Bobbs-Merrill, 1952.

Havnevik, Hanna. *Tibetan Buddhist Nuns.* Oslo, Norway: Norwegian Univerity Press, n.d.

Heschel, Abraham Joshua. *The Sabbath.* Cleveland and New York: Meridian Books and the Jewish Publication Society, 1951.

Hirakawa, Akira, trs. *Monastic Discipline for the Buddhist Nuns: An English Translation of the Chinese Text of the Mahasamghika-Bhishuni-Vinaya.* Patna, India: Kashi Prasad Jayaswal Research Institute, 1982.

Hoffmann, Helmut. *The Religions of Tibet.* London: George Allen & Unwin Ltd., 1961.

Hookham, S. K. *The Buddha Within.* Albany: State University of New York Press, 1991.

Hopkinson, Deborah. *Not Mixing Up Buddhism: Essays on Women and Buddhist Practice.* Fredonia, New York: White Pine Press, 1986.

Horner, I.B., trs. *The Book of Discipline (Vinaya Pitaka): Volume V: (Cullavagga).* London: The Pali Text Society and Routledge and Kegan Paul, 1975.

————, trs. *The Book of Discipline (Vinaya-Pitaka): Volume VI: (Parivara).* London: The Pali Text Society and Routledge & Kegan Paul, 1986.

————. *Women under Primitive Buddhism: Laywomen and Almswomen.* New York: E.P. Dutton, 1930.

Howard, Jane. "Margaret Mead, 'Self-Appointed Materfamilias to the World.' " *Smithsonian* XV:6 (September 1984), pp. 122–32.

Humphries, Christmas, ed. *The Wisdom of Buddhism.* New York: Harper and Row, 1960.

Hunt, Mary E. *Fierce Tenderness: A Feminist Theology of Friendship.* New York: Crossroad, 1991.

Hurvitz, Leon, tr. *Scripture of the Lotus Blossom of the Fine Dharma (The Lotus Sutra).* New York: Columbia University Press, 1976.

Jacobsen, Thorkild. *The Treasures of Darkness: A History of Mesopotamian Religion.* New Haven: Yale University Press, 1976.

Jiyu-Kennett, Roshi. *The Wild White Goose,* 2 vols. Mount Shasta, CA: Shasta Abbey, 1977.

Jones, Ken. *The Social Face of Buddhism.* London: Wisdom, 1989.

Kabilsingh, Chatsumarn, trs. *The Bhikkuni Patimokkha of the Six Schools.* Bangkok: Chatsumarn Kabilsingh, 1991.

————. *A Comparative Study of Bhikkuni Patimokkha.* Varanasi: Chaukhambha Orientalia, 1984.

———. "The Future of the Bhikkuni Samgha in Thailand." In *Speaking of Faith: Global Perspectives on Women, Religion, and Social Change.* Ed. by Diana L. Eck and Devaki Jain. Philadelphia: New Society Publishers, 1987.

Kajiyama, Yuichi. "Stupas, the Mother of Buddhas, and Dharma Body." In *New Paths in Buddhist Research.* Ed. by A. K. Warder. Durham, NC: The Acorn Press, 1985.

———. "Women in Buddhism." *Eastern Buddhist* (New Series) XV:2 (1982), pp. 53–70.

Kalff, Martin M. "Dakinis in the Cakrasamvara Tradition." In *Tibetan Studies.* Ed. by Martin Brauen and Per Kvaerne. Zurich: Volkerkundemuseum der Universitat Zurich, 1978, pp. 149–62.

Kalupahana, David J. *Buddhist Philosophy: A Historical Analysis.* Honolulu: University of Hawaii Press, 1976.

———. *The Principles of Buddhist Psychology.* Albany, NY: State University of New York Press, 1987.

Kapleau, Philip. *Three Pillars of Zen.* Boston: Beacon Press, 1967.

Katz, Nathan. "Anima and mKha-'gro-ma: A Critical Comparative Study of Jung and Tibetan Buddhism." *The Tibet Journal* II:3 (Autumn 1977), pp. 13–43.

Kaufman, Gordon. "God and Emptiness: An Experimental Essay." *Buddhist-Christian Studies* IX (1989), pp. 175–87.

Keller, Catherine. *From a Broken Web: Separation, Sexism, and Self.* Boston: Beacon Press, 1986.

Kern, H., tr. *Saddharma-Pundarika or The Lotus of the True Law.* New York: Dover Publications, 1963.

Kern, H. *Manual of Indian Buddhism.* Dehli: Motilal Barnasidass, 1974.

Keyes, Charles F. "Mother or Mistress but Never a Monk: Buddhist Notions of Female Gender in Rural Thailand." *American Ethnologist* XI:2 (1984), pp. 223–41.

Khantipalo, Bhikku. *Banner of the Arahants: Buddhist Monks and Nuns from the Buddha's Time Till Now.* Kandy, Sri Lanka: Buddhist Publication Society, 1979.

King, Sallie B. *Buddha Nature.* Albany, NY: State University of New York Press, 1991.

King, Winston L. *A Thousand Lives Away: Buddhism in Contemporary Burma.* Oxford: Bruno Cassirer, 1964.

Kitagawa, Joseph M., ed. *The History of Religions: Retrospect and Prospect.* New York: MacMillan, 1985.

Klein, Anne. "The Birthless Birthgiver: Reflections of the Liturgy of Yeshe Tsogyel, the Great Bliss Queen." *The Tibet Journal* XII:4 (1987), pp. 19–37.

———. "Finding a Self: Buddhist and Feminist Perspectives." In *Shaping New Vision: Gender and Values in American Culture*. Ed. by Clarissa W. Atkinson, Constance H. Buchanan, and Margaret R. Miles. Ann Arbor, MI: UMI Reserach Press, 1987.

———. "Gain or Drain?: Buddhist and Feminist Views of Compassion." In *Spring Wind. Women and Buddhism: A Special Issue of the Spring Wind Buddhist Cultural Forum*. VI:1-3 (1986), pp. 105-16.

———. "Nondualism and the Great Bliss Queen: A Study in Tibetan Buddhist Ontology and Symbolism." *Journal of Feminist Studies in Religion* I:1 (Spring 1985), pp. 73-98.

———. "Primordial Purity and Everyday Life: Exalted Female Symbols and the Women of Tibet." In *Immaculate and Powerful: The Female in Sacred Image and Social Reality*. Ed. by Clarrissa W. Atkinson, Constance Buchanan, and Margaret R. Miles. Boston: Beacon, 1985.

Kongtrul, Jamgon. *The Torch of Certainty*, trs. by Judith Hanson. Boulder, CO: Shambhala, 1977.

Kunsang, Erik Pema. *Dakini Teachings: Padmasambhava's Oral Instructions to Lady Tsogyal*. Boston: Shambhala, 1990.

LaFleur, William R. *Buddhism: A Cultural Perspective*. Englewood Cliffs, NJ: Prentice-Hall, 1988.

Lame Deer, John, and Erdoes, Richard. *Lame Deer: Seeker of Visions*. New York: Simon and Schuster, 1972.

Lang, Karen Christina. "Lord Death's Snare: Gender-Related Imagery in the Theragatha and Therigatha." *Journal of Feminist Studies in Religion* II:2 (Fall 1986), pp. 63-79.

Law, B.C. "Lay Women in Early Buddhism." *Journal of the Asiatic Society of Bombay* (New Series) XXXI & XXXII (1956 & 1957), pp. 121-41.

Law, Bimala Churn. *Women in Buddhist Literature*. Varanasi, India: Indological Book House, 1981.

Lerner, Gerda. *The Creation of Patriarchy*. New York: Oxford University Press, 1986.

Lester, Robert C. *Buddhism: The Path to Nirvana*. San Francisco: Harper and Row, 1987.

Levering, Miriam L. "The Dragon-Girl and the Abbess of Mo-Shan: Gender and Status in Ch'an Buddhist Tradition." *Journal of the International Association of Buddhist Studies* V:1 (1982), pp. 19-35.

Lhalungpa, Lobsang P., trs. *The Life of Milarepa*. New York: E.P. Dutton, 1977.

Li, Jung-hsi, trs. *Biographies of Buddhist Nuns: Pao-Chang's Pi-chiu-ni-chuan*. Osaka, Japan: Tohokai, Inc., 1981.

Lopez, Donald S. *The Heart Sutra Explained: Indian and Tibetan Commentaries.* Albany, NY: State University of New York Press, 1988.

Lowe, Marion. "Sociobiology and Sex Differences." *Signs: Journal of Women and Culture* IV:1 (1978), pp. 118-25.

Macy, Joanna. *Mutual Causality is Buddhism and General Systems Theory.* Albany, NY: State University of New York Press, 1991.

————. "Perfection of Wisdom: Mother of all Buddhas." In *Beyond Androcentrism: New Essays on Women and Religion.* Ed. by Rita M. Gross. Missoula, MT: Scholars Press, 1978, pp. 315-33.

Marshall, George N. *Buddha: The Quest for Serenity.* Boston: Beacon, 1978.

McFague, Sallie. *Metaphorical Theolgoy: Models of God in Religious Language.* Philadelphia: Fortress Press, 1982.

————. *Models of God: Theology for a Nuclear Age.* Philadelphia: Fortress Press, 1987.

McGuire, Brian Patrick. *Friendship and Community: The Monastic Experience, 350-1250.* Kalamazoo, MI: Cistercian Publications, 1988.

McLaughlin, Eleanor. "The Christian Past: Does It Hold a Future for Women?" In *Womanspirit Rising.* Ed. by Carol P. Christ and Judith Plaskow. San Francisco: Harper and Row, 1979, pp. 93-106.

Miller, Barbara Stoler. "Ballads of the Early Buddhist Nuns." *Zero* V (1981), pp. 68-77.

Miller, Beatrice D. "Views of Women's Roles in Buddhist Tibet." In *Studies in History of Buddhism.* Ed. by A.K. Narain. Dehli: B.R. Publishing Corporation, 1980, pp. 155-66.

Mullin, Glenn H., trs. & ed. *Selected Works of the Dalai Lama II: The Tantric Yogas of Sister Niguma.* Ithaca, NY: Snow Lion, 1985.

Murti, T.R.V. *The Central Philosophy of Buddhism.* London: George, Allen and Unwin, 1974.

Neumann, Erich. *The Origins and History of Consciousness.* New York: Pantheon Books, 1954.

Ortner, Sherry B. "The Founding of the First Sherpa Nunnery, and the Problem of 'Women' as an Analytic Category." In *Feminist Re-Visions: What Has Been and What Might Be.* Ed. by Vivian Paraka and Louise A Tilly. Ann Arbor, MI: The University of Michigan Press, 1983.

Nagarjuna. *The Philosophy of the Middle Way*, trs. by Kalupahana, David J. Albany NY: State University of New York Press, 1986.

Nalanda Translation Committee, trs. *The Life of Marpa the Translator.* Boulder, CO: Prajna Press, 1982.

————. *The Rain of Wisdom.* Boulder, CO: Shambhala, 1980.

Nagao, Gadjin. *The Foundational Standpoint of Madhyamika Philosophy.* Albany, NY: State University of New York Press, 1989.

Nakamura, Kyoko, trs. *Miraculous Stories form the Japanese Buddhist Tradition: The Nihon Ryoiki of the Monk Kyokai.* Cambridge: Harvard University Press, 1973.

Norbu, Thinley. *Magic Dance: The Display of the Self-Nature of the Five Wisdom Dakinis.* n.p.: 1981.

Norbu, Thubten Jigme Norbu, and Turnbull, Colin M. *Tibet.* New York: Simon and Schuster, 1968.

Norman, K. R., trs. *The Elders' Verses I: Theragatha.* London: Pali Text Society and Luzac and Company, Ltd., 1969.

————. *The Elders' Verses II: Therigatha.* London: Pali Text Society and Luzac and Company Ltd., 1971.

Paden, William E. *Religious Worlds: The Comparative Study of Religion.* Boston, Beacon Press, 1988.

Paul, Diana Mary. *The Buddhist Feminine Ideal: Queen Srimala and the Tathagatagarbha.* Missoula, MT: Scholars Press, 1980.

Paul, Diana Y. "Kuan-Yin: Saviour and Saviouress in Chinese Pure Land Buddhism." In *The Book of the Goddess.* Ed. by Carl Olson. New York: Crossroad, 1983, pp. 161-75.

————. *Women in Buddhism: Images of the Feminine in Mahayana Tradition.* Berkeley: Asian Humanities Press, 1979.

Plaskow, Judith. *Standing Again at Sinai: Judaism from a Feminist Perspective.* San Francisco: Harper and Row, 1990.

Powell, Andrew. *Living Buddhism.* New York: Harmony Books, 1989.

Prebish, Charles S. *Buddhist Monastic Discipline.* University Park, PA: Pennsylvania State University Press, 1975.

Rahula, Walpola. *What the Buddha Taught.* New York: Grove Press, 1974.

Ray, Reginald A. "Accomplished Women in Tantric Buddhism of Medieval India and Tibet." In *Unspoken Worlds: Women's Religious Lives.* Ed. by Nancy Auer Falk and Rita M. Gross. Belmont, CA: Wadsworth, 1989.

————. "Response to John Cobb." *Buddhist-Christian Studies* VII (1988), pp. 83-101.

Reis, Ria. "Reproduction or Retreat: The Position of Buddhist Women in Ladakh." In *Recent Research on Ladakh: History, Culture, Sociology, Ecology.* Ed. by Detlef Kantowsky and Reinhard Sander. Munich: Weltforum Verlag, 1983.

Rhys-Davids, C.A.F. and Norman, K.R., trs. *Poems of the Early Buddhist Nuns: (Therigatha).* Oxford: The Pali Text Society, 1989.

Rhys-Davids, Mrs. *Psalms of the Early Buddhists I: Psalms of the Sisters.* London: The Pali Text Society and Oxford University Press, 1948.

—————. *Psalms of the Early Buddhists II: Psalms of the Brethren.* London: The Pali Text Society and Luzac & Company, Ltd., 1951.

Rhys-Davids, C.A.F. trs. and ed. *Stories of the Buddha: Being Selections from the Jataka.* New York: Dover Publications, 1989.

Rhys-Davids, T.W., tr. *Buddhist Suttas.* New York: Dover Pulications, 1969.

Richman, Paula. "The Portrayal of a Female Renouncer in a Tamil Buddhist Text." In *Gender and Religion: On the Complexity of Symbols.* Ed. by Caroline Walker Bynum, Steven Harrell, and Paula Richman. Boston: Beacon Press, 1986, pp. 143-65.

Robinson, Richard H. and Johnson, Willard L. *The Buddhist Religion: A Historical Introduction*, Third Edition. Belmont, CA: Wadsworth, 1982.

Ruether, Rosemary Radford. "Motherearth and the Megamachine." In *Womanspirit Rising.* Ed. by Carol P. Christ and Judith Plaskow. San Francisco: Harper and Row, 1979, pp. 43-52.

—————. "Misogyny and Virginal Feminism in the Fathers of the Church." In *Religion and Sexism: Images of Women in Jewish and Christian Traditions.* Ed. by Rosemary Ruether. New York: Simon and Schuster, 1974, pp. 150-83.

—————. *Sexism and God-Talk: Toward a Feminist Theology.* Boston: Beacon, 1983.

—————. *Women-Church: Theology and Practice.* San Francisco: Harper and Row, 1986.

Ruddick, Sara. *Maternal Thinking: Toward a Politics of Peace.* New York: Ballantine Books, 1989.

Saiving, Valerie. "The Human Situation: A Feminine Perspective." In *Womanspirit Rising.* Ed. by Carol P. Christ and Judith Plaskow. San Francisco: Harper and Row, 1978, pp. 25-42.

Sakya, Jamyang, and Emery, Julie. *Princess in the Land of Snows: The Life of Jamyang Sakya in Tibet.* Boston: Shambhala, 1988.

Sangharakshita, Bhikshu. *A Survey of Buddhism.* Boulder, CO: Shambhala, 1980.

—————. *The Three Jewels: An Introduction to Modern Buddhism.* Garden City, NY: Anchor Books, 1970.

Saunders, E. Dale. "A Note on Shakti and Dhyanibuddha." *History of Religions* I:2 (1962), pp. 300-06.

Sayers, Dorothy. *Are Women Human?* Grand Rapids, MI: Eerdmans, 1971.

Schaef, Ann Wilson. *Women's Reality*. Minneapolis: Winston Press, 1981.

Schuster, Nancy. "Changing the Female Body: Wise Women and the Bodhisattva Career in Some *Maharatnakutasutras.*" *Journal of the International Association of Buddhist Studies* IV:1 (1981), pp. 24-69.

————. "Striking a Balance: Women and Images of Women in Early Chinese Buddhism." In *Women, Religion, and Social Change.* Ed. by Yvonne Yazbeck Hadda and Ellison Banks Findly. Albany, NY: State University of New York Press, 1985.

————. "Yoga Master Dharmamitra and Clerical Misogyny in Fifth Century Buddhism." *The Tibet Journal* IX:4 (1984), pp. 33-46.

Seneviratne, Maureen. *Some Women of the Mahavamsa and Culavamsa.* Colombo, Sri Lanka: H.W. Cave & Co., 1969.

Shantideva. *A Guide to the Bodhisattva's Way of Life*, trs. by Stephen Batchelor. Dharamsala: Library of Tibetan Works and Archives, 1979.

Sharma, Arvind. "Can There Be a Female Buddha in Theravada Buddhism?" In *Bucknell Review: Women, Literature, Criticism.* XXIV:1 (Spring 1978), pp. 72-79.

————. "How and Why Did the Women in Ancient India Become Buddhist Nuns?" *Sociological Analysis* XXXVIII:3 (1977), 239-51.

Sidor, Ellen S. *A Gathering of Spirit: Women Teaching in American Buddhism.* n.p.: Primary Point Press, 1985.

Snellgrove, David and Richardson, Hugh. *A Cultural History of Tibet.* Boulder, CO: Prajna Press, 1980.

Snellgrove, David. *Himalayan Pilgrimage.* Boulder, CO: Prajna Press, 1981.

————. *Indo-Tibetan Buddhism: Indian Buddhists and their Tibetan Successors,.* 2 vols. Boston: Shambhala, 1987.

Spretnak, Charlene. "Feminist Politics and the Nature of Mind." In *The Politics of Women's Spirituality: Essays on the Rise of Spiritual Power within the Feminist Movement.* Ed. by Charlene Spretnak. Garden City, NY: Doubleday, 1982, pp. 565-73.

Speyer, J.S., trs. *The Jatakamala: or Garland of Birth Stories of Aryasurya.* Dehli: Motilal Banarsidass, 1982.

Spring Wind—Buddhist Cultural Forum. *Women and Buddhism.* n.p.: Zen Lotus Society, 1986.

Starhawk. *The Spiral Dance: A Rebirth of the Ancient Religion of the Goddess.* San Francisco: Harper and Row, 1979.

Stein, R.A. *Tibetan Civilization.* Stanford, CA: Stanford University Press, 1972.

Stevens, John. *Lust for Enlightenment.* Boston: Shambhala, 1990.

Streng, Frederick J. *Emptiness: A Study in Religious Meaning*. Nashville: Abingdon, 1967.

Stryk, Lucien, ed. *World of the Buddha: A Reader from the Three Baskets to Modern Zen*. Garden City, NY: Doubleday, 1969.

Suzuki, Daisetz Teitaro, tr. *The Lankavatara Sutra*. London: Routledge and Kegan Paul, Ltd., 1973.

Suzuki, Shinryu. *Zen Mind, Beginner's Mind*. New York: Tuttle, 1974.

Swearer, Donald K. *Wat Haripunjaya*. Missoula, MT: Scholars Press, 1976.

Tabrah, Ruth M. "Reflections on Being Ordained." *Eastern Buddhist* (New Series) XVI:2 (Fall 1983), pp. 124–33.

Talim, Meena V. "Buddhist Nuns and Disciplinary Rules." *Journal of the University of Bombay* 1965, pp. 93–137.

Taranatha, Jo-nan. *The Origin of Tara Tantra*. Trans. and ed. by David Templeman. Dharamsala, India: Library of Tibetan Works and Archives, 1981.

Tay, C.N. "Kuan-Yin: The Cult of Half Asia." *History of Religions* XVI:2 (1976), pp. 147–74.

Tendzin, Osel. *Buddha in the Palm of Your Hand*. Boulder, CO: Shambhala, 1988.

Thomas, Edward J. *The Life of the Buddha as Legend and History*. London: Routledge & Kegan Paul, Ltd., 1969.

Thurman, Robert A. "Guidelines for Buddhist Social Activism Based on Nagarjuna's *Jewel Net of Royal Counsels*." *The Eastern Buddhist* (New Series) XVI:1 (1983), pp. 19–51.

———, trs. *The Holy Teaching of Vimalakirti: A Mahayana Scripture*. University Park, PA: Pennsylvania State University Press, 1976.

Tiger, Lionel. *Men In Groups*. New York: Vintage Books, 1970.

Tong, Rosemarie. *Feminist Thought: A Comprehensive Introduction*. Boulder, CO: Westview Press, 1989.

Treblicott, Joyce, ed. *Mothering: Essays in Feminist Theory*. Totowa, NJ: Rowman and Allenheld, 1983.

Tribe, Fran. "Ordinary Practice." *Kahawaii* V:1 (1983), pp. 3–7.

Trungpa, Chogyam. *Born in Tibet*. Boulder, CO: Shambhala, 1977.

———. *Crazy Wisdom*. Boston: Shambhala, 1991.

———. *Cutting through Spiritual Materialism*. Berkeley: Shambhala, 1973.

————, ed. *Garuda IV: The Four Foundations of Mindfulness*. Berkeley: Shambhala, 1976.

————. *Glimpses of Abhidharma*. Boulder, CO: Prajna Press, 1978.

————. *The Heart of the Buddha*. Boston: Shambhala, 1991.

————. *Journey without Goal: The Tantric Wisdom of the Buddha*. Boulder, CO: Prajna Press, 1981.

————. *Meditation In Action*. Berkeley: Shambhala, 1969.

————. *The Myth of Freedom and the Way of Meditation*. Berkeley: Shambhala, 1976.

————. *Shambhala: The Sacred Path of the Warrior*. Boston: Shambhala, 1988.

————. *Visual Dharma: The Buddhist Art of Tibet*. Berkeley: Shambhala, 1975.

Tsai, Kathryn A. "The Chinese Buddhist Monastic Order for Women: The First Two Centuries." In *Women in China: Current Directions in Historical Scholarship*. Ed. by Richard W. Guisso and Stanley Johannesen. Youngstown, NY: Philo Press, 1981.

Tscherbatsky, Th. *The Conception of Buddhist Nirvana*. London: Mouton and Co., 1965.

Tsomo, Karma Lekshe, ed. *Sakyadhita: Daughters of the Buddha*. Ithaca, New York: Snow Lion, 1988.

————. "Tibetan Nuns and Nunneries." In *Feminine Ground: Essays on Women and Tibet*. Ed. By Janice Dean Willis. Ithaca, NY: Snow Lion, 1987, pp. 118-34.

Tulku, Tarthang, trs. *Mother of Knowledge: The Enlightenment of Ye-shes mTsho-rgyal*. Berkeley: Dharma Publishing, 1983.

————. *Sacred Art of Tibet*. Berkeley: Dharma Publishing, 1972.

Uchino, Kumiko. "The Status Elevation Process of Soto Sect Nuns in Modern Japan." In *Speaking of Faith: Global Perspectives on Women, Religion, and Social Change*. Ed. by Diana L. Eck and Devaki Jain. Philadelphia: New Society Publishers, 1987.

Van Esterick, Penny, ed. *Women of Southeast Asia*. De Kalb, IL: Northern Illinois University Center for Southeast Asian Studies, 1982.

————. "Laywomen of Theravada Buddhism." In *Women of Southeast Asia*. Ed. by Penny van Esterick. De Kalb, IL: Northern Illinois University Press, 1982, pp. 55-78.

Warner, Marina. *Alone of All Her Sex: The Myth and Cult of the Virgin Mary*. New York: Alfred A. Knopf, 1976.

Waldron, William S. "A Comparision of the Alayavijnana with Freud's and Jung's Theories of the Unconscious." *Annual Memoirs of Otani University Shin Buddhist Comprehensive Research Institute* VI (1988), pp. 109-50.

Warren, Henry Clarke, trs. and ed. *Buddhism in Translations*. New York: Atheneum, 1968.

Wayman, Alex and Hideko, trs. *The Lion's Roar of Queen Srimala*. New York: Columbia University Press, 1974.

Wayman, Alex. "Female Energy and Symbolism in the Buddhist Tantras." *History of Religions* II:1 (1962), pp. 73-111.

Welbon, Guy. *The Buddhist Nirvana and Its Western Interpreters*. Chicago: University of Chicago Press, 1968.

Wiebe, Donald. "The Failure of Nerve in the Academic Study of Religion." *Studies in Religion* XIII:4 (1984), pp. 401-22.

Wijayaratna, Mohan. *Buddhist Monastic Life According to the Texts of the Theravada Tradition*. Cambridge: Cambridge University Press, 1990.

Williams, Paul. *Mahayana Buddhism: The Doctrinal Foundations*. London: Routledge, 1989.

Willis, Janice Dean. "Dakini: Some Comments on its Nature and Meaning." In *Feminine Ground: Essays on Women and Tibet*. Ed. by Janice Dean Willis. Ithaca, NY: Snow Lion, 1987, pp. 57-75.

―――. *The Diamond Light: An Introduction to Tibetan Buddhist Meditations*. New York: Simon & Schuster, 1972.

―――, ed. *Feminine Ground: Essays on Women and Tibet*. Ithaca, New York: Snow Lion, 1989.

―――. "Nuns and Benefactresses: The Role of Women in the Development of Buddhism." In *Women, Religion, and Social Change*. Ed. By Yvonne Yazbeck Haddad and Ellison Banks Findly. Albany, NY: State University of New York Press, 1985, pp. 59-85.

―――. "Tibetan Ani-s: The Nuns Life in Tibet." In *Feminine Ground: Essays on Women and Tibet*. Ed. by Janice Dean Willis. Ithaca, NY: Snow Lion, 1987, pp. 96-117.

Willson, Martin. *In Praise of Tara: Songs to the Saviouress*. London: Wisdom Publications, 1986.

Wilson, E.O. *Sociobiology: The New Synthesis*. Cambridge: Harvard University Press, 1975.

Woodward, F.L., trs. and ed. *Some Sayings of the Buddha According to the Pali Canon*. London: Oxford University Press, 1973.

Yeshe Tsogyal. *The Life and Liberation of Padmasambhava*, 2 vols., trs. by Kenneth Douglas and Gwendolyn Bays. Berkeley: Dharma Publishing, 1978.

INDEX

INDEX

364 BUDDHISM AFTER PATRIARCHY